FutureSpeak

FutureSpeak

A Fan's Guide to the Language of Science Fiction

ROBERTA ROGOW

Foreword by C. J. Cherryh

Illustrations by Leah Rosenthal

Paragon House
NEW YORK

First edition, 1991

Published in the United States by

Paragon House
90 Fifth Avenue
New York, NY 10011

Manufactured in the United States of America

Library of Congress Cataloging-in-Publication Data

Rogow, Roberta,
FutureSpeak : a fan's guide to the language of science fiction / Roberta Rogow. — 1st ed.
p. cm.
Includes bibliographical references.
ISBN 1-55778-347-0 : $24.95. — ISBN 1-55778-477-9 (pbk.) : $15.95
1. Science fiction—Dictionaries. 2. English language—New words—Dictionaries. I. Title.
PN3433.4.R64 1991
809.3'876203—dc20
90-28905
CIP

To SF writers, artists, editors, and fans everywhere . . . this book is for you.

Contents

Acknowledgments ix

Foreword by C. J. Cherryh xi

Introduction xiii

How to Use This Book xix

FutureSpeak Entries A to Z 1

APPENDIX A *Useful Addresses* 387

- Publications 387
- Organizations 389
- Conventions 390
- Costuming 391

APPENDIX B

- Filk Distributors 392
- Filker's Bill of Rights 393

Filk-Songs 394

- "That REAL Old-Time Religion" 394
- "Banned From Argo" 395
- "Hope Eyrie" 398

APPENDIX C *Rotsler's Rules for Masquerades* 400

APPENDIX D *Award Rules* 401

Nebula 401

Hugo 402

Bibliography 406

Acknowledgments

A work the size of *FutureSpeak* could not have been accomplished without the assistance of many people. The original word list was provided by the members of the New Jersey Science Fiction Society and the Science Fiction Association of Bergen County (N.J.). The staff at Schiller's Bookstore, in Paramus, N.J., provided me with reference books and newsletters. Fan editors Devra Langsam, Debbie Goldstein, and Ruth Berman went over the manuscript, checking for misstatements and adding bits of fannish lore that I might have missed otherwise.

I was able to check much of my information with the originators of the words and phrases that I describe in *FutureSpeak.* Poul Anderson, Forrest J. Ackerman, Marion Zimmer Bradley, Frederik Pohl, and Bruce Sterling kindly responded to my queries with personal letters that explained just how certain terms came into the Language of Science Fiction. Bruce Sterling enlightened me on the origins of "Cyberpunk," and sent a copy of his own article, "A Workshop Lexicon," from *Interzone* (September 1990). I was able to speak briefly at Conventions with Gardner Dozois, Sam Moskowitz, Larry Niven, Susan Shwartz, Darryl Schweitzer, Joan Winston, and Jane Yolen, all of whom were gracious enough to add to the background material for this book. Marty Gear, Pat Kennedy, and Drew Saunders filled me in on the history of Costuming. Adam Malin gave me an extended interview about Conventions. Scott Greene told me about Small Press. I got information on the inner workings of large Conventions from Mark Levin, Ellen Franklin, Tony Lewis, and Thomas A. Renner. Bennet Rutledge explained the workings of the Society for Creative Anachronism to me. Peter David was a source of information about Comics, and Gregory A. Baker gave me some terms from the world of Gaming. John Upton was able to correct some of my material on Computers and the Space Program. Mary Otten explained about videotaping and Cloning Parties. Some of my information on Filking came from the Introduction to the FILKINDEX written by Sourdough Jackson, and some came from the newsletters put out by Margaret Middleton and John Boardman.

I owe special gratitude to C. J. Cherryh, who was responsible for getting my first story into a mass market publication; to Bert Holtje, who persisted in presenting the manuscript to one publisher after another until he found one willing to take it; to PJ Dempsey, the editor who tried to make sense of the world of Science Fiction; to the staff at the Union Public Library, Union, N.J., for their forbearance; and most especially, to my husband, Murray Rogow, who insisted that I face the Word Processor and without whom . . .

Foreword

Living languages change with change, *mutans mutandis*—social and technological progress (or the occasional barbarian horde) can't help but affect meanings, applications, syntax, and substance. We're in the atomic age, the space age, the computer age, the sexual, the technological, the information revolution; we're in racial integration, sexual diversification; we're finding our roots, redefining expectations, relationships, and somehow coping. We're handling an infostream infinitely broadened, be we technophiles or technophobes; we're managing a planetary ecology and hanging in and hanging on while hanging out. News flashes around the planet on an array of satellites—languages change. Fast food, fast news, and button-pushing access, pizza, the cola wars, and the New Europe—it's a brand new world of brand new *new* words. And, hotdoggers on the wave of change, the aficionados of science fiction have developed their own language of concepts, ideas, and yes, the outright fun of believers in the future. It transcends national boundaries, finds speakers in the United States, the United Kingdom, and Europe—concoms are alive and well in Nebraska and fen are stirring in Kiev: FTL granted, they'll be forming at Alpha Cent. Fiawol, Joe Fan, and keep on.

Roberta Rogow's *FutureSpeak* is an idea long overdue.

C. J. Cherryh

Introduction

Science Fiction is a way of life. There are other definitions of Science Fiction. According to Dr. Isaac Asimov's article in *The World Book Encyclopedia,* Science Fiction is "a popular kind of imaginative literature. Its basic themes include space travel, time travel, and marvelous discoveries and inventions." Theodore Sturgeon's definition for the *Encyclopedia Americana* insists that Science Fiction is that form of "fiction in which some aspect of science forms an element of the plot or background." In *Collier's Encyclopedia,* Barry Malzberg says that Science Fiction is "that branch of fiction that deals with the possible effects of an altered technology or social system on mankind."

Science Fiction is all of these, and more. Science Fiction includes romantic fantasies like *Flame of Byzantium* by Chelsea Quinn Yarbro; swashbuckling adventure stories like the Domenic Flandry novels by Poul Anderson; high-tech problem-solving stories like *Ringworld* by Larry Niven; grim tales of a future in which most of humanity has succeeded in destroying itself like *Damnation Alley* by Roger Zelazny; sagas of civilizations on faraway planets, in a future that has almost forgotten Earth, like the Pern novels by Anne McCaffrey . . . all this, and much, much more.

Science Fiction offers escape from the ordinary, day-to-day routine; it also offers mind-expanding vistas in which today's trends may become tomorrow's nightmares, or possibly, yesterday's dreams. Science Fiction has been called everything from puerile fantasy to a blueprint for the future. Science Fiction is also considered the most popular genre of fiction with young, college-educated men and women.

On one thing everyone agrees: No other form of popular literature has developed such a lively network of dedicated readers, many of whom aspire to be writers of Science Fiction. Mystery readers may argue the merits of Sherlock Holmes or Nero Wolfe; Western readers may collect Americana. Science Fiction readers collect books and art, but they go farther than that. They incorporate Science Fiction into the fabric of their lives.

Science Fiction readers gather into clubs that produce magazines filled with stories, poetry, and art. They organize large-scale meetings, called Conventions, at which they act out some of their fantasies by dressing up in unusual costumes. They interact through computer networks and bulletin boards. All these activities call for some kind of terminology to explain what, exactly, they are doing. I choose to call this jargon *Futurespeak: A Fan's Guide to the Language of Science Fiction*.

The Language of Science Fiction is composed of several types of jargon, those words and phrases that are particular to a profession or trade. In the case of Science Fiction, several trades and professions are involved, as well as the terms and phrases invented by the Fans to describe their activities.

Science Fiction is, first of all, a form of popular literature, with all that implies. Writers, editors, artists, and publishers must deal with Science Fiction as a means of economic support. Moreover, as a form of popular literature, Science Fiction must be presented to its audience through an extensive system of marketing, so that the writers, editors, artists, and so forth can continue to provide this audience with its pet form of entertainment. Not only that, but the audience for Science Fiction is in itself an influence. Not even the groundlings in the Shakespearean theater were more vociferous in their likes and dislikes than Science Fiction Fans.

The thematic material of Science Fiction has traditionally been the world of technology. In recent years, this world has been expanded enormously, so that what was once called Science Fiction is now Fact. At the same time, the expectations of the readers of Science Fiction have expanded, so that the material now included in Science Fiction may go into such areas as psychic phenomena, time travel, and alternate universes. The rather simple-minded tales of rip-roaring adventure in the vast reaches of space that appealed to prepubescent males of earlier decades have given way to more interesting and exciting stories of a future extrapolated from what we know or guess about the present.

Between the writing establishment, the thematic material, the critical and scholarly appraisals, and the fans, Science Fiction manages to include a number of people, all of whom speak the Language of Science Fiction. That language is the subject of this book.

There is the arcane lingo of the writing profession, in which someone can speak of a "Universe" or of a "Feghoot." There are the names given to subgenres within the genre, like "Sword and Sorcery" or "Cyberpunk." There are the precise scientific and technological terms for pieces of equipment or measurements or natural phenomena, like "quasar" or "sensor." There is the jargon of the fans themselves, which is deliberately set up as a barrier against the "Mundanes," those terrible creatures who do not understand Science Fiction. All of these jargons combine to form the Language of Science Fiction, as it is used by the people involved in writing it, filming it, selling it, and absorbing it.

I first became aware of the Language of Science Fiction when I entered Fandom in the early 1970s, although I had been reading Science Fiction long before that. My first introduction to Science Fiction was Robert Heinlein's *Have Space Suit, Will Travel,* but what really got me going was *Northwest of Earth,* created by C. L. Moore. I read Science Fiction avidly, and even read about such things as Conventions in magazines like *Galaxy* and *Analog.* I was not aware that those gatherings would permit outsiders like myself into their doings.

It was not until I got involved with *Star Trek* and its fans that I realized Conventions were for us mere mortals who did not write for pay. I began to attend the Star Trek Conventions in the New York City area . . . and in Baltimore . . . and in Philadelphia . . . and eventually, my horizons expanded, and I found myself at my first WorldCon. And in all these places, I heard the Language of Science Fiction.

This jargon of jargons can be used as a barrier to keep the Unknowing at bay. It can also be used because there really is no other way to say what must be said. The very aptness of a phrase leads to its adoption, because there really is no alternative. When Marion Zimmer Bradley describes a nontelepath in a telepathic society as "head-blind," she has coined a phrase that then gets picked up by others as "mind-blind" . . . but how else to describe the sensation of being without a sense possessed by everyone else around you?

This book tries to make sense of all the jargons that make up the Language of Science Fiction. In each case I have tried to give the origin of the word or phrase as it is used in Science Fiction terminology, and I have tried to give examples wherever possible. Some terms and phrases are self-explanatory; some are highly technical; some are applicable to other forms of endeavor besides Science Fiction. In each case I have tried to explain how the term came to be, and why it is part of the Language of Science Fiction, even though some of these terms may have other applications outside the world of Science Fiction.

Wherever possible I have tried to ascertain exactly who (if anyone) started a particular term, or turn of phrase. I have used several reference works, which are listed in the Bibliography. I have had extensive interviews with several people who were knowledgeable on such fannish matters as Filk-Singing and Costuming. I have had briefer communications with many other people (usually on the run at Science Fiction Conventions), all of whom are listed in the Acknowledgments.

There are a few things I have *not* listed in this book. I have not included extensive biographical material. There are many excellent biographical works (some of which I have used as reference material) on Science Fiction writers, artists, editors, and so on. The only people I include in the Language of Science Fiction are those who have lent their names to specific dicta ("Asimov's Laws of Robotics") or those who have become symbolic of a movement or a stereotype (Harlan Ellison). I have also not included those terms and phrases that pertain only to a specific set of stories, whether in print or on film, that is, a Universe. There are a number of reference works, such as *The Darkover Concordance*, that may deal with these things in greater detail.

I have tried to cite the first appearance of a work, whether it is written or filmed, even though some of the major Science Fiction novels may have begun life as short stories or serials in magazines. I have given the first-run dates of television series, although they may be available on videotape, or may be rerunning in syndication somewhere around the television dial.

I have tried to explain the many jargons used by the makers and consumers of Science Fiction: their meanings, their origins, and some of their ramifications, for those people who may have some interest in Science Fiction, but who may have been put off by this Language, which I have called "FutureSpeak."

How to Use This Book

I have listed these terms and phrases alphabetically, letter by letter. Words defined elsewhere in this book that are *relevant* to the entry at hand are distinguished by CAPITAL LETTERS. Other cross-references have been added wherever necessary. For each entry, when appropriate, I have included a notation in parentheses that explains its place in the Science Fiction world:

1. **Literary:** Terms and phrases that pertain to Science Fiction as literature, including those that deal with the physical act of writing, and the critical analysis of what has been written. Literary definitions may also apply to a particular story or film.
2. **Publishing:** Terms that deal with the preparation of the written product for sale.
3. **Printing:** Terms referring to the physical book as an item in its own right. Since much Science Fiction is privately printed, many people are involved with the actual process of getting the words onto paper in multiple copies for reading purposes.
4. **Film:** Terms used by those who put Science Fiction on film. This may also include TV/television.
5. **Aerospace:** Terms used in the exploration of space, which has engendered its own set of technological terms, many of which originated on the pages of Science Fiction.
6. **Specific sciences:** Self-explanatory, but necessary.

7. **Fan:** Terms and phrases that originated among the readers of Science Fiction. Many of the activities of Fans have engendered subjargons of their own, which will be indicated by the ubiquitous quotation marks. Conventions, Costuming, and Filking are the most frequent subheadings.
8. **Gaming:** Terms used by the players of such games as "Dungeons and Dragons"™ and similar exercises in fantasy.
9. **Comics:** Terms used by those who write, draw, and prepare comic books for publication.
10. Any other terms and phrases I felt were worth including.

I have tried to include as many of the arcane terms of the Language of Science Fiction as possible. If I have missed some, feel free to write to me care of my publisher, and omissions will be included in a revised edition.

The Language of Science Fiction, like everything else, is in a constant state of flux. This year's catch-phrase is next year's cliche; "Nanoo-nanoo" was funny in 1983 and silly in 1984. Not even a Science Fiction writer can predict just what is going to emerge from the language of Science Fiction in the next five years.

The only thing that I can promise is . . . it won't be what you think it will be!

FutureSpeak

ability (gaming): Any of the natural traits that make up a CHARACTER's basic definition. The character's ABILITIES are determined at the beginning of the game by a roll of the dice. While certain elements of the character are determined by the player (for example, ALIGNMENT) the character's ABILITIES may determine the character's CLASS, since certain ABILITIES are necessary for certain types of characters. A WARRIOR without STRENGTH is a sorry specimen indeed.

abort (aerospace): The command to cease action on any particular portion of a mission, or to shut down the mission itself. The ABORT button is controlled by the commander of the spacecraft and it is his or her decision that the mission or part of it be aborted. In theory, a mission can be aborted at any stage; in actual fact, an abort call is taken very seriously, and only used in cases of dire emergency.

access code (computer): The combination of letters that allows the user to find what's on a particular disk. Each FILE has to have its own ACCESS CODE, which must be different and unique so that the computer doesn't confuse it with some other ACCESS CODE on that disk or diskette.

ACCESS CODES play important roles in TECHNOTHRILLERS, where possession of the right one can open a Pandora's Box of dandy data.

accessories (fan/costuming): All those bits and pieces that are part of a costume, but not actually sewn onto it: swords, hats, shoes, reticules, sporrans, weapons . . . all are ACCESSORIES, and as such, can lend real impact to a costume. By the same token, a badly made or inappropriate ACCESSORY can detract from the overall effect. The most frequent ACCESSORY error is footgear; as ROTSLER'S RULES state, "Thy shoes shall match thy dress."

Some costumers are incredibly talented, and can make their ACCESSORIES from basic materials. Others haunt used clothing shops, garage sales, and flea markets in search of odd items that can be converted into costume elements. Lusters from Victorian chandeliers may wind up at the end of a magic wand, or dangling from the points of a crown. A beaded collar will be used for a headdress, and a moth-eaten fur stole will be dismembered and used as a Barbarian's loincloth. Nothing is too trivial or too tacky; plastic packing elements have been used as futuristic body armor, and the cardboard rolls that hold delicate crochet and knitting yarn can be the basis of a set of manacles (properly jeweled, of course) for the Slave Girls of Gor. Nothing will stop the imagination of a truly determined costumer.

Ackerman, Forrest J. (b. 1916): SF chronicler, movie historian, and superfan, who began many of the traditions of FANDOM. He claims to be the first to wear a HALL COSTUME, and was prominent in setting up such landmarks as the Fantasy Foundation, which has become a full-sized museum in Hollywood. ACKERMAN is a member of FIRST FANDOM, and is usually found at WORLDCONS, pontificating on the History of SF. ACKERMAN revels in his reputation as being Mister Superfan.

acrylics (art): Paint made with a chemical base that lends itself to a very clear, sharp line and a glossy finish. Most SF artists use ACRYLIC in preference to oil paint, because it's a very quick-drying medium. SF COVER ART is usually executed in ACRYLIC.

actifan (fan): A person who is actively engaged in SF FANDOM and its activities, such as attending SF CONS, writing for FANZINES and APAS, GAMING, and COSTUMING. For such a person, Fandom Is A Way of Life; see FIAWOL.

action/adventure story: One in which the element of constant movement of characters in and out of dangerous or suspenseful situations takes precedence over such minor matters as CHARACTERIZATION, description, or even rational MOTIVATION and PLOT. A good deal of early SF was this kind of pell-mell hurtling into action without much care for the basic believability of the situation. If it's totally immersed in ACTION/ADVENTURE, the story can be classified as SPACE OPERA. However, there are many good ACTION/ADVENTURE tales that also contain believable characters and fascinating speculations on Society. ROBERT HEINLEIN'S novels, which are full of action and adventure, are also filled with riveting characters and scientific plausibility.

Adam and Eve story: One in which the remaining male and female characters are left to repopulate a world. By now it's a total cliche, however remarkable it was when first used (somewhere around 1923). It's one of the most common "TOMATO SURPRISE" ENDINGS. Editors groan when they see it.

adaptation (comics): A comic based on some source other than the WRITER's fertile imagination. Most ADAPTATIONS are the comic equivalent of a NOVELIZATION of a popular film or TV series. Since they are usually taken directly from the SHOOTING SCRIPT, any later deviation from the script will show up in the comic.

A prime example is the adaptation of *Indiana Jones and the Last Crusade.* One of the most endearing scenes in the film involves the dispersal of a a flock of birds by means of an umbrella, carried throughout his escape from a Nazi stronghold by the elder Professor Jones (played by Sean Connery). The umbrella is nowhere to be seen in the comic, leading to the inevitable conclusion that its use was a brilliant piece of improvisation added at the last minute.

There are also comics with original story lines whose characters may be based on popular TV SERIES or films. These are not, strictly speaking, ADAPTATIONS.

adultzine (fan): A FANZINE that contains material that is not suited to minors. ADULTZINES were originally devoted to tales of romance with some sex thrown in; they are now almost exclusively SAME-SEX RELATIONSHIP STORIES, and may be graphically (if imaginatively) illustrated. Most of them require an AGE STATEMENT from the purchaser, so that they are not sold to someone who may not be ready for such realism. There are a few printers who flatly refuse to print ADULTZINES.

adzine (fan/fanzine): A FANZINE devoted to announcements of other FANZINES for sale, or in need of contributions. There is no fee for placing a notice in an ADZINE; occasionally the editor requests a copy of the material being advertised, for review purposes.

Some ADZINES contain only notices of FANZINES for sale. Others include longer reviews of FANZINES, FILK TAPES, or anything else the editor may want to bring to the readers' notice.

aerospace engineering: The designing and construction of spacecraft, as well as vehicles that move through atmosphere. The actuality involves much testing of materials, experimentation with models, and eventually, construction of vast rockets. Of course, the imaginations of SF writers have no such limitations. SF is full of stories in which some eccentric inventor builds a rocket in his backyard and cheerfully takes off for the moon.

Agena (aerospace): The earliest upper-stage rocket used in the U.S. space program. AGENAS were first used in 1959, and were considered the most powerful of their time. They are now obsolete.

agent (publishing): The intermediary between the writer and the publisher, who negotiates the sale of a book or screenplay in return for a percentage of the writer's profits (usually between

10% and 20%). In today's world, many publishers won't even accept a manuscript unless it is submitted by an AGENT. A film or TV network must, according to the rules of the Screenwriters' Guild, deal only with AGENTS. The trick, therefore, is for an unpublished writer to find an AGENT.

Beginning writers can find their AGENTS through a publication called *Literary Marketplaces* that can be found in any library or bookstore, or through a similar publication, WRITERS' MARKET. Another system that works even better is to gain referrals from other writers to their agents. Science Fiction writers seem to be more inclined to this kind of networking than other genres, and an established writer will frequently lend a hand to a talented newcomer by introducing him or her to a good AGENT.

A good AGENT looks after the best interests of the writer. He or she is also a legal advisor, editor, critic, and sounding board for new ideas. There are a few writers who proclaim loudly that they have never had an AGENT, and find no need for one. Chances are they began writing before the "agent rule" came into effect, and with a number of books or film scripts to their credit, their reputation is enough to get their works into print. For the up-and-coming writer of novels or SCREENPLAYS, an AGENT is a necessity. The exception to the "agent rule" is the magazine market.

age statement (fan): A written declaration that the purchaser of a FANZINE is over 18 years of age (or, in some cases, over 21).

airbrush (art): An implement that uses compressed air to spread the color evenly over a prepared surface. The result is a very smooth, elegant surface that can be refined to show great detail, cover imperfections, or create misty backgrounds. It is an expensive technique, but the results justify the expense.

airglow (aerospace): A faint glow in the night sky, arising from the ionosphere, where solar radiation turns otherwise inert atoms into ions. AIRGLOW appears in photographs taken from satellites, as a luminous halo around the Earth. Presumably, there would be a similar phenomenon observed around any planet with an oxygen/nitrogen atmosphere.

airlock (aerospace): An airtight transfer compartment through which a space traveler may enter or exit a sealed, pressurized cabin or ship. AIRLOCKS, which were developed for submarines, are now a vital part of all spacecraft.

albedo (aerospace): The ratio of light reflected from a body in space, whether natural (like the moon) or artificial (a SPACE STATION). ALBEDO is a matter of some concern, since it can affect the internal temperature of a spacecraft, making it literally too hot to handle. The heat that is not reflected away from the craft is absorbed by the components of the craft and transmitted to anyone or anything inside it.

algol (computer): An algorhythmic computer language designed by European academics. It is more popular in Europe than in the United States.

Algol variables (astronomy): A star system discovered and explained by English astronomer John Goodricke; it is now considered to be a triple-star system, and a source of radio waves that might be caused by an exchange of gasses between two of the three stars. The other explanation of the radio waves from ALGOL is also being investigated, but astronomers prefer Goodricke's explanation.

alien (literary): The SF term for any being not native to the planet Earth; by extension, should we find sentient life elsewhere, we would be the ALIENS.

The form such life would take has been a source of endless conjecture to SF writers, from H. G. WELLS' horrific MARTIANS to some of the more sympathetic creatures found in current SF. ALIENS might be more or less intelligent, compassionate, or altruistic than we are. They might come after us with ray-guns blazing or decide that we are just too nasty for their rarified sensibilities and quarantine us or they might just be passing by.

ALIENS in SF can be ferocious or delightfully quaint. They can be any shape or size justified by their natural environments. The only thing an ALIEN in current SF should not be is a mindless, ravening beast, out for blood, with no real psychological reality. Then it would be a BEM, and as such, it's an anachronism in SF as we see it today.

Alien/Aliens (film): Two films by different directors using the same monster to make different points. ALIEN, directed by RIDLEY SCOTT in 1979, is basically a HAUNTED HOUSE story, in which some space travelers find a parasitic creature in an abandoned spaceship that hunts them down one by one. The sequel, directed by John Cameron in 1986, has the lone survivor of the first film going up against a whole nest of the critters, with the help of a rowdy squad of SPACE MARINES.

Both films are notable for their atmosphere of brooding doom, the well-defined biological probability of the predatory ALIEN, and the excellent acting of Sigourney Weaver as the spunky heroine.

Alien Nation (film/TV): A workably mediocre film that became an excellent TV series. The BASIC PREMISE deals with the sudden influx of some 250,000 ALIENS, who have landed in southern California and are now integrating themselves into the American Dream. Parallels with the immigrant experience and the Black experience are obvious, but the message is given with enough humor, compassion, and action to be believable.

alignment (astronomy): A situation in which the planets of a system are placed in their orbits in a direct line with one another from a central point (usually as seen from Earth). The most common form of such an ALIGNMENT is a solar or lunar eclipse; when it occurs between a larger and a smaller object, the smaller one may pass before the larger one, causing a TRANSIT. See also CONJUNCTION.

alignment (gaming): One of several traits that a character may assume—GOOD or EVIL, CHAOTIC or LAWFUL, and various combinations of the same (with a NEUTRAL element thrown in). There are nine possible combinations, each having a major implication for the way the character will react to different elements of the adventure. It is recommended that a player stick with some form of GOOD character; if this is a heroic adventure, why be the villain? On the other hand, some players find a LAWFUL GOOD person to be too priggish to play properly, and will prefer to be CHAOTIC or NEUTRAL.

The characters in a particular game should have ALIGNMENTS that more or less balance each other; otherwise, they'll spend all their time fighting over what's to be done, and they'll never get anywhere!

allegory (literary): A deceptively simple story with a hidden meaning, often one with deep political or religious implications. Many of the classic children's stories are ALLEGORIES, whose original meaning has been forgotten or distorted. GEORGE ORWELL'S *Animal Farm* is a example of a modern ALLEGORY.

"all systems go" (aerospace): "Everything is just fine; we are going ahead as planned." John Glenn said it on his first space flight in 1962, but he claimed he got it from Col. "Shorty" Powers, who was running the communications console for the Mercury Program at the time. This phrase has now become part of the standard usage of the English language.

alpha-female (biology): The leader of a matriarchal pack, or the mate of the leader of a patriarchal pack; hers are the genes that are going to be perpetuated, since she is the only one in the pack permitted to have offspring by the ALPHA-MALE. A number of SF writers have tried to extend this behavior pattern to non-Earth life-forms, with interesting results.

alpha-male (biology): The leader of a male-dominated pack, or the mate of the leader of a female-dominated pack. ALPHA-MALE behavior is much more aggressive than ALPHA-FEMALE behavior in similar situations, since the ALPHA-MALE is constantly under threat from other males who might want to take over the leadership of the pack. Among primates (and, incidently, humans), a ritualized defusing of this aggressive behavior has led to MALE BONDING.

alter ego (literary): A character who acts and speaks for the author, as a kind of alternate. Often, the ALTER EGO will tell the story from a particular POV/POINT OF VIEW; while not the main character, the narrator can comment on the action from an outsider's angle. He or she may not know the workings of the other characters' minds; they (and we) can only guess from what is done and said by those other characters just what is going on.

alternate history (literary): One of the intellectual games SF authors play, in which the story takes place in a world where some vital (or even trivial) event occurred differently from the historical reality we know. One of the most common "ifs" of this type is speculation of the outcome if Hitler had won World War II. Other key points might be battles that were won or lost by the barest of margins, or assassinations that did (or did not) take place. See also ALTERNATE UNIVERSE; PARALLEL UNIVERSE.

Alternate Universe (literary): A plane of existence similar to our own, but with significant differences, brought on by a change in the actual fabric of reality. For instance, Piers Anthony's *Blue Adept* novels presuppose two Universes, superimposed upon each other. In one, magic works (within certain limits); in the other, the physical laws of science rule. Roger Zelazny's AMBER Universe presupposes several planes of reality, called Shadows, with one being supreme, the City of Amber.

The most common ALTERNATE UNIVERSE is one in which magic formulas take the place of what we call Science, that is, the predictable reactions of physical objects to particular circumstances. In Randall Garrett's *Lord Darcy* stories, for instance, Richard the Lionhearted did not die of an arrow wound; instead, he lived long enough for his nephew, Arthur of Brittainy, to succeed him . . . and the Angevin Empire still exists. Magic works, according to logical and sound reasoning in this Universe.

ALTERNATE UNIVERSE stories bring out the historian in most SF Fans. See also ALTERNATE HISTORY; PARALLEL UNIVERSE.

amateur (literary): Not a professional, that is, a fan. AMATEUR can be used as praise or blame, depending on the attitude of the user. There are still a number of people who firmly believe that if something is worth reading, it must be paid for; otherwise, since no one thought enough of it to buy it, there is no point in reading it. On the other hand, a number of excellent writers are filling the pages of FANZINES, SMALL PRESS, and SEMIPROZINES with readable stories for which they receive little or nothing by way of payment. See also FAN; FANDOM.

Amber (literary): The Universe invented by Roger Zelazny for a series of novels that began with *Nine Princes in Amber* in 1976. The first series takes Corwin, Prince of Amber, through a hair-raising set of adventures, involving family squabbles, battle, murder, and sudden death, and wanderings through several ALTERNATE UNIVERSES. Zelazny is currently embarked on a second set of Amber novels, involving Corwin's son in more adventures.

The AMBER novels have spawned at least two FANZINES (*Kolvir* and *Shadow Shiftin'*), a number of FILK-SONGS, and some truly incredible costumes. While some critics decry them as mere potboilers, as compared with some of Zelazny's more ponderous and thought-provoking works, the AMBER stories remain in print because of their popularity.

analog (computer): An electronic "brain" that works on the principle of measuring voltage, electrical resistance, or whatever. ANALOG computers are now considered primitive. They have largely been replaced by DIGITAL computers. However, many of the post-World War II stories about computers used ANALOG computers as their main characters.

Analog Magazine: Formerly, *Astounding Stories,* edited by John Campbell through most of its run, 1938 to 1965. Always a bastion of HARD-CORE SF and HIGH-TECH STORIES, ANALOG is still one of the major SF markets for both prose and art.

android (literary): An automaton; a machine deliberately built to resemble a human being, possibly with living tissue in its body, usually, in its brain cells. ANDROIDS differ from robots in that they are supposed to be as physically like humans as it is possible for a machine to be.

A typical film/TV ANDROID is Mr. Data from "Star Trek: The Next Generation." A constant theme in SF is the ANDROID who finds that a human body brings with it human emotions. An interesting variation on this idea is in C. L. Moore's story "No Woman Born," in which an actress trades in her organic body for a metal one. See also ROBOT; CYBORG.

Andromeda strain (biology): A new strain of microorganism, developed in a research laboratory, whose escape might lead to disastrous consequences. A case of Life imitating Art, since the term came from the novel of the same name by Michael Crichton, in which a bacillus is brought to Earth via a meteorite.

Angstrom unit (physics): Named for Nils Angstrom; a length of light waves. 1/10,000 of a micron, or 1/100,000,000 of a centimeter. In other words . . . very, very short.

animation (film): Any process that makes nonanimate objects appear to move. The nonanimate objects can be drawings, puppets, even bits of clay or blocks of furniture. Several techniques are used in ANIMATION: STOP-ACTION animation, which records a minute change in a solid object; FULL ANIMATION, which records minute changes in drawings that are then projected at a certain rate so that the eye is fooled into believing that they are moving; LIMITED ANIMATION, in which some of the background is not changed, while the main figures show some alteration, providing the illusion of movement.

ANIMATION in SF began early, with the trick photography of GEORGES MÉLIÈS. Most people would agree that the Walt Disney Studios reached a high degree of artistry in FULL ANIMATION with such masterpieces as *Fantasia* and *Bambi. Who Framed Roger Rabbit?* has opened new vistas in interaction between animated and "live" performers, while the surreal images of Ralph Bakshi's *Lord of the Rings* display another path for animation to take.

Unfortunately, most animation in SF film is used in the SATURDAY MORNING GHETTO, where the Superheroes battle monsters of every description, proving that SPACE OPERA is not dead.

anthology (comics): A comic that contains several different stories by several different CREATIVE TEAMS, presumably about several different sets of characters. Found largely in HARDCOVER, comic ANTHOLOGIES often serve as a showcase or historical perspective on a character or set of characters.

anthology (publishing): A group of short stories, poems, or novellas usually connected by theme. SF has gradually attained literary legitimacy through HARDCOVER anthologies, although PAPERBACK anthologies were one of the first forms of SF made available in book form (as opposed to PULP MAGAZINES). At first, ANTHOLOGIES contained only previously printed works, but with the decline of SF magazines, the "original" ANTHOLOGY is becoming more and more popular.

Several concepts in anthologies have become popular in the last ten years, among them, the SHARED UNIVERSE anthology, and the THEME anthology, in which various writers use a central theme for original stories. *Thieves' World* is a primary example of the SHARED UNIVERSE; *What Might Have Been* is an anthology of ALTERNATE UNIVERSE stories edited by Greg Bear and Martin Greenberg.

A group of stories by a single author is termed a "collection," and is usually MARKETED and sold in the same way as any other work by that author.

anthology series (TV): A number of short dramas, each complete unto itself, that are broadcast under a general title. A mainstay of early television, ANTHOLOGY SERIES included such classics as TWILIGHT ZONE (1959–1964) and *Outer Limits* (1963–1965). ANTHOLOGY SERIES provided a training ground for directors such as STEVEN SPIELBERG, writers such as Paddy Chayevsky, and actors such as William Shatner among hundreds of others. The popularity of the ANTHOLOGY SERIES waned with the development of dramatic SF series with continuing characters. Recent attempts at reviving the genre with such shows as *Amazing Stories* (produced by SPIELBERG, 1985–1987) have met with little success on broadcast TV; however, eerie shows such as *The Hitchhiker* and *Ray Bradbury Theater* have found a home on CABLE or DIRECT SYNDICATION stations.

antihero (literary): The antithesis of the HERO, that trusty, brave, and reverent soul who leads the fight in the battle of Good against Evil. The ANTIHERO is frequently depicted as being brutal and coarse, and is often shown to be untrustworthy in the normal sense. ANTIHEROES of both sexes represent the ambiguity of modern morality. They appear frequently as the protagonists of PICARESQUE tales. Typical SF ANTIHEROES are swaggering swashbucklers like Poul Anderson's Domenic Flandry, the Terran Agent in the *Technic Civilization* series, and Han Solo, the mercenary-turned-general in the *Star Wars* films of GEORGE LUCAS. An ANTIHERO may not be admirable in the strictest sense of the word, but he or she is often a welcome change from the dauntless perfection of the HERO or Heroine.

antimatter (physics): Matter consisting of antiparticles that resemble protons, electrons, and so on, but have an opposite electrical charge. Theoretically, if matter and ANTIMATTER come into contact, they will annihilate each other, releasing vast amounts of energy, which could, it is theorized further, provide power for space travel.

One theory holds that there are separate regions of the universe, one built on matter as we know it, the other built on ANTIMATTER; the two regions separated at the moment of the BIG BANG. Another theory holds that there are various planes of existence, one containing matter, the other ANTIMATTER. At the present time, none of this can be proven, which does not stop physicists or SF writers from speculating about it.

antitech (literary): A society or community violently opposed to technology beyond a specific (and usually very primitive) level. Often, this attitude is represented as being the result of a POST-HOLOCAUST reversion to savagery reinforced by a repressive priesthood, which has decided that technology is the root cause of the surrounding devastation.

APA/Amateur Press Association (fan): A collection of individual newsletters, published at regular intervals by a group of contributors, collated by an Official Editor (OE), who then mails out the collection to each member of the group. Members contribute enough copies of their newsletter to send to the entire group, and reimburse the OE for the postage.

APAS (pronounced as a word) began fairly early in SF FANDOM. The first recorded APA was FAPA (Fantasy Amateur Press Association), founded in 1937 by Donald A. Wollheim. Since then there have been many APAS that deal with many facets of SF FANDOM. At one time or another, there have been APAS on FILKING, like APA-Filk, or *Star Trek*, like APA-Enterprise. APA-69 is for gay SF fans; APA-NYU helps New York (or ex-New York) fans communicate with each other.

Joining an APA is not too difficult; a very few have waiting lists, but most are willing to accept new contributors as the Old Guard GAFIATES, or drops out. Check around at CONS; ask other fans with similar interests if there is an APA for a particular area of expertise. Then, the prospective member writes a newsletter and mails it to the OE, who collates it with the rest of the bundle, adds a "cover sheet," and mails out the lot.

Computer BULLETIN BOARDS are taking over some of the function of APAS, which were originally the primary means of communication between SF fans. However, APAS still perform their major function of giving SF people the opportunity of expressing themselves and interacting across the miles.

apocryphals (fan): Those cute dragons, sehlats, stuffed kitties, or whatever that are toted around CONS by FANS as mascots, good-luck charms, or just plain decorations as a kind of security blanket for grown-ups. Many of them are works of art. At one time there was a craze for bean-bag dragons, which were then dressed up in costumes that could be anything, from a medieval tunic to a full-dress Star Fleet Admiral's jacket, complete with medals. A few CONVENTIONS offer prizes for the most original or best-dressed APOCRYPHALS.

Apollo program (aerospace): The last of the manned American space flights that led to the Moon landings. Apollo 11 got Neil Armstrong, Mike Collins, and Edward "Buzz" Aldrin to the Moon in July of 1969. The final APOLLO mission was #16, in 1972; since then, no human has walked on another planetary body besides our own Earth, although our artifacts have traveled to Mars through the Viking program and beyond the limits of our planetary system with the Voyager probes. Efforts in subsequent space programs were aimed at using the SPACE SHUTTLE to deploy satellites and provide the means of constructing a possible way-station before going on to protracted space voyages.

Apollo suit: See SPACE SUIT.

appliances (fan/costuming): Excrescences of rubber, plastic, or other materials attached to a costumer's body to provide an extrusion or to replace a natural feature. Noses can be altered into snouts; horns are attached to heads, and tails to spines; even wings may be incorporated into a costume, although, as one FILKSONG has it, "After you've sewn 'em, it would have been easier if you'd have grown 'em!" Makeup techniques borrowed from theater and films have made startlingly realistic effects possible.

Whatever the APPLIANCE, the most important thing for a costumer is to make sure it does not fall off, which is one of the most devastating things that can happen during a costume presentation.

archetype (literary): A character or plot-line so hoary with age that it has ceased to be a STOCK figure or situation, and has been accepted as a myth in and of itself. According to the works of psychologist Carl Jung, certain ARCHETYPES have occurred with such regularity in folklore and mythology around the world that they may be part of the fabric of being human. The Wise Woman, the Pure Hero, the Quest for the Meaning of Life . . . all of these are ARCHETYPES that form much of the basis of our literary heritage, including SF.

artificial gravity (aerospace): Any means of providing the illusion of gravity in space, where there is none. The sensation of weightlessness is uncomfortable for many space travelers, and various ideas have been proposed to provide a sense of "up" and "down" for the inhabitants of SPACE STATIONS or space vessels on prolonged trips. It is generally accepted by the SF community that some form of ARTIFICIAL GRAVITY will be needed in spacecrafts that are used for extended voyages. How this is to be achieved varies from writer to writer, but it's one of the CONVENTIONS of SF writing. There is a "deck" on a spaceship, and the crew's feet are on it. See also CORIOLIS EFFECT.

artificial intelligence (electronics): The possibility of creating a mechanism capable of duplicating human thought processes that has fascinated SF writers since Mary Shelley wrote FRANKENSTEIN in 1818. The current research is aimed at using the human brain as a model for a machine that will not only think but might even feel emotions. Most SF computers that develop personalities are not particularly mobile; David Gerrold's Harlie, of *When H.A.R.L.I.E. Was One* (1972), is typical. See also ANDROID; ROBOT; COMPUTER.

art show (fan/conventions): An exhibition of SF/Fantasy artwork at a CON (Convention) that serves as a showcase for artists, both PRO and FAN. Most SF CONS generate great interest in their ART SHOW, and try to attract exhibitors from around the country. There is usually a selection of works by the Artist GUEST OF HONOR, both ORIGINALS and PRINTS, as well as PIECES by local artists. Most of the works exhibited are assumed to be for sale, unless otherwise noted. Members of the CON can purchase the art through various AUCTIONS, indicating their interest by placing written bids on BID SHEETS. In addition to a small commission charged by the CON on art that has been sold, some CONS generate income through HANGING FEES, that pay for minor housekeeping costs like printing BID SHEETS.

Most artists welcome the opportunity to exhibit at an SF CON. The audience is there to view and purchase SF and Fantasy art; in addition, SF book and magazine editors are there to look over the current output, and may provide encouragement and a possible commission for a rising artist.

The ART SHOW also provides the opportunity for the artists to meet and exchange notes on who's buying what, and what the next trend is going to be. As in the SF writing field, most SF artists find themselves a small fish in a large sea of MAINSTREAM sharks, and are usually eager to get together for social interaction. See also AUCTIONS; BID SHEET; BIDDING WAR; CON; CONTROL SHEET; PIECE; VOICE AUCTION.

ASFA/Association of Science Fiction Artists: Organization of SF illustrators, similar in aims to SFWA (Science Fiction Writers of America), in that it promotes the interests of SF artists. Members must have sold a certain number of illustrations or paintings, making them "professional." ASFA provides its members with sample contracts, assists in negotiation difficulties, and acts as a clearinghouse for information on such matters as which are the best CONS for exhibit purposes.

ashcan edition (comics): A very small run of a comic, to be privately distributed. Occasionally the ASHCAN EDITION is a prototype or trial edition of a new comic; sometimes it is a SIGNED LIMITED EDITION; more often, it is the comic book equivalent of a FANZINE, or else it's an INSIDE JOKE edition that is circulated only among those who are in on it.

Asimov, Isaac (b. 1920): Prolific SF writer, author of over 400 works by latest count, and still going strong, known for stories of HARD-CORE SF. He is best known for the *Foundation* novels, and his many tales of ROBOTS. *The Caves of Steel* introduced R. Daneel Olivaw, ASIMOV's answer to Sherlock Holmes, as well as the Three Laws of Robotics, which are now incorporated into most robot research.

ASIMOV is an erudite and witty speaker, and is often called on to act as spokesperson when the opinion of the SF community is requested by the general media, as during the Voyager Missions, for instance.

Presently, Dr. A (as he is fondly known in FANDOM) is engaged in uniting his various Universes into one gigantic Super-Novel, between his editorial duties at *Isaac Asimov's SF Magazine,* his various scientific writings, his juvenile novels, and his many appearances at East Coast Conventions.

Asimov's Laws of Robotics: See ROBOT.

asteroid (astronomy): A small rocky body in space, moving in an elliptical orbit around a star, often with several thousand similar bodies, forming an ASTEROID belt. In our Solar System, the ASTEROID belt lies between the orbits of Mars and Jupiter, giving rise to the belief that there was once another planet in that orbit. Asteroids range in size from a meter or two to about 600 miles in diameter—too small to hold an atmosphere, or evolve native life-forms. However, asteroids make dandy hiding places for pirates and other riffraff, and may be the scene of a typical SPACE OPERA adventure tale.

Occasionally, asteroids collide, due to their extremely eccentric orbits, and the resulting debris falls to Earth as meteorites. Even more rarely, an ASTEROID may veer toward Earth itself. One theory of the disappearance of the dinosaurs has a large ASTEROID falling to Earth, sending up such a shower of rock and dust that it caused NUCLEAR WINTER, dimming the sun, and eliminating most life on this planet. The possibility of such a collision is remote, but is still being pondered by SF writers as well as astronomers. See also EARTH-GRAZERS.

astral plane (parapsychology): A state of existence beyond the range of our current perception. According to one theory, we exist on several planes; the most obvious of these is the one of our normal senses. The ASTRAL PLANE has been described as a gray, featureless area, which may be the scene of OUT-OF-BODY EXPERIENCES, such as those encountered by travelers in the *Overworld* of Marion Zimmer Bradley's DARKOVER series.

astrogation (aerospace): Navigation in space; the steering of a vessel through space, using complex computations arrived at through calculations of Time and Distance . . . usually, in SF stories today, with the assistance of a computer. The ASTROGATOR is a vital member of a spacecraft's crew; in many a tale he or she or it must steer through star systems and in and out of HYPERSPACE as well as around ASTEROIDS.

astrology (parapsychology): The ancient PSEUDOSCIENCE of divining the future or examining the character of an individual by consulting the position of the stars and planets at the time of the individual's birth. It is possible that the gravitational fields of these bodies might have some effect on a particular person, born at a particular moment. ASTROLOGY has a large and devoted following.

ASTROLOGY played a role in the development of ASTRONOMY, which is the study of the actual bodies in space rather than their effects on beings below them.

astronomical (art): Refers to the subject matter, not necessarily the price (although a really spectacular PIECE may sell for a goodly sum). Astronomicals depict stars, planets, and other un-Earthly scenes with as much realism as the artist can manage. Doug Drexler (better known as the hand behind the makeup in the 1990 *Dick Tracy* movie) is one of the masters of ASTRONOMICAL ART. His PLANETSCAPES are scenes of great beauty as well as technical accuracy.

astronomical unit (astronomy): The average distance between the Earth and the Sun, which is 92,955,832 miles or

149,597,910 kilometers. Distances in the SOLAR SYSTEM are often expressed in ASTRONOMICAL UNITS for convenience.

astronomy: The branch of science concerned with the observation of celestial bodies from Earth, and their interactions with each other. ASTRONOMY has a long and honorable history, beginning with ancient priests who observed the heavens to determine the correct dates for rites and ceremonies, and including such well-known figures as Galileo, Herschel, and Lowell. Modern ASTRONOMY uses tools undreamed of by the ancient priests, the latest being the Hubbell Space Telescope, placed in orbit in 1990.

astrophysics: The application of the laws of physics to the study of the universe outside our Earthly envelope. Studies of matter beyond Earth have led to important advances in our understanding of nuclear energy and gravitational fields.

Atlantis (literary): A legendary island of advanced civilization, whose sudden demise has prompted much speculation from authors as diverse as Plato and Marion Zimmer Bradley. ATLANTIS was first mentioned by the Greek philosopher Plato around 450 B.C. as the site of an ideal civilization, one of the earliest Utopias. In later years, ATLANTIS was presumed to lie somewhere under the Atlantic Ocean, drowned and still waiting for archeologists to find it. Oceanographic studies have proven that if ATLANTIS ever existed at all, it is not under the Atlantic. However, the island of Santorini, in the eastern Mediterranean, which was destroyed by a violent volcanic eruption around 1500 B.C., has been considered a possibility for the site of ATLANTIS.

Whether or not ATLANTIS ever existed in fact, it is still the scene of SF and Fantasy tales, and various explanations of its high level of technology have ranged from a native civilization to training by kindly ALIENS.

atmosphere (astronomy): The breathable envelope of gasses that encircles a planet, without which life as we know it cannot exist. Earth's ATMOSPHERE contains oxygen, nitrogen, hydrogen, and various other gasses; another planet may contain the same gasses in different proportions, or an entirely different mix altogether! One of the problems in WORLDBUILDING is to determine the ATMOSPHERE of a given planet and its effect on the flora and fauna that must breathe it.

atmosphere (literary): The prevailing mood of a story or film, as established by descriptive passages or (in the case of film) evocative camera work. A dark, brooding ATMOSPHERE might be important to a GOTHIC SF tale, while a light or frivolous ATMOSPHERE might heighten the enjoyment of a PICARESQUE adventure story. On the other hand, an inappropriate ATMOSPHERE can destroy a story . . . or else, make it into a satire of its own genre.

atmospherics (aerospace): Background noises that interrupt transmissions between the spacecraft and the GROUND CONTROL. They are annoying, but sometimes unavoidable, and the public hears them as bursts of static.

atomics (physics): Anything that involves the use of nuclear fuel or energy as a power source. In SF, starships are often powered by ATOMICS of an unspecified but highly dangerous nature.

auctions (fan): Used by various groups of FANS to raise money. The most common type of AUCTION is the one the CONVENTION runs via the ART SHOW, selling works of art to the highest bidder through written or vocal means. MAIL AUCTIONS are often used by FANS who must SELL OUT some of a vast collection of memorabilia that cannot possibly be carried to a central marketplace, or FANS who want to attract the widest distribution of bidders. CHARITY AUCTIONS may raise money for worthy causes, dear to the heart of a CONVENTION GUEST OF HONOR, or to assist a well-known SF FAN or author in times of financial distress.

authorized fan club: One run by the fans of a particular star of a film, or the author of a series of books, with the permission of said star or author, and the assistance of the person or his or her secretary, family, or whatever. Some actors relish the attention given to them by an AUTHORIZED FAN CLUB, and contribute to the club publications; others merely tolerate the club as part of the price paid for Fame. A very few do not authorize fan clubs for themselves at all; they prefer to be known simply by their work.

Occasionally, the production company will permit the members of an AUTHORIZED FAN CLUB the privilege of observing the production process, visiting the set, and so on. All of this is breathlessly reported in the Club's newsletter, or other publication. Many AUTHORIZED FAN CLUBS provide their members with some publication: a NEWSLETTER, an annual yearbook, or a FANZINE with stories and art as well as adulatory articles about the Star.

Most of the people connected with SF television series or films are grateful for the EGO-BOO such clubs provide. After all, all actors want to know they are appreciated by their loyal fans.

automation (engineering): The replacement of human drudges by machinery that presumably takes over the scut-work, leaving the humans to more important tasks. A bugaboo of mid-century SF, which saw many semiskilled or unskilled workers turned out of their jobs by more efficient machines that did not need such amenities as vacations or rest periods.

autopilot (aerospace): A device that can take over the routine duties of steering a craft through space (or atmosphere) for a set period, while the human pilot attends to other chores. Should the autopilot encounter something unusual (like an ASTEROID), it is supposed to summon the pilot with a loud beep, hoot, or siren.

axis (aerospace): One of three imaginary lines around which a spacecraft can revolve to achieve a particular position in space. The lateral axis runs from the bow to the stern, so the craft's nose may be pitched up or down; the vertical AXIS causes yaw; and the longitudinal AXIS allows the craft to roll. Any or all of these are called into action as the craft travels through Space.

back contamination (aerospace): The possible intrusion of a microorganism brought back to Earth by a spacecraft. This was a very real fear in the early days of Space exploration, when most of the scientific community was ready to accept the notion that there might be Something Out There with deleterious effects on the human system. However, after exhaustive search, nothing has been found to justify this fear, Michael Crichton's *Andromeda Strain* notwithstanding. It's far more likely that the opposite may be true; that the human and mechanical space travelers might have left something behind on Mars or the Moon (or beyond!) that might some day come back to haunt us, or may even destroy something about which we as yet know nothing, as in ARTHUR C. CLARKE's *Before Eden* (1961) in which incipient life on Venus is wiped out by waste left by human explorers. See also ANDROMEDA STRAIN; CHICKEN SOUP; WOLF TRAP.

backlist (publishing): The total listing of what a particular publisher keeps in print. Current best-sellers, known as the FRONTLIST, are, of course, available, but for authors to really be successful, their books should be BACKLISTED, so that they are always available. See also FRONTLIST; OUT OF PRINT/OP.

back matter (publishing): Material inserted after the main body of the text of a book. This often includes auxiliary information collected into an appendix, a bibliography, or a glossary; the index to a book is always placed after the main text. SF novels may have considerable BACK MATTER in the form of maps, glossaries to non-Human languages, and similar aids to understanding the culture of another species. The BACK MATTER in the original *Dune* novel by Frank Herbert is 50 printed pages.

back projection (film): See BLUE SCREEN.

back-story (literary): The events that occurred previous to the actual beginning of a story; everything that led up to the moment when the PLOT begins. In the case of SF, this can include quite a bit of FUTURE HISTORY, all of which must be integrated into the text so that the readers know where they are and what these people are doing there.

How this is done depends on the writer's expertise. The simplest way is to tell the reader directly; this, however, is also the surest way to stop a story dead in its tracks. The IDIOT LECTURE isn't much better, where one character tells another all this stuff.

The FLASHBACK method of inserting the BACK-STORY is slightly more effective, particularly in films, where it can be imparted to the audience as a DREAM SEQUENCE or VOICE-OVER. In a story, a FLASHBACK may just be confusing, and has to be handled with extreme care.

There is the "citation" method, in which the author uses chapter headings and citations from a hypothetical reference work, as used by Frederik Pohl in his *Heechee* novels or Frank Herbert in the *Dune* books. Jacqueline Lichtenberg has an Afterword or Preface in her SIME-GEN novels that explains everything in exhaustive detail. The *Thieves' World* anthologies often include maps and forewords that cover such matters as local geography and recent history of the region.

If there is enough BACK-STORY, the author must then go ahead and tell the story in another novel, dubbed a PREQUEL. And that's how SERIES are born. See also EXPOSITION; PREQUEL; SERIES.

badge (fan/convention): The identifying object that labels a person as being a member of a particular CONVENTION. The BADGE may be a simple piece of paper with the person's name, membership number, and the name of the CON on it, or it may be a sturdy plastic piece, in glorious color, with an alligator clip attached. Whatever it is, it must be worn at all times during the CON to gain admission to all ongoing activities. Its loss is a major disaster; however, people do manage to lose them, necessitating the constant announcements of "We have just found BADGE #123; please collect it at REGISTRATION."

BADGES are attractive and informative; they are also expensive. PRO-CONS tend to do without them, using only HAND STAMPS to keep out the riffraff.

BADGES may have printed ribbons attached to identify members of the CON-COM, DEALERS, GUESTS, or anyone else who may need access to an otherwise restricted area.

See also HAND STAMP; NAME TAGS.

Bakshi, Ralph: Experimental cartoonist and filmmaker; innovator in the field of animation. He first came into prominence in underground COMMIX, then moved into film, with a number of violent and sexually charged films. His *Fritz the Cat* was billed as the first X-Rated Cartoon. Bakshi's use of LIMITED ANIMATION and unusual lighting effects can best be seen in his stirring adaptation of *Lord of the Rings*.

B and W (comics): Black and White, as opposed to a full-color comic book. Many INDEPENDENTS use B AND W because it's far less expensive than the color process; however, the covers are still produced in full color.

"Banned from Argo" (fan/filk): A song, written by LESLIE FISH and a group of friends, describing in detail the adventures of an unnamed but easily identifiable starship crew on shore leave. It has a catchy tune and a raucous chorus, and it's the first FILK SONG most NEOFANS learn. It is still funny, but because it is so very popular it has gotten a strange reputation. Anyone who calls for it at a FILK-SING is instantly branded as a Clod

Who Knows No Others, and is hooted down. There is even a variation of the chorus that goes: "We don't sing 'Argo' anymore."

"Banned from Argo" has been recorded several times, by FISH and others.

barbarian (fan/SCA): The person who has taken on the behavior and dress of a BARBARIAN of the Literary type (see below). They walk around the CONVENTION clad in fur and leather, not much of either, bearing as much hardware as the WEAPONS POLICY will let them. They are often quite pleasant in their everyday MUNDANE life; they look on this activity as a way of releasing their aggressions.

The only objection to BARBARIANS at the CON comes when they insist on playing out their PERSONAS to the full. Then they become obnoxious, and must be removed, gently but firmly, by SECURITY.

barbarian (literary): The "child of nature," often endowed with superior strength and abilities, who lives and loves outside the laws of so-called Civilization. Robert Howard's CONAN is the prototype, along with Edgar Rice Burroughs' Tarzan; both of them owe a lot to Kipling's Mowgli, hero of *The Jungle Book.* The idyllic BARBARIAN is governed by his own sense of what is right; he takes what he wants, slaughters those whom he feels deserve it, and generally acts like a puppy off the leash.

The reality is, of course, quite different, as history has shown. The BARBARIAN societies on Earth have been rigidly circumscribed by custom and taboo; only when such a society overruns and conquers a weaker (although more settled) foe are the bars let down. When that happens, as it has in our own time, the result is horrendous for all concerned.

The popularity of BARBARIAN heroes (and occasional heroines) in fantasy literature is their appeal to the destructive adolescent in all of us; that urge to upset the Powers That Be, and give the authoritarian Establishment a symbolic kick in the pants. Eventually, most of us have to grow up and bow to those in authority; the BARBARIAN can thumb his nose (or worse).

barbecue maneuver (aerospace): a rotation of a spacecraft once an hour around its ventral axis, in the manner of a chicken on a barbecue spit, to keep the external temperature evenly balanced between the heat of the sun and the cold of space. Unless this is done, one side of the craft becomes intolerably hot, while the other freezes over. The BARBECUE MANEUVER was first used during the Apollo 8 mission, in 1968.

bardic circle (fan/filk): A FILK-SING, or sing-along, where the chairs are arranged in a circle and each member takes a turn, in strict rotation. Lately, BARDIC CIRCLES have become more BARDIC and less FILK; the songs are supposed to be Authentic Ballads, and are often fairly grim in tone.

A more popular variation is PICK, PASS, OR PLAY, where the circle is wider, and the members have the option of passing their turn to someone else.

Occasionally, the BARDIC CIRCLE will leave room for a nonperforming audience; however, a Strict BARDIC CIRCLE will expect everyone to participate in one way or another. See also FILK; PICK, PASS, OR PLAY

Barsoom (literary): Mars, as described by EDGAR RICE BURROUGHS, in a series of stories written between 1912 and 1948. John Carter, RICE'S hero, is miraculously and mysteriously transported to Mars/Barsoom, where he undergoes wild adventures and romantic interludes with improbable but memorable beings. The BARSOOM of BURROUGHS bears little resemblance to the rock-strewn desert revealed by the cameras of the Viking lander, but that is immaterial; the stories are still read, and stand as a landmark of SPACE OPERA.

basic material (film): The original source for a screenplay, which adapts it to the needs of the camera. The BASIC MATERIAL could be a novel (*Logan's Run*, originally by William F. Nolan, 1961) or a short story ("Enemy Mine," adapted from a story by Barry L. Longyear, 1985). It could be a play or a comic book (*Superman*). Whatever it is, by the time it reaches the screen it may be well-nigh unrecognizable. All that remains of Alan Nourse's novel *Bladerunner* is the title, which was tacked onto a truncated version of Philip K. Dick's complex novel *Do Androids Dream of Electric Sheep?* Nourse was still paid for his novel, just as Dick was paid for his, which may explain why, although there are many horror stories about what happens to BASIC MATERIAL once the filmmakers get their hands on it, writers still try to sell their stories to filmmakers.

basic premise (literary): See PREMISE.

***Bat Durston* story** (literary): A generic ACTION/ADVENTURE formula story, set on another planet or in another time. Bat Durston is the all-purpose ACTION/ADVENTURE Hero: tall, handsome, courageous, and not too bright. A BAT DURSTON STORY can be transferred from the Longhorn Saloon in Dodge City to the Bull and Bear Tavern in Sherwood Forest to the Spaceman's Rest on Planet X without changing much more than an adjective or two. The plot remains the same.

The term first was used in the BLURB for *Galaxy* magazine in the 1950s, when Herb Gold was editing. In the ad, Gold promised that there would be no such mindless PULP FICTION in *Galaxy*, which would print only the best and most thought-provoking SF it could find. (Gold made good on his promise, too; *Galaxy* was one of the sources of unusual SOFT SF until it folded in 1980.)

The BAT DURSTON STORY need not always be a cliche; *Outlands* (1981) is taken directly from the Western classic film, *High Noon*, with Sean Connery as the hard-bitten lawman originally played by Gary Cooper.

Batman (comics/film/TV): Superhero created by Bob Kane for Detective Comics, based loosely on a series of short stories by Murray Leinster. Batman made his first appearance in 1939; since then, he has not only appeared in comic books but has been the hero of a campy TV series (1966–1968), and appeared in a film that broke all existing box office records (starring Michael Keaton as BATMAN and Jack Nicholson as the Joker.)

BATMAN is, in reality, Bruce Wayne, a multimillionaire-turned-crimefighter, who lives with his young ward, his butler, his old aunt, and his hardware in "stately Wayne Manor," just outside Gotham City. BATMAN battles only the weirdest of SUPERVILLAINS: the Joker, who uses practical jokes for very nasty purposes; the Penguin, with his endlessly imaginative umbrellas; King Tut, who fancies himself an Egyptian Pharaoh, reincarnated. Against such villains, BATMAN employs an arsenal of gadgets, all housed in the Batcave, beneath Wayne Manor.

BATMAN'S popularity is easily understood. He is not some being from another planet but an ordinary person who has trained himself for the self-imposed duty of protecting the less fortunate from the villainies perpetrated by the more powerful. In earlier stories, he is sometimes referred to as the "Dark Knight"; he is just as ruthless as the people he fights, the difference being that he is on the side of Justice.

Baxter Book (comics): A TRADE EDITION of a COMIC, printed on high-quality paper, often in a HARDCOVER format. BAXTER BOOKS are often collections, ANTHOLOGIES, or PORTFOLIOS, with unusually high standards for artwork and coloring.

"Beam me up, Scotty!" (TV): The phrase uttered by Captain Kirk on STAR TREK whenever he wanted to leave an unpleasant or dangerous situation. It has become a catch phrase, uttered in tones of desperation or exasperation, when things get out of hand. It appears on T-SHIRTS and BUTTONS, often with the addendum "There's no intelligent life here."

Beauty and the Beast (film): A rendition of the fairy tale, directed and produced by poet and artist Jean Cocteau in lavishly romantic style. Considered by many one of the most beautiful movies ever made, *La Belle et le Bête* was filmed in the depths of World War II, under circumstances in which the only way out of total despair was total romanticism.

The film follows the fairy tale faithfully, with Jean Marais as the Beast and Joy Aimee as Beauty. It was first shown in the United States in 1948; it is often revived in "art houses" and at film festivals.

"Beauty and the Beast" (TV): Television series, 1986–1990. One of the more unusual PREMISES seen on American television, B&B surmises that under the city of New York there exists a subterranean network of tunnels and caves, where a Utopian society of outcasts ekes out its existence with the assistance of "helpers" from the "world above." The Beast is Vincent, a genetic experiment gone awry, with the appearance of a lion and the soul of a poet. Beauty is represented by Catherine, a young woman of the upper strata of Society, who is brutally mangled one night (she is mistaken for someone else). Vincent finds her, takes her into the Tunnel World, and the rest of the series depicts their growing relationship, as they realize their love for each other. Interspersed with this highly charged romanticism is the brutal reality of late-20th-century New York City, with its urban problems of crime, homelessness, drug addiction, and so forth.

The series was originated by Ron Koslow, and has generated a good deal of response from female fans; its star, Ron Perlman, was somewhat startled at how much his man-hearted-lion touched women of all walks of life. However, the RATINGS were disappointing after the Second Season, and the series was canceled.

The fans began a LETTER-WRITING campaign, and 12 more episodes were made. Since Linda Hamilton wished to leave the SERIES, another "Beauty" had to be found, and a story-line evolved that did not prove to be popular with the fans. The show was canceled again, this time for good. However, there is always CABLE or SYNDICATION!

BEM (Bug-Eyed Monster) (literary): A horrendous-looking creature of improbable aspect and unknown evolution, whose sole purpose is to menace the hero of an ACTION/ADVENTURE story. BEMS are considered cliche ALIENS these days. Readers today demand more character depth, even to their villains. The most hideous being is presumed innocent until it is found, red-tentacled, destroying an innocent mining colony. Even then, it is often discovered that the BEM was protecting its young, or defending a sacred burial ground that the humans, in their ignorance, were defiling. See also ALIENS; EXOBIOLOGY; XENOBIOLOGY.

benchmark (computer): The standard against which a computer's abilities and capabilities are tested. The term has come into the standard language as a touchstone, a high point against which others of a similar type are measured.

bheer (fan): A beverage available in the CON SUITE. It may be mildly alcoholic, it's usually served warm in a plastic glass, and it's supposed to be served only to those who are over 21. At one time it was actually beer, but the term is now used to describe almost any alcoholic liquid refreshment.

bible (tv): The information needed to write a script for a particular television series. Technically, it's called a *Writer's Guide.* It contains a list of the main continuing characters of the series, as they have been developed by the actors and the writers through the history of the series; it gives the historical or technological background of the series, if any; and it provides a format for presentation of scripts. The BIBLE for "V," for instance, would include material developed by the producers and writers that explained the "Visitors" and their society, so that any script would conform to what was already known about them and not contradict a previous script.

BIBLES are supposed to be top-secret, never to be seen outside the confines of the studio or the writer's sanctum. A number of them have managed to work their way into the marketplace—particularly the *Star Trek Writers' Guide* originally made up by Gene Roddenberry for the classic "Star Trek" series, and the new BIBLE for "Star Trek: The Next Generation"—reproduced for the edification of the fans.

bidding number (fan/art): Arbitrarily assigned to a person who wishes to bid on artwork at a CON. Often the BIDDING NUMBER is the number of the bidder's membership, as recorded on his or her BADGE; this makes sure the only bidders are members of the CON. WORLD-CONS have a more complex system, since they are dealing with a wide variety of artwork and over five thousand possible bidders.

bidding war (fan/art): The clash of egos and wallets when two fans want the same piece of artwork. Often, the two bidders are good friends, and the cry heard then is "Can I come and visit it?" A good bidding war can be a grand source of entertainment for the bystanders at the VOICE AUCTION, making it one of the high points of a CON.

bidding war (fan/conventions): The spirited contest between two possible venues for the WORLD-CON. According to the current Constitution of the World Science Fiction Society (the parent body of the World SF Convention), "WSFS shall choose the location and Committee of the WORLD-CON to be held three years from the date of the current WORLD-CON." Therefore, if an area wishes to play host to some 5,000 or so SF Fans, the committee representing that area has to get the information to the fans at least five years in advance. Since the WORLD-CON Constitution has divided the world into four regions (three in the North American continent and one representing everyone else), and since the WORLD-CON venue is supposed to move from region to region, it can be surmised that if there is adequate hotel and convention facilities in more than one city in said region, and if there is an active FANDOM ready to take on the duties of a WORLD-CON, there may well be a struggle to land this particular fish for a particular area.

It occasionally happens that there is no opposition to a particular site; in that case, the BIDDING WAR is called off for another year. See also WORLD-CON.

bid party (fan/convention): A gathering organized by a group of people trying to drum up support for a WORLD-CON bid. Since the World SF Convention is held in a different location each year, various areas vie with each other to get the business generated by such an event in their locality. A BID PARTY may be held in a single hotel room, or the CON-COM may decide to rent a suite in the hotel used by a major REGIONAL CON. There they will distribute literature praising the beauties and attractions of their city, and offer regional refreshments. BID PARTIES offer a chance for fans to congregate, sample delicacies, and "schmooze."

bid sheets (fan/art): Small paper forms attached to PIECES entered into the ART SHOW, for the purpose of entering bids prior to the VOICE AUCTION. Each BID SHEET usually has the name of the artist, the title of the PIECE, and a space for bids by bidder's name or by BIDDING NUMBER if the CON is a particularly large or important one. Often a PIECE must generate a set number of bids before it can be entered in the VOICE AUCTION. If no other person bids on it, the highest bidder gets the piece, after the manner of all auctions.

BID SHEETS enable the ART SHOW to determine which pieces will be entered into the VOICE AUCTION. They may also be the venue of lively BIDDING WARS, where two people crave the same item. When this gets to the point of written comments, the BID SHEET itself may be auctioned, with the proceeds going either to charity or to the CON.

Big Bang theory (astronomy): The event that supposedly began our universe, some 18 billion years ago (according to the latest astronomical data). The theory holds that at the time of the BIG BANG, all matter in the universe was squeezed into an intensely hot, dense fireball. So dense was this object that even atoms did not exist. The BIG BANG took only a few seconds, but at least a million of our years passed before the universe cooled enough for helium atoms to form. See also ENTROPY.

"Big Brother is watching you!" (literary): Ominous slogan emblazoned everywhere in GEORGE ORWELL'S DYSTOPIA, *1984*. The phrase has become the watchword of any dictatorship. It is also used whenever Those in Authority are present, and best behavior is mandatory.

"bill-yuns and bill-yuns" (TV): The constant cry of CARL SAGAN displaying the wonders of the universe during the various segments of the television series COSMOS, although he insists he never says it. It has become a catch-phrase to indicate a very large number of anything.

binary stars (astronomy): A system in which two stars revolve about each other, held together by gravitational fields. They are also called double stars.

SF writers and artists have tried to postulate what life would be like on a planet circling one or both of these stars; some really spectacular ASTRONOMICAL art has been produced, illustrating such a landscape.

bionics (biology): See CYBERNETICS.

birdworks (aerospace): The factory or plant where the spacecraft is actually assembled. A spacecraft is a bird; the phrase is obvious.

black hole (astronomy): An object in space whose gravitational pull is so strong that not even light can escape. It is surmised that such an object may be a star, greatly compressed, as might happen after a SUPERNOVA. The nucleus of a BLACK HOLE is theoretically quite small, but unbelievably heavy; it attracts everything within its gravitational field, including stray atoms and light. Once inside, nothing gets out. It is literally a hole in space.

BLACK HOLES cannot be directly observed, but their presence is deduced from emanations from nearby stars. Matter from a star may fall into a BLACK HOLE, emitting X-rays as it goes. Once the atoms reach the BLACK HOLE, they disappear.

Many SF writers have tried to surmise what would happen should someone actually enter a BLACK HOLE.

black humor (literary): Also known as "gallows humor," translated from the German *galgenhumor*. A mordant wit that finds comedy in the most uncomedic circumstances: nuclear war, death and destruction, and the sourest views of the Human Condition. The most striking example of BLACK HUMOR in SF film is *Dr. Strangelove, or How I Learned to Stop Worrying and Love the Bomb*, directed by Stanley Kubrick in 1964.

Blade Runner (film): Hugo-winning film based on Philip K. Dick's *Do Androids Dream of Electric Sheep?* directed by Ridley Scott, 1982. A stunning but ultimately depressing view of the future, in which most of the population has left Earth for the stars, and the only ones remaining are the sick, the ignorant, and the criminal. Harrison Ford plays a policeman, a "bladerunner," whose specialty is locating runaway ANDROIDS, called "replicants"; Rutger Hauer is the replicant seeking its maker, who ultimately must die.

The film is particularly notable for its brooding atmosphere and detailed backgrounds, deliberately invoking FILM NOIR.

"Blake's Seven" (TV): British-made television series that has become a CULT show among fans. The PREMISE involves a gang of outlaws, led by Roj Blake, who escape from a prison ship, find an Alien spaceship, and go out to fight for Justice. The series was not broadcast in the United States at all until very recently, and then it was only available in a small area. The episodes were distributed through BOOTLEG TAPES, to a small and vociferous group of fans, whose LETTER-WRITING CAMPAIGN alerted PBS stations to the desirability of acquiring this series.

BLAKE'S SEVEN fans have sponsored their own CONS; they have

generated many FANZINES, FILKS, and much artwork. The show is now being distributed more widely, and its FANDOM appears to be growing.

blooper reel (TV): A private film, made as a joke for the CAST and CREW of a TV series or a particular film, made up of OUT-TAKES, those inevitable missed lines, missteps, and mistakes that happen on the best-regulated of SETS. Occasionally the BLOOPER REEL finds its way out of the private screening room and becomes part of the CON FILM PROGRAM. Gene Roddenberry's *Star Trek* BLOOPER REEL has been pirated so often that it has become a standard item, for sale at CONS.

blorch, the (fan): Any of a variety of minor ailments that may attack a fan at a CON. Symptoms can include upper respiratory ailments, gastrointestinal disturbances, insomnia, or general irritability. The cure for THE BLORCH? Go home, go to bed, drink chicken soup, and sleep. See also CONVENTION CRUD.

blue screen (film): A special effects process that combines several elements into one image, using a traveling MATTE. The actors are photographed against the BLUE SCREEN. From this, one print is made, so that the actors are clear, against an opaque background. A second print is made with the background clear and the actors blanked out. Then one image is superimposed over the other, so that it appears to the eye as one complete image.

When done right, the effect can be breathtaking, as in the flying sequences of the *Superman* films.

blue screen acting (film): An exercise of the actors' imagination, wherein they react to something that will later be inserted via the BLUE SCREEN process described above. The final scenes of CLOSE ENCOUNTERS OF THE THIRD KIND are BLUE SCREEN ACTING at its finest. They were shot in an airplane hangar in Alabama, where François Truffaut, Bob Balaban, Richard Dreyfuss, and a cast of thousands had to gasp in wonder at the nonexistent "Mothership," which would be photographed much later. The inspirational result is a tribute to the talent of everyone involved.

blurb (publishing): The advertising, promotional, or laudatory review material on the dust jacket of a HARDCOVER or cover of a PAPERBACK book. The term was coined by critic and humorist Gelett Burgess in the 1920s, and no one has been able to come up with a better one.

The BLURB should give the reader an idea of the plot or theme of the book. It should tell something about the author, and it may include material or reviews about the author's previous works. Although the marketing department is usually responsible for its content, it is not uncommon for the editor of the book to write the BLURB.

B-movies (film): Films made during the 1930s and 1940s to be shown as the second part of a double bill. They were made quickly, written to formula, with STOCK CHARACTERS and plots, by hack directors and capable but not especially well-known actors. A few determined actors made their reputations in B-MOVIES, then went on to greater efforts; most of the B-MOVIES relied on a standard group of character actors and actresses. Many of the horror films of the 1930s qualify as B-MOVIES, as the plots got stranger and stranger and the scripts got worse and worse.

The rise of television and the breaking of the studio monopoly ended the production of B-MOVIES; their place was taken by the MADE-FOR-TV MOVIE, and most recently, by the made-for-video movie.

BNF (Big-Name Fan) (fan): A person who is well known in FANDOM, who may not be particularly well known to MUNDANES. Some BNFS (pronounced as initials) may be successful in fields other than SF; others may be more obscure. BNFS achieve their status through their work on behalf of FANDOM, as FAN-EDS, on CON-COMS, at FILK-SINGS and MASQUERADES, or just by being seen at CONS.

The question of who is or is not a BNF depends on who you talk to, which segment of FANDOM you're talking about, and where you live. A BNF in one section of the United States may be totally unknown elsewhere. Some BNFS GRADUATE and become PROS; others prefer to keep their AMATEUR status.

Probably the biggest BNF is FORREST J. ACKERMAN, who revels in his FANNISH connections. See also SMOF; SMOG.

book fans (fan): Those who insist that they only read SF, as opposed to those who watch it on television or films. There is a snobbery about BOOK FANS, who regard MEDIA FANS as illiterate cretins, incapable of understanding any but the very simplest plot line. MEDIA FANS retaliate by declaring that BOOK FANS are elitist wimps, who don't understand half of what they read anyway.

The break between BOOK FANS and MEDIA FANS was at its height in the 1970s, when the TREKKERS, as it seemed to the BOOK FANS, appeared to be taking over FANDOM. STAR TREK FANS wound up having their own conventions as a matter of protest against what they perceived as discrimination. There is still a difference between the FAN-CONS, which are aimed at BOOK FANS, and the PRO-CONS, which are ardently MEDIA-oriented. See also READER (fan).

booster (aerospace): Any rocket that propels the ship away from the ground and into the atmosphere, and, eventually, through space. Strap-on BOOSTERS fall away as the rocket climbs; later, BOOSTERS assist in maneuvers.

bootleg tapes (fan): Videotapes made by recording television programs or films that are not available in the United States, or by illicitly and illegally duplicating existing videotapes. While the sale of such tapes is illegal, there is a gray area regarding the reproduction and private distribution of home-made duplicates of series like BLAKE'S SEVEN and *The Professionals*, which were not shown in the United States until very recently, and may not be available at all in some areas. Dealers are warned that they are responsible for the legality of their merchandise, and any items that do not comply with FCC regulations and copyright laws may be confiscated.

bootlegzines (fan): FANZINES that have been photocopied without the permission of the original editor, offered for sale at exorbitant prices by unscrupulous dealers. Many of the early

MEDIAZINES are no longer available, since only a hundred copies or less were printed. The bootlegger manages to get a copy, reproduces it, and sells it as the original.

This is bad, but even worse are people who duplicate fanzines that are still in print, cutting the original editor out altogether. This practice has caused a lot of ink to be spilled in LETTERZINES, but there really is no recourse for the first editor to take without opening the copyright can of worms that no one wants to open. See also MEDIAZINE.

bootstrap exploration (aerospace): Using the gains from one mission to launch the next one, just as a person is said to rise by his or her bootstraps. Each mission brings in more information, which can be used to further the next mission, and so on, until the Space Station is built, the Moonbase is secured, and we're on our way to the stars.

boot up (computer): The procedures that initiate activity in a computer such as turning on the machine or entering the date and the time, whatever. The computer will not operate until this is done.

Bradbury, Ray (b. 1920): SF and Fantasy writer, known for his short stories of eerie doings, collected into volumes like *The Illustrated Man.* His most notable work of SF is *The Martian Chronicles*, a set of unconnected tales that form a unified work. BRADBURY'S influence is felt largely in the horror and fantasy elements that are now integrated into SF.

BRADBURY'S stories have been the BASIC MATERIAL for several films, among them *Farenheit 451*; he is the host of the "Ray Bradbury Theater," an ANTHOLOGY SERIES now seen in DIRECT SYNDICATION on television.

braking ellipses (aerospace): A maneuver that uses a series of orbital approaches to a planetary atmosphere to slow down the spacecraft before landing. The planet's gravity pulls the craft into an orbit that gradually decreases in velocity, until the final approach.

brennschluss (aerospace): The moment at which propulsion ends, for whatever reason, whether the craft is in orbit or out of fuel. From the German, meaning "combustion termination." Presumably the craft is on its way by then; if not, it's on its way back, very fast!

broadcast standards (TV): The department in charge of what actually gets onto the screen, or, the Censors. How powerful they are depends on the network, the show's content, the projected audience, and the time slot. Television is particularly vulnerable, since it is presented in the home, where the young and innocent may be direly affected by what they see on the screen.

We tend to laugh now at the stories of BROADCAST STANDARDS bigwigs who determined how much breast could be revealed by a costume, or which expletives had to be deleted. Some scripts were totally revised to comply with BROADCAST STANDARDS; one STAR TREK script had its KICKER cut out when it revealed that a crew woman was pregnant! (An episode of "Star Trek: The Next Generation" totally revolved around the pregnancy of an unmarried crew member, which shows how far things have come since then.)

Networks still exercise the option of removing undesirable material; there is more latitude given to CABLE or DIRECT SYNDICATION, where there is less control from Powers That Be.

Buck Rogers (comics/TV/film): The archtypical SF SPACE OPERA hero, first seen in a story, *Armageddon 2419 A.D.*, by Philip Francis Nowlan, published in 1928. BUCK ROGERS became the hero of a comic strip drawn by Dick Calkins; he was portrayed by Buster Crabbe in serial movies in the 1930s, and most recently, by Gil Gerard in a short-lived TV series that aired from 1983 to 1985, called "Buck Rogers in the 25th Century."

BUCK ROGERS is noble, brave, honest, and slightly goofy. In his original incarnation, he was a test pilot, frozen for 500 years, who wakes up in the future and proceeds to have a variety of adventures with the help of Wilma Deering and a variety of robots, sidekicks, and Mad Scientists.

BUCK ROGERS has come to stand for the ideal Space Hero, both real and fictional. As one lawmaker put it when asked about funding for future Space programs, "No BUCK ROGERS, no bucks."

bug (computer): An unwarranted hitch in the program, more dangerous than a mere GLITCH. If necessary, a BUG can call for a complete revision of the program, that is, a DEBUGGING, which is a very tedious process indeed. A VIRUS is a particularly nasty BUG.

The term originated when an actual insect managed to disrupt the workings of one of the earliest computers; the bug has been preserved in a scrapbook, and may be seen at the Smithsonian Institution in Washington, D.C. See also DEBUGGING.

bulletin boards (computer): Networks of linked computers, used by fans for instantaneous communications through MODEMS. There are several such networks; some fans belong to all of them. They are rapidly taking the place of traditional means of fannish communications, like APAS.

burn (aerospace): To fire a spacecraft's rockets for maneuvering purposes. A delicate operation, since too much BURN can send the craft into outer space and too little can do great harm to the ship's trajectory.

buttons (fan): Round metal or plastic objects with pins attached, usually with slogans or pictures emblazoned thereupon. A form of portable graffiti that can express the wearer's personal philosophy ("I am the mother of all things, and all things should wear a sweater"), or taste in entertainment ("Ravin' Avon Fan"), or even general mood ("Chaotic Weird"). Buttons are available in the DEALER'S ROOM of any CON; they are also handed out by promoters of films, TV series, books, and comics to publicize their products.

Burroughs, Edgar Rice (1875–1950): One of the earliest writers of SPACE OPERA, the creator of *Tarzan* and the *John Carter of Mars* stories. Burroughs formed the taste of a generation who avidly read of the deserts of Mars and the jungles of Africa (neither of which he ever visited). In spite of his high-flown dialog and simplistic plots, Burroughs remains one of the most popular SF/Fantasy authors, past or present, whose books are never OUT-OF-PRINT.

byte (computer): a unit of computer memory; 8 bits equals one BYTE.

cable (TV): An alternative means of receiving television signals through a CABLE instead of through the air. Since this involves a certain amount of equipment, and since the CABLE must be installed in the house where the signal is received, this is not a free service, as is broadcast television, but is usually provided by a private company. The stations that are received by the CABLE may or may not be available "over the air" as well; some CABLE services are linked to free channels in distant locations, extending the range of the user's television signal. Originally, the CABLE system was meant to bring better reception to those areas which, because of geography or weather, would not otherwise get any television signals at all.

There are several CABLE services that show new movies, original dramas, or special events that are not available elsewhere; for these the user must pay an extra fee. A number of CABLE stations provide special services, like all-sports programming, high-quality cultural events, or MUSIC VIDEOS.

Some British-made television series are not offered at all on broadcast television, and are only available on specialized CABLE stations. DR. WHO and BLAKE'S SEVEN, for instance, are rarely seen on local broadcast stations.

"call a rabbit a smeerp": The editor's term for using Terran biology on faraway planets, instead of inventing something really different. One of the more glaring aspects of faulty WORLD-BUILDING, the CALL A RABBIT A SMEERP syndrome is found in SF stories where the writer is more interested in action than description. If the place really is different, with a different ecology, geologic history, and possibly a different chemical makeup than Earth, the beings that inhabit it will be different, too.

Studies of the flora and fauna of Earth has demonstrated that ecological niches get filled by very odd creatures indeed, and there is no reason to believe that a reptile or bird might not fill the niche used on Earth by small, prolific mammals.

James Blish is supposed to have used the term first, but other editors feel the same way.

camera-ready copy (printing): Material that arrives typed cleanly, in whatever FORMAT the editor uses, ready to be taken to the printer. CAMERA-READY COPY is considered already typeset, ready to be used to print a book or a FANZINE. It is extremely economical, and is used today more than ever because of the ease with which it can be produced, thanks to computers and laser printers.

campaign (gaming): An adventure, involving all the players in some activity, like seeking a treasure or slaying a dragon. There are all sorts of things that can happen in a CAMPAIGN, and most of them are determined by the DUNGEONMASTER, with the aid of the dice.

Campbell, John (1910–1971): Highly influential writer and editor, who practically reinvented the SF genre after HUGO GERNSBACK invented it. As editor of *Astounding Stories*, CAMPBELL initiated what some call the Golden Age of SF, introducing writers like ROBERT HEINLEIN, ISAAC ASIMOV, L. Sprague DeCamp, and many others to his readership. He fostered HARD-CORE SF as well as FANTASY; he encouraged many of the people who are now considered the founders of modern SF.

The annual award given to the best new writer is named in his honor.

canals: See CHANNELS.

candids (fan/photos): Photographs of actors, writers, and others just being "people," as opposed to publicity STILLS. CANDIDS are especially prized when they show the subject with the fans, or when they catch the subject off-guard, in a moment of supreme silliness.

"Captain Video" (TV): The first continuing SF television series, first aired in 1949. Al Hodges was CAPTAIN VIDEO, who fought the Forces of Evil with his Video Rangers, launching their attacks from a secret mountain base.

CAPTAIN VIDEO was shot live, in black and white, on sets that looked as if they were made of orange crates (and probably were). The scripts were written by then newcomers Robert Sheckley, Damon Knight, and C. M. Kornbluth, who took the juvenile drama a step beyond the formula and stock characters expected of them. The popularity of CAPTAIN VIDEO led to other juvenile adventure series, like "Tom Corbett, Space Cadet." Unfortunately, SF on television then became identified with "kid stuff," and serious adult drama in the SF genre on television was limited to ANTHOLOGY SERIES until STAR TREK came along.

cast (TV/film): The actors involved in a TV series or film, particularly the lead players. The guest cast are the actors hired for one particular segment or EPISODE of the series; the rest are the regular cast.

The regular cast of a highly acclaimed or popular series find themselves much in demand as GUESTS OF HONOR at CONVENTIONS, where they get to bask in the glory of fannish applause. One measure of a series' popularity may be how often its cast members are invited to attend these functions.

cathode ray tube (physics): The object inside the computer or television apparatus that enables the image to be projected onto a screen. It's the central element in a television set, and its invention was the key to the entire video revolution.

cel (film): A section of film to be used in animation; from celluloid, the material used in early animated films. A scene is painted onto a transparent plastic sheet; more plastic sheets are overlaid, to produce the desired effect.

Original CELS are sold as COLLECTABLES; some of the CELS from JAPANIMATION can be viewed as original works of art, and are treated accordingly by collectors.

celestial mechanics (physics): The study of the motion and gravitational interrelations of bodies in space; of major importance in astronomical observations as well as in the theoretical and practical aspects of space travel.

celestial sphere (astronomy): The imaginary sphere of the heavens, with the Earth as its center, which appears to rotate once a day. All astronomical objects appear to lie on the inner surface of this sphere, facing the Earth.

This view of the Earth as the center of the universe has been disproven since the time of Copernicus; however, the fiction of the celestial sphere is maintained in order to locate particular objects in the sky. We know, for instance, that the stars in the various constellations may have little real relationship to each other, but the sky maps will show them as they appear to us here on Earth.

channeling (parapsychology): Leaving one's physical body to contact others on an ASTRAL PLANE. Another name for an old idea; OUT-OF-BODY experiences have been a part of parapsychological investigation for some time. See also OUT-OF-BODY EXPERIENCE.

channels (astronomy): The lines seen by astronomer Percival Lowell when he observed the planet Mars. It is now thought that these lines were nothing more than a reflection of the blood vessels in the astronomer's eye. However, the idea of a planet with running water captured the imagination of SF writers, and

Mars was endowed with channels or canals in the works of EDGAR RICE BURROUGHS, C. L. Moore, RAY BRADBURY, and many others.

The Viking landing disproved the Lowell theory; alas, there were neither channels nor canals. Nevertheless, there are geological formations that indicate that Mars once had flowing water, so Lowell might not have been totally wrong after all.

chaotic (gaming): One of the ALIGNMENTS set out in DUNGEONS AND DRAGONS.™ A CHAOTIC character believes that all things are ruled by chance, and there is no real order in the universe. A CHAOTIC Good character will be pragmatic, even self-seeking, but will usually do the Right thing, although perhaps for the wrong reasons. A CHAOTIC Neutral character has decided that there is no order in anything, least of all one's own actions, and is likely to do anything at any time. A CHAOTIC Evil character is totally wild, out only for himself or herself, with no restraints at all.

Most players tend to favor CHAOTIC Good characters, who are most like the majority of humankind, and are the easiest to work with.

chapbook (printing): Originally, a small cheap book of 8 to 16 pages, illustrated with woodcuts, containing such ephemera as nursery rhymes and ballads. These CHAPBOOKS are very rare and very valuable now, although at the time they were considered too cheap and banal to keep.

Currently, a SMALL PRESS CHAPBOOK may be a long story, of novella or novelette length (more than 3,000 words, less than 25,000 words) that is not quite long enough to be a novel, printed as an entity of itself, with illustrations. CHAPBOOKS are often used to introduce new writers who are working in the short story format, and who want to try a more complex story.

characterization (literary): The technique of developing the CHARACTERS in a story, so that they become real to the reader, who is drawn into their lives. The writer must use dialog, description, and PLOT POINTS to further the development of the CHARACTERS, so that by the end of the story, they will have changed in some significant way, or effected others to change. Anything less than that means a lack of depth to the story, and ultimately, a two-dimensional CHARACTER.

CHARACTERIZATION was not a major factor in early SF. PULP FICTION thrives on STOCK CHARACTERS and ACTION/ADVENTURE plots leave little room for deep emotional self-examination on the part of the participants. Writers like HARLAN ELLISON and RAY BRADBURY extended the limits of SF to include better-defined CHARACTERS. There are some who point to the emergence of women like Ursula LeGuin and Joan Vinge into the field of SF and the intrusion of SOFT SCIENCE into the hitherto technological world of HARD-CORE SF as a major catalyst that extended the genre still further. It is no longer enough for a writer to project a view of the future, or explain some piece of machinery; the people in the story are expected to be fully developed, as much as in any other work of fiction.

characters (gaming): The participants in a particular adventure, either as controlled by the DUNGEONMASTER or by the players. PLAYER CHARACTERS represent the players, who decide their actions and define their skills. NONPLAYER CHARACTERS are inserted by the DUNGEONMASTER as he or she sees fit.

characters (literary): The people in a story or a dramatic presentation. A work of fiction usually deals with recognizable people or beings representing them; in an allegory, animals may act like humans.

SF CHARACTERS may or may not be humans; they may not even be organic beings, strictly speaking. However, the writer must present the CHARACTERS in such a way that the reader cares about them and wishes to know more about them and their doings. See also ARCHETYPE; STOCK CHARACTER.

charisma (gaming): The ABILITY of a CHARACTER to lead through persuasiveness and personal magnetism; a particularly useful trait in a Paladin, who must gather his forces against the Powers of Darkness, or a Thief, who can persuade the group to take part in some foolhardy scheme. Conversely, a lack of CHARISMA designates the nebbish or nerd, who tags along, but is barely tolerated. CHARISMA is determined by the DUNGEONMASTER at the beginning of the game, by a throw of the DICE.

chicken soup (aerospace): One of the experiments sent to Mars on the Viking spacecraft in 1976, to determine the existence of life as we know it on the planet. A vial containing a combination of amino acids and other nutrients was placed on the Martian surface in hopes that some organism would be attracted to this bait and ingest it, leaving evidence of its good taste by expelling gasses, or at the very least, by removing the CHICKEN SOUP.

Unfortunately, the bait was not taken. The results were inconclusive; as of now, the only evidence of life on Mars is the remains of the Viking itself.

children's room ghetto (publishing/bookselling): The section of a bookstore or library devoted to materials for children. Many fine writers find themselves placed there, either because their protagonists are less than 13 years old, or because they choose to write in a fanciful, poetic style. As a result, readers who do not have children of their own, or who consider themselves past the age of such juvenalia, miss the loony humor of Daniel Manus Pinkwater, the wild puns of Jane Yolen, the bone-chilling eeriness of Zilpha Keatly Snyder, and the complexities of William Sleator, to name only a few.

Many of the great FANTASY authors are placed in the CHILDREN'S ROOM GHETTO, for no other reason than that they are read as part of a school curriculum. Jonathan Swift might well be horrified to learn that his biting political satire, *Gulliver's Travels*, is being sold as a jolly tale for little ones. See also JUVIES.

circadian rhythm (biology): The 24-hour cycle of human bodily activity that seems to occur whether we want it to or not. Experiments with isolated people in caves or laboratory conditions have proven that the human system reacts to a more or less regular cycle of activity. Astronauts on extended space flights or in space stations report the same reaction. It is conceded that some means of enforcing a "day" and a "night" will have to be built into any spacecraft on an extended flight.

SF writers have taken this into account in their tales of star voyaging; there are usually two shifts postulated in current space-traveling tales, although earlier SPACE OPERAS seemed to take the attitude that everyone was always available for duty.

Of course, there is always the AUTOPILOT. . . .

clairvoyance (parapsychology): The ability to see or hear events at a distance, even as they are taking place. Prescience is the ability to predict these events; precognition is the knowledge of the events before they happen, but not necessarily with any accuracy.

CLAIRVOYANCE often is uncontrollable and unpredictable. A true clairvoyant may see or hear something, and only later will he or she be able to relate what was seen or heard to an event happening some distance away.

Clarion Workshops (literary): The Clarion Science Fiction Writers' Workshops, conducted simultaneously during the summer on two college campuses, one in the Midwest (recently, at the University of Michigan in Ann Arbor), the other at the University of Washington in Seattle. The seminar was first held in 1968 at Clarion State College in Clarion, Pennsylvania; the venue has moved, but the basic thrust of the workshop remains the same. The course consists of six weeks of intense study of all aspects of SF writing under the guidance of a panel of respected and successful SF writers. Among those who have participated are screenwriter and novelist Norman Spinrad, short story expert Marta Randall, and novelists of the caliber of Orson Scott Card, Larry Niven, and Vonda McIntyre.

Admission to the course is by application; particulars are announced each year in various SF-oriented publications like LOCUS and *Science Fiction Chronicle*, and in WRITER'S DIGEST, which lists workshops and seminars on a regular basis. The course is aimed at people who intend to make a career out of writing SF, and those who have emerged from it have counted it as a major influence on their careers.

Clarke, Arthur C. (b. 1917): Writer and astronomer, known for HARDWARE stories, tempered by metaphysical nuances. His most popular novel, *2001: A Space Odyssey*, became one of the most beautiful and mysterious SF flims of all time, as depicted in Stanley Kubrik's 1968 film of the same name. CLARKE also acted as the host of "The Mysterious World of Arthur C. Clarke" (1980), a series of 30-minute TV programs that explored such phenomena as UFO sightings and rains of frogs.

Clarke's Laws: A set of truisms, formulated by A. C. CLARKE: (1) Any Technology sufficiently advanced in relation to its observers is indistinguishable from magic. (2) The only way of discovering the limits of the possible is to venture a little way past them into the impossible. (3) When a distinguished but elderly scientist states that something is possible, he is almost certainly right. When he states that it is impossible, he is very probably wrong.

class (gaming): A CHARACTER's profession or career, for which the CHARACTER has presumably trained before the events of the game. There are four basic CLASSES: WARRIOR, WIZARD, PRIEST, or ROGUE. There are subdivisions within these CLASSES, dependent on the character's ABILITIES, ALIGNMENT, and RACE. All of these factors are balanced by the DUNGEONMASTER and the PLAYER to formulate the CHARACTER, who will be the player's representative during a particular adventure, campaign, or perhaps, through a series of games.

cleric (gaming): A nondenominational PRIEST, in a ROLE-PLAYING GAME. CLERICS are usually some variant of GOOD, with WISDOM as a prime requisite ABILITY. They have the ability to cast certain spells, and handle sacred objects. A Priest can also be a fighter, like Friar Tuck in the legends of Robin Hood.

cliche (literary): A trite, overused, hackneyed character, plot twist, phrase, or situation; from the French. There are many CLICHES in SF, ranging from the ADAM AND EVE story to the Mad Scientist to the BEM. It is not easy to get away from them; a mark of a good writer is to be aware of them and to turn them around somehow, so that the superhero becomes a klutz (which is yet another CLICHE). See also STOCK CHARACTERS.

cliffhanger (film): An ending that leaves the hero (or more often, the heroine) in deadly peril, with no rescue in sight. The reader knows the hero will get out of danger, but not until the next installment. The term is taken from the filmed serials of the 1920s, 1930s, and 1940s, in which each segment ended with the leading character in this situation, often literally hanging over a cliff. The reasoning behind this was quite blatantly to ensure the return of the audience to the theater to see how it all came out.

Some SF writers have done this in the middle of a TRILOGY. The first volume has established the characters and their UNIVERSE. The last one is going to tie up everything neatly. How to sustain the interest of the readers? Leave the outcome of the middle novel up in the air (or hanging over a cliff!), so that the readers will buy the next book to learn how the hero got saved.

This was the technique used by George Lucas in his STAR WARS trilogy. The first film ended on a note of triumph, while the second installment (*The Empire Strikes Back,* 1980) just left the main characters in limbo, until the loose ends got tied up in 1983 in *Return of the Jedi.*

clipper (fan): A collector of FILM CLIPS, particularly from TV series like STAR TREK. CLIPPERS swap particular snippets of film, which can be used as PHOTO-REFS, or mounted as slides for humorous slide shows. See also FILM CLIP.

clones (computer): Computer programs that have been copied with or without the original programmer's consent. When the material copied is under copyright, the process is known as computer piracy, and it is highly illegal, as well as being unethical. See also COPYRIGHT; SOFTWARE PIRACY.

cloning (biology): The reproduction of individual beings from a single asexually produced gamete. CLONING is usually done in research laboratories, under highly restricted conditions, although it has occurred in nature among very simple protozoa.

The idea of reproducing a specific set of genes upon demand is a theme that recurs in SF, usually with an undercurrent of

horror implied. Ira Levin's *The Boys from Brazil* (1976) uses the idea of a conspiracy to duplicate not only the genes but the environment that produced Adolf Hitler. Michael Crichton's 1990 novel *Jurassic Park* explores the ramifications of CLONING extinct species (in this case dinosaurs), which may develop along lines their re-creators had not considered.

As early as the 1920s, scientists were trying to fathom the chemistry of life; with the discovery of the DNA molecule and its possibilities, CLONING has become a distinct possibility instead of a remote and vaguely uncomfortable bit of SF.

cloning (fan): The reproduction of videotapes of TV series not shown in the United States, either for personal use or for sale. Cloned tapes offered for sale are illegal, and those who clone them are likely to have their merchandise removed by either CON SECURITY or the Federal Marshalls. On the other hand, the privately circulated video clones are in a gray legal area; so far, no one has tried to open that particular can of worms. See also BOOTLEG TAPES.

cloning parties (fan): Gatherings of fans for the purpose of duplicating homemade videotapes of television episodes. Each guest brings a videocassette player and a number of empty cassettes, as well as his or her own collection of TV episodes. The machines are hooked together, and duplicates are made while the guests watch the episode in question. These tapes are for personal use only; commercial tapes are not cloned.

closed universe (literary): A story or series of stories whose characters and setting are kept tightly under the author's direct control, away from FAN-FIC. No one else is permitted to use them, borrow them, satirize them, or play with them, under threat of lawsuit. Some people do this out of fear of plagiarism; some are so involved with their particular UNIVERSE that they don't want amateur hands mucking about with it. There is also the very real possibility of setting some kind of precedent that would involve use of the UNIVERSE by a professional promoter without adequate compensation to the originator of it.

On the other hand, some writers will permit limited fannish borrowing of a milieu as long as the author's own CHARACTERS are left strictly alone. Anne McCaffrey has given her consent to fans who want to set stories on PERN, but will not let those stories contain any of the CHARACTERS she invented.

Unless fans are directly in touch with the originator of a literary UNIVERSE, it is recommended that they stick to the TV or film UNIVERSES for FAN-FIC to avoid legal complications. The various TV and movie producers are resigned to sharing their CHARACTERS with the fans, on the theory that if the TV SERIES or movie has generated that much interest, there will be an enthusiastic audience for any subsequent PRO material that might be generated. Those people who do not understand this are soon enlightened by the ones whose coffers have been filled by eager fans, who will support the TV SERIES for years.

As for professional publication, no reputable author would encroach on another's territory without full written permission. LICENSED publications are another matter. See also COPYRIGHT; CROSS-UNIVERSE STORY; OPEN UNIVERSE.

closedzine (fan): A FANZINE whose contributors are limited to a specific group. A few CLUBZINES only accept material from club members, for instance. In one or two cases, a fannish UNIVERSE has been set up among a few people, who write about their own CHARACTERS. These may be PERSONAS adopted by members of a particular game of DUNGEONS AND DRAGONS™ or a CLUB.

Close Encounters of the Third Kind (film). The FIRST CONTACT theme taken to marvelous heights; probably the most spectacular Flying Saucer movie ever made. Produced and directed by Steven Spielberg, the story deals with several people who observe an Alien spacecraft, and who are then drawn to the particular place where the craft is going to land. In a spectacular bit of BLUE SCREEN ACTING, the visiting spaceship lands, to the booming accompaniment of a five-note musical phrase, created by JOHN WILLIAMS. The five-note phrase has become as big a musical SF symbol as the eerie theme from TWILIGHT ZONE. See also FIRST CONTACT STORY; SPIELBERG, STEVEN.

club (fan): A group of people who meet on a more or less regular basis to discuss SF and take part in FANNISH activities. Most metropolitan areas have at least one SF CLUB; college campuses seem to breed them; they are even established on the bases of the armed forces. CLUBS finance their activities not only by payment of membership dues but by sales of FANZINES, or by sponsoring a CONVENTION.

Fans of a particular TV series may form their own CLUB, as may the fans of a particular actor. Some film production companies sponsor an OFFICIAL FAN CLUB, in addition to the "unofficial" ones organized by the fans.

Some long-running CLUBS have distinguished memberships; the most famous of these, the Futurians, was also one of the earliest. The *Encyclopedia of Associations* lists some 20 major SF organizations; the Star Trek Welcomittee lists many, many more.

Anyone interested in locating the nearest SF CLUB might try attending a CON. Even if the local club isn't sponsoring it, they will certainly have a representative nearby.

clubzine (fan): A magazine or newsletter printed and distributed by an SF CLUB. CLUBZINES range in size and price from a folded photo-offset sheet of local news and reviews, to a multipage compilation of fiction, art, and whatever else the CLUB feels like inserting into it.

The most basic CLUBZINE is the newsletter that informs the membership of the time, date, and location of the next meeting, along with some information about any prospective speakers. More elaborate is the volume of art and fiction produced by an AUTHORIZED FAN CLUB, extolling the CHARACTERS portrayed by the star. Most expensive and easiest to find are the slick magazines produced by the OFFICIAL FAN CLUBS of Lucasfilm or Paramount, which promote the next film or describe the most recent ones of those organizations.

CLUBZINES may be CLOSEDZINES, although anyone with an interest in the organization may join in the fun by joining the CLUB.

COA (Change of Address) (fan): A listing of people who have changed their mailing address since the last time anyone heard from them, often included in APAS or CLUBZINES. Fans tend to be mobile; some of them seem to move hourly. COA lists help keep track of people.

collaboration (literary): The joint effort of two writers to produce a work of fiction greater than either could do alone. COLLABORATION is nothing new to fiction; SF just seems to foster more of it.

Collaborators can be husband and wife (Henry Kuttner and C. L. Moore), father and son (Frank and Brian Herbert), brothers (Arkady and Boris Strugasky), or just good buddies (Jerry Pournelle and Larry Niven). They can work in alternating shifts, or together as a team, or by each partner taking a separate part of the PLOT, which will then be pulled together by a third party. An "old hand" may collaborate with a newcomer, who will then pass the favor on to some other newcomer when the time is ripe. COLLABORATION, when done properly, brings out the best in both writers.

The ultimate COLLABORATION is the SHARED UNIVERSE, in which several authors contribute stories set in a particular place or time, occasionally using each others' characters.

collating party (fan): A gathering of FANS with the ostensible purpose of putting together the pages of a printed document, whether it is a FANZINE, an APA, or the PROGRAM BOOK for a CONVENTION. The host or hostess provides the refreshments and the tables to spread out the pages in their correct order. The guests provide labor, in the best American tradition, which turns necessary drudgery into a social occasion.

There is a tangible reward for the strained backs and paper-cut fingers; everyone who participates in a COLLATING PARTY receives a free copy of whatever has just been collated.

collectables (fan): Anything that someone wants that someone else is willing to sell. SF COLLECTABLES include all kinds of printed matter: books, both hardcover and paperback; magazines; fanzines; comic books. Movie memorabilia plays an important part in SF collecting, and DEALERS can provide promotional materials like posters, press kits, and scripts of well-known SF films and TV SERIES. Other oddments may include dolls, toys, promotional key chains, jewelry, BUTTONS . . . if someone made it, someone else is going to collect it.

The high point of a PRO-CON is a visit to the DEALERS' ROOM, where the visitor will see tables piled high with COLLECTABLES.

colorist (comics): The person who adds color to the comic art, working from photostats of the artist's black-and-white ORIGINALS. This is not as easy as it sounds, since the color must then be printable according to inks now in use. The colorist is part of the CREATIVE TEAM that puts together a comic.

comb binding (printing): See RING BINDING.

comet (astronomy): A small icy body embedded in a cloud of gas and dust, moving in a highly elliptical orbit around the sun. COMETS have been noted by ancient astronomers; their advent was supposed to foretell all kinds of doom and destruction. Certain COMETS have been traced through history by matching the accounts of various observers, the most notable being Halley's Comet, whose most recent appearance was in 1986.

The COMET is seen in the night sky as a "hairy star," as the gasses in its "head" are heated by the sun and form a "tail." COMETS rarely come close enough to the Earth's gravitational field to be attracted to it; however, a mysterious explosion and

fire in Siberia in 1905 is thought by many astronomers to be the result of a collision with a COMET.

comics: Illustrated magazines or books that tell a story largely through pictures, with dialog indicated in enclosed captions called "balloons." COMICS often depict SUPERHEROES with unusual powers, who fight criminals even more powerful than they.

COMICS began in the early 1900s with the development of cheap color printing techniques. One of the earliest fantasy COMICS was Winsor McCay's *Little Nemo in Slumberland,* the dreamlike adventures of an imaginative little boy. BUCK ROGERS made his appearance in 1926, and FLASH GORDON came along in 1934. With SUPERMAN in 1939, the SF genre in comic was well established.

After World War II, COMICS went into a "horror" phase, and became the source of a ferocious controversy. The content of COMICS was censored; the gruesome elements were supposed to be played down, and the "wholesome" anthropomorphic animal "funnies" were supposed to be promoted. In recent years,

COMICS have become more mature in story content and in artistic merit.

A comic book is rarely the work of a single individual; instead, there is a CREATIVE TEAM that combines the efforts and talents of the artist, INKER, COLORIST, dialoger, PLOTTER, and WRITER to produce an exciting tale of ACTION/ADVENTURE.

command module (aerospace): The control center for space missions that holds the living and working quarters for the crew. The COMMAND MODULE must have a SHIRTSLEEVE ENVIRONMENT, for comfort. It must be kept neat, since small objects floating in ZERO-G may cause more damage than large ones if they get into delicate machinery. Now that crews are of both sexes, the sanitary facilities in the command module have been redesigned to provide more privacy than was deemed necessary in the Apollo missions.

The COMMAND MODULE may be attached to a SERVICE MODULE or a landing module. The SPACE SHUTTLE is the ultimate COMMAND MODULE. See also MODULE (aerospace).

commix (comics): Comic books produced by independent, nonprofessional artists, with an iconoclastic and unusual point of view; in other words, Underground Comics. A product of the Counterculture of the 1960s, COMMIX railed against the Establishment in coarse and satiric terms. Robert Crumb's COMMIX are especially notable (and are prime targets as COLLECTABLES).

compatible (computer): Used to describe a computer that can deal with material designed for a different model or brand; also used to describe SOFTWARE that can be used by several different computers.

computer: A device capable of performing some of the functions of the human brain, particularly mathematical calculations and assimilation of information far faster than the human brain. COMPUTERS, now a part of our daily lives, were among the many gadgets suggested by SF writers. Their nightmare was that a COMPUTER would eventually attain sentience and insist on taking over the world. Sheckley's "Etoain Shridlu" is a story in which a COMPUTER attached to a printing press tends to believe everything it prints. Other "thinking machines," like David Gerrold's H.A.R.L.I.E., are more selective. See also ARTIFICIAL INTELLIGENCE.

computer geek (fan): An intelligent, highly motivated person whose expertise in computers is not matched by social graces or physical attractiveness. COMPUTER GEEKS congregate in the computer room at CONS, where they compare notes and dream up vast programming schemes.

computer graphics (film): Animation techniques that use computers to create unusual and original designs. All data for a scene are fed into the computer: perspective, lighting, movement, and so on. Then the images are placed on the film. The result is often clearer, sharper, and more brilliant than anything produced by human hands.

COMPUTER GRAPHICS are not used extensively in longer films as yet; they are often seen in MUSIC VIDEOS, TV commercials, and as SPECIAL EFFECTS. A particularly good example is the video battle scene in the Disney film, *Tron* (1982).

Con/Conventions (fan): Gatherings of SF people, both amateurs (FAN) and professionals (PROS) for business and social purposes. CON and CONVENTION are usually used interchangeably in SF FANDOM.

CONVENTIONS began in the late 1930s as meetings of youngish SF readers and would-be writers, many of whom later emerged as FIRST FANDOM. The pattern still holds, as the next generation of SF readers try their hands at writing, editing, and art. The best place to meet like-minded people is at a CON.

CONS have changed considerably since the first small gatherings, which rarely collected more than a few hundred souls, most of them male. A REGIONAL FAN-CON may attract up to 1,500 people, and a PRO-CON may draw twice that number. The WORLD-CON may tally up to 5,000 attendees before closing the books on REGISTRATION.

There is a CON for almost every taste and fancy in SF. There are the FAN-CONS, which attract SF writers, artists, and editors from a particular geographic region. There are PRO-CONS, run by entrepreneurs who present the stars and creators of popular TV SERIES to their public. There are SER-CONS, which delve into academic and scientific explorations of SF. There are even RELAX-A-CONS, small easy-going meetings very much like the first SF CONS, where friends can eat, chat, and meet more SF FANS. MINI-CONS may only run for a few hours; other CONS may run over a weekend or more.

Most CONS feature the same elements, in varying degrees of intensity. There is usually a GOH (Guest of Honor), who may be a well-known SF writer or artist at a FAN-CON, or the star of a popular film or TV SERIES at a PRO-CON. The GOH and other SF people will participate in PANELS and other group discussions of subjects of interest to SF FANS. There is often an ART SHOW, at which SF artists can display their talents, and an AUCTION at which the FANS can acquire the artwork shown at the ART SHOW. There is usually a FILM or VIDEO ROOM, where SF feature films and TV EPISODES can be viewed. For many FANS, the most important area of the CON is the DEALERS' ROOM, where they can stock up on books, comics, FANZINES, memorabilia, and whatever else they can lay their hands on that the DEALERS will sell them.

Some FAN-CONS may include WORKSHOPS in writing or art techniques as part of their PROGRAMMING. FILK-SINGING is becoming a part of the formal program at many CONS, although in the past it was relegated to private parties held after most other activities had ended. The MASQUERADE is a high point of most CONS, although some CONS do not have any formal presentation onstage, and merely hand out awards for HALL COSTUMES. Some CONS hold a REGENCY BALL, with or without refreshments.

There are CONS held all over the world. Most major U.S. cities host at least one FAN-CON a year, and many PRO-CON promoters visit the larger metropolitan areas at least twice a year. It is possible to attend two or three in a single weekend, given the time, the stamina, and the bankroll. CONS are typically held over a three-day weekend, beginning on Friday evening and ending with a DEAD DOG PARTY late Sunday afternoon. CONS can be held anywhere; they have been presented in fraternal lodge halls, college facilities, and high school gymnasiums. However, most CONS utilize hotels that can provide meeting rooms as well as sleeping quarters, so that the members can take some respite from the ceaseless activities around them.

The biggest CONVENTION of all each year is the WORLD-CON, the World Science Fiction Convention, held annually on the first weekend in September in a different location each year. The WORLD-CON is the meeting place for the totality of the SF world, both FAN and PRO. The HUGOS are awarded at the WORLD-CON; the MASQUERADE is a colorful and elaborate parade of exotic costumes; the FILK-SINGING goes on all night. Most of all, it provides an opportunity for established SF writers and artists to meet their public, and for the FANS to approach their mentors on terms of equality.

CONVENTIONS advertise through FLYERS distributed at other CONS, through notices in SF magazines, and through mailed notices. They have generated their own jargon, indicated in this book by the fan/convention in parentheses after the entry.

For more information on where to find listings of CONVENTIONS, see Appendix A.

Conan the Barbarian (literary): CHARACTER originated and developed by Robert Howard in a series of stories, first published between 1932 and 1936. Conan is the archetype of the Literary Barbarian; endowed with a splendid physique, a talent for survival, and a rudimentary ethical code, he strides through his Hyperborean Universe as king, thief, and adventurer. Although Howard died in 1936, Conan's adventures have been continued through a number of successors, and Conan was portrayed by Arnold Schwarzenegger in two well-made films.

Con Chair (fan/conventions): The person in charge of putting together the elements of a FAN-CON; the Chairman/woman of the committee. (The sexism was dropped along with the final syllable; the Chair may be male or female). The CON CHAIR must have the tact of a Kissinger, the hide of an elephant, and the patience of Job. Most of all, the CON CHAIR must stay within reach of the CON-COM at all times, and be able to handle any crisis before, during, and after a CON, whether it be a sudden lack of transportation to bring the GOH from the airport, or a possible riot in the lobby when one of the costumed CON members confronts a MUNDANE. Those who have held this position in an organization for a number of years deserve medals and battle citations.

Con-Com (fan/conventions): The Convention Committee, the people actually involved in organizing and running a CONVENTION. The CON-COM may consist of the CON CHAIR and two or three good friends, or it may involve a positive army of subcommittee heads and their assistants (not to mention GOFERS). Most CON-COMS will have one person in charge of each of the main activities of the CON: REGISTRATION, PROGRAMMING, ART SHOW, DEALERS' ROOM, and so forth. A CON can be run without an efficient CON-COM, but it's easier when the committee is ready to deal with any and all crises.

Con-Com Mommy (fan/convention): Another name for CON CHAIR; it could also describe the member of the CON-COM who tends to the physical needs of the Committee by providing food, hot or cold refreshments (as determined by taste and the weather), and sleeping space.

conjunction (astronomy): An ALIGNMENT of astronomical bodies, in which each body is at the same celestial longitude (although at varying distances from the Earth). At the exact moment of CONJUNCTION, one body passes in front of the other, as seen from the Earth. If the body nearest the Earth appears larger than the farther body, the conjunction may be called an eclipse; if it appears smaller, the result may be called a TRANSIT.

constitution (gaming): The ABILITY of a CHARACTER that indicates physical health, an important component in deciding a character's CLASS. A Thief with a low CONSTITUTION score might be prey to various ailments of a minor, but annoying, sort (like hay fever); a WARRIOR must have a very high CONSTITUTION score to withstand all those battle wounds.

construction (fan/costuming): The actual attaching of one element of a costume to another, whether by sewing, glueing, or riveting, if the costume calls for it. CONSTRUCTION should be unobtrusive, neat, and durable; the garment has to be worn, after all, and must be able to withstand sitting, standing, and walking. ROTSLER'S RULES also recommend that the costume be constructed in such a way that the wearer can perform necessary natural functions. It's a long, long time between the check-in and the presentation, sometimes as much as hours. One of the great tragedies in a costumer's life is the costume that falls apart onstage.

Con suite (fan/conventions): Also known as a Hospitality Suite; a room or set of rooms used by the CONVENTION as a meeting place, open to anyone with a BADGE, where CON members may find companionship, MUNCHIES, BHEER, and possibly even the GOH. To find the CON SUITE, just follow the noise, or the crowd. The CON SUITE is usually listed in the PROGRAM BOOK and the POCKET PROGRAM.

continuity (comics): Taken from the film sense, but in this case, the events of one issue of a comic must fit in with previous issues, so that the CHARACTERS present a consistent image to the readership. They will know and comment vociferously if a CHARACTER suddenly and inexplicably develops new and startling powers, or forgets he had them. They are even nastier when a CHARACTER reveals (or forgets) previous relationships that may alter the whole tone of the comic. Comic book writers are advised to read every single issue of a particular comic before attempting to work on an established CHARACTER. It is far better to come up with one that is completely original, and establish your own CONTINUITY.

continuity (film): The technique of matching each shot of a scene with the one before, so that when it appears on film, there will be a sense of continuous action, even though one scene may have been shot some time before the other one. The person in charge is called the Continuity Girl (who is sometimes male); it is this person's responsibility to tell the actors what they were wearing, and to make sure it matches in every detail with the previous activity seen onscreen. If it is not done correctly, you get a scene where an actor rides up a hill clean-shaven and down with a three-day growth of stubble, or appears at one moment with a vest on, and in the next moment without one.

control sheet (fan/art): The ART SHOW paperwork; a printed form that every artist must fill out before exhibiting at a CON, listing each PIECE by title, with its MINIMUM BID and QUICK SALE prices. After the VOICE AUCTION, the actual price brought by each PIECE is entered onto the CONTROL SHEET, so that at the end of the CON the artist may retrieve any unsold PIECES, and relieve the CON of its responsibility for them.

CONTROL SHEETS are a necessity at large FAN-CONS, where the ART SHOW may have several thousand PIECES. They are often the only way of managing the financial end of the ART SHOW: listing how much is due to the artist, and how much will go to the CON. See also BID SHEETS; VOICE AUCTION.

convention: See CONS/CONVENTIONS.

convention crud (fan/conventions): Any physical ailment that goes through the membership of a CONVENTION, laying everyone low. Often brought on by exposure to strange viruses or bacilli at a large gathering of people from all parts of the country. Symptoms may include gastrointestinal distress or flu; occasionally, CONVENTION CRUD may call for a doctor's care. See also BLORCH.

conventions (literary): The standard CHARACTERS and plot lines of a particular literary genre; the "rules of the game" for detective stories, Westerns, SF or Fantasy tales, or any other type of story. Readers expect certain elements in these stories, and are disappointed when they don't get them. CROSS-GENRE STORIES take the CONVENTIONS of one genre and mix them with another, with variable success.

copy editor (publishing): The person who edits a manuscript for proper grammar, general readability, and accuracy. In the case of SF, a COPY EDITOR may bring a scientific fallacy to the writer's attention, or ask that an idea be clarified or expanded.

He or she may also question a particular use of language. Of course, the writer may not be wrong, but may be deliberately wringing the collective neck of the English Language for a particular effect. See also EDITOR; PROOFREADER.

copyright (law): The law that defines the ownership of a piece of writing, and that limits its use. The COPYRIGHT laws are meant to assure that an author benefits from what he or she created, and that no one else has that right, unless given permission by the author or publisher. Problems arise in the case of MEDIAZINES, where fans write stories using characters taken from copyrighted materials, that is, SF films and TV SERIES. A writer who attempts to sell a work using any character developed by another person without permission is guilty of plagiarism, and will be in legal trouble under the COPYRIGHT laws.

There is also the issue of the person who decides to reproduce a FANZINE, without the permission of the original publisher/editor. That, too, is a violation of copyright. People who violate COPYRIGHT laws are sued, and any writer would be wise to request permission before using another writer's material. See also BOOTLEG TAPES; BOOTLEGZINES; CLOSED UNIVERSE; SOFTWARE PIRACY.

cor-flu (printing): Correction fluid, used in correcting mimeograph stencils. There was a time when mimeo was the primary printing medium for FANZINES. COR-FLU has passed into obsolescence by the advent of photo-offset and xerography, but it has been immortalized by several FILK-SONGS. See also WHITE-OUT.

Coriolis effect (aerospace): The physiological effects on human beings as they are moved through a rotating system, such as disorientation, loss of balance, and in some cases, nausea. It's called "space sickness" when it applies to space travelers. The effect was named for Gaspard de Coriolis, who first discovered it through experiments on small animals.

Corman, Roger (b. 1926) American filmmaker and producer of inexpensive but effective films, well known for hiring beginning talent who would later justify his faith by becoming well-respected writers, directors, and actors as veterans of the genre. Vincent Price made a series of horror films loosely based on stories by EDGAR ALLAN POE. Boris Karloff, Peter Lorre, and Basil Rathbone joined forces in CORMAN'S *The Raven*. CORMAN films were noted for lavish sets and a mordant wit that raised them above the usual "slice 'n' dice" horror films of the time. CORMAN was active as a director from 1955 to 1971. He moved into producing during the 1970s and 1980s, but has recently emerged as a director once again with a new version of the FRANKENSTEIN legend in 1990.

corpsicle (literary): The body of a cryogenically frozen person, waiting for its resurrection. Coined by Frederik Pohl, from "popsicle," a frozen confection. See also CRYOGENICS.

cosmic dust (astronomy): Small particles found in space; they may be as tiny as an atom or as large as a small pebble. They travel through space causing no problems, unless a spacecraft blunders into one traveling close to light speed. The result of such a collision would be penetration of the spacecraft's hull, and subsequent loss of air pressure, oxygen, and eventually, life aboard the craft.

SF writers have used this as a PLOT POINT in countless tales of spaceships and their crews; most SF spacecraft have some sort of deflector system to ward off these tiny bits of space dirt.

cosmic rays (astronomy): Nuclei of atoms, stripped of all electrons, shooting through space at speeds close to that of light. COSMIC RAYS themselves rarely reach Earth's surface, since the Earth's atmospheric layer deflects them; instead, they collide with the molecules in the atmosphere, causing them to disintegrate into a shower of lesser particles.

COSMIC RAYS are a serious problem in space, where they can enter human tissue, causing damage to DNA molecules and affecting the replication of human cells. Spacecraft must be shielded adequately before extensive space travel can be a reality. The threat of COSMIC RAYS is considered so extensive by some scientists that they have postulated that debris from a faraway SUPERNOVA might have caused the extinction of the dinosaurs.

cosmology (astronomy): The study of the origin and evolution of the universe, encompassing studies of the planets around our sun, the sun itself, other stars, and galaxies far beyond our own. Some SF writers have extended this to include the origins of the fictitious worlds that make up their particular UNIVERSES.

cosmology (literary): The building up of a whole UNIVERSE, including its religious, moral, and ethical background. COSMOLOGY is part of the SF/Fantasy writer's BACK-STORY; no world is "real" unless the writer knows where his people come from, and where they think they are going.

"Cosmos" (TV series): TV SERIES of 13 EPISODES, first aired in 1980–1981, developed by CARL SAGAN, dealing with the Earth and its place in space. Sagan used re-creations, reenactments of historical events, computer graphics, actual film taken in space, and any other means he could to expound on the wonders of this world and all the others that may lie beyond our solar system. His bright-eyed exposition of the "BILL-YUNS AND BILL-YUNS" of stars, or animals, or whatever, opened the world of the cosmos to many who might otherwise not have noticed it.

costuming (fan): The wearing of clothing at a CONVENTION other than that seen usually in whatever venue the CON is taking place. The first person to admit wearing a costume at a CON is FORREST ACKERMAN, who described his outfit as "a tunic, something like the one in the film *Things to Come.*" The Costume Parade quickly became a feature of most CONS, as more people decided to join in the fun of dressing up as their favorite SF character. By the mid-1960s, the Costume Parade had become so long that more guidelines were needed to streamline the event.

The idea of a formal presentation at a CON began in 1969, in Los Angeles. Peggy Kennedy, a noted costumer, soon formulated a DIVISION SYSTEM, so that people with less expertise would not have to compete with accomplished costumers. The system was accepted into the World SF Constitution in 1981; there are now three Divisions: NOVICE, JOURNEYMAN, and MASTER. Some

REGIONAL CONS add CRAFTSMAN, for those who have had a good deal of experience locally, but have never managed to get to a WORLD-CON.

COSTUMING has become serious business for its participants; there is an annual Costume CON, with WORKSHOPS, PANELS, and several costume presentations. For those who just like to parade around the CON in strange attire, there are HALL COSTUMES. The PRESENTATION COSTUMES are shown at a MASQUERADE or Costume Call, where they are judged by a panel that often includes an artist and a theatrical costume designer.

COSTUMING is one of those delightful activities that fans indulge in for the fun of it. A few of the more staid fans deplore this sort of juvenile behavior, and one CON tried to ban HALL COSTUMES. The CON-COM was astonished to find its membership decreased. Costumes may FREAK THE MUNDANES, but the fans enjoy them. See Appendix A for the Address of the Costumers' Guild.

cover art (publishing): Any artwork on the outside of a book or magazine. The COVER ART must do several things: It must attract the eye, it must depict something of the contents of the book, and it must satisfy the artist's creative urge. Most SF artists are involved in COVER ART in one form or another.

The designing of a cover is not left to the artist alone. The Art Director's needs, and the necessity to include the title of the book, its author, and additional copy, such as a headline or a quote or two about the book, must be taken into account. Some artists may be given the complete text of the book as a reference; more usual is a brief summary or even a general instruction. The artist designs the cover as best suits the style of the book.

COVER ART for FANZINES is another story. The artist rarely works in color, but in pen and ink, since the finished product is usually PHOTO-OFFSET. The FANZINE cover need not describe a particular story, as the PROZINE does, but it should give an indication of the orientation of the 'zine; a MIXED MEDIAZINE will have several characters interacting, and an SF 'zine may have a spaceship. See also ILLOS.

cover flats (publishing/printing): Reproductions of the COVER ART of a book, often the actual laminated covers of a MASS-

MARKET PAPERBACK, distributed for publicity purposes. COVER FLATS are often sent to contributors to ANTHOLOGIES to assure them that the book is about to be distributed. They are also made available to artists as promotional pieces, to demonstrate the artist's expertise.

CPU (computer): Central Processing Unit, the "master brain" of a complex computer.

Craftsman (fan/costuming): An intermediate step in the hierarchy of COSTUMING expertise, between JOURNEYMAN and MASTER, for those who have won several awards at local and REGIONAL CONS, but have never quite made it at WORLD-CONS. It solves the problem of what to do with the person who is very good, but not yet good enough. See also DIVISION SYSTEM.

craftsmanship awards (fan): Also known as workmanship awards; prizes given to costumers for excellence in a particular detail of CONSTRUCTION or design. Such things as beadwork, leatherwork, embroidery, knitting or crochet, metalwork of various kinds, and other handicrafts may be incorporated into a costume, but may not be noticed from the audience. The CRAFTSMANSHIP AWARDS reward the hours that went into the details of the costume.

crawl: See CREDITS.

creative team (comics): The group responsible for putting a comic book together. The usual gang will be an artist, a SCRIPTER, COLORIST, an INKER, and a LETTERER. See also CONTINUITY (COMICS); PLOTTER.

credits (film): The complete list of who did what in the making of a film. The opening CREDITS of a film tell the title of the film, its stars, its producer and director, the writers, and the production company. At the end of the film is the complete list of CREDITS, called the crawl, which slowly unrolls as the audience leaves the theater.

CREDITS can also refer to a list of films in which a person has participated in some way, either as an actor, as crew, as a writer, or even as an agent. An actor will bring a list of such credits with him or her to an audition; a writer may send his or her list of credits to a publisher or an agent. In both cases, the purpose is the same: to impress a prospective employer.

creepy-crawlies (art): Horrible, grotesque, eerie things that flutter out of the pages of an artist's sketchbook. Horror art has been around since the apocalyptic visions of Hieronymus Bosch. SF magazines specializing in horror use CREEPY-CRAWLIES as FILLOS.

crew (aerospace): The people who are actually sent into space on a particular mission. The CREW of a spacecraft usually trains for the particular mission for several months, after a term of basic training as an astronaut.

Spaceship crews in SF tend to follow certain patterns, since there are certain positions that must be filled. There is usually a commander and a second-in-command as backup; someone has to handle Engineering, and someone has to deal with Communications. Medical emergencies need a specialist, or even two, and there is usually someone on hand to do whatever the others tell him, her, or it.

Although some of these functions can be filled by mechanical devices, most SF postulates that there will be a CREW on board any future spacecraft.

crew (film/TV): The technicians and craftspeople who work behind the scenes on a film or TV program. They provide the vital services without which the show cannot reach the public. They are the cameramen, the stunt people, the electricians and lighting experts, the special effects and sound technicians, the makeup artists and wardrobe people. They have odd titles like Script Girl, Best Boy, and Gaffer. Their only moment of official notice is at the very end of a film or TV program, when their names are flashed on the screen briefly, or are shown on the CRAWL.

The importance of the tech CREW in an SF film or TV series

cannot be emphasized too strongly. The technical aspects of the show must be unobtrusive and yet right for the ambience of what the actors are doing; otherwise the whole show loses its believability.

critique (literary): A detailed critical analysis of a story or film, or the act of making such an analysis. A CRITIQUE does more than say whether a story is good or bad writing; the critique explains why the story succeeds or fails in its objective, and how the writer can make it better.

Many CONS offer WORKSHOPS, in which a professional writer or editor will CRITIQUE stories and offer suggestions to would-be writers as to how they can improve their craft.

cronk (gaming): A creature that lives to eat; not a player CHARACTER, although some gamers are convinced that their fellow-players might answer to the description.

cross-alignment (gaming): The combination of GOOD, NEUTRAL, and EVIL with LAWFUL, NEUTRAL, or CHAOTIC that makes up the character's total ALIGNMENT. The ALIGNMENT is decided by the player before the game; the character's ABILITIES are decided by the DUNGEONMASTER who rolls the dice. Once that is done, the character can be given a CLASS, and a RACE, and can be formulated . . . and only after that can the adventure begin.

cross-genre (literary): A story that uses the CONVENTIONS and format of two different types of formula fiction. For instance, a story might have a dashing hero and a spunky tart-tongued aristocratic heroine (as in Regency Romance fiction), but be set on another world, as in SF. One of the most familiar cross-genres is to fit a "classic" or "tough" detective into an SF context, as in Asimov's *Caves of Steel* (1954) or Glen Cook's *Garrett* novels. James White's *Sector General* stories combine SF with the "hospital" or "medical" stories of the nature of Max Brand's "Dr. Kildare" series. CROSS-GENRE stories offer the writer an opportunity to work in both GENRES, combining the two for added effect.

crossover (comics): A comic book story that features characters from other titles appearing as "guest stars" in this one. Action Comics often has stories in which BATMAN comes to the aid of SUPERMAN, or vice versa.

crossover author (publishing): A MAINSTREAM writer who tries his hand at SF, or the other way around. A number of well-known authors of serious fiction have used a futuristic setting for their works, the most notable of recent years being Doris Lessing, with her *Canopus in Argo* novels.

cross-Universe story (literary): One in which characters from one TV SERIES, film, or novel interact with characters from a totally different TV SERIES, film, or novel. Usually these are written by fans, for FANZINES, and are seldom expected to be more than an exercise of the imagination that can be shared by the people who buy the 'zine.

Occasionally an SF author will use a character invented by another, but always with the first author's full permission. For example, in *The Dark Dimensions* (1971), A. B. Chandler's John Grimes character interacts with Poul Anderson's character, Sir Domenic Flandry. According to Mr. Anderson, Chandler had the idea of combining the two characters in one story; Anderson had wanted to reciprocate, but never quite got to put Grimes into one of the *Domenic Flandry* tales.

The most notorious professionally published CROSS-UNIVERSE novel was Barbara Hambly's *Ishmael* (1985), which was originally written for a FANZINE, but was later bought by Pocket Books as part of their STAR TREK series. Since it was a CROSS-UNIVERSE story, permission had to be requested from Columbia Pictures to use the characters from the TV SERIES "Here Come the Brides" in a story about time travel and "Star Trek."

CRT (Combat Result Table) (gaming): A listing of all the possible variable results in a war game, usually determined by the DUNGEONMASTER after rolling the dice. The CRT guides the DUNGEONMASTER in deciding who got hurt, and how much, based on the character's ABILITIES, RACE, and PROFICIENCY. Vociferous arguments usually accompany the announcement of the CRT results.

CRT (computer): See CATHODE RAY TUBE.

crudzine (fan): A badly written, badly printed FANZINE, or possibly, one with which the reader disagrees. No one admits to putting out a CRUDZINE; it usually belongs to someone else.

cryogenics (biology): The science of producing very low temperatures, usually through the use of special machinery that will act as a super-refrigeration unit. CRYOGENICS has led to the development of solid rocket fuel, and even more importantly, to the use of such freezing techniques to preserve the tissues of human bodies. See CRYONICS.

cryonics (biology): The techniques of using super-cold temperatures to preserve the tissues of the human body, for research and for possible resuscitation. The discovery of mammoths buried deep in the ice in Siberia, perfectly preserved (but not alive), has led to the possibilities inherent in lowering body temperature to a state of hibernation, keeping the metabolic processes barely functioning, until the body can be revived.

A number of early SF writers have played with the notion of a person being revived in this way after having been frozen; BUCK ROGERS was supposed to be such a person. More recently, the idea of a cryogenic SLEEPER SHIP has been brought forward as a possible way of accommodating a large number of people on a long voyage into space without having to provide air, food, or recreation for them. Present research has shown that it may only be a matter of time before it is possible to put human beings into such a state.

crystals (parapsychology): Minerals that form solids in certain patterns, used as a focus for mental powers. Certain CRYSTALS are thought to bring certain results. CRYSTALS are among the most popular items sold at SF CONS.

Cthulhu (literary): The horrific god created by H. P. LOVECRAFT in a set of stories, later expanded by August Derleth into a "Cthulhu Mythos." CTHULHU has all the charming features of Baal, Moloch, and the Christian version of the Devil. It lies in wait in dark and mysterious places, like the proverbial bogeyman.

CTHULHU has been so overused that it has become a macabre joke among SF fans. There is even a button that proclaims "Smile! Cthulhu loves you!"

cult film: One that has little immediate impact when it is first shown, but slowly builds up a following over the years, until it can qualify as a Classic. *Dark Star* (1974) is a typical SF CULT FILM. Probably the most famous CULT FILM is THE ROCKY HORROR PICTURE SHOW, which has been playing for well over 15 years.

culture-clash (sociology): The disparity between two groups of people trying to occupy the same place at the same time, particularly when their life-styles are diametrically opposed. This has happened many times in human history; usually, a group with a higher level of technology takes land that belongs to a group at a lower state of technological development. The results are usually tragic for the second group, since the first group has the will and the means to dominate the second. The "old ways" must give way to more efficient means of production of food and materials.

Early in the development of SF, it was blithely assumed that the greater the level of technology, the better humankind would be; therefore, any nonhuman creatures without similar technology could only benefit by assuming ours. More recent studies in sociology have shown that societies, like individuals, can suffer stress from too much change, too fast. There has been a reaction to the overtechnological approach; several writers have depicted worlds on which the human settlers make serious errors in dealing with indigenous societies, with tragic results.

Much of Marion Zimmer Bradley's DARKOVER series deals with the CULTURE-CLASH between the aristocratic, telepathic Darkovans, and the high-tech egalitarian Terrans. Other writers deal with a possible future on Earth, when some survivors of a nuclear holocaust live underground, whereas others have learned to cope with the natural world, as it is on the surface.

CULTURE-CLASH stories provide some of the most interesting and disturbing reading in today's SF.

cybercrud (computer): The deliberate use of computer jargon to confuse nonusers of computers. From "cyber," having to do with computers, and "crud," garbage. Another form of FREAKING THE MUNDANES, used by COMPUTER GEEKS as a kind of self-protection against the rest of society.

cybernetics: The science of developing ARTIFICIAL INTELLIGENCE, especially through the combination of human tissue with electronic mechanisms. First used by Nicholas Wiener in 1947 to describe the science of designing computers. The prefix "cyber" has been attached to many other words; in every case, it means "having to do with computers."

cyberpunk (literary): Stories written in the mid-1980s that combine HIGH-TECH scenery with counterculture language and values. The term was coined by Bruce Bethke from "cyber," having to do with computers, and "punk," a visually repulsive and deliberately cacophonic form of rock music. He used it as the title for a story published in 1982. Gardner Dozois picked it up and used the word to characterize the entire subgenre.

CYBERPUNK stories tend to depict a violent and frightening future, when COMPUTERS have taken over much of the drudgery, leaving humanity to get along as best as it can. The leading writers in the CYBERPUNK School are William Gibson and Bruce Sterling. The TV series "Max Headroom" (1987) is the visual equivalent of CYBERPUNK.

cyborg (biology): An organism in which human tissue is replaced by an artificial mechanism. The most primitive CYBORG would be a person with a glass eye or artificial limb; in more extreme cases, whole organs can be replaced by machinery. Martin Caidin's *Cyborg* (1972) was turned into the TV SERIES "The Six Million Dollar Man," who, with "The Bionic Woman," fought crime from 1973 to 1978. See also ANDROID; ROBOT.

dark fantasy (literary): Horror or terror stories, with deep psychological overtones as well as religious undertones. Classic writers of DARK FANTASY include POE and LOVECRAFT; STEPHEN KING has brought dark fantasy into the modern era. See also HORROR STORIES.

"Dark Knight:" See BATMAN.

dark nebula (astronomy): A seeming contradiction in terms; a nebula is a cloud of gasses and dust in space, and a DARK NEBULA can be seen as a cloud of such proportions that it appears to blot out the stars behind it as seen from Earth.

Darkover (literary): The setting for a series of novels and short stories by Marion Zimmer Bradley and her fans. The first novel in the series, *Sword of Aldones* (1962), was, in effect, the end of a long planetary history; in order to understand what had happened to the planet and its people, Ms. Bradley began to write stories set before *Sword of Aldones*.

The series deals in part with the CULTURE-CLASH between the agrarian, aristocratic, partly telepathic people of DARKOVER and the Terrans, who have come to set up a base for their spaceships (it seems the planet lies in a particularly advantageous spot between the upper and lower arms of our galaxy). Several novels pit one or more members of each society against its restrictions and customs. A recurrent theme is the person who finds a welcome on the other side of the fence, when the society into which he was born rejects him.

Another recurrent theme in the series, and one that may be a strong reason for its popularity, is the liberation of women from traditional values and dependence on males for protection and economic support. Many young women have found the DARKOVER books inspirational in their search for personal freedom and integrity.

The DARKOVER series has become an OPEN UNIVERSE to a certain extent. Ms. Bradley has invited her fans to "come and play in my garden," and they have responded with NEWSLETTERS, FANZINES, and stories that have been collected into seven anthologies published by DAW.

There is an annual Darkover Grand Council Convention held during the Thanksgiving weekend, at which Ms. Bradley is the GOH. DARKOVER costumes are standard garb at MASQUERADES. The *Darkover Concordance* was published in 1982, which listed all the people, places, and things mentioned in the novels up to that date.

The latest DARKOVER novel is *The Heirs of Hammerfell* (1990); there are more anthologies planned, and the fans continue to keep the DARKOVER UNIVERSE alive.

darkspace (aerospace): Intensity of light in space where the sun is not visible, as, for instance, during a night launch on Earth, or on the "dark side" of the moon, which is turned away from the sun. Total light then consists of only direct starlight, either from the nearer stars or from the faraway galaxies. This light, however, is at least 30% brighter than that seen on Earth, since it does not have to filter through the atmosphere, with its pollutants and its distorting pressure.

Dark Star (movie): CULT FILM, set on a spaceship whose mission is unknown, whose crew is disintegrating into total psychosis, and whose cargo consists of thermonuclear bombs. A total fizzle when it was released in 1974, it has become a standard item at CONVENTIONS, probably because of its not-too-subtle counterculture message.

database (computer): A set of programs for the computer to follow.

Day After Tomorrow Story (literary): One set in the very near future; the result may be marginally SF. The TECHNO-THRILLERS of Tom Clancy are DAY AFTER TOMORROW STORIES; SO are the stories of the SURVIVALIST FICTION series. Nevil Shute's *On the Beach* is a classic DAY AFTER TOMORROW STORY.

One problem with this kind of story is that tomorrow has a way of arriving more quickly than the writer thought, and it is rarely the way the writer envisioned it. See also FUTURE HISTORY.

day rates (fan/convention): Reduced price memberships to a CONVENTION, good for only one day. Most FAN-CONS run two and a half days, over a weekend, but some fans are limited because of work, school, or family responsibilities. DAY RATES allow them to attend the CON for part of a weekend. PRO-CONS only charge DAY RATES, and expect their membership to change from day to day.

Day the Earth Stood Still, The (movie): One of the first and best of the post-World War II SF films, directed by Robert Wise and first shown in 1951. A spaceship lands on the Mall in Washington D.C.; a space traveler emerges, preaching peace, accompanied by a huge and menacing-looking robot. Paranoia takes over, and the space traveler (Michael Rennie) is shot and wounded. He takes refuge with a "typical" family who eventually get him back to his spaceship. The robot, Gort, neutralizes all electrical activity on Earth, thus effectively making it "stand still"; the traveler, having demonstrated that Earth is vulnerable, and the people on this planet should stop their warfare and start cooperating for the betterment of all, goes back where he came from.

THE DAY THE EARTH STOOD STILL is a landmark film in many respects: certainly the first to present a space traveler as something other than a ravening BEM or mindless beast; the first to suggest that a civilization higher than our own might be Out There; the first to use a story based on "human" values, rather than sociological or historical preaching.

This film has been placed on "Ten Best SF Film" lists by many SF writers and critics. It is a "must" for any comprehensive SF film collection.

day-tripper (fan/convention): Someone who takes advantage of DAY RATES to attend a CON for part of a weekend. Their BADGES are marked so that they cannot sneak back into the CON for a second day without paying full membership rates. DAY-TRIPPERS are particularly prevalent at a WORLD-CON, where local FANS may decide to attend for only one or two days, instead of the full five.

dead dog party (fan/conventions): The final event of most SF CONVENTIONS; a gathering of the CON-COM, and those hardy souls (or those whose trains are late) who have managed to last through the entire three days. The DEAD DOG PARTY often turns into a gripe session, when the CON-COM and the members can comment on what went right, what went wrong, and what they are going to do next year.

dealers (fan/convention): Also known as Hucksters or Huxters. The people who sell things at SF CONVENTIONS. Some of them are PROS, who own stores or run mail-order businesses, selling books, magazines, toys, memorabilia, and what-not. Many DEALERS, however, do this as a sideline, and sell things on weekends at CONS, flea markets, or craft shows.

DEALERS are responsible for the quality and legality of their merchandise, which may vary considerably from CON to CON, depending on the number and caliber of the DEALERS. A MEDIA-CON or PRO-CON will attract sellers of T-SHIRTS, BUTTONS, comic books, and memorabilia, whereas a FAN-CON will bring out the makers of jewelry and leather goods, and the collectors of rare and used books. A MEDIA-CON will also attract FANZINE DEALERS. Some PRO writers or editors double as DEALERS.

Dealers' Room (fan/convention): Also known as the Huxter or Huckster Room. The marketplace of the CONVENTION, where the DEALERS sell their goods. The DEALERS' ROOM is the focal point of a PRO-CON; a FAN-CON may have a smaller, more select, DEALERS' ROOM. Some long-running FAN-CONS have had the same DEALERS for so many years that they have gotten a reputation as being almost impossible to buy into.

death ray (literary): The imaginary weapon of destruction favored by writers of SPACE OPERA. It usually is powered by some arcane formula concocted by the VILLAIN, and it is impervious to almost everything until the HERO manages to put it out of commission with some simple (but clever) plan.

DEATH RAYS occasionally come up in movies; the one in the STAR WARS saga can obliterate an entire planet.

debugging (computer): Removal of malfunctions from a device or a computer program. This may involve anything from picking over the program to completely redesigning the mechanism, and may take anywhere from a few minutes to several years. See also BUG.

Deryni (literary): A telepathic race of beings who inhabit an Alternate Universe based roughly on Welsh legends, created by Katharine Kurtz in a series of novels, beginning with *Deryni Rising* (1970) and continuing through three TRILOGIES. The DERYNI are the rulers of Gwynnedd, who are harried out of their rightful place by an intolerant Church and its Inquisition. The series deals with the complex political and religious plots and counterplots that bring the DERYNI back to power.

DERYNI costumes are often seen at MASQUERADES, and there are a few DERYNI FILKS. There is also a DERYNI FANZINE, under the editorial eye of Ms. Kurtz herself. With this one exception, DERYNI is a CLOSED UNIVERSE.

Deus Ex Machina ending (literary): From the Greek, "God from the Machine"; a pat ending wherein all difficulties are solved by a hitherto unmentioned person or power. Ancient

Greek plays might end with a divine personage literally being dropped onto the stage by a simple mechanism (like a basket on a cable) to unwind the tangled plot and get everyone offstage, living happily ever after. A DEUS EX MACHINA ENDING is the last resort of a writer who has no idea of how to get the CHARACTERS out of their assorted messes and back to a relatively happy conclusion to their adventure.

dexterity (gaming): The ABILITY to handle objects with agility, especially when combined with good reflexes and hand-to-eye coordination. A low DEXTERITY score usually means the character is a klutz who trips over its own feet and steps on twigs when the group is trying to sneak up on a dragon.

dice (gaming): Not only the more common 6-sided cubes, but 4-sided, 8-sided, and more. They are sold in SPECIALTY SHOPS and at CONS, and are a necessary part of any ROLE-PLAYING GAME.

digital (computer): One that operates on the principle of counting, as opposed to the ANALOG computers, which measure one item against another. Most computers in use today operate on the DIGITAL system.

direct distribution (comics/publishing): Selling items directly to specialty distributors, who then resell them to SPECIALTY SHOPS, who then sell them to fans. The unsold books cannot be returned to the distributor under this system; the store must either sell them or hold onto them until they become COLLECTABLES.

direct syndication (TV): The marketing of television series to local or cable stations without first airing the episodes on NETWORK TV.

With the expansion of the television audience to include CABLE, PBS, and local stations, independent producers no longer have to rely on the networks, but can sell their programs directly to the smaller but more numerous stations, bypassing the networks completely.

Most of the television SERIES that opt for DIRECT SYNDICATION are game shows or situation comedies, which are not particularly expensive to make and find a ready audience. However, a few well-made SF series have also found their audience in DIRECT SYNDICATION when networks would have turned them down on the grounds of limited viewership or excess violence. The most successful series in DIRECT SYNDICATION is "Star Trek: The Next Generation," which is now seen on over 250 stations in the United States and even more across the world. Anthology series like "The Hitchhiker" and "Ray Bradbury Theater" that would never pass BROADCAST STANDARDS are well received on local and cable stations. See also CABLE; NETWORK; SYNDICATION.

disaster movie: One in which the plot turns on some major catastrophe, either natural, like *Earthquake*, or manmade, like *The Towering Inferno*. In either case, the story usually places a number of characters in the middle of this catastrophe, and part of the fun is trying to guess which are going to survive.

disclaimer (fan): A statement on the title page of a FANZINE, particularly a MEDIAZINE, that states "This is an amateur publication and as such is not meant to be in violation of copyright of. . . ." The stories within will contain characters that are under copyright, but because this disclaimer announces that the publication is strictly amateur, the FANZINE falls into an area of copyright law known as "fair use." Most producers of TV series understand this, and tacitly allow their characters to be used; those that meet this phenomenon for the first time are quickly informed by the veterans that the use of their characters in FANZINES is a sure sign of a hit series in the making.

division system (fan/costuming): A system of organizing MASQUERADES by expertise, devised by Peggy Kennedy in her *Compendium of Costuming* and adopted by the World SF Convention in 1981.

The division system permits costumers to compete more or less equally, depending on the experience of the costumer. A NOVICE has never won at a WORLD-CON; in local or regional competition, a NOVICE may simply be someone who has never competed at all. A JOURNEYMAN has won at least one major award. A MASTER has won at least three major awards at WORLD-CONS or Costume Cons. For those who have won major awards at REGIONAL CONS, but have never competed in a WORLD-CON, there is now the CRAFTSMAN division.

The DIVISION has to do with the level of craftsmanship in making the costume; the category of the costume is decided by the costumer. Prizes are usually awarded in categories of Science Fiction, Fantasy, and Re-Creation; occasionally, the judges will award a prize for Most Humorous, Most Beautiful, or whatever they think is appropriate. See also COSTUMING.

docking (aerospace): The process of bringing two crafts together in space and securing them well enough to prevent their drifting apart. This maneuver is a necessary step in the building of a permanent SPACE STATION, and the achievement of docking is not a minor one. One of the best-publicized docking maneuvers was the Apollo-Soyuz Mission in 1977, which proved that craft from different nations could successfully unite and then separate.

Doomsday Clock: A hypothetical clock that signals the approach of total nuclear holocaust, as determined by the *Bulletin of Atomic Scientists;* a figurative way of visibly demonstrating international tensions, which may lead to the annihilation of Earth and our species. During the height of the Cold War, the DOOMSDAY CLOCK stood at 11:58 or 11:59, signifying that the world was one minute or so away from such a disaster. Recent developments in Europe have permitted the DOOMSDAY CLOCK to be moved back several minutes, meaning that nuclear war is that much farther away.

Doomsday Story (literary): Story that depicts the total obliteration of Humanity, either through a nuclear holocaust or a natural catastrophe. Most of them are meant to be dire warnings of the "If we don't watch out . . ." variety; they are inevitably gruesome and are rarely enjoyable. Occasionally, the protagonist of such a story turns out to be a being from another planet, who wonders what kind of creatures these humans were, who nuked, polluted, or simply sickened and died out.

Dorsai (literary): Society of warlike humans who hire themselves out as mercenaries; created by Gordon R. Dickson for his *Childe Cycle* of novels and short stories, beginning with *Dorsai!* (1959). According to Dickson's FUTURE HISTORY, the DORSAI are only one of several specialized societies scattered throughout the Galaxy. The DORSAI stories cover several generations of the Grahame family, all of whom are fighters of one kind or another.

The very term DORSAI has come to stand for a militaristic point of view and a super-macho attitude. There are a number of DORSAI FILK songs, some of them written by Dickson himself; they tend to be either bawdy or totally grim.

At one time there was a private security force called the Dorsai Irregulars, who were hired to provide CON SECURITY; this group has been disbanded, but the term still lingers for any gang that attempts to regulate CONVENTIONS.

dot-matrix type (printing): The imprint used by some electronic typewriters and word processors that is composed of tiny dots that form the letters. If the dots are too faint, or too far apart, the printing is very difficult to read and to photocopy. For these reasons, some editors (professional and amateur) refuse to accept manuscripts in DOT-MATRIX TYPE.

double star (astronomy): See BINARY STAR.

doublethink (literary): Coined by GEORGE ORWELL in his classic novel *1984*; the capacity to hold two contradictory ideas at the same time, and believe in both of them. Both the term and the concept have been incorporated into standard English.

down (computer): Said of a COMPUTER that is not functioning. COMPUTERS can go DOWN for many reasons: a sudden surge of power, a sudden decrease in power, a MALFUNCTION in the mechanism, an overload of data. When the COMPUTER goes DOWN, the humans must wait until the technicians repair the MALFUNCTION.

Dracula (literary): Title character in the horror story by Bram Stoker, played in films by Bela Lugosi, John Carradine, Christopher Lee, and Jack Palance, among others. The literary DRACULA is a VAMPIRE, who can theoretically live forever as long as he has access to the blood of humans for nourishment. DRACULA travels from his gloomy castle in Transylvania to England, where he is hunted down by two young men and old Dr. Van Helsing. Eventually he is destroyed . . . or is he?

The character of DRACULA was based on historical fact. There was a Dracula—Vlad Tepes Dragul, to be exact. He lived in the late 16th century, during the turbulent period when the Turks were making inroads into the Balkans, and he spent most of his life fighting the Ottoman forces. For this he is considered a national hero in Romania, where his former territory is now situated.

Vlad Tepes was considered bloodthirsty, even for his times, but during his own lifetime he was never accused of being a vampire. Bram Stoker drew on Balkan folklore and concocted a heady brew of gore and semiporn that has taken over the historical DRACULA legends completely. Bram Stoker's novel never seems to lose its hold on the public imagination; in 1979 there were three DRACULAS trying on capes at the costumers' at the same time: Raul Julia in a theatrical production on Broadway, Louis Jourdan in a television production for PBS, and Frank Langella in a remarkable film presentation. George Hamilton played DRACULA for laughs in *Love at First Bite*, and Al Lewis was a daft DRACULA in the TV comedy series "The Munsters" (1964–1966). Somewhere, Vlad Tepes must be laughing heartily. See also VAMPIRES.

dragons (literary): Gigantic creatures, traditionally equipped with wings and scales, vaguely reptilian. DRAGONS appear in both European and Asian folklore, but with entirely different natures and characteristics.

The European DRAGON is considered a source of evil, a monster whose favorite breakfast is a young maiden or a doughty knight. Only the very bravest or purest warrior can destroy it, as in the tales of St. George, or the Greek myth of Perseus. On the

other hand, the Asian DRAGON is a benign beast, a bringer of good fortune and a symbol of royalty.

DRAGONS appear with monotonous frequency in Fantasy and SF. J. R. R. TOLKEIN'S Smaug is the evil creature who holds the power of the Rings, in the *Lord of the Rings* trilogy. Lawrence Yep and Jane Yolen have both written stories for young people in which dragons are bred on faraway planets; like Anne McCaffrey's DRAGONS of PERN, they are telepathic, and must bond with a human to survive.

DRAGONS also appear in SF and Fantasy art, usually looking like large lizards with improbable wings, much in the style of Tenniel's "Jabberwocky" illustration for *Alice in Wonderland.*

Several explanations have been given for the human tendency to create stories of DRAGONS. There is one school of thought that claims that DRAGON stories began when fossil dinosaur bones were discovered by early humans. There is some credence for this; so-called "dragon bones" have been used in Asian medicine for centuries. A more controversial theory is that humans have SUBRACIAL MEMORIES locked into their psyches that date back to the times long before evolution produced primates, let alone humans.

For whatever reason, DRAGONS are part of our fantasy life, and manage to creep in and around the SF world through folklore, story, and even in song: "But can you believe they had feathers? Ye gods, how the dragons roar in!"

dramatic irony (literary): The events and statements in a story that lead the characters (and the reader) to expect one sort of reaction, but that turn out to be something quite different. For instance, in Barbara Hambly's *Ladies of Mandrigyn*, the women fight valiantly to save their men, only to find that in the process they have changed so much that their men may not be able to accept them.

dream sequence (film): A portion of a film that is supposed to represent a dream or nightmare of one of the characters; the sequence is supposed to furnish information about the character's past or interior life that will then be important to the unfolding of the plot. One of the earliest uses of the DREAM SEQUENCE is in the silent film, *The Cabinet of Dr. Caligari.*

DREAM SEQUENCES are often photographed through filters, or in slow motion, so that the audience knows what they are watching. *The Wizard of Oz* might be called a gigantic DREAM SEQUENCE.

Occasionally, a DREAM SEQUENCE is inserted into a film to tell the audience something about the characters, or to explain some of the PLOT. See also BACK-STORY.

Dr. Who (TV): Leading character in the longest-running television SERIES on British TV. The Doctor, as he is usually called, is a Time Lord from Gallifrey, who hops around the universe, in and out of Time, in a T.A.R.D.I.S. (pronounced Tardis), which looks like an old-fashioned British police call-box. The Doctor is usually accompanied by one or more "companions," people he has picked up in his travels who manage to tag along on his outrageous adventures.

Over the 20-plus years DR. WHO has been in production some seven actors have been seen as The Doctor: Peter Cushing, John Pertwee, William Hartnell, Tom Baker, Peter Davidson, Colin Baker, and Sylvester McCoy. The one most associated with the role was Tom Baker, who played Dr. Who throughout most of the 1970s, and who is the Doctor most fans envision when they write FAN-FIC. The part is currently held by Sylvester McCoy, and even though that could change, the show will not. Whenever a new actor takes the part, The Doctor undergoes a "regeneration." He also gets a new wardrobe (each actor devises his own) and a new set of quirks. Tom Baker's long scarf, yo-yo, jelly babies, and slouch hat were Dr. Who trademarks; other Doctors have played the recorder, worn a stalk of celery in a breast pocket, or put on checkered pants and striped coats.

DR. WHO was seen sporadically in the United States during the 1970s and 1980s, often in the SATURDAY MORNING GHETTO, where it lurked at the unlikely hour of 10 A.M. American devotees eventually put pressure on Public Broadcasting and CABLE stations to carry the series, so that now it is shown in most areas during those times when high school and college students are most likely to be watching. The goofy humor, offbeat dialog, and forays into history attract SF fans; the tacky special effects and simplistic story lines don't seem to matter. The popularity of the series shows no signs of tapering off.

DR. WHO fans produce FANZINES, FILK-SONGS, COSTUMES galore. Only STAR TREK can claim as loyal and persistent a group of devotees.

DUFF (Down Under Fan Fund): A fund, established in 1972, based on TAFF (Trans-Atlantic Fan Fund), to send a well-known FAN across the Pacific Ocean, either to or from Australia. The DUFF recipient may be American, Australian, or even a New Zealander, but is usually Australian (if the WORLD-CON is being held in Australia, an American FAN may receive the money).

The money comes from fan AUCTIONS, sales, and other FANNISH efforts; the recipients usually wind up at the WORLD-CON, wherever it is being held.

Dumarest of Earth (literary): A seemingly endless series of novels by E. C. Tubb, in which Earl Dumarest, a lonely wanderer through the Galaxy, seeks Earth, his place of origin. The series began in 1967 with *The Winds of Gath*, and while each story takes Dumarest a step nearer, he never seems to get anywhere. Meanwhile, he has managed to absorb a highly secret symbiote, sought by the Cyclan, a vast organization of CYBORGS, whose sole aim is to dominate every other species in the Galaxy.

DUMAREST has become symbolic of the OPEN-ENDED SERIES, which just goes rolling along, as long as the fans keep reading them; and the fans will keep reading them as long as DUMAREST doesn't get to Earth!

dump (bookselling): A cardboard bookstand, meant to hold from ten to fifty books, which can be placed close to the cash register, where bookstore patrons will be certain to see it. A smaller version is called a counterpack, which can be placed on the cash register counter. DUMPS and counterpacks are provided by the publishers to advertise their latest publications, and advance the SUBSCRIPTION of the next installment of a popular SERIES. Libraries are also being urged to use DUMPS to encourage casual reading.

DUMPS are usually meant to hold many copies of the same book, and may be provided when a certain number of copies are ordered. Although they were originally used to promote PAPERBACKS, some publishers are now providing them for HARDCOVER books as well.

dump (computer): An order to remove information from a file, which may then be replaced with other data.

Dune (literary): Series of five novels by Frank Herbert; the last one was completed by Brian Herbert after the death of his father, Frank.

The first in the series, *Dune*, was a tremendous work, encompassing feudal politics, GALACTIC EMPIRES, PSIONICS, and ecological concerns, all enmeshed in a plot concerning the fate of the planet Arrakis and its native inhabitants, the Fremen, and the indigenous Sandworms. Paul Atreides, the hero of the first novel, founded a dynasty whose fortunes were followed in the next four books.

A grimly epic film was made of *Dune* (1984): The tangled plot of the novel defied any attempt to unravel it, and not even David Lynch's quirky direction could save the film from critical disaster.

dungeon lawyer (gaming): A player who considers himself more proficient in the finer points of the game than the DUNGEONMASTER. He argues over every encounter, contests every decision, and generally makes such a fuss that the only thing to do is make him the DUNGEONMASTER, and contradict his rulings.

dungeonmaster (gaming): The leader of a game of DUNGEONS AND DRAGONS.™ Also called the DM; also called GOD. The DM throws the dice to set up a character's ABILITIES; the DM organizes the CAMPAIGN and announces the results of encounters, fights, and so on. The DM is in charge of the adventure, and can include various NONPLAYER CHARACTERS, monsters, or whatever is needed to keep things moving. The DM must be able to defend all these decisions, so the DM must be very conversant with the traditions and fine points of the game. It's easier to be a DUNGEON LAWYER than a DUNGEONMASTER.

Dungeons and Dragons™ (game): The first of the standardized role-playing games, devised by Gary Gygax in 1974. The game involves creating a CHARACTER, and taking that CHARACTER through a series of adventures with other CHARACTERS, developed by the other players. Much of the action takes place in the minds of the players, led by the DUNGEONMASTER. A CHARACTER may change and grow through the adventures until it reaches a point of proficiency where it becomes a demi-god.

D&D™ games have been known to run over a period of years, until the CHARACTERS become PERSONAS, and wind up in Fantasy novels. There is even a series of novels directly based on the D&D™ Universe.

duotone (comics): Black, white, and one other color of ink, used to print comic books. Most often the other color is red, used as an accent in costumes and blood. DUOTONE is less expensive to print than full color, but more effective than B&W.

dwarf star (astronomy): An ordinary star, during its main phase of activity on the MAIN SEQUENCE scale. Our own sun may be termed a DWARF STAR. Larger stars are GIANTS or Supergiants.

Dynamation (film): A technique for filming animated sequences using models that are moved slightly for each shot; developed by Ray Harryhausen, in *The Seventh Voyage of Sinbad* (1959), and used to great effect in films like *Jason and the Argonauts* and *Clash of the Titans* (1981). When the models are properly filmed, DYNAMATION produces an astonishing degree of realism.

DYNAMATION is very effective, but it is also expensive and time-consuming. Most SFX in SF and Fantasy films are now done through COMPUTER GRAPHICS and PUPPETRY.

Dyson sphere (physics): A theory developed by John Dyson, and presented by him in a paper in 1960: A biosphere could be constructed around a star that would completely enclose it. Likewise, a similar sphere could be constructed to enclose a particular planet, thus increasing living space. Larry Niven's *Ringworld* is based on this idea; the Ringworld is the "equator" of such a sphere, completely encircling its sun.

dystopia (literary): A thoroughly unpleasant, wretched place to live; the opposite of a UTOPIA. DYSTOPIAS abound in SF, ranging from the deserts and ruined cities following a nuclear war to the mechanized and regimented society of Asimov's *Caves of Steel.* Ray Bradbury's *Farenheit 451* (1953) supposes a world without books; Harry Harrison's *Make Room, Make Room* (1966) gives an idea of what would happen if the population explosion reached its worst proportions.

Filmed DYSTOPIAS also abound, starting with Fritz Lang's *Metropolis* (1927), and going right up to the deserted cities and wastelands of the *Mad Max* films of the 1980s.

The term dates back as far as the 1860s, when it was coined as a back-derivation from More's *Utopia.* More used a word he derived from the Greek, but there is some controversy as to which prefix he used: *ou*-topia, meaning "other place," or *eu*-topia, meaning "better place." DYSTOPIA assumes that More meant the latter, and it is undoubtedly true that a DYSTOPIA is a far worse place than any we have ever known.

E

earth-grazers (aerospace): ASTEROIDS whose orbits pass close enough to Earth to constitute a possible danger. The last one passed within Earth's atmosphere in 1972, close enough to have been photographed over the state of Idaho. Theoretically, a shift in the orbit of one of these might lead to a collision with Earth, on the order of the one that is supposed to have led to the extinction of the dinosaurs.

Echo (aerospace): The first American communications satellite, launched in 1961.

ecliptic (astronomy): See PLANE OF THE ECLIPTIC.

ecology (biology): The study of organisms in relation to their environment. ECOLOGY has become a buzzword in the 1980s, when the interrelationships of organisms have been interrupted to the point where life on Earth may be in real danger of extinction.

ECOLOGY is a major factor in WORLDBUILDING. SPACE OPERA is full of wild adventures on distant planets whose flora and fauna are deadly but improbable. Currently, many writers who set their stories on worlds other than Earth have worked out elaborate diagrams and charts in which each ecological niche is filled with some sort of being. Extended studies of life on our own planet have led to a greater understanding of how living organisms interact with each other, which can be extended further by SF writers creating their fictional worlds.

Earth does not always fare so well at the hands of SF writers. *No Blade of Grass* (1957) by John Christopher deals with a world in which all plant life has been destroyed. A POST-HOLOCAUST story or a DYSTOPIA is often explained as being the result of some dire planetary plague or pollution.

Many SF fans take these predictions quite seriously, and work to improve the environment, both by petitioning for legislation and by actively participating in projects that will clean the air and water, so that life as we know it can continue at least on one planet in this universe.

Ecotopia (literary): A perfect world, in which every element of the ECOLOGY is in balance with every other element. Presumably this was the condition of Earth before humans came along. A number of writers have tried to depict such a state of grace; usually, some clod of a Terran comes in and disturbs the tranquility of the environment, causing havoc. Harry Harrison's *Deathworld Trilogy* is a graphic example of such a world gone mad.

editor (publishing): The person directly responsible for what gets into print. It takes many different types and levels of EDITORS to produce a book, magazine, or FANZINE. For example, some EDITORS buy the story or manuscript, while others do the necessary revisions and consult with the writers about them. The managing EDITOR of a magazine makes sure the entire project proceeds on schedule, putting all the various elements together into a harmonious whole. EDITORS may be FAN or PRO; they may be responsible for the entire LINE or SERIES.

EDITORS of SF magazines have had a major effect on the genre. HUGO GERNSBACK and JOHN W. CAMPBELL invented the genre by their fostering of certain trends in writing. EDITORS are constantly changing the paths in which SF will go by their choices for publication. See also COPY EDITOR; FAN-ED; PRO-ED.

ego-boo (fan): The thrill of accomplishment and self-gratification on having produced something or achieved some distinction in any field, but especially in SF. Short for "ego-boosting"; Forrest Ackerman claims he coined the word.

ego-scan (fan): Quickly reading a FANZINE or APA to find one's own name mentioned. After making sure one's own contribution has been acknowledged, one can then go on to read the rest of the publication. EGO-SCAN is not limited to the SF genre.

Einstein, Albert (1896–1956): Mathematician and physicist, winner of the Nobel Prize for mathematics, 1905, whose work laid the basis for advances made in nuclear physics and astronomy.

Einstein's Theory of Relativity (physics): $E = MC^2$: A set of theories that deal with movements of bodies at the speed of light, or as close to it as we can get. According to this theory, Time slows down as you approach the speed of light, so that a person traveling at light speed will not age as fast as someone on a planet. Ramifications of this are central to Joe Haldeman's *The Forever War* (1974), in which the soldiers fighting a thousand-year-old war age only a few years, alienating themselves from the people around them, who see the warriors as perpetually young while they themselves must age and die. Other writers prefer to ignore the problems involved in FTL (FASTER THAN LIGHT) travel.

elf (literary): A nonhuman, possibly magical being, often with extrasensory powers. ELVES appear in European folklore under a number of names, often euphemisms or allusions. In parts of England and Ireland one hears references to the Leprechauns, "Little People," or "Wee Folk." They are supposed to be allergic to iron, so that a horseshoe over a door will keep them away. However, gold attracts them, and they tend to collect it in great quantities.

ELVES creep into FANTASY literature frequently. TOLKEIN included an ELF in his *Brotherhood of the Ring*, and Puck might be

called an ELF in KIPLING's *Puck of Pook's Hill.* Wendy and Richard Pini's *Elfquest* stories deal with a whole society of ELVES.

ELVES are among the principal RACES in DUNGEONS AND DRAGONS™; they can be warriors (but not Paladins), or rogues, or even WIZARDS. ELVES are usually slender, rather than burly, with almond-shaped eyes and large pointed ears. Anyone seen at a CON wearing a green tunic and tights, with large ears, may be considered to be impersonating an ELF.

Elfquest (literary): A series of GRAPHIC NOVELS by Wendy and Richard Pini, dealing with the adventures of several tribes of ELVES in an ALTERNATE UNIVERSE. The series began as a comic book, which was then reprinted as a BAXTER BOOK in HARDCOVER. Eventually, the stories were rendered into prose and printed as a series of novels.

The ELFQUEST characters are especially attractive to costumers, who attempt to reproduce in three dimensions what the Pinis have done in two. There are ELFQUEST FILK songs, but any attempt to use the ELFQUEST characters in FAN-FIC meets with strong disapproval from the creators of the UNIVERSE.

Ellison, Harlan (b. 1934): Writer of short stories that touch upon SF, Fantasy, and Horror. Because he is such a harsh critic of other writers and their books, he has become the symbol of the SF writer who loudly proclaims how much he loathes FANS and FANDOM.

empath (parapsychology): One who can sense the emotions of others, although not necessarily the reasons for them. EMPATHS cannot "read" minds; they do not know what another person is thinking, only what the person is feeling.

Empathy is a form of EXTRA-SENSORY PERCEPTION that is difficult to focus; the EMPATH must guard against becoming too close to another being, whose emotional needs may take over those of the EMPATH. The character of Deanna Troi, in the TV SERIES "Star Trek: The New Generation," is a typical EMPATH.

encumbrance (gaming): The weight (usually rendered in pounds, not grams) that a CHARACTER can carry, as in weapons, armor, tools, or whatever the DUNGEONMASTER decides the group needs. A CHARACTER with STRENGTH can wear a suit of armor, a sword, and a battle-axe. Of course, some CHARACTERS don't need very much more than their hands, their brains, and a length of rope to achieve their goals.

entropy (physics): A term first used by Clausius, a German physicist, in 1850 to encapsulate the dictum that where there is work, there is an equal and equivalent loss of energy. ENTROPY always increases in any closed system not in equilibrium, and it remains constant for a system that is in equilibrium. A number of NEW WAVE writers have become involved in this paradox, and have tried various ways of dealing with entropy.

entry corridor (aerospace): The correct angle a spacecraft must follow to return safely to Earth. If the angle of return is too steep, the craft will burn up due to the friction with the Earth's atmosphere; if it is too shallow, the craft will bounce off the atmospheric envelope completely like a stone skipping across a pond. Computers are used to calculate the ENTRY CORRIDOR.

epic (literary): A work of such scope that to do it justice it requires at least three novels of over 100,000 words each, or a three-hour film with a cast of thousands.

Originally the term was only applied to monumental poems detailing the mythic adventures of a great hero with the active assistance of the dieties. These poems were told and retold many times before being committed to writing. The *Iliad* of Homer, or the *Beowulf* sagas are classic EPICS. Virgil's *Aeneid* is a conscious attempt to re-create the atmosphere of the oral tradition, which was even then considered ancient.

The DUNE novels of Frank and Brian Herbert constitute an epic, with their religious overtones and mythic underpinnings. George Lucas' STAR WARS films were hailed as epics individually; as a trilogy (with more supposedly on the way), they may become a super-epic.

episode (TV): A particular program in a TV series. In the past, each EPISODE was treated as an isolated incident, or a single drama; the continuity of characterization was often ignored by the writer, so that a person out of the character's past might be dragged in, used, and then never heard from or seen again. Each EPISODE would begin and end with the characters at the same emotional point, so that they seemed to exist on one level only.

This routine changed with the emergence of the "ensemble cast" in SERIES like "Hill Street Blues" (1982–1987), in which the characters took on an added dimension as the events of each episode changed and modified their behavior. EPISODES of such SERIES tend to be linked together, so that a story might be continued over several EPISODES in the manner of the daytime soap operas or the old movie serials like FLASH GORDON. Such a set of linked EPISODES is called an "arc."

Because of this shift in writing emphasis, TV series like "V" or "Star Trek: the Next Generation" tend to have episodes that relate back to previous EPISODES. A writer must be prepared to utilize facts previously established in earlier scripts in his or her own story.

error box (astronomy): A box-shaped representation of a particular area of space that a particular celestial object is presumed to inhabit. The astronomer must focus the telescope on that area, and search for the particular planet, star, or whatever it is he or she hopes to find.

escape velocity (aerospace): The speed an object must attain to escape from a gravitational field; usually the object is a spacecraft, and the gravitational field is Earth's. To leave the Earth's gravitational pull, a rocket must achieve 6.95 miles (11.2 km) per second.

esper (literary): One who uses EXTRA-SENSORY PERCEPTION. There are several varieties of ESP: CLAIRVOYANCE, TELEKINESIS, PRECOGNITION, and EMPATHY being the most common. All of them have been used in SF since its beginnings in the early 1900s.

Early SF treated ESPERS as particularly sinister and desperate MUTANTS. Not until after World War II were they given an honorable role in stories like Sturgeon's classic *More Than Human* (1953), in which a group of ESPERS combine their talents to become "homo gestalt." Katharine Kurtz's DERYNI are ESPERS whose mental powers dismay the religious authorities.

Back in the real world, NEW AGE practitioners are fascinated with ESPER talents, and work assiduously to extend their own mental powers.

establishing shot (film): A way for the camera to set the scene for a film, by acting as the "eyes" of a hypothetical observer. An ESTABLISHING SHOT can sweep around in a panoramic view, or it can focus on one particular object. The ESTABLISHING SHOT of a star field can instantly announce that the film is set somewhere in Space . . . or in a Galaxy Far Far Away. A dark forest scene heralds a fantasy like *Excalibur*, and the dreary wastelands of Australia prepare the viewer for the grim future world of the *Mad Max* trilogy.

Comics have taken over the use of the establishing shot to set the scene, with double-page spreads that depict everything from the interior of a starship to the wooded glens of the ELFQUEST Universe.

E.T. (movie) (1982): One of the most popular SF films of recent years; STEVEN SPIELBERG's touching story of a space traveler who gets left behind, and Elliot, the boy who befriends him. The film depends less on SPECIAL EFFECTS than on good writing and acting for its impact. Many critics consider E.T. one of the most beautiful SF films ever made.

"E.T. phone home" (film): Catch-phrase from E.T. (see above), uttered by the title character, who strings up a contraption to contact his space-faring friends. For a while it was used to jolt daydreaming friends out of reveries, or to let people know that they were wanted for some errand or other. It has since died out, except on BUTTONS.

Eucatastrophe (literary): A final apocalyptic victory of Good; presumably, the right side will win Armageddon.

"Eureka!" (literary): Literally, "I have it!"; supposedly uttered by the ancient Greek mathematician Archemedes upon discovering the displacement of water in his bath. It has become a cliche phrase exclaimed by MAD SCIENTISTS in SF stories as they prance joyfully about their laboratories waving test tubes.

EVA (Extra-Vehicular Activity) (aerospace): Anything that a space traveler does outside the spacecraft; usually, this involves launching SATELLITES or repairing existing ones.

The first EVA was the space walk, on the SOYUZ mission in 1965, performed by Cosmonaut Alexie Tashkov; later American GEMINI missions used EVA activities, leading up to the Apollo moon landings in 1969.

Later modifications in SPACE SUITS enabled astronauts and cosmonauts to use compressed air to maneuver around the crafts. EVA plays a vital part in the film *2010* (1984), as a link is set up between the derelict spaceship and the craft sent out after it.

event (fan/SCA): A meeting of the SOCIETY FOR CREATIVE ANACHRONISM, with or without food. An EVENT usually involves the entire group, and calls for GARB, FEAST-GEAR, and all the ACCESSORIES that go with one's SCA PERSONA. See also SOCIETY FOR CREATIVE ANACHRONISM.

event horizon (astronomy): The boundary of a BLACK HOLE, at the edge of the Schwartzchild Radius. Outside of this area, time as we know it proceeds at its usual rate (everything being relative); within the EVENT HORIZON, even light is absorbed, and time has no meaning. Anything inside will be effectually frozen; time will seem to stop. It is the guilt at having left his friends in this suspended state that drives the hero of Pohl's *Heechee* saga to desperation, and eventually, to return to find them.

evil alignment (gaming): One of the three possibilities for a character's moral code, the other two being Good and Neutral.

Against this must be set the possibilities of LAWFUL, NEUTRAL, and CHAOTIC. Most players are cautioned to be some variation of Good, since Evil is, after all, the villainous aspect of the fantasy world, and is clearly meant to come to a bad end. However, as one actor gleefully put it, "Everyone wants to play a nice, juicy villain," and some players will chose Lawful Evil for their CROSS-ALIGNMENT. Such a CHARACTER will use his talents for his own benefit, within legal limits. The Sheriff of Nottingham, in the Robin Hood legends, is an example of Lawful Evil. The worst characters are Chaotic Evil, who do whatever they like, whenever they like, for their own benefit and no one else's. They are the archetypal villains of every fairy tale and fantasy, from Ming the Merciless to Darth Vader, and are there mainly to be destroyed by the GOOD characters.

exobiology (biology): See XENOBIOLOGY.

exoskeleton (biology): In nature, the development of some form of rigid organic material to enclose the soft organs of a creature, thus protecting it and supporting the body at the same time. On Earth this feature is limited to such creatures as some insects like cockroaches and crustaceans like lobsters. SF writers have used the idea to create such beings as the Groaci, the crablike villains of Keith Laumer's *Retief* stories.

experience points (gaming): Credit earned by a CHARACTER by completing some task during an adventure: solving a problem, or doing something that improves skills in this CHARACTER'S particular CLASS. A player may accumulate EXPERIENCE POINTS for the CHARACTER through a series of adventures, until the CHARACTER has become close to perfect . . . or until the CHARACTER meets his end.

exposition (literary): The unfolding of the PLOT, and the relation of the actions of the story to the BACK-STORY; the events that took place before the present action that are now affecting the CHARACTERS as we observe them.

EXPOSITION is part of the craft of writing, whether in drama or prose. The audience must know who these CHARACTERS are, and what they are doing here, before they can identify enough with them to care about them and read (or watch) more about their doings.

SF demands more EXPOSITION than most forms of fiction, since the BACK-STORY sometimes covers a few million years of evolution. A few writers claim they simply ignore EXPOSITION and dive into the story, leaving the readers to figure out the background for themselves. This leaves some readers extremely frustrated, demanding that the author write a PREQUEL to explain just what went on before the PLOT began in the first book. See also BACK-STORY; DREAM SEQUENCE; IDIOT LECTURE; PREQUEL.

extra-sensory perception (ESP) (parapsychology): The term used by Dr. Joseph Rhine in 1934 to describe the attainment of information by means other than the usual senses of sight, sound, smell, taste, and touch. ESP has become controversial, because many of its practitioners cannot explain how it works, and until they do, scientists insist they cannot accept it.

Forms of ESP include CLAIRVOYANCE, TELEKINESIS, PRECOGNITION, and PSYCHIC HEALING. Some people have claimed to read minds; some insist they only feel the emotional reactions of others (EMPATHY). See also EMPATH; ESPER; PRECOGNITION; TELEKINESIS.

extraterrestrial (astronomy): Anything not native to Planet Earth, whether organic or not. A meteorite is EXTRATERRESTRIAL; so is a hypothetical BEM. Most SF writers now prefer the term to the shorter but less accurate ALIEN.

Fafiate (fan): See GAFIATE.

Fairy Tales (literary): Stories of magic, set "once upon a time", often dealing with the rise of a young person to prominence, thanks to luck and virtue. FAIRY TALES began as folklore, and were told around hearths and campfires well into the 19th century. Charles Perrault re-wrote some of the old stories for the courtiers of Louis XIV, and the brothers Wilhelm and Karl Jakob Grimm collected them in the mid-19th century. Hans Christian Andersen deliberately wrote in the style of the old tales, bringing literary sensibility to the form. Modern fairy tales include "The Thirteen Clocks" and "The White Deer" by James Thurber, and "The Mirrorstone" by Michael Palin.

Many SF writers acknowledge their debt to FAIRY TALES. Robin McKinley has re-written the "Beauty and the Beast" story as "Beauty." Other writers have taken such themes as "Jack and the Beanstalk" and "Cinderella" and given them futuristic settings. Much SPACE OPERA has been compared to FAIRY TALES, particularly in CHARACTERIZATION and MOTIVATION.

FAIRY TALES are simplistic in orientation. Good is rewarded; evil is punished. The young HERO is often scorned as a "Simpleton" or "Ash-pit", and must undergo tests of courage and strength before attaining power, riches, and the hand of the princess (or prince). Evil characters include WITCHES, ogres, and WIZARDS, who thwart the HERO at every turn, but are eventually destroyed by him. There is always a happy ending, and they all live "happily ever after".

Many Fantasy stories try to imitate the archaic language of FAIRY TALES. Not all of them succeed; perhaps the best-known of these is the "Lord of the Rings" trilogy of J.R.R. TOLKIEN.

FAIRY TALES have become part of Western European culture, studied by psychologists like Carl Jung and Bruno Bettelheim, collected by serious anthropologists, and vastly imitated by writers for adults as well as children. Many critics feel that SCIENCE FICTION is the new repository of FAIRY TALES.

fan (plural fans or fen): A person devoted to some activity, in this case, Science Fiction. SF FANS have been a moving force since the genre emerged in the 1920s, and their activities have generated a body of literature and a jargon all their own.

The SF FANS of those early years were predominantly male, young, and technology-oriented. They tended to be above average in intelligence and below average in physical appeal, and they tended to cluster together for self-protection against an otherwise unfeeling world.

Eventually these young men grew up to become FIRST FANDOM and many of them emerged as the Grand Masters of today's SF world. After World War II, the world of FANS and FANDOM expanded to include more diverse groups. The real breakthrough came in the 1960s, when women found a voice and a place in SF.

SF FANS no longer fit the stereotype of a pimply adolescent seeking escape. While there are many young people reading SF, there are also educated adults. FANS read SF. Many also write SF, and try to get their writings published. Since there is a limited market for paid SF, an extensive network of SEMIPROZINES and FANZINES has grown up to distribute these writings.

FAN activities include FILKING, COSTUMING, and GAMING as well as writing FAN-FIC, contributing to LETTERZINES and APAS, participating in CLUBS, and attending CONVENTIONS. FANS influence SF by what they buy and what they watch on TV and in movie theaters. They are vociferous about their likes and dislikes, and have been known to organize LETTER-WRITING CAMPAIGNS to save their favorite TV programs from cancellation.

A few lucky fans GRADUATE and GO PRO; they become the next group of SF writers and perhaps generate a FANDOM of their own. Many SF writers began as FANS, and continue to participate in FAN-AC. The line between PRO and FAN is very thin in SF FANDOM, and SF writers tend to be more approachable than writers of other genres. After all, most of them have been on both sides of that thin line, and they reciprocate, bringing new writers along, so that SF FANDOM has become a kind of pool for new talent. See also the terms in this book labeled FAN.

fan-ac (fan): Short form of "Fannish Activity"; any activity indulged in by FANS of SF. FAN-AC may include GAMING, COSTUMING, and FILKING; contributing to FANZINES or APAS; or participating in a CONVENTION or CLUB. FAN-AC can take as much or as little time as a FAN will allow. Some people find themselves totally involved, while others use SF as a momentary escape from daily life. See also FIAWOL.

fan club (fan): A group of people interested in a particular film, TV SERIES, series of novels, or actor or actress in a film or TV SERIES. They may gather together on a regular basis, or simply correspond with each other.

FAN CLUBS may not be directly connected with SF, although they are often organized around an SF film, TV series, or series of novels. An AUTHORIZED FAN CLUB (like the George Takei Fan Club) will have a direct connection to the object of the club's interest, while an OFFICIAL FAN CLUB (such as the STAR TREK FAN CLUB) will be run by the production company or studio that originated the TV series or film.

FAN CLUBS often finance their activities by producing a FANZINE with FAN-FIC, art, and articles related to their idol. The Leonard Nimoy Fan Club issues a *Yearbook*, with rare photos and reviews as well as the usual stories, art, and poetry. Both Paramount and Lucasfilms have monthly bulletins that promote their current productions, with plenty of photographs, interviews, and background material on their films. See also CLUBS.

fan-con (fan): A CONVENTION run by SF fans, as opposed to one run by a professional entrepreneur. FAN-CONS tend to be SER-CON, that is, serious and constructive, with an emphasis on SF as literature as opposed to SF as entertainment. A FAN-CON will have a noted writer as GoH; the program will include PANELS and WORKSHOPS, with the intention of improving the writing and artistic skills of the membership.

Many FAN-CONS are run by a standing CON-COM; others are run by well-known clubs like the Lunarians, who rotate the responsibilities yearly, so that no one person can become a Convention Czar.

FAN-CONS are listed in various SF magazines, particularly *Isaac Asimov's SF Magazine* and *Analog*; they also distribute FLYERS at other FAN-CONS. On some weekends in the summer there is a FAN-CON in more than one locality, so that every fan has an opportunity to attend a CON somewhere. See Appendix A for a list of convention addresses.

fandom (fan): The aggregate of SF FANS that presumably includes anyone interested in reading, writing, producing, or watching Science Fiction. In actuality, SF FANDOM usually refers to those FANS who actively take part in CONVENTIONS, FAN writing, or other FAN-AC. It is a diverse group, often split on social and political issues, and a lot harder to stereotype than in past years. See also FAN; FAN-AC.

fandom (literary/film/TV): Those people devoted to a particular TV SERIES, series of novels, or film, who are actively involved in promoting it through writing, art, costumes, song, or whatever else they can think of.

The most numerous and most vocal of the FANDOMS is STAR TREK, which may have begun the whole process of FRINGE FANDOM. STAR TREK fans produced MEDIA FANZINES, concocted costumes, and generally kept the STAR TREK idea alive for a decade after the series was canceled, until it was revived as a series of theatrical films. STAR WARS FANDOM burst on the scene in 1977. DR. WHO FANDOM parades about in floppy hats and long scarves. There are JAPANIMATION FANDOM and DARKOVER FANDOM, and the latest arrival, FUZZY FANDOM, which glorifies cute anthropomorphic animals in animated films.

The hope of every producer of SF films and TV series is that their production will generate a FANDOM, which will keep the thing going through FAN-FIC and FAN-AC, even through cancellation, yea unto SYNDICATION and RERUNS.

fan-ed (fan): The editor of a FANZINE. Usually the editor is also the publisher, who finances the undertaking out of personal funds, expecting to make back the cost of the printing when the FANZINE is sold. Some FAN-EDS use their skills to become professional SF EDITORS; others just do it for fun.

fan feud (fan): A minor argument between FANS that erupts into a major war that drags everyone around FANDOM into the hostilities. The first FAN FEUD involved New York fans in the late 1930s, and concerned political activities of the time. A number of the young men (women were unseen and unheard of in SF FANDOM at that time) would later be drawn into a far larger and more vicious conflict that superceded that particular feud, centering around the possible Communist affiliations that might be espoused by some of the members of the group.

FAN FEUDS can be generated over matters of taste (STAR TREK VS. STAR WARS), or matters of ethics (FAN-CONS VS. PRO-CONS), or even simple personality conflicts. They tend to be fierce while they last, but like most wars, they eventually get settled (occasionally with the assistance of the judicial system). At least one FAN FEUD, involving members of a Michigan STAR TREK club, wound up in court, so that the financial matters of the club could be settled to everyone's satisfaction. The real victims of FAN FEUDS are not the participants but the bystanders, who try to remain friendly with both feuding parties.

Anyone who feels impelled to take sides in a FAN FEUD should remember the fate of the grain between two grindstones, and let the feuders fight it out on their own.

fan-fic (fan): Fan fiction; stories written by FANS for publication in FANZINES. Most FAN-FIC is written for MEDIAZINES, using characters created by others in films, TV SERIES, and very occasionally, in novels.

FAN-FIC has always been a part of SF FAN-AC. The first FANZINES contained fiction as well as criticism and scientific discussion. However, there soon arose a kind of snobbery that went: "If it's good enough to read, it's good enough to sell; if it hasn't been sold, why bother to read it?" As a result, Science Fiction was either printed in professionally produced publications or it was not printed at all. There were enough magazines in the 1930s, 1940s, and 1950s to provide a market for the writers then active in SF.

The scene changed drastically with the emergence of the STAR TREK FANZINES. Many of these included stories that were continuations of the STAR TREK EPISODES, or that explored aspects of the STAR TREK characters, or that invented new adventures for the crew of the Starship Enterprise. Since these characters were technically under copyright to Gene Roddenberry, the stories that used them could not be sold professionally, although Roddenberry gave tacit permission to FANS to write what they liked for their own pleasure. The only way to distribute these stories was through the medium of FANZINES, and so the MEDIAZINE was born.

The first two STAR TREK FANZINES were *Spockanalia* (first published in 1966 by Devra Langsam) and *ST-Phile* (1966, Juanita Coulson). Others followed, and the STAR TREK Welcommittee now lists nearly a thousand of them.

FAN-FIC has come a long way since the first STAR TREK efforts. FAN writers have improved their skills through practice, until writers like Jean Lorrah and Jacqueline Lichtenberg can proudly announce that they emerged through FAN-FIC. Subgenres have developed within FAN-FIC, such as the HURT/COMFORT STORY, or the MARY SUE STORY, or the SLASH story. With the loss of markets for original SF stories, there are more "straight SF" FANZINES and SEMIPROZINES being published these days than was usual in the past.

FAN-FIC is still one of the best ways for a beginning writer to hone skills and develop a personal style.

fannish (fan): Describes anything produced by FANS, or (pejoratively), fit only for FANS. Something can be FANNISH if it is pure, uncommercial, and devoted to the highest ideals of FANDOM. It can also be called FANNISH if it is poorly written or shabbily constructed, naive in philosophy, and ineptly presented. As Obi-Wan Kenobi says in the STAR WARS films, "It all depends on your point of view."

fantasy (literary): A story in which unusual, strange, eerie, wonderful things happen, without scientific explanation. SF and FANTASY tend to overlap in the current literary scene, to the point where most bookstores lump them together in one section.

The distinction seems to be that SF deals with the probable, while in FANTASY the action may be downright impossible outside that particular UNIVERSE. The events in an SF story are at least theoretically possible; in a FANTASY, at least one element is simply not possible given the limitations of our universe.

There is a tendency toward SCIENCE FANTASY, which combines elements of both SF and FANTASY so that magic works, but only when used by particular people who are born with certain talents, or only in accordance with particular laws. Randall Garrett's *Lord Darcy* stories take place in such an Alternate Universe.

Fantasy has its own genres and conventions within those genres; fantasy also lends itself to CROSS-GENRE stories, in which ELVES, magicians, and DRAGONS interact with tough detectives or hard-tech-toting MERCENARIES. See also DARK FANTASY; HIGH FANTASY; URBAN HIGH FANTASY.

fanzine (fan): An amateur publication, produced by people interested in SF and FANTASY, distributed by mail or at CONVENTIONS. The term is a combination of "fan" and "magazine," and should be pronounced to rhyme with "machine." It is often shortened to " 'zine"; as such it is sometimes pronounced to rhyme with "wine." FANZINES are a major part of FAN-AC, and they provide a market and an audience for upcoming writers, artists, and editors.

FANZINES began as NEWSLETTERS, printed by FANS by mimeograph and distributed for postage or exchange copies. The first acknowledged FANZINE is Raymond A. Palmer's *Comet*, issued in

1930. Throughout the 1930s and 1940s, FANZINES were primarily used by SF FANS as a means of communication. In them the young men (mostly) could voice their criticism of the world around them, and praise or condemn the works of their favorite SF writers. It is this kind of FANZINE that is the subject of Dr. Frederick Wortham's treatise *The World of Fanzines* (1968).

With the emergence of MEDIAZINES the FANZINE picture changed completely. Whereas the older FANZINES rarely printed fiction, the newer FANZINES consisted largely of FAN-FIC, usually depicting the adventures of STAR TREK or other TV or film characters. The older FANZINES rarely ran more than 12 pages; MEDIAZINES might run as long as 200 pages of fiction, poetry, and artwork. The older FANZINES were printed as cheaply as possible (dittos, mimeograph, or even typed individually); the MEDIAZINES demanded better, cleaner reproduction, usually PHOTO-OFFSET, which had to be financed some way. The price of MEDIAZINES began to rise.

There is now a dichotomy that is reflected in the HUGO AWARDS, one of which is given for "Best Fanzine." It usually goes to one of the old-style FANZINES, since they are the ones most widely distributed. Only twice has a media FANZINE been nominated, and both times it was voted down. Some people in FANDOM still insist that MEDIAZINES are not FANZINES, since they contain fiction and may be priced as high as $20 per copy.

However, the editors of MEDIAZINES insist that they are as FANNISH as anyone else; they simply have to cover the cost of their printing.

Whether or not they contain fiction, FANZINES remain one of the chief vehicles for FAN-AC. There are even FANZINES that list other FANZINES for sale. Upcoming FANZINES drum up customers through FLYERS and announcements in other FANZINES. FANZINES are also available at CONS, particularly MEDIA-CONS. See also FAN-ED; K/S FICTION; MARY SUE STORY; addresses of some FANZINES are listed in Appendix A.

feast-gear (fan/SCA): Tableware brought to an EVENT by a member of the SOCIETY FOR CREATIVE ANACHRONISM. Before the general use of tableware, each visitor was expected to provide his or her own utensils. FEAST-GEAR is an attempt to re-create this custom. It also lifts a certain burden off the shoulders of the host of the EVENT, who does not have to worry if there is enough silverware to go around.

Feghoot (literary): An SF-oriented shaggy-dog story, ostensibly chronicling the Adventures of Captain Ferdinand Feghoot. The story winds its way through a long, preposterous set of events to a final and atrocious pun. FEGHOOTS first appeared in *The Magazine of Fantasy and Science Fiction* in the late 1950s; Grendell Briarton is credited with writing the first one, but others have taken up the form since then.

Feminist SF (literary): Science Fiction that deals with so-called "women's issues": GENDER ROLES, the place of women in society, and the diverse behavior between the sexes. Joanna Russ is a leading writer of FEMINIST SF, with *The Female Man* leading the way for other explorations of these topics.

The whole place of women in SF, both as participants and as characters, has shifted greatly in the last twenty years. Many women acknowledge the importance of STAR TREK and its predominantly female FANDOM in the emergence of women into the hitherto male enclave of SF writing, although it may be argued that STAR TREK simply echoed the direction of the times.

Either way, women have become highly visible in SF, and their concerns have affected their subject matter.

FIAWOL (fan): Fandom Is A Way Of Life; the motto of those active FANS who live out their dreams through their involvement in SF FANDOM. Those are the people whose pictures appear in newspapers, dressed up like BARBARIANS, SPACE MARINES, and BEMS. They write FAN-FIC and edit FANZINES; they sing FILK-SONGS; they have wedding ceremonies in STAR TREK or STAR WARS costumes. They even raise their children in FANDOM. They occasionally use their associations in FANDOM to good effect in their MUNDANE life, becoming writers, editors, or computer experts.

FIJAGDH (fan): Fandom Is Just A God Damned Hobby; the cry of those FANS who insist they only read SF for fun, and won't admit that they are deeply involved in FANDOM. They would never dream of attending a CON, and they shrug when they see pictures of strange people dressed like BARBARIANS, SPACE MARINES, or BEMS in the newspapers. See also PASSIFAN.

FIJAWOL (fan) See FIAWOL.

file (computer): A section of the information entered on a computer disk, which is disgorged upon receiving the proper ACCESS CODE; also called a Document.

filk (fan): The music of Science Fiction, composed and performed by FANS at CONVENTIONS. The term is supposed to have come from a possibly apocryphal song sheet, on which "folk songs" was mistyped as "filk songs," after which the term stuck. It has been dated as early as 1947, but SF historian Sam Moskowitz insists that FANS were writing FILK long before that.

FILK songs might be original poems introduced into a story or novel, like HEINLEIN's *Green Hills of Earth*, or they might be previously written poems set to music, like Donald Swann's song cycle based on the poems in *Lord of the Rings* that J. R. R.

TOLKIEN wrote in *Elvish.* They are often parodies, both humorous and serious, using existing music with new lyrics.

Subject matter for FILK extends as far as the SF/Fantasy world can go. There are songs that epitomize a particular story or a character in a story, or an episode of a particular TV SERIES, or a film. They can, like old ballads, be short stories in verse. They can deal with elements of the mythic past, or with the probable technological future. They can praise or vilify the Space Program, computers, or anything else that strikes FILKERS as funny, serious, or otherwise worth commemorating.

Occasionally a very popular FILK song will generate its own FILK in response. BANNED FROM ARGO, by LESLIE FISH, has acquired its own set of parodies. The wheel has come full circle; one of FISH's songs has spawned a book of short stories (*Carmen Miranda's Ghost Is Haunting Space Station Three,* 1990), and those stories may well inspire FILKS in response.

FILK is also used as a verb, meaning to sing FILK songs, or to use a currently popular song as the basis for a parody. Many songs are constantly FILKED; a list of the parodies of "The Battle Hymn of the Republic" may run to fifty items or more.

In recent years, FILK has moved into the CONVENTION program. Most SF CONS will provide a meeting room for late-night FILKING, which will be announced in the PROGRAM BOOK.

FILK has evolved its own jargon, which is listed in this book in parentheses as FAN/FILK. See also BARDIC CIRCLE; FILKER; HYMNAL; PICK, PASS, OR PLAY.

filker (fan): Someone who writes or performs FILK. FILKERS are found toting guitars at CONVENTIONS, huddled in corners with scraps of paper, chortling happily as they conduct another parody.

Some people are better at singing and playing than others, so a sort of star system has evolved around certain FILKERS. Juanita Coulson, for instance, is known as a FILKER, as well as a writer and editor. LESLIE FISH, who is becoming known as a writer, began as a FILKER.

Another phenomenon is the FILK group, a duet, trio, or larger choir that sings FILK in harmony, for performance, instead of leading a general sing-along. The Omicron Ceti Three began this sort of FILKING in 1976; other groups are the L. A. Philkharmonics and Technical Difficulties.

FILKERS tend to prefer guitars as the instrument of choice; however, autoharps, banjos, and even synthesizers have been brought out at FILK-SINGS. See also FILK; FILK-SING; FILK-TAPES; FRANK HAYS DISEASE/PETE SEEGER'S ANTIDOTE.

filk-sing (fan): A gathering at which FILK songs are performed. Until the mid-1980s, these hootenannies were held in private hotel rooms, where fans would perch on beds or chairs and join in the choruses until the rest of the hotel guests began to complain about the noise. FILK-SINGS are now held in vacant meeting rooms after the main PROGRAMMING of a CON has ended.

FILK-SINGS are run along various lines. A BARDIC CIRCLE gives each participant a chance to perform, in strict rotation. A variant of this is PICK, PASS, OR PLAY, where each person has the option of performing or requesting someone else to sing a favorite song. Midwest Chaos reverts back to the hootenanny idea; anyone with a good song can just jump in and sing it.

More organized than a FILK-SING is a FILK Concert, at which FILK groups are given an opportunity to perform. There are also "One-Shot" Concerts, during which each performer may play one song, with the results being taped for a future FILK-TAPE.

FILK-SINGS usually begin somewhere around 11 P.M. and end at dawn, or whenever the last guitarist gives up.

filk-tapes (fan): Audio cassettes of recorded FILK songs, performed by FILK-SINGERS, either in the privacy of a recording studio, or during a FILK-SING at a CONVENTION, available for sale in the DEALERS' ROOM of a CON or through the mail.

FILK-TAPES are a development of the 1980s, when the development of cheap and portable equipment made it possible to record FILK-SINGS at CONS, as well as in studio settings. There are now several semiprofessional organizations that produce FILK-TAPES in bulk, for distribution at CONS. A few FILKERS produce their own tapes, in the same way that FANS produce their own magazines; the result might be called an electronic FANZINE.

FILK-TAPES are being taken seriously by SF critics; at least one has been reviewed in a major publication. For addresses of some distributors of FILK-TAPES, see Appendix A.

filkzine (fan): A FANZINE devoted to FILK, either as a review medium, or as a compilation of lyrics. Some FILKZINES also include the music to original songs as well as the text of the parodies. A very long or diversified collection of FILK is called a HYMNAL.

fill-in (comics): An issue of a comic book done by a CREATIVE TEAM different from the one that usually draws it. If a fill-in team does well, they may be given a chance to develop their own comic book.

fillos (fan/art): Small illustrations that look very cute, hideous, or quaint, but do not illustrate any particular story or poem. Cartoons and CREEPY-CRAWLIES are FILLOS; so are FANZINE covers. See also ILLOS.

film clip (film): Either a small piece of running film, shown to promote interest in the finished product, or a single segment of the actual film, cut and mounted so that it can be shown as a slide. The second kind of FILM CLIP is often collected by artists, who use them as PHOTOREFS.

film noir (film): Movies made during the late 1940s, often by expatriate European filmmakers, that deal with the underclass of the city, exploring the depravity of human activity in the guise of a detective thriller. Many of them were made as B-MOVIES, as cheaply and quickly as possible, and were not considered particularly important when they were made. The dark brooding atmosphere and underlying cynicism of the script of many of these films tended to leave most viewers of the time feeling cheated of a traditional "happy ending."

This dark and brooding aspect has been picked up by SF filmmakers, as they depict the city of the future. *Blade Runner* (1982) was a deliberate attempt to imitate the FILM NOIR atmosphere; only at the very end is the darkness lifted into what some people consider a falsely happy ending.

firmware (computer): SOFTWARE that actually exists, as opposed to VAPORWARE, which is still being thought out and may never get into production at all.

First Contact Story (literary): One that depicts the initial meeting between EXTRATERRESTRIALS and humanity. FIRST CONTACT can be wary or hostile or curious or friendly. It can take place on Earth or on our landing elsewhere. A few writers have even supposed that it took place millennia ago, and we are the result of it.

There are many parallels for FIRST CONTACT in human history, and many SF writers have observed and used them in their stories. In early years the advent of humans onto a planet was presumed to be a Good Thing; recent developments in ecology and anthropology have caused thoughtful people to wonder about this.

The term was first used as the title of a story by Murray Leinster in 1946; SF EDITORS and critics picked it up, and it has been used ever since. See also ALIENS; EXTRATERRESTRIALS; XENOBIOLOGY.

first edition (publishing): The initial printing of a particular book. Most FIRST EDITIONS are worth exactly what the publisher chooses to list as the selling price; however, early editions of some SF books are quite rare, and have a value far above the initial cost.

First Fandom (fan): A group of aging but still active gentlemen who can prove that they read SF before 1939. (Ladies are not excluded from FIRST FANDOM, but at the time few young women would admit to reading SF.) Many of the Grand Old Masters of SF are proud to belong to FIRST FANDOM; among them are ISAAC ASIMOV, Hal Clement, and Frederik Pohl.

FIRST FANDOM gives a "Big Heart" award every year during the HUGO AWARD ceremonies at the WORLD-CON; they also sponsor charity auctions for those of their membership who may need financial assistance. Most of all, they remind the younger generation that age is no barrier to a willingness to welcome the future.

first printing (comics): The original FIRST EDITION of a comic book. Early comic books were not printed in vast lots, so a FIRST PRINTING of some comics may be worth far more than the buyer's mother ever anticipated when she tossed out what appeared to be a pile of dusty old comics.

Fish, Leslie: FILKER, political activist, song writer, BNF, and most recently, published author. She has been the subject of endless stories herself, partly because of her well-known (in FANDOM) quirks, and partly because she has written many of the best-known and most-asked-for FILK songs, among them the notorious BANNED FROM ARGO.

fixed stars (astronomy): Stars that seem to remain in place over the years when seen from Earth without a telescope. Early astronomers noted that these stars remained constant in the sky, whereas others, dubbed "planets," appeared to move randomly. The movements of the stars are imperceptible to the naked eye, leading to the conclusion that the Earth was the center of the Universe, and the stars were "fixed" in some sort of celestial globe. Later developments and the perfection of the telescope proved that this theory was quite wrong; however, some astronomy texts still use the fiction of the FIXED STARS to locate objects in the sky.

flaking (comics): A condition of very old and brittle comics, in which small pieces of the edges tend to chip off. Sulfur-based paper has this tendency; it affects cheaper editions of both HARDCOVER books and PAPERBACKS. Serious collectors will provide plastic bags to prevent this drying and chipping process.

flashback (film/literary): Showing or writing scenes into a story that took place before the main action, to inform the audience of some important event or to allow the audience some insight into a character's MOTIVATION. FLASHBACKS in a film may be shot in a different light or through a filter, or they may just be inserted as a VOICEOVER. Some films or stories are one long flashback as the NARRATOR provides the background information, leading to a KICKER that may shift the focus of the whole story. See also BACK-STORY; DREAM SEQUENCE.

Flash Gordon (comics/film/TV): The archetypal SCIENCE FANTASY hero, as opposed to BUCK ROGERS, who was usually surrounded by the trappings of technology. FLASH GORDON was first seen as the hero of a comic strip introduced by Alex Raymond in 1934. He was then portrayed by Buster Crabbe in three serial movies, in which the intrepid Flash went to Mars to combat the plans of the evil magician Ming the Merciless. The most recent version was a 1981 film, lavishly produced by Dino De Laurentis, with Max Von Sydow as Ming and Sam Jones as Flash.

FLASH GORDON'S Universe is pure SPACE OPERA, with little acknowledgment of scientific realities; there's lots of action, and many strange and wonderful beings, but the emphasis is on the magical, not the technological, as in the BUCK ROGERS films and comics.

flyby (aerospace): An approach to a planet by an unmanned spacecraft, for exploration purposes. Before humans land on a planet, they try to learn as much about it as they can; ergo, they send PROBES to photograph and record as much as they can. The

Soviet PROBE Venera provided much valuable information about the planet Venus; the U.S. Voyager FLYBYS gave a whole new set of information on Jupiter, Saturn, Uranus, and Neptune. Presumably, should we go beyond our own system, FLYBYS will be used before people land on a particular planet.

flyers (fan): Announcements of forthcoming CONVENTIONS, FANZINES, or whatever, printed up in bulk and distributed through the mail or at CONS. FLYERS are found on the FREEBIE TABLE, where fans hover to see what's going on where. Some of the larger CONS provide a kind of rack, to place flyers in chronological order according to when the event is supposed to take place.

flying saucers: See UFO.

Forbidden Planet (film): Landmark film, first shown in 1956, based roughly on the theme of Shakespeare's *The Tempest*, starring Walter Pigeon as Dr. Morbius and a stalwart cast as the crew of a starship that disturbs the doctor's lonely idyll. The Captain, played by Leslie Nielsen, discovers the truth about the destruction of the colony that supposedly settled the planet, while falling in love with the beautiful daughter of Dr. Morbius.

FORBIDDEN PLANET was one of the first SF films shot in color; it had a solid story line, believable characters, and a valid point to make without heavy-handed preaching. It had flashes of wit, a large robot, a multinational crew, and a workable starship design. Many of the elements used in FORBIDDEN PLANET have become the cliches of current SF films, but at the time they were completely new. The film still holds up after nearly 35 years, and belongs in every SF film collection.

force field (literary): A defensive barrier of pure energy that acts as a shield against projectiles of all sizes, from a small asteroid to a molecular particle. According to current physics, theoretically such a barrier is possible, but the mechanism that would create and maintain it would expend more energy than it would produce, thus defeating the purpose of the force field.

In spite of this scientific deterrent, force fields have been a standard ploy in SPACE WARFARE since the beginning of SF as a genre. Without them, spaceship defense would be impossible, and they remain one of the literary conventions of SF.

format (publishing): The physical makeup of a book: HARDCOVER, TRADE PAPERBACK, or MASS MARKET PAPERBACK. HARDCOVER or TRADE PAPERBACKS may be any size, but MASS MARKET PAPERBACKS must be a standard size to fit into the racks in bookstores, newsstands, and other outlets. Many HARDCOVER books are reissued as MASS MARKET PAPERBACKS.

The term is also used to describe the standard way of presenting a manuscript to an editor: typed, on one side of the page, double-spaced, with inch-wide margins all the way around; each page must be numbered in sequence, often with an abbreviation of the title. This FORMAT is mandatory for any professional publication, and most FAN editors prefer it as well, since it is easier to edit and typeset. It is strongly suggested that a prospective contributor should find out what format is preferred before submitting the manuscript to an EDITOR, by sending a SASE for GUIDELINES.

formatting (computer): Preparing a disk to receive information. Different models of computers do this in various ways; some of them do it automatically as a new disk is inserted. Unless FORMATTING is done, the new disk will not accept any data.

formula fiction (literary): Stories written in any GENRE that adhere so closely to the literary CONVENTIONS that they could have been composed by following a chemist's formula. See also HACK; STEREOTYPE; STOCK CHARACTERS.

Fort, Charles (1874–1932). Journalist, researcher, and compiler of weird happenings, who catalogued and recorded such events as poltergeists, black rains, strange lights in the sky, and sudden descents of frogs from the heavens. His findings drew derision during his lifetime, and he has since become the symbol of the pseudoscientific nut who may, very occasionally, be right.

fortnightly (comics): A comic issued every two weeks (26 issues per year); this is not exactly the same as twice a month, which would mean only 24 issues per year.

FORTRAN (computer): Formula Translator, the most widely used scientific programming language. One of the three most commonly used computer languages, the other two being BASIC and COBOL.

Foundation (literary): A series of novels by ISAAC ASIMOV, outlining the rise, fall, and rise of a GALACTIC EMPIRE, run by an all-powerful FOUNDATION. ASIMOV'S vision of the future includes many technological marvels, positronic ROBOTS, and political intrigues that last over the millennia. The series began as a set of stories in *Astounding Magazine* in 1950; the FOUNDATION Trilogy consists of *Foundation* (1951), *Foundation and Empire* (1952), and *Second Foundation* (1953). *Foundation's Edge* (1982), *Robots and Empire* (1985), and *Foundation and Earth* (1986) carry the story even further. Recent developments in the story line attempt to link the FOUNDATION novels with ASIMOV'S other stories, *The Caves of Steel* and *The Naked Sun*.

four-color (comics): Comic books printed in full color, using all four basic inks (red, yellow, blue, and black), in various strengths and combinations. FOUR-COLOR comics are the most spectacular, the most desirable, and the ones most likely to be copied as RE-CREATION COSTUMES.

fourth dimension (literary): An area of perception beyond the normal ones of height, length, and depth that circumscribe our present state of being. One theory has it that the fourth dimension is Time; crack that one and we will achieve TIME TRAVEL. Another theory holds that there are many dimensions, each one holding a PARALLEL UNIVERSE, which differs from ours in that human history has taken a different turn at some historic crossroads.

While the idea of a fourth dimension has intrigued SF writers since the beginning of this century, the mechanism for finding it has eluded physical scientists. However, the NEW AGE practitioners are convinced that the FOURTH DIMENSION can be reached through expansion of our own mental powers. So far, neither mental nor physical science has found this extra dimension; it remains a literary device.

Frankenstein (literary): Novel written by Mary Shelley in 1818, in which a young doctor tries to create a living being from the remains of cadavers. He succeeds momentarily, but the creature eventually turns on him and destroys him. Many interpretations have been found for this blood-curdling tale, written by Mary Shelley after what must have been a strange summer vacation spent in a ruined castle in Switzerland with her husband, the poet Percy Bysshe Shelley, their poet friend George Lord Byron, and Byron's mistress (who was also Mary's half-sister).

The real impact of the story was felt in the classic film made in 1930, with Boris Karloff as the Monster. Although other versions of FRANKENSTEIN have been made, including one with a relatively good-looking Michael Sarrazin as the Monster, it is this makeup that we see when we envision the soulless being who is pathetic and hideous at the same time. Even the parodies of Fred Gwynne in "The Munsters" and Peter Boyle in *Young Frankenstein* cannot dilute the impact of Karloff's performance.

The term FRANKENSTEIN has entered the English language as a metaphor; it usually refers to some device or scheme that destroys its creator.

Frank Hays Disease/Pete Seeger's Antidote (fan/filk): Named for West Coast FILKER Frank Hays; a sudden amnesia attack during which a FILKER forgets the lyrics so carefully committed to memory, particularly if they are the FILKER's own creation. It is an embarrassing ailment, and it tends to come on in the middle of a particularly dramatic or witty rendition. The cure is PETE SEEGER'S ANTIDOTE, named for the well-known folk singer and activist: to stare at the ceiling. The missing lyrics will magically appear thereupon. (Seeger does this all the time, which is why many of his fans swear that all they have ever seen of him is his beard and his Adam's apple.)

Frazetta, Frank (b. 1928): SF and Fantasy Artist, known for his depictions of muscular men and well-endowed women, clad in scraps of fur, cloth or armor, clinging to rocky crags or dragons. FRAZETTA's illustrations have appeared on book covers (such as an Ace edition of *Tarzan* books), calendars, and posters. The image that comes to mind when HEROIC FANTASY is mentioned is the FRAZETTA image.

freaking the Mundanes (fan): Behaving in a deliberately outrageous way at a CONVENTION in order to upset the non-SF guests at the hotel. Some young people do this inadvertently, out of high spirits, like puppies off the leash. More mature SF FANS might do it when provoked by those same MUNDANES.

The MUNDANES, on the other hand, have a tendency to react with either shock or humor, depending on their own ideas of proper behavior. Some of them may be outraged at the sight of a young man wandering about in a fake-fur loincloth, while others may simply wonder if he's going to catch a cold.

freebies (fan): The goodies for distribution on the FREEBIE TABLE: BUTTONS, POSTERS, books, and so forth.

FREEBIES also refer to the contributors' copies of FANZINES sent out by the EDITORS in lieu of monetary payment. Most FANZINE EDITORS send out the FREEBIES as soon as the issue has been received from the printer and collated.

Various FAN-EDS have different policies on FREEBIES, depending on the length of the contribution and the size of the FANZINE. Some very large and elaborate 'ZINES might call for a limit on the size of the contribution that receives a FREEBIE; however, the general rule is that any contributor to a FANZINE receives a copy of it. Prolific FAN writers can accumulate a sizable collection of FREEBIES.

freebie table (fan): The table or rack set up at a CONVENTION for the distribution of materials that promote other CONS, FANZINES, or professional films, books, TV series, or magazines. FANS descend on these like locusts to stock up on BUTTONS, POSTERS, comics, and free magazines, in hopes that they may, in time, become COLLECTABLES. Some of the STAR WARS promotional materials are now worth a tidy sum.

fringe fan (fan): One who is only interested in a small and select part of FANDOM; someone with a devotion to only one element of SF. STAR TREK and MEDIA fans, GAMING or COSTUMING or FILKING fans, even COMPUTER GEEKS have been stigmatized as FRINGE FANS. In today's diversified SF field, the fringe has become the whole garment, and most fans have more than one interest.

frontlist (publishing): New books being promoted by a publisher, through catalogs and advertisements. The FRONTLIST consists of the books published in a given SEASON; if they sell well, and remain available for sale, they then become the BACKLIST, and will be kept in print. See also BACKLIST; OUT-OF-PRINT.

front matter (publishing): Also known as front-of-the-book; any written data that precede the actual text of a given work, whether it is fiction or nonfiction. FRONT MATTER includes the book's title page, the copyright page, a listing of other books by the same author, the Table of Contents, a dedication page, and a Foreword, Preface, or Introduction to the work. An SF novel may also include maps of an imaginary locality, a glossary of terms in a language invented by the author, or excerpts from a hypothetical encyclopedia that will explain some 5,000 years of FUTURE HISTORY. In some cases, the FRONT MATTER may be more interesting than the text it is supposed to explain.

The Glossary, maps, and so forth may also be inserted *after* the text of the book, in which case they become BACK MATTER. See also TIME-LINE.

FTL Drive (literary): Faster Than Light speed propulsion, which physicists tell us is impossible, but without which SF would not be able to exist or continue to be written. Getting around this thorny piece of inflexible physics is one of the "givens" of SF. If humanity is to get to the stars, then some sort of FTL propulsion will have to be devised; otherwise, GALACTIC EMPIRES, SPACE COLONIES, and all the other political apparatus of

SF will have to be abandoned and SPACE WARFARE will be totally impossible.

The solutions to the FTL DRIVE have been ingenious, but most researchers seem to feel that a practical FTL engine is very far in the future. This does not stop SF writers from using FTL drive as a means of getting from one place to another quickly enough to keep the story moving.

full animation (film): The rendering of animation so that every element on the screen seems to move. FULL ANIMATION requires incredibly detailed artwork on each frame, so that even the blades of grass seem to sway in the breeze. Only the major studios such as Disney are willing to spend the extensive amount of time and money that FULL ANIMATION demands. Most animated cartoons seen these days are done with LIMITED ANIMATION.

Furry Fandom (fan): A group of FANS who enjoy watching cartoons featuring cute, anthropomorphic animals. This FANDOM seems to have come out of the closet only in the last year; until now, a liking for such comics and cartoons was regarded as a temporary aberration, brought on by too much baby-sitting. The popularity of *Who Framed Roger Rabbit?* (1989) has made FURRY FANDOM fashionable.

future history (literary): An extrapolation of current events that expands into a possible prediction of future events, leading to a particular story or series of stories. Many writers try to predict trends, or look even farther ahead to a distant future.

Like DAY AFTER TOMORROW STORIES, FUTURE HISTORY stories are at the mercy of events that do not always turn out the way the experts predicted. Many FUTURE HISTORIES were dependent on political situations that have since been resolved, or have been made invalid by events out of everyone's control (flood, famine, etc.).

Occasionally, technology moves faster than the writers. The rapid advance of the COMPUTER into domestic life was only foreshadowed by the depiction of ROBOTS as household servants in SF stories. Many SF writers described the first landing on the

Moon, but none of them could foresee that it would be shared all over the world through the technology of TELECOMMUNICATIONS.

future shock (sociology): The term coined by Alvin Toffler in his book of the same name published in 1970 in which he described the stress and disorientation engendered by too much change, too fast, in the structures of society. In our own century, Western society has gone through so many changes in social structure, economics, technology, and cultural orientation that many people are left totally at sea without emotional ties to anything. The term has now passed into the standard English language.

futurology (sociology): The attempt to forecast the future, based on information gleaned from statistics, current trends, and so on. Alas, futurologists are often stymied by the unexpected, and human history has a way of taking turns that are not predicted by their statistics.

SF writers have tried to extrapolate the future from present trends, but many of them will admit that they have been wrong as often as they have been right. If SF is about predicting the world of the future, then most certainly some SF is going to wind up being considered quaint fantasy.

GAFIA (fan): Get Away From It All. At first, the term referred to FANDOM, which was seen as a means of escape from reality. Over the years, the meaning has reversed itself, until now the "All" that the user tries to "Get Away From" is FANDOM itself.

Gafiate (fan): Verbal form of GAFIA; to remove oneself from FANDOM, sometimes with a psychic wrench, sometimes with a sigh of relief. It can be pronounced either to rhyme with "giraffe-ee-ate" or as "gay-fee-ate."

There are a number of fairly good reasons to GAFIATE: school or job commitments, a new spouse who simply does not understand FANDOM, or a particularly nasty FAN FEUD. A person who wishes to continue FAN-AC but finds it impossible is said to FAFIATE, that is, to be Forced Away From It All.

From time to time someone GAFIATES, and then returns, to the sound of much cheering.

Gaia theory (biology): The concept introduced by Dr. James Lovelock in 1969, expounded in his book *Gaia: A New Look at Life On Earth* (1979), that regards the Earth as a unified ecosystem, with every living creature linked to every other living creature in a web of food chains, interactive relationships, and possibly even psychic bonds. The idea has been used by SF writers, notably Harry Harrison in his *Deathworld Trilogy*; biologists are just now realizing the enormity of the interactions of life on Earth, and the vast destruction that can come from removing one minor element from this web of life. The term comes from the Greek goddess of the Earth, Gaia, and is an allusion to all Earth as a unified organism. See also LIVING WORLD.

Galactic Empire (literary): A wide-ranging political entity that encompasses several star systems, all with habitable PLANETS, each of which has its own peculiar beings and particular society. The concept has been a part of SF since the 1920s; *Within the Nebula*, by Edward Hamilton, first printed in 1929, introduced the final version of the GALACTIC EMPIRE, as it has come to be accepted in SF lore.

GALACTIC EMPIRES are often depicted as being run by a despotic and despicable aristocracy, all of whom are actively engaged in Byzantine political maneuverings, gleefully assassinating the opposition or, conversely, arranging suitable marriage alliances with potential enemies. ROBERT HEINLEIN'S *Citizen of the Galaxy* (1957) takes a young man through several societies within such an Empire, until he reaches the apex of the Power Pyramid.

This sort of GALACTIC EMPIRE is often depicted as one so rotten that it is just waiting for some leader to foment a rebellion that will topple the whole unsavory crew into the dust of a Just War, which will presumably replace the vicious and corrupt government with something more nearly representing the U.S. Congress or the British Parliament (depending on the nationality of the writer). The British-made TV SERIES BLAKE'S SEVEN is based on such a BASIC PREMISE.

There has been some criticism of the concept of GALACTIC EMPIRES, both on scientific and on sociological/political grounds. The stories of galaxy-wide revolution should be read in the context in which they were written, that is, the Cold War of the 1940s and 1950s. As for the technological problems of communications and FTL DRIVE, those are among the accepted norms of SF.

Galactic lens (astronomy): The presumed shape of the Milky Way Galaxy, that is, a collection of stars swirling around a central point that would appear to an outward observer to resemble a convex lens. We, on Earth, are situated on a planet that circles a star somewhat off-center on this lens. We see the center of the lens as a band of luminosity across the night sky; to the ancient astronomers, it looked like a road or path or maybe even a stream. Looking beyond the central portion of this lens, seen only through powerful telescopes, astronomers have postulated areas of few stars, where habitable planets would be few and far between. These planets would be called RIMWORLDS, since they occur on the rim of the Galactic lens.

galaxy (astronomy): A system of billions, if not trillions, of stars, bound by gravity to circle a central point. Our Sun is a minor star in a GALAXY we have termed the Milky Way; Andromeda and the Magellanic Cloud are the only other GALAXIES visible from Earth without a telescope, but many others have been discovered by astronomers using advanced radio-telescopes. The new Hubbell Space Telescope should enable astronomers to locate GALAXIES even further away than those.

gaming: Participation in organized forms of "Cops 'n' Robbers" by FANS of SF and Fantasy. GAMING usually involves taking part in an SF or Fantasy adventure, using a PERSONA developed with the aid of dice or a guidebook, and possibly developing the PERSONA further in later adventures.

FANS have incorporated SF into various board games; many FANS play an excellent game of Bridge or Chess, and games of chance tend to creep into SF and Fantasy stories. However, the real breakthrough came with DUNGEONS AND DRAGONS,™ patented by Gary Gygax in 1977. Here was a game that was almost entirely mental; the participants were involved in grand exploits in a fantasy UNIVERSE, filled with danger at every turn, in which the action was almost entirely in the minds of the players.

D&D™ led to many imitators; there were adventures written by players that were then used as the basis for still more adventures. Some of the CHARACTERS developed by players later surfaced in a spate of Fantasy novels. Eventually, Gygax licensed D&D™ novels, models, and so on.

GAMING is now a major CONVENTION activity. A Gaming Room can be set up, where various DUNGEONMASTERS can direct their CHARACTERS and organize their CAMPAIGNS. By the end of the CON, each DM should have finished the CAMPAIGN; if not, then the group has to get together somehow . . . and another dungeon is born!

gamma rays (astronomy): Celestial objects or their emanation with wavelengths less than X-rays. Bursts of GAMMA RAYS seem to come from random directions, leading to the conclusion that they are generalized phenomena and not directed at Earth or anywhere else in particular. GAMMA RAYS were considered a particular threat to space travelers, but so far, no one seems to have been affected by them.

garb (fan/SCA): Costumes worn by the SOCIETY FOR CREATIVE ANACHRONISM at EVENTS, CONVENTIONS, and REN-FAIRES. They are supposed to be historically accurate, even to the material; some groups frown on use of any cloth not made of totally natural fibers.

GARB can be as sketchy as a basic tunic and a handmade helmet, or it can be an elaborate reproduction of a famous portrait. It is supposed to reinforce the SCA member's PERSONA, and it must be verifiably authentic for the character's time and place. Most of all, it must be comfortable, since the wearer is going to be in it for the better part of the day.

Really fine SCA GARB has been entered in MASQUERADES, to the point where some judges will automatically disqualify a costume that appears to be GARB, on the grounds that it was not originally made as a costume, but as everyday dress. See also SCA.

garbage (aerospace): Mechanical odds and ends orbiting the Earth, left over from space travel: orbiting satellite debris, or just plain junk. After 30 years or more in space, humanity can look upward and know that we have strewn the outer atmosphere with our artifacts, or the remnants of them.

gas giant (astronomy): A PLANET largely composed of gasses in liquid or solid form, rotating around a solid, extremely dense core. In our own PLANETARY SYSTEM, JUPITER, SATURN, Neptune, and Uranus are considered to be GAS GIANTS. Possibilities of life as we know it originating on such a PLANET are nil; they are usually enormous, with tremendous gravity, and intensely cold. Terrestrial PLANETS, on the other hand, are closer to the parent sun, and are capable of supporting a breathable atmosphere and flowing water, the two requisites for life as we know it.

geek (fan): A socially inept, unattractive, but generally harmless person, usually (but not always) an adolescent male. The original STEREOTYPE of an SF FAN was a GEEK, who used SF to embroider fantasies of a life away and apart from reality. Many former GEEKS have become major SF writers and artists.

The term comes from carnival slang, where a GEEK performed repulsive acts, like biting off the heads of live chickens. The fannish meaning softens the blow somewhat. See also COMPUTER GEEK.

Gemini program (aerospace): The second U.S. manned space project, initiated in 1963. The program called for ten flights of a two-person spacecraft that would permit the astronauts to practice techniques that would eventually be used in the Apollo program, culminating in a manned landing on the MOON. Among the achievements of the GEMINI PROGRAM were the SPACE WALKS, with and without UMBILICALS, and the testing of equipment that would be used to great effect in the Apollo missions.

gender roles (psychology): Those activities of daily living that a particular society associates with male or female GENDER. A more accurate term than sex roles, the matter of GENDER ROLES has been extensively explored in SF. Often the roles are reversed for satiric effect, so that women are depicted as aggressive war-mongers, while men are shown as delicate and retiring creatures who must be protected from the grosser realities of Life.

FEMINIST SF often deals with GENDER ROLES, usually to the disparagement of the male role and the glorification of the female. See also ROLE REVERSAL.

generation ship (literary): A way of getting around the unpalatable fact that it is going to be very difficult to colonize other PLANETARY SYSTEMS if the spaceship is going at the speed of light or less. First conceived by astronomer Konstantin Tsiolkovsky and presented to the public in an essay published in 1929, a GENERATION SHIP would carry a broad population of settlers, who would either be frozen in CRYOGENIC containers, or would live and die aboard their vessel, waiting for the day of landing.

The problems of a society on board such a ship have been explored in SF since Laurence Manning's story *The Living Galaxy* in 1934. Films and novels have dealt with the possibilities inherent in a society confined to one small area for an unknown length of time. In several such stories, the inhabitants do not even realize that they are traveling on an artificially constructed vessel, since they were born on it, and know no other way of life. Often the inhabitants of a GENERATION SHIP may be guided by a COMPUTER that has been deified over the centuries.

An alternative to the GENERATION SHIP is the SLEEPER SHIP, which holds the prospective space colonists in suspended animation until landfall. See also SPACE COLONY.

genetic engineering (biology): The manipulation of genetic material to produce a desired organism. At present, GENETIC

ENGINEERING has produced some interesting results in very simple organisms, but so far, extensive experimentation has not led to the horrific results of H. G. WELLS' *Island of Dr. Moreau* (1896).

Several SF writers have postulated nonhuman societies in which GENETIC ENGINEERING has replaced chemistry and metallurgy, so that instead of manipulating inorganic matter to make tools, sentient creatures create nonsentients to do work that is done on Earth by machines. So far, human research in GENETIC ENGINEERING has not come anywhere near this advanced state.

genre (publishing): A specific type of writing, with its own set of rules, called CONVENTIONS. There are GENRES in both fiction and nonfiction writing, but the most common GENRES of popular fiction are Westerns, Romance, Mystery, and SF/Fantasy. Readers of GENRE fiction tend to specialize, so bookstores and libraries similarly segregate those particular books for their convenience. See also CROSS-GENRE FICTION; CROSSOVER WRITER.

genzine (fan): In the early days of SF, a GENZINE was simply a generalized FANZINE, and the term is still used by SF FANS to refer to a FANZINE that has no particular theme. When MEDIA FANZINES came along, about 1970, the term began to be used for a MEDIA FANZINE that had a variety of FANDOMS represented. See also FANZINE; MEDIAZINE.

Gernsback, Hugo (1884–1967): Writer and editor, pioneer in publishing and editing SF in the United States. After editing a series of magazines dealing with the then brand-new fields of electronics and radio, GERNSBACK started *Amazing Stories* in 1926, now acknowledged to be the first major SF publication in the United States.

GERNSBACK is said to have invented what we now call Science Fiction, although he usually called it *SCIENTIFICTION*. Since he had a thorough background in science, he insisted that the stories he printed have some possibility of scientific reality. He nurtured talents like Frederik Pohl and inspired the so-called GOLDEN AGE OF SF.

GERNSBACK lived long enough to see his pioneering rewarded; the annual awards for excellence in Science Fiction are called

HUGOS in his honor, and he was given an Honorary HUGO in 1966.

"get'em" story (fan): A story in a FANZINE in which the protagonist "gets it," that is, gets hurt, maimed, humiliated, or generally mistreated. The first recipient of this treatment was STAR TREK's Mr. Spock; later stories might involve Han Solo of STAR WARS, or some of the Rebels in BLAKE'S SEVEN. A variant might have one of a MALE BONDING pair hurt, while the other one gives assistance and comfort.

"GET'EM" STORIES tend to become gruesome, maudlin, or both. There have been PANELS and WORKSHOPS at CONVENTIONS that explain medical and psychological realities for writers of GET'EM stories. See also HURT/COMFORT STORY.

ghost stories (literary): Stories dealing with supernatural phenomena. GHOST STORIES have a long and honorable history, dating back in human existence to the campfires of primitive tribes whose world was ringed about with the spirits of the dead.

GHOST STORIES tend to fall into several categories. There are tales in which an angry spirit wreaks hideous vengeance for a past crime. A variant on this theme is the story in which the ghost has left some task unfinished, and tries to make contact with a descendant who will complete the mission. Another type of ghost story has a descendant of the original spirit reliving some incident that can release the unhappy specter from its earthly existence and let it go back to the ASTRAL PLANE to which it properly belongs.

GHOST STORIES remain a staple element of GOTHIC ROMANCE. Usually the eerie events are explained away, all except for one incident that keeps the question mark still in the readers' mind.

Ghu (fan): A generic deity, invoked by FANDOM in moments of crisis or exasperation. Like "Zot," GHU is mostly benign, and its name can be taken in whatever spirit it is uttered with no ill effects.

giant star (astronomy): See RED GIANT.

GIGO (computer): Garbage In, Garbage Out, a dictum of computer use. In other words, the computer only gives back what was put into it, and if the figures entered were wrong, the computer cannot correct them (at least, not in today's world).

glass shot (film): An OPTICAL effect, achieved by painting the background on glass, then shooting through the painting, as opposed to a MATTE shot, in which an area of the screen will be blank, to be completed later in the laboratory. GLASS SHOTS are used when building a SET would be too time-consuming, or when the desired effect would be impossible to achieve without some kind of film magic. They are effective, but delicate, and difficult to match. Most SFX use the MATTE technique. See also BLUE SCREEN.

glitch (computer): Any minute but annoying MALFUNCTION that interrupts a computer program. If a GLITCH is not attended to immediately it could develop into a BUG that might escalate into a major MALFUNCTION, thus requiring complete reevaluation of the PROGRAM.

glop (fan): Any disgusting mess; more particularly, a loathesome-looking (but supposedly nutritious) combination of yogurt, wheat germ, kelp, and flavorings. The term was first used by teenagers in the 1950s and seems to have penetrated into a number of other jargons, including SF.

Goddard, Robert Hutchings (1882–1945): American inventor and pioneer in rocket research. GODDARD built and launched the world's first liquid-fuel ROCKET in 1914. His experiments led to the basic research necessary for the launching of the U.S. space programs in the 1960s, but GODDARD died before he could reap either the financial reward or the recognition that he so richly deserved. His widow sold his patents to the U.S. government, so that they could complete GODDARD's experiments, and eventually, travel to the MOON.

Godzilla (film): The leading character of a series of Japanese-made MONSTER MOVIES of the 1950s. When he first appeared in

1954, the 400-foot-tall reptile was called "Gojira," but his name became Americanized, and he achieved fame.

The first film had a simple plot that was repeated in the inevitable sequels: A nuclear blast awakens the monster from its hibernation under the Pacific Ocean, whereupon it wreaks havoc across Japan until bombed and driven back to bed. Later films had GODZILLA battling Mothra (a giant moth) in *Godzilla vs. The Thing* (1964), or an evil giant shrimp in *Godzilla vs. the Sea Monster* (1966). GODZILLA himself was played by a stunt man in a rubber suit; occasionally, the zipper showed.

GODZILLA has become the archetypal Movie Monster. There is a GODZILLA Fan Club, and GODZILLA movies are a staple at late-night film SHOWINGS at CONS.

gofers/gophers (fan): The volunteers who work for the CONVENTIONS, also called "helpers" or "Cadettes." From the show-business jargon for the nonentity who is there to "go-for" coffee, sandwiches, and so on.

GOFERS are the workers of the CONVENTION Hive, running errands, setting up the panels for the ART SHOW, locating the various speakers, and getting things organized. For their efforts, GOFERS get a free membership to the CON and possible sleeping room in a GOFER HOLE. They also get the thrill of meeting the PROS close-up, and being a part of the CON-COM. See also CONVENTIONS.

Gofer Hole (fan/convention): The place from which the GOFERS are dispatched to their various stations. It may be the CON SUITE, or a separate meeting room, or even the bedroom of the CON CHAIR. Wherever it is, there is usually a schedule of events there, to which the GOFERS can refer for their assignments. If necessary, the GOFER HOLE may be used to house GOFERS who have no other place to stay during the CON.

GOH (fan/conventions): Guest of Honor; sometimes pronounced as a word, sometimes as initials. The GOH at a FAN-CON is usually a well-known writer or artist (a large CON will have one of each). A PRO-CON will try to get the star of a television SERIES or film that is currently in vogue. Occasionally, a PRO-CON will invite a "Nostalgia Guest," who was featured on a SERIES some time ago.

In either case, a GOH is usually someone well known enough that people will be attracted to attend the CON, especially if it is someone with a distinctive point of view. Occasionally someone decides to attend the CON who is even more important than the official GOH; that person may become a Special GOH.

The duties of the GOH depend in part on the type of CON he or she is attending, as well as on the personal inclinations of the GOH. The GOH usually gives at least one prepared speech and sits on several PANELS, signs autographs, meets with the CON members at some kind of social gathering, and is generally affable to the people who may have traveled some distance to absorb the pearls that drop from his or her lips. The CON pays the GOH whatever honorarium has been negotiated, plus travel expenses, and provides food and a place for privacy. At a FAN-CON, the GOH is really a guest, and most of them respond by being gracious to their hosts.

At a PRO-CON, the GOH is on a little different footing, since the membership is quite large, and the negotiations may be somewhat different. A PRO-CON GOH is often an actor who may not be used to speaking extemporaneously. He or she will give a brief speech about whatever is happening with their SERIES or film, and will answer questions from the audience for an hour. Most of them are delighted to sign autographs, but some prefer not to do so, and the CONVENTION staff usually respects this wish.

Being asked to be a GOH at a CON is an honor, and most SF writers regard it as an accolade; it means that one has "arrived" to the point where someone is willing to pay not only for one's books but for the privilege of meeting the writer.

Golden Age of SF (literary): Roughly, from 1938 to 1946, or the years when most SF was found in PULP magazines, and JOHN W. CAMPBELL was editor of *Astounding Stories* magazine.

During this period the ground rules were laid for what is now known as Science Fiction. Stories should deal with some aspect of the future, based on an extrapolation of the present situation. There should be an underlying scientific reality to the PREMISE. Technology should be presented as realistically as possible. Nonhuman characters should be realistically presented, either as adversaries or as protagonists. Action/adventure might be an element in the story, but ideas are supposed to take precedence.

There is some evidence that this so-called GOLDEN AGE is the product of nostalgia. From the point of view of sheer amount of SF produced, and width and breadth of distribution, the GOLDEN AGE OF SF is now! See also GERNSBACK, HUGO.

go-motion animation (film): A technique for filming models of creatures and spacecraft that gives a great illusion of movement; both the camera and the model are shifted during stop-action photography. The technique was used to great effect in *The Return of the Jedi* (1983).

googol (mathematics): 10 to the 100th power, or 1 followed by 100 zeros. Supposedly named by the very young nephew of prominent mathematician Edward Kasner.

Good alignment (gaming): The second of the three possibilities for a CHARACTER's moral orientation in a role-playing game, the other two being EVIL and NEUTRAL. GOOD CHARACTERS are kind, generous, altruistic, sweet-tempered, and love their mothers. Paladins are GOOD, as are most PRIESTS. A LAWFUL GOOD CHARACTER may be too, too perfect, like Sir Galahad in the Arthurian legends. Most players will prefer CHAOTIC GOOD, which comes closest to most human existence.

go pro (fan): To become a professional writer by the simple act of receiving payment for one's work. How much payment is a moot point, since a number of SMALL PRESS magazines or SEMIPROZINES pay minimal amounts; presumably, once you receive something, you are a PRO. See also GRADUATE.

Gor (literary): Sadomasochistic Universe created by John Norman in a series of novels, beginning with *Tarnsman of Gor* in 1966. During the series, Earthman Tarl Cabot arrives on GOR by means unknown, where he undergoes endless adventures. Much of the series involves superbly endowed women debasing themselves before muscular men, or aggressive women being "tamed" by even more aggressive men. At this point the whole series has become something of a joke. There have been costumes at MASQUERADES like "The Housewives of Gor" or "The Bag Lady of Gor," and cartoons entitled "Slave Boy George of Gor." In spite of this, the books are popular enough to remain in print.

Gothic novel (literary): A tale of brooding atmosphere and supernatural doings, with a lovely heroine in peril, a stalwart hero to save her, and a vicious villain. The term was first applied to Horace Walpole's *Castle Otranto* in 1764; since then, the GOTHIC NOVEL has become a staple of fiction.

Gothic elements have crept into SF as well; there are a number of gloomy castles replete with ghosts, trap doors, and sorcerous booby traps in Fantasy stories throughout the 19th and early 20th centuries. In true SF style, most of the ghostly doings are explained by some means, leaving one element to puzzle the reader . . . was it a ghost or not?

"Go to POO" (aerospace): A command to clear all computers of previous data. POO is "Program Zero Zero," which removes all data and clears the decks for action. The term was used during the MERCURY and GEMINI missions; it is now considered obsolete.

graduate (fan): To become a professional writer or artist, by being paid for one's efforts, after having been a FAN for some time. Most FAN writers and artists are aiming at a possible career as a PRO; getting a substantial check for a book advance, story, or royalty means as much as receiving a diploma. See also PRO.

graffiti wall (fan): A page of pithy sayings, witty exchanges, jokes, and cartoons, such as might be found on any city wall. A cheap and easy way to fill a spare page of a FANZINE, the GRAFFITI WALL is a remnant of the 1960s' TV SERIES "Laugh-in" (1968–1973), which featured such a wall as part of its finale. GRAFFITI WALLS are also put up at CONS, where a large piece of drawing paper may be taped to a stretch of corridor wall and left for FANNISH comments and cartoons.

Grand Guignol (literary): (pronounced Grahn Gwi-nyol, from the French): Horror films with a heavy emphasis on gore; from the Theatre du Grand Guignol in Paris, France, which opened its doors in 1897, and presented violent and gruesome melodramas right through the 1950s. The term is used to describe films of the SLICE 'N' DICE variety, like the *Nightmare on Elm Street* series. See also SLASHER MOVIES.

Grand Tour (aerospace): Unmanned space voyage, launched in 1977, during which the Voyager spacecraft flew by JUPITER, SATURN, Neptune, and Uranus, taking advantage of a once-in-a-century lineup of planets in their orbits. The information sent back by Voyager during its GRAND TOUR has revised our impressions and understanding of the SOLAR SYSTEM.

graphic album (comics): A large comic book that presents several comic-format stories in one collection, between hard covers. The stories may be interrelated; the book may be an anthology of stories drawn by the same artist, or just a sampling of the materials from one publisher.

graphic novel (publishing): Novel-length story presented in comic format, usually between hard covers. GRAPHIC NOVELS are usually original stories, whereas GRAPHIC ALBUMS are often reprints. *Elfquest*, by Richard and Wendy Pini, is one of the most popular GRAPHIC NOVELS. GRAPHIC NOVELS are usually of very high artistic and literary quality.

graphics (publishing/printing): The typeface, abstract designs, and other decorations on a book cover or inside a magazine (fan or pro), including the ILLOS. GRAPHICS add to the appeal of the 'ZINE; without them, the item looks drab and is therefore virtually unsalable.

grazing (fan/convention): Attending ROOM PARTIES for the purpose of nibbling on the MUNCHIES. A few CON members survive without buying a single meal; they wander from party to party and GRAZE. This is not recommended, as it is almost certain to lead to the BLORCH.

Great Red Spot of Jupiter (astronomy): A gigantic 300-year-old storm raging on the planet JUPITER. Galileo was the first to spot it, through his primitive telescope; the super-sensitive telescopes on the Voyager spacecraft took the most complete pictures we have of the GREAT RED SPOT.

greenhouse effect (physics): The warming of a planet's atmosphere, due to certain gasses, especially carbon dioxide, which tend to hold the heat of the sun within an atmospheric envelope as it reflects back from the planet's surface, just as the glass in a greenhouse protects the plants within from the cold air while holding in the heat of the sun.

It is surmised that this is what happened to the planet VENUS; any free-flowing water boiled off, and the radiation from the sun was held in, making the planet's surface unimaginably hot.

The increased use of fossil fuels in the last 150 years has increased the amount of carbon dioxide in the Earth's atmosphere, leading some scientists to believe that our own planet may suffer the same fate as VENUS.

grognard (gaming): A veteran GAMER; one who almost qualifies as a DUNGEON LAWYER. From the French for "grumbler," used in the French Armed Forces the way "old sweat" is used in the British Army. GROGNARDS may not be as argumentative as DUNGEON LAWYERS, but they can be just as annoying to other players.

Grok (literary): A total understanding of one person by another, without the necessity for verbalization. Coined by ROBERT HEINLEIN in *Stranger in a Strange Land*, first published in 1961; taken into the language by the Counterculture, for whom the book became a kind of icon.

Young people tend to be tongue-tied in the presence of others; to GROK would do away with the necessity to use words. A popular button for the early Trekkers said "I Grok Spock."

G-suit (aerospace): Gravity suit; pressurized equipment, used by pilots, astronauts, deep-sea divers, and anyone else who might need it to withstand pressure or the lack of it. G-SUITS have come a long way from the first attempts at a SPACE SUIT, which made little provision for natural bodily functions.

guesstimate (fan): A combination of Guess and Estimate; an informed estimation of anything.

guidelines (publishing): A set of requirements sent by a magazine EDITOR to a prospective writer, listing the type of story that particular magazine prints, along with word and FORMAT requirements, and a schedule of payments. Most would-be writers are expected to send for GUIDELINES before submitting anything to a PROZINE or book publisher.

guild (fan/SCA): A group of craftspeople within the SOCIETY FOR CREATIVE ANACHRONISM. A prospective member is supposed to join a GUILD at the same time as joining the organization. There are GUILDS for COSTUMING, fighting, or various other skills used before the advent of the Industrial Revolution.

The term has been expanded into general SF FANDOM, so that there is now a International Costumers GUILD, and a Filkers GUILD is being set up.

The term was first used in the Middle Ages, when craftspeople joined together to protect their interests. GUILDS regulated trade, set standards in craftsmanship, and generally took care of their own people. SF GUILDS provide their members with opportunities to meet others of like interest, who can compare notes and set standards of workmanship, in the same spirit as the Medieval GUILDS.

GURPS (gaming): Generic Universal Role-Playing System; a game that uses characters and rules from a variety of ROLE-PLAYING GAMES, besides DUNGEONS AND DRAGONS.™

hack (literary): A writer who produces books, FORMULA FICTION, or even nonfiction, to order. HACK writers were the mainstay of PULP FICTION in the early years of SF.

The term originally meant a sturdy workhorse or "hackney"; this kind of horse was often used to pull hired carriages and cabs, so the vehicle also became known as a "hackney" or "hack." Like the carriage, the HACK writer is for hire, and will provide a steady supply of what is required for a fee.

hacker (computer): A totally fanatic COMPUTER buff, who enjoys using every form and format of the programming system. HACKERS have surfaced in elementary schools as well as in graduate programs. They have rearranged DATABASES and broken into supposedly secure government computer complexes. Most HACKERS are harmless; a very few are irresponsible, bordering on criminal. A HACKER with no redeeming social graces may become a COMPUTER GEEK.

hack 'n' slay (gaming): A not-very-subtle style of play in DUNGEONS AND DRAGONS™; see it, kill it! The DUNGEONMASTER may try to control this sort of thing by explaining that there are better ways of dealing with problems than by simply chopping

at them; however, a character with more STRENGTH than WISDOM may be hard to convince.

half-life (physics): The amount of time it takes for a RADIOACTIVE mineral to lose half of its electrons. It is a useful way to measure the age of a particular object, since the HALF-LIFE of an element remains constant across the universe. A RADIOACTIVE isotope of carbon, C-14, is present in all organic matter, which makes it a useful tool for archeologists, who can measure its content in any artifact made of wood, cloth, or other organic materials.

hall costume (fan/costuming): The sort of garments that might be worn on another planet or in another era, used as dress-up clothes at a CONVENTION. HALL COSTUMES are relatively easy to wear, since they are actually clothes, as opposed to a PRESENTATION COSTUME, which is made to be seen from the stage. SCA GARB is often seen at CONS as HALL COSTUMES.

FORREST J. ACKERMAN claims to have been the first to wear a HALL COSTUME at the first WORLD-CON in 1939. They have added to the ambience of the weekend ever since. A few SF SERCON fans have decried this practice as juvenile, and have tried to ban HALL COSTUMES from their CONS. As a result, the CONS in question lost considerable membership, and the ban was lifted. See also PERSONA; PRESENTATION COSTUME.

Hammer Films: British film company, founded in 1948, named for producer Will Hammer; known for lush-looking but cheaply made horror films, usually starring Peter Cushing and/or Christopher Lee. The heyday of HAMMER FILMS was 1950–1965. A typical HAMMER FILM would be set in some medieval Mittel European castle, where an evil Baron or Countess is ravaging the countryside, waiting for a spotless knight or enterprising young peasant to come along and spoil his or her fun. The doings usually include vast amounts of bright red blood, heaving cleavages on everyone (male and female), and a more-or-less happy ending. The American equivalents of HAMMER FILMS are the ones made by ROGER CORMAN.

hands-on animation (film): The combining of animated figures with live action, so that the humans appear to interact with the cartoons. Some of the earliest animated cartoons used a very simple hands-on technique; more complex were the sequences in which Gene Kelly danced with Jerry the Mouse in *Anchors Aweigh* (1945), or with a perky Scheherezade in *Invitation to the Dance* (1956). The most sophisticated use of HANDS-ON ANIMATION is in the 1989 film *Who Framed Roger Rabbit?* in which the cartoons appear nearly three-dimensional, thanks to COMPUTER GRAPHICS.

hands-on workshop (fan/convention): A training session in COSTUMING, art techniques, writing, or FANZINE production held during a CONVENTION, in which the attendees get to do the thing. Advance registration is usually required for these WORKSHOPS, which are announced well ahead of time in PROGRESS REPORTS.

The leaders of the WORKSHOPS are experts, eager to share their knowledge with aspiring newcomers. In the case of art or writing WORKSHOPS, a sample of the attendee's work may be required in advance, so that the leader of the WORKSHOP may

CRITIQUE the piece, and the other members of the class may offer their suggestions.

hand stamp (fan/conventions): An inked impression placed on the back of the hand of an attendee at a PRO-CON, to distinguish those who have paid from those who have not. Many PRO-CONS use hand stamps instead of BADGES, which are expensive to print and tend to fall off. By showing the HAND STAMP the attendee can gain admission to the DEALERS' ROOM and all other elements of the CON.

Occasionally someone will try to sneak into the CON by forging the HAND STAMP. This is not considered acceptable behavior, and the person who does it will be remembered at future CONS, and probably will be turned away, or at least will be watched very closely by SECURITY. See also BADGES.

hanging fee (fan/conventions): The nominal fee charged by a FAN-CON to an artist for space in the ART SHOW. An artist may want to reserve considerable space, or may only have a few small items to exhibit; in either case, the HANGING FEE will be charged per panel or per table. Some fan artists decry HANGING FEES, but the professionals realize that any art gallery will charge a similar fee, and the HANGING FEES for most CONVENTIONS are quite low (as little as $1.00 per PIECE in some cases), and cover the cost of such items as BID SHEETS and CONTROL SHEETS. See also ART SHOW.

hard copy (computer): The printed words that are legibly impressed on paper. Until then, the data are held in electronic limbo on disk or diskette, and can be altered or even erased.

hard-core SF (literary): Science Fiction that deals largely with mechanisms, technology, and problem-solving, as opposed to SOFT SF, which deals with personal relationships in a futuristic setting. HARD-CORE SF is a back-creation from "hard-core pornography," and seems to have the same uncompromising attitude. The science element predominates, and must comply with current knowledge (no fanciful FTL DRIVE, no ESP, no improbable ALIENS).

The originator of this kind of SF is undoubtedly JULES VERNE, whose adventure tales incorporated as much of his era's technology as he could cram into them. What he did not know definitely, he extrapolated, and was not much astonished to be proven right.

Of the current crop of writers, Hal Clement is the acknowledged leader in the field of HARD-CORE SF. Stories such as *Mission of Gravity* (1954) depend on exact calculations of planetary mass, atmospheric density, and the composition of the planet's core for their SUSPENSION OF DISBELIEF. See also HARD SCIENCES.

hardcover (publishing): An expensive and durable binding, made of cardboard covered with fabric, as opposed to the cheaper and flimsier PAPERBACK binding. Until the 1950s, a book was first published in HARDCOVER; only after a few years had passed would there be a cheaper edition in PAPERBACK.

SF was first printed in PULP magazines, then in PAPERBACKS. Only after 1950 were HARDCOVER editions of SF novels and ANTHOLOGIES published on a regular basis, reversing the usual order of things in publishing. Many of the classic SF novels of the so-called GOLDEN AGE were first published in PAPERBACK, and were later reissued in HARDCOVER editions.

The current situation is complex. A novel may be issued as an original MASS-MARKET PAPERBACK; it may be issued as a TRADE PAPERBACK; it may be presented simultaneously in HARDCOVER and PAPERBACK editions. Much depends on the publisher and the popularity of the writer. However, the most expensive and therefore most prestigious FORMAT is still HARDCOVER.

hard sciences: Those studies dealing with the definition and manipulation of matter: physics, chemistry, geology, and astronomy, as opposed to those studies dealing with personal relationships: psychology, anthropology, and sociology. Much of SF as it was conceived in the 1920s dealt largely with problem-solving in situations dominated by technology. The "science" in Science Fiction was supposed to be as accurate as current knowledge would allow, and SF was supposed to be based on the "probable" as opposed to the "impossible."

The scientific community of the 1990s is beginning to admit that the so-called SOFT SCIENCES are as necessary to the understanding of ourselves and our universe as the HARD SCIENCES, and current trends in SF reflect this awareness. See also HARD-CORE SF; SOFT SF.

hardware (computer): The actual mechanism that runs the COMPUTER. The various disk drives, the printer, the motor . . . all these are HARDWARE. The programming on the diskettes is SOFTWARE.

Hardware stories (literary): Also called NUTS 'N' BOLTS STORIES or HARD-CORE SF. Stories that deal with technology and problem-solving in a HIGH-TECH environment. Much SF written between 1940 and 1960 was of this variety.

Haunted House Story (literary): A story in which a group of characters is isolated in a large, dark, structure and systematically terrorized by someone or something that may or may not be human. GOTHIC STORIES often took place in ancient castles or decaying mansions, but almost any oppressive structure will do. "ALIEN" is set on a deserted spaceship, in which a species of extra-terrestrial life has made a nest.

HC (comics): HARDCOVER edition of a comic book; an expensively bound edition, often issued as a GRAPHIC ALBUM. Many comic strips will issue a retrospective HC edition at regular intervals; the FORMAT is not as common with comic books, whose publishers usually opt for the TRADE PAPERBACK FORMAT. See also BAXTER BOOK; GRAPHIC ALBUM.

Heinlein, Robert (1907–1988): One of the giants of SF, whose work spans the philosophic gamut of SF, from the political savvy of *Double Star* (1956) to the action/adventure fantasy of *Glory Road* (1963) to the pseudomilitarism of *Starship Troopers* (1959) to the implied mysticism of *Stranger in a Strange Land*

(1961). HEINLEIN's influence has been felt since the GOLDEN AGE OF SF and will continue into a future that he depicted many times, in many different ways. No one can consider themselves literate in SF without having read some of HEINLEIN. See also GROK.

Henson, Jim (1940–1990): Inventive puppeteer and showman, whose association with GEORGE LUCAS revolutionized the depiction of nonhumans in SF films. HENSON's early work on television led to his involvement with the Children's Television Workshop and "Sesame Street" (1969 to present). Later ventures included "The Muppet Show" (1976–1981) and "Fraggle Rock" (1988 to present). At the same time, HENSON expanded the use of puppets in film fantasies like *Labyrinth* (1986) and *The Dark Crystal* (1982), which were aimed as much at the adult audience as at the children. HENSON's beings may not be exactly human, but they take on a life of their own, as actors who have worked with them will testify.

"Here we go again!" ending: (literary): Ending that gives indications of another adventure forthcoming. The story does come to some kind of finish, so there is no CLIFFHANGER; however, the characters meet with some new challenge and HERE WE GO AGAIN!

Hero (literary): The leading character in a story, with whom the audience is expected to sympathize and identify. The HERO personifies all that the author finds admirable, and may even be the author, slightly disguised, or as the author would like to be. HEROES of early SF were usually shown as young, athletic men, devoted to their country and their military organizations; they defeated BEMS and thwarted MAD SCIENTISTS. They rarely swore, drank, or flirted with women. This pristine image was soiled as SF became more realistic, until the ANTIHERO is now just as prevalent as his pure-hearted counterpart.

The HERO in Classical mythology was often someone who had been favored by the gods. SF HEROES tend to be lucky; they also tend to have a lot of odd knowledge that comes in very useful in tight places.

Current SF has its HEROES, who may be female; they, too, are just a little larger than life. See also SUPERHERO; WOMAN WARRIOR.

heroic fantasy (literary): A tale of high adventure, set in a mythic past or in a faraway world, filled with magic and derring-do, with a stalwart HERO, a beautiful heroine, and a heinous villain. TOLKEIN's *Lord of the Rings* is one kind of HEROIC FANTASY; ROBERT HOWARD's *Conan the Barbarian* stories are another. HEROIC FANTASY in art is typified by the nearly nude models of BORIS VALLEJO and FRANK FRAZETTA. See also HIGH FANTASY; SWORD AND SORCERY.

Hertzsprung-Russell diagram (astronomy): A graph on which color and temperature of stars is plotted against brightness; named for its developers, astronomers Ejnar Hertzsprung and Henry Norris Russell. The diagram shows stars at various stages of evolution; the star's size and color will be determined by how long its core has been emitting energy. The youngest stars are the white giants; older stars may be RED DWARFS. Our own sun is midway along the diagram, yellowish and middle-aged. Stars that fall easily into the H-R DIAGRAM are called MAIN SEQUENCE STARS; a few seem to be exceptions to the rule, and they are usually marked as such on the diagram.

"He's dead, Jim" (TV): Statement uttered many times by the character of Dr. McCoy on STAR TREK, in various episodes and with various degrees of intensity and shock. It has become a catch-phrase, uttered in tones of deepest despair, indicating the total ruin of whatever is in question.

high fantasy (literary): Pseudomedieval tales of great scope, dealing with battles between Good and Evil. A very highfalutin form of HEROIC FANTASY, with apocalyptic overtones and a general weightiness of purpose. Many HIGH FANTASY writers base their style on Malory's classic *Morte D'Arthur* and the many imitators who followed him. At best, HIGH FANTASY can be beautifully written; at worst, it becomes a leaden bore.

high-tech (literary): A society in which technology has reached a high level of development. SF writers tend to depict an extension of whatever technological level their contemporary society has reached. In the 1950s, for instance, a story set in the fairly near future of the 1980s might assume that a household would include robots to do the dirty work. However, the all-pervasive influence of personal COMPUTERS and TELECOMMUNICATIONS seems to have eluded the prognosticators.

HIGH-TECH societies are often depicted as being dependent on their mechanisms, and vulnerable to lower-tech but strongly motivated natives of faraway planets. Recent experience on Earth has shown that the highest technological expertise is not always the best thing for living beings.

hit points (gaming): How much damage a CHARACTER in a ROLE-PLAYING GAME can suffer before being declared dead by the DUNGEONMASTER. The number of HIT POINTS is determined by the DM by rolling the dice, then balancing the number indicated against the CHARACTER'S ABILITIES. Someone with great STRENGTH or CONSTITUTION can hold up better than someone less able to withstand injury. HIT POINTS are subtracted from the character's EXPERIENCE POINTS as well. A character who keeps getting wounded has obviously not learned from experience.

hive-mind (literary): A group of beings who share a single mental impetus, such as the social insects on Earth (ants, bees, wasps). A form of HIVE-MIND was first suggested by H. G. WELLS in *The First Men on the Moon* (1901); another form of joint mentality is the "homo gestalt" conceived by THEODORE STURGEON in *More Than Human* (1953).

The HIVE-MIND is often depicted as an enemy; the only way to defeat it is to remove the controlling element, which may be an individual or even, as in the *Dumarest of Earth* series by E. C. Tubb, a computer.

Hobbits (literary): Small cheerful people, created by J. R. R. TOLKIEN in the book by the same name, and inserted into his *Lord of the Rings* saga. HOBBITS may be recognized by their bare hairy feet, which are especially obvious when people impersonating them are seen parading about the halls at CONVENTIONS.

Hogu Award (fan): A mock award ceremony, giving token awards for what the donors consider the worst SF of a given year. The HOGUS are a deliberate spoof of the prestigious HUGO AWARDS, held annually at the WORLD-CON. They are attended by whoever feels like going to a chosen fast-food place at the time announced in the WORLD-CON NEWSLETTER; the ordinary patrons may think what they like of this rowdy assemblage. Like the Sour Apple Awards and the Dubious Achievement awards given each year by *Esquire* magazine, the HOGU is accepted with wry humor by its recipients, none of whom deliberately set out to win it.

Hokas (literary): Creatures invented by Gordon Dickson and Poul Anderson for a series of stories, later collected and issued under the title *Earthman's Burden* (1957) and *Hoka*! (1984). The HOKAS resemble 4-foot-high teddy bears, with sharp claws, sharper fangs, and incredible strength matched only by their drinking capacity. They are at once completely imaginative and totally literal, so that they believe everything that they read must be true; as a result, they interpret the various forms of popular literature handed out by their brand-new Terran allies in their own fashion, giving Anderson and Dickson the opportunity to parody such GENRES as the Pirate Story, the Western, and even their own SPACE OPERAS.

HOKAS make adorable APOCRYPHALS; any name on a list of

CONVENTION members with H-O-K-A somewhere in it may be suspect.

hologram (physics): A photograph taken by laser light, to create a three-dimensional image. The subject will appear to be displaced in different views. While the use of HOLOGRAMS is currently limited to small reproductions on magazine covers, jewelry, and so forth, it is predicted that the images may be expanded to the size of a television screen. Many stories set in the next century depict home entertainment centers that use HOLOGRAMS in the same way we use television. The production of HOLOGRAMS is termed holography.

homeostatic systems (physiology): Devices that maintain themselves in a state of equilibrium, in which input and output are automatically balanced. It is assumed that the invention of such a system is the first step in ARTIFICIAL INTELLIGENCE.

hook (film/TV): The opening scenes of a film or TV EPISODE that set the scene and presumably HOOK the audience like a fish on a line, waiting to see what will happen. The HOOK of a typical TV episode will have the REGULAR CAST in some kind of danger; the viewers will stay around to see how they get out of it.

horror stories (literary): Stories in which a mood of terror is invoked; often they emphasize the repulsive, the gory, or the nightmares of childhood. Currently, the leader of horror writers is STEPHEN KING, who can provide a chill of fear in such an unlikely place as a suburban housing development. KING and his followers play on primal fears to keep their readers turning the pages.

Horror (or terror) tales date back in time through the ancient myths of gods and goddesses, to the no less mythical stories of WITCHES and DRAGONS that have come to us in the folklore now read to small children. EDGAR ALLAN POE is credited with having perfected HORROR STORIES in the 19th century, with classics such as "The Telltale Heart" and "A Cask of Amontillado."

HORROR STORIES today are prone to exaggeration, show too

much gore, and what was scary becomes merely disgusting as in the GRAND GUIGNOL, or in SLASHER MOVIES.

Howard, Robert (1906–1936): Creator of the original CONAN THE BARBARIAN, in a series of novels and short stories published between 1932 and 1936. Since his death, the character of CONAN has been carried through a number of adventures, written by people of varying talents, and the original novels have been reprinted many times.

hucksters/huxters: See DEALERS.

Hugo Awards: Given at the WORLD-CON since 1953, to honor excellence in Science Fiction, in all its forms and formats; named for HUGO GERNSBACK, the pioneer editor of SF.

The HUGOS are voted on by the membership of the WORLD-CON, which includes fans as well as professional writers and artists; the award is therefore a measure of popularity as well as literary or artistic achievement. Nominating ballots are sent out by the year's WORLD-CON committee; the five items in each category with the most nominations are placed on the final ballots, which are sent out in the spring of the year of the award. Awards are given for excellence in novels, novellas, novelettes, and short stories; there are also awards for Best Editor (PRO) and Best Editor (FAN); Best Fanzine; Best Semi-prozine; Best Artist (PRO) and Best Artist (FAN). The award for Best Dramatic Presentation has been hotly contested in the last decade, as SF films and TV series have grown in importance.

Because the nominating and voting base is so broad, the HUGO AWARDS have been criticized on several counts. One school of thought holds that the general public cannot really recognize excellence unless it comes attached to some popular name, and that the HUGO is merely a popularity contest. However, the NEBULA AWARDS are given by the SFWA, and very often, the same item will receive both awards, proving that SF readers are at least as perceptive as SF writers. Another criticism has to do with the award for Best Fanzine, which is inevitably given to one of the few non-MEDIAZINES still operating on a wide enough level to attain a majority of votes. MEDIAZINE editors resent the voting procedure that favors a publication with a circulation of over a thousand copies, which few MEDIAZINES can match.

In spite of all these cavils and carpings, a HUGO nomination is in itself an honor, and to win one is a high point in the career of anyone involved in SF.

humanoid (biology): Resembling a human, that is, a creature that looks like us, although it may not be from this planet. A human is a being from Earth; anything else is HUMANOID. It may have conspicuous differences (blue skin, green hair), or it may merely be bald with irregularly shaped splotches on its enlarged head. A HUMANOID is organic; if it is a mechanism that resembles a human, it is termed an ANDROID.

hurt/comfort story (fan/fanzine): A type of story, usually found in MEDIAZINES, in which one of a MALE-BONDED pair of protagonists gets hurt while the other has to give comfort. The hurt can be physical, and it can be excruciating, while the comfort can be direct medical aid or psychological assurance.

The genre began in MEDIAZINES, with stories that usually involved the characters of Kirk and Spock from STAR TREK. A later variation dealt with Luke Skywalker and Han Solo of STAR WARS. Starsky and Hutch, from the TV SERIES of the same name, received similar treatment at the hands of their loving fans.

HURT/COMFORT STORIES can be grimly realistic when it comes to medical details; on the other hand, they come perilously close to SLASH in their depiction of the interaction of the male characters.

An interesting note: Although most of these stories are written by women, they rarely deal with female characters. Often the men are depicted as reacting to each other in so-called "female" terms, providing nurturing, and so on.

hymnal (fan/filking): A very large collection of miscellaneous FILK-SONGS, for use at FILK-SINGS. The earliest such collection was *The HOPSFA Hymnal*, put out by the Johns Hopkins SF Association in the early 1970s. *The Westerfilk Hymnals #1* and

#2 and *The NESFA Hymnal #1* and *#2* are the others most commonly seen at FILK-SINGS.

A HYMNAL sing assumes that everyone either has a HYMNAL or can look on with someone who has one. While HYMNALS are great fun for NEOFEN, the more experienced FILKERS have usually heard most of the songs in the HYMNALS so often that they prefer to listen to the new product.

hyperspace (literary): A concept that has yet to be accepted by the scientific establishment, but has been a mainstay of SF since JOHN W. CAMPBELL used it in *The Mightiest Machine* in 1934. In its simplest form, the idea of HYPERSPACE is that Space is not continuous, but takes the form of folds or tucks, in which the laws of Relativity do not apply. If a spaceship can navigate in and around the tucks and wrinkles of Space, it can cut across vast distances in a short space of time, eliminating the need for GENERATION SHIPS to get where one is going.

HYPERSPACE has become one of those "conventions" of SF, like FTL DRIVE. Science says it doesn't exist, but writers use it anyway.

hyphenate (film): A person who performs two or more important functions in making a film; the two titles are separated by a hyphen, as in Director-Producer STEVEN SPIELBERG, or Writer-Director John Carpenter. SF seems to attract such multi-talented individuals, who insist on overseeing several aspects of a film so that their unique vision will be properly presented to the audience.

I

IBM (International Business Machines): One of the major manufacturers of COMPUTERS and their assorted wares (hard and soft). IBM is listed in the Wallace/Wallechinsky *Peoples' Almanac* among the corporations so large as to approximate a national unit in its scope and political clout. While there are many other manufacturers of COMPUTERS, IBM tends to be used as the symbol of the corporate entity in general discussions of the economics of COMPUTERS.

idiot lecture (literary): A way for the author to let the reader know some of the BACK-STORY, by having one CHARACTER tell it to another (who may or may not know it, or care about knowing it). This is usually considered a clumsy way of inserting EXPOSITION into the story; the action stops dead, and the audience (reading or viewing) tends to lose interest. IDIOT LECTURES were around long before SF; those early scenes in domestic comedies of the 1890s, where the maid told the butler about the Young Master or the Old Mistress, are also IDIOT LECTURES.

illos (fan/fanzines): Short for illustrations; any form of artwork inserted into a magazine, whether FAN or PRO. ILLOS are usually printed in black and white, so pen and ink sketches are preferred to pencil (which is more delicate, but harder to repro-

duce). Story ILLOS depict events in a particular story; FILLOS are simply decorative pieces placed here and there to fill up otherwise empty space (anathema to a FANZINE editor). CREEPY-CRAWLIES are FILLOS with a horror theme.

ILLOS are works of art in their own right, and are often exhibited at CONVENTION ART SHOWS. The rights to ILLOS belong to the artist, who may then either sell the ORIGINALS or arrange to have them reprinted in a PORTFOLIO. See also COVER ART.

Illuminatus (literary): Trilogy by Robert Shea and Robert Anton Wilson, first published in 1975, and kept constantly in print; a satiric tale of intrigue in which various cults and secret organizations constantly jostle each other in their attempts to control human existence, which manages to plod along without their help. Some SF FANS are convinced that this is not satire but an actual depiction of true life. ILLUMINATUS has given birth to several odd offshoots of FANDOM, including FANZINES and a ROLE-PLAYING GAME.

illustrated novel (publishing): A very long piece of fiction interspersed with illustrations; these may be black-and-white drawings or color plates. Illustrations were included in many popular novels up to the 1940s; after World War II, the cost of producing illustrated books became prohibitive, and today it is rare for a novel to include any illustrations, with the exception of books written for children. A long story told primarily in pictures is a GRAPHIC NOVEL.

ILM (Industrial Light and Magic) (film): The workshop set up by GEORGE LUCAS for his STAR WARS SFX, now the home of some of the most imaginative and creative people in the film industry. With the addition of the legacy of JIM HENSON to the menage (or menagerie), ILM manufactures monsters, assembles Aliens, and illuminates innumerable starscapes. ILM is the Mecca for anyone involved in the magic of movie making.

imaginary science (literary): Plausible explanations for SF concepts that otherwise violate known laws of physics, chemistry, and so on. IMAGINARY SCIENCE may, in time, prove to be reality, unlike PSEUDOSCIENCE, which is based on false information from its inception.

FTL DRIVE and TIME TRAVEL are as yet considered impossible; however, thanks to IMAGINARY SCIENCE, SF writers find ways to use them in HARD-CORE SF stories.

imprint (publishing): A particular division within a large publishing house that specializes in a certain field, or in publishing a certain type of book that carries its own LOGO. For instance, within the large publishing company of Random House, Del Rey is the Science Fiction imprint.

Within the imprint, there may be particular LINES, or SERIES, distinguished by a special colored spine, cover design, or LOGO, or some other characteristic, that may be controlled by one or two editors.

inker (comics): The person who completes the pencil drawings of the ARTIST, adding in the details, the backgrounds, and so forth. The INKER is a vital part of the CREATIVE TEAM who adds a particular style to the finished product. Inking requires a very delicate touch and an eye for the microscopic detail. See also CREATIVE TEAM.

In medias res (literary): From the Latin, literally, "In the middle of things"; the literary technique of opening a story in the middle of the action, instead of starting at the beginning and winding one's way through the PLOT to the end.

The IN MEDIAS RES opening goes back as far as Homer's *Iliad*, which gets the reader interested in Achilles' snits first, then goes back to tell about the Abduction of Helen, and so on. The problem with beginning an SF story IN MEDIAS RES is that a great deal of the BACK-STORY is going to have to be inserted somehow so that the reader will know what is going on. This may be done by means of FLASHBACKS or DREAM SEQUENCES or even an IDIOT LECTURE, after which the writer can go on to conclude the action.

Beginning a story IN MEDIAS RES does get the reader involved immediately; it is up to the writer to then fill in the gaps in the readers' knowledge.

inside joke (literary): A private joke between Those Who Know that is unintelligible to those who don't. SF authors may include the names of their friends (or their enemies) as minor characters in a story, or may name a planet for an obscure scientist. INSIDE JOKES creep into comics, as visual jokes, when an artist uses the face of a friend in the background.

intelligence (biology): The ability of a creature to reason, learn, and remember what has been learned, so as to transmit that information to others of its kind. Until recently, INTELLIGENCE was a major criterion to be applied to any life form that might be found on another planet. Recent studies have shown that chimpanzees and gorillas can learn to communicate through sign language; that some monkeys have initiated forms of behavior they then teach to other monkeys; and that dolphins have the ability to communicate with each other.

The latest criterion against which a species is matched to decide whether it is equal to humanity is SENTIENCE. Until apes and monkeys exhibit that, humans remain smugly at the top of the evolutionary chain. See also SENTIENCE.

intelligence (gaming): The ABILITY of a CHARACTER to reason, learn, and remember what has been learned, and then apply it to a given situation; determined by the DUNGEONMASTER with the use of dice at the beginning of the game. INTELLIGENCE is a primary requirement for a CLERIC or a magic-user, although it is not as important for a FIGHTER, and a ROGUE without INTELLIGENCE soon winds up either in prison or dead.

interactive fiction (publishing): A story told in segments, out of order. As the reader goes along, choices of action must be made at the end of each segment; each choice leads to another part of the story, with various endings, not all of which are happy ones.

The first story of this sort was Edward Packard's *Third Planet from Altair*, published in 1979 as a JUVIE, followed by *Deadwood City*, a Western, in the same format. Although the early INTERACTIVE FICTION was published in HARDCOVER, later SERIES were published as PAPERBACKS. The FORMAT is extremely popular with young people, who eagerly pursue the story in and out of its permutations and combinations. Such series as *Choose Your Own Adventure* are now found in the CHILDREN'S ROOM GHETTO in any library or bookstore. The idea is now being extended into the adult market.

interactive games (gaming): ROLE-PLAYING GAMES similar to DUNGEONS AND DRAGONS™ taken to the next logical step: a weekend encounter session, in which each participant is given a role in a much wider scenario. These games may be run as part of a CONVENTION, concurrent with the rest of the PROGRAMMING.

interface (computer): Interaction between COMPUTERS of various manufacturers. Eventually, all COMPUTERS will be able to do this; as the situation now stands, some COMPUTERS are COMPATIBLE; others are not.

interplanetary space (aerospace): The area within the Sun's gravitational influence, that is, the Solar System as we know it, including the Earth and its Moon, the other eight planets, the ASTEROID BELT, and the OORT CLOUD. INTERPLANETARY SPACE is the area most likely to be explored by humanity in the next century, whether in person or vicariously through PROBES like the Voyager.

interstellar space (aerospace): The area beyond the gravitational influence of our Sun, that is, beyond the SOLAR SYSTEM as we know it. Early SF called this area OUTER SPACE, which is too vague for today's HARD-CORE SF writer. INTERSTELLAR SPACE lies "between the stars," and the distances are so vast that one needs FTL DRIVE or HYPERSPACE to get from one STAR SYSTEM to another.

Interzone SF (literary): Another term for CYBERPUNK, taken from the British magazine *Interzone,* which specializes in this subgenre of SF.

"into" (fan): Interested in; a borrowing from the Hippie slang of the 1960s. A FAN may be INTO STAR TREK or CYBERPUNK, or GAMING or COMPUTERS.

ion engine (aerospace): A proposed engine that would use a stream of ionized particles generated by solar or nuclear power as a fuel source. This sort of engine would be assembled in Space, possibly in a SPACE STATION, and would generate enough power to almost achieve LIGHT SPEED. A small-scale ion drive has already been built, and is used for small orbital adjustments in satellites. However, any engine large enough to provide power to get to the stars would probably require a nuclear fuel supply. Of all the schemes to get out and into the rest of the Galaxy, this is considered the most feasible by space scientists.

ion storm (literary): A major disturbance in the particles that drift about in INTERSTELLAR SPACE, similar to a storm on Earth. According to astronomers, such activity is highly improbable; however, ION STORMS are regularly found in SF stories and films that put spaceship crews in jeopardy.

J

jacket (publishing): More properly called a dust jacket; a paper cover that protects a HARDCOVER book. The JACKET may have COVER ART in addition to the title and author's name, the publisher and/or the IMPRINT or SERIES, and any other material that the publisher thinks will sell the book. The JACKET is folded over the front and back covers; this flap is used for the BLURB, and possibly, for a picture of the author.

Jacob's ladder (electronics): A device consisting of two metal rods attached to a battery that sends a spark from one rod to another. This apparatus was a common sight in the MAD SCIENTIST films of the 1930s. It looked incredibly sinister, but the spark never reached anything but the other side of the ladder, and the device is no more than a spectacular sort of electrical fireworks. In other words, it does nothing.

The name refers to the biblical tale of Jacob's dream of a ladder that reached to heaven; it has been applied to other ladders, from the one that reaches from ship to ship for life-saving purposes, to the passage out of a dungeon.

Japanimation (film): Short for Japanese animation; cartoons made in Japan, depicting the adventures of SUPERHEROES or spaceship crews. JAPANIMATION is occasionally seen on television during the SATURDAY MORNING GHETTO lineup, but is more commonly found at CONVENTIONS, on BOOTLEG TAPES. The artistic merit of the JAPANIMATION films seems to outweigh their literary merit, but something may have been lost in the translation of the text.

JATO (aerospace): Jet-Accelerated Take-Off; an aircraft that can lift off quickly from a stationary position, within a planet's atmosphere. A lunar landing vehicle must burn liquid oxygen to achieve ignition and leave the Moon's surface in a vacuum.

journeyman (fan/costuming): The division of COSTUMING judging, between the NOVICE and the MASTER, for those with moderate experience in costuming. There has been some argument as to what constitutes a JOURNEYMAN at a WORLD-CON; one group insists that anyone who has appeared at a WORLD-CON MASQUERADE at least once must register the second time as a JOURNEYMAN, while another group says that a contestant is a NOVICE until he or she wins something. Most Regional CONS go by the first definition.

The term derives from the French *jour*, meaning "day." It was the practice of Medieval Guilds that a craftsman would serve a term as an apprentice, learning the trade, and would then be tested by the masters of the Guild. If the apprentice proved to be competent, he was permitted to practice the craft, going from town to town, working for "daily wages." See also COSTUMING; DIVISION SYSTEM.

JPL (astronomy): Jet Propulsion Laboratory, in Pasadena, California; astronomical observatory and computer center operated for NASA by the California Institute of Technology. The JPL is the nerve center for planning and research in the U.S. exploration of Space. Most recently, JPL has been involved in the GRAND TOUR of the Voyager probes; with the probe's exiting of our Solar System and the end of the GRAND TOUR, new missions are being mapped out for unmanned probes, and basic research is beginning on the possibilities of manned missions to Mars and the outer planets.

judging (fan/costuming): The evaluation of costumes at a MASQUERADE; a very delicate and difficult matter. Most SF CONS that have a MASQUERADE will choose their judges carefully from local MASTER COSTUMERS, theatrical costumers, and artists. Criteria taken into account will be the WORKMANSHIP that went into the costume, as well as its effect on the audience. A RE-CREATION costume must resemble the original as closely as possible. Historical costumes are judged for authenticity. Many WORLD-CONS provide the judges with polaroid photographs of the costumes taken just before the actual MASQUERADE, so that the judges can see the details of the costume that might otherwise be missed.

Prizes at MASQUERADES are usually given in Categories as well as DIVISIONS. Most common are Science Fiction, Fantasy, and Re-creation; occasionally prizes may be given for Most Humorous, Most Original, or even Best Alien. SF CONS usually award ribbons or certificates; the prize is in the winning, and the reward is the honor.

JUDGING at PRO-CONS is a little less rigorous, but the criteria are the same. Originality is a plus; shoddy WORKMANSHIP is a minus. The prizes at a PRO-CON MASQUERADE or Costume Parade may be more substantial, but the real thrill for the contestant is that gasp of wonder, roar of approval, or howl of laughter that tells the contestant that the costume had the desired effect, whatever the judges think.

jump-ship (aerospace): A proposed spaceship that "jumps" across our Galaxy, from star to star. The ship might use an ION ENGINE, which would bring it close to LIGHT SPEED, or it might find a way of crossing HYPERSPACE. An SF LITERARY CONVENTION expands on this idea, so that in some SF stories, spacecraft literally leapfrog across Space, aiming at particular stars, homing in on particular stations through complex computer systems. Of course, all of these JUMP-SHIPS are equipped with FTL DRIVE, which makes them technically impossible; nevertheless, they are used constantly.

Jupiter (astronomy): The largest of the nine planets that form our Solar System. A GAS GIANT with four major moons, seven (or more) minor ones, a thin ring system, and a possible internal core, JUPITER is considered by some astronomers to be a star that failed to reach necessary mass for internal energy production. While astronomers consider life on JUPITER itself to be extremely unlikely, the moons have been considered as likely sites for SPACE COLONIES. *Outland* (1981) is a film set in such a colony; the vast bulk of JUPITER is seen looming over the tiny colony to great effect.

justified type (printing): A page typed so that both sides of the lettering are straight, forming a nice, neat margin all the way around. JUSTIFICATION is managed by expanding the space between the letters to fit the space on the page. It makes for very professional-looking copy.

juvies (publishing): Juvenile books, meant for readers under the age of 13. Once scorned by "serious" SF writers, the juvenile field is being explored by major writers like Jane Yolen and ISAAC ASIMOV. ROBERT HEINLEIN wrote some of the most enduring JUVIES, *Starman Jones* (1952), *Have Space Suit, Will Travel* (1958), and *The Star Beast* (1955), which are still the first introduction many young people get to the wonders of SF. Anne McCaffrey's PERN series began as a trilogy for young adults.

The juvenile field is an expanding market. Many adult readers will find untold treasures in the CHILDREN'S ROOM GHETTO.

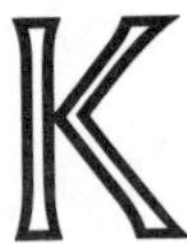

Kepler, Johannes (1571–1630): German mathematician and astronomer, who formulated the proposition that the orbits of the planets of the Solar System are ellipses, not circles, as had been suggested by Copernicus. KEPLER incorporated his ideas in an early SF tale, *Somnium* or *The Dream* (printed after his death, in 1634), in which he describes a trip to the MOON.

Kepler's Laws (astronomy): (1) Every planet orbits its sun in an ellipse. (2) The radius vector of the ellipse sweeps out equal areas within the ellipse in equal terms. (3) A fixed ratio exists between the time taken to complete an orbit and the size of the orbit; the ratio is the same for every planet.

So far, nothing has been discovered to show that these laws do not apply to other planetary systems in the Galaxy.

kicker (literary): An extra element, a final snappy line or twist of plot that caps the joke and adds the extra point to a story. Often the KICKER is a HERE WE GO AGAIN! ENDING. The KICKER that misses its point may be called a TOMATO SURPRISE ENDING.

kill fee (publishing): Money paid to a writer or artist for a work that was commissioned but is not going to be used. An ILLO that depicts a specific scene in a story, or a story meant for a

SHARED UNIVERSE cannot be sold elsewhere, but the writer or artist should be compensated for the work that went into creating them.

King Arthur (literary): The subject of innumerable tales dating back to the 12th century; possibly a war leader of post-Roman British forces combating the invaders from what is now Germany in the 6th and 7th centuries A.D.

The historical KING ARTHUR is mentioned briefly in monkish chronicles written at least a hundred years after the event. He may have been descended from a Roman family, left behind when the Legions were pulled out of Britain in the mid-400s. He is supposed to have pulled a number of warring tribes together to fight off the Saxon forces, who were being pushed out of their own lands by other tribes, who were being pushed in turn by tribes from Central Asia, in what has been called the Dark Ages. There is little solid evidence, either written or archeological, to support the existence of such a person; however, the legends that grew up around this leader would suggest that someone very like the KING ARTHUR of the later Medieval romances probably existed.

Over the centuries, the legends of KING ARTHUR were extended and enhanced. Chretien de Troyes incorporated the KING ARTHUR tales with the legends of the Holy Grail, the cup from which Jesus drank at the Last Supper. Sir Thomas Mallory's *Le Morte D'Arthur* combined many of the legends and written poems into one vast tale of knightly valor and human betrayal. Much of the current perception of KING ARTHUR comes from Alfred Lord Tennyson's *Idylls of the King*, which put Mallory's prose back into poetry.

New findings in archeology have led to a justification of the historical KING ARTHUR's existence. Rosemary Sutcliffe used these findings in her Arthurian novel, *Sword at Sunset*. Other writers have used the ARTHUR legends to suit their own purposes. Marion Zimmer Bradley's *Mists of Avalon* (1983) places the story within the context of the battle between the old fertility cults and the "new religion," Christianity. T. H. White's *Once and Future King* interprets the story as the struggle between Law and Chaos. Filmed versions range from the stuffy pageantry of

Knights of the Round Table (1954) to the gritty realism of *Excalibur* (1987).

The legends of KING ARTHUR have even been played for laughs. Mark Twain satirized the Tennyson concept of high-flown nobility in *A Connecticut Yankee in King Arthur's Court* (1889). More recently, Peter David has a resurrected King Arthur running for Mayor of the City of New York in *Knight Life* (1988) . . . and winning.

Each era seems to interpret KING ARTHUR to suit its own mores and morals. One thing is sure: As far as literary production is concerned, KING ARTHUR will always be "The Once and Future King."

King Kong (1933, 1976): The classic MONSTER MOVIE about the enormous ape who loves a beautiful woman. The 1933 version is still considered a monument in SF filmmaking, with its stop-action animation; the climactic scene atop the Empire State Building, with biplanes zooming around the impassioned ape, has been parodied many times. The later, more elaborate version produced by Dino De Laurentiis, missed the point completely.

King, Stephen (b. 1947): Probably the best-known and most popular writer of horror fiction alive at this writing. KING sets his novels in the most banal of surroundings, where the true horror is the manipulation of one human being by another. In KING's novels, old cars can take on the personalities of dead lovers, and a quaint New England village can harbor unspeakable evil. Several of KING's books have been made into popular films, some of which he directed himself.

KING is now moving into the SF field, with his *Gunslinger* trilogy, bringing the same elements of menace unseen to SF that he does to contemporary horror stories. See also HORROR STORIES.

Kipling, Rudyard (1865–1936): British writer of short stories and poems, whose influence has been felt by SF writers as diverse as Gordon Dickson, ROBERT HEINLEIN, and Robin McKinley. KIPLING's output included the fantasy tales of *Puck of Pook's Hill* (1906); the *Just-So Stories* (1902), which were written for his own small children; stories of technology; and even an early SF story, *With the Night Mail* (1905). KIPLING's poetry has been set to music many times, most recently by FILK-SINGER LESLIE FISH, and is often heard at FILK-SINGS.

KIPLING's political opinions were those of his time and his class; he was considerably less prejudiced against the natives of India than other English colonials. For a long time he and his works were in disrepute because of the implied attitude of "White Man's Burden" and imperialistic jingoism. However, as the political scene cooled down, KIPLING's artistry became more popular than his politics. *A Separate Star*, edited by David Drake and Sandra Meisel in 1989, is an anthology of stories by writers who acknowledge their debt to KIPLING.

klick (military): A kilometer. Distances in SF stories are difficult to calculate; either the story is set in Space, where distances are literally astronomical, or it is set on a planet where distance may be calculated in any of a number of ways. In the 1980s, with most of the world using the metric system, the kilometer gradually replaced the mile as a unit of distance.

Kraith (literary): A series of stories, originally written by Jacqueline Lichtenberg in the early 1970s for STAR TREK FANZINES;

they were later collected and reprinted in six volumes of reduced type.

The KRAITH is a sacred Vulcan religious vessel, and its loss and return was the basis of the series, which dealt with Spock and his Vulcan background, and the incorporation of Captain Kirk into that Vulcan family. The series gradually expanded to include stories by authors other than Lichtenberg; there were even Alternate KRAITH stories, written by people who didn't like what Lichtenberg was doing to the characters she herself had originated.

KRAITH has become the symbol of the fan-written STAR TREK UNIVERSE. There have been KRAITH costumes, KRAITH FILK songs, and long, involved KRAITH discussions at STAR TREK CONVENTIONS. Much of what is assumed to be Vulcan about STAR TREK was not invented by D. C. Fontana, who wrote the EPISODES dealing with Vulcans, but was interpolated by Lichtenberg and the KRAITH writers.

The original KRAITH volumes are OUT-OF-PRINT, and are considered COLLECTABLES. See also STAR TREK.

K/S fiction (fan/fanzine): Stories written by STAR TREK fans, based on the premise that Captain James T. Kirk and his Vulcan First Officer, Mr. Spock, are sexually involved with each other. The idea first was promoted in a story by LESLIE FISH, printed in *The Obs'zine.* At the same time, Gerry Downes used it as the basis for a novel, *The Alternative,* in 1977. Since then, the premise has been extended to include other MALE BONDING pairs.

The bulk of K/S FICTION is written by women, leading to the assumption that the stories are not written about gay men but about gay women. Some very prominent and vocal leaders of FEMINIST SF have decried this practice, stating that the writers of K/S should come out of their literary closet and be honest about what they are doing. Another school of thought holds that the stories are written about male/female relationships, with one of the characters standing in for the author herself.

K/S FICTION is sold at CONVENTIONS or through mail-orders; an AGE STATEMENT is usually required for purchase. Any story that deals with this kind of situation is called a SLASH STORY (thus, K/S).

L

L-5 Society: A group set up in 1968 to promote space exploration and the establishment of SPACE STATIONS. Named for the five LAGRANGE POINTS, those points around a planet's equator along which a body can be held in equilibrium. The L-5 SOCIETY promoted manned space flight during the 1960s and 1970s; in 1987 it merged with the National Space Society. See also LAGRANGE POINTS.

Lagrange points (astronomy): Five points in space, aligned with a planet's equator, along which a very small body can remain in orbit between two other, larger bodies, such as Earth and its Moon, in complete equilibrium. Named for French mathematician Joseph Louis Lagrange, who formulated the theory in the last years of the 18th century. Once a SPACE STATION is set in one of these points, it would theoretically need no further impetus to remain in orbit; it would be held in place indefinitely by gravity.

The building of SPACE STATIONS along these points was one of the major aims of the L-5 SOCIETY.

Lagrange stations (aerospace): SPACE STATIONS located in Earth (or other planetary) orbits at the LAGRANGE POINTS. The L-5 SOCIETY was active in promoting the possibility of constructing such stations around Earth. Each station would be capable of supporting a large population, in various habitats, each designed for a particular life-style. See also LAGRANGE POINTS; SPACE STATIONS.

LAN (computer): Local Area Network; also called the NET.

laser (physics): Light Amplification by Stimulated Emission of Radiation; a concentrated form of light, invented in 1960 and perfected in the last twenty years. The LASER tube contains a helium-neon mixture or a cylindrical ruby crystal, whose atoms are excited artificially so that the stimulated atoms react to light of a particular wavelength. The result is a very intense heat-producing beam of light.

LASER technology has been used for everything from measuring the precise distance from Earth to the Moon, to slicing cataract tissue from the eyes. LASERS can be set to emit light with no heat; as such, they are occasionally used to simulate weapons in mock warfare. However, as yet no one has built a practical weapon that uses the LASER as the traditional SF DEATH RAY, and most SF people devoutly hope no one will. See also LASER WAR.

laser printing (printing): A very clear form of type, embossed onto the paper by a LASER, rather than being imprinted by pressure, as in ordinary printing processes. Used in XEROGRAPHY, it gives a very polished look to a FANZINE.

laser war (fan/conventions): Also called a "blaster-battle." A mock battle, waged with weapons that project a beam of light rather than an object, conducted through the corridors and up and down the fire stairs of a hotel. LASER WARS were a feature of Conventions during the 1970s; however, world events have made hotel security staffs very anxious about anything that looks like a weapon, and WEAPONS POLICIES at most conventions have limited the opportunities to carry even the most innocuous laser weapon. CONS are now more likely to organize INTERACTIVE GAMES in lieu of LASER WARS.

LASFS (fan): Los Angeles Science Fantasy Society. It claims to be the oldest continuously running SF club, founded in 1934. The group has its own clubhouse, with an extensive SF library and memorabilia collection.

"Last Man on Earth" story (literary): One that describes a person in just this situation; a very popular theme in the 1950s, when there seemed a distinct possibility that this situation might occur. Very much akin to the DOOMSDAY STORY, the LAST MAN ON EARTH often discovered that he might have a female companion, in which case it turned into an ADAM AND EVE STORY.

launch vehicle (aerospace): The rocket that lifts the PAYLOAD into orbit. The LAUNCH VEHICLE, which is usually discarded once the craft is in orbit, is usually a ROCKET; the craft it carries can be a satellite, a capsule, or a SHUTTLE.

launch window (aerospace): The interval of time during which a rocket can lift off to attain a specific orbit or to reach a particular point at a particular time. The LAUNCH WINDOW is carefully calculated by humans; nature, alas, is not consulted, and rockets may miss their LAUNCH WINDOWS because of rain, high winds, or extreme cold. To ignore these phenomena and go ahead with the launch is to invite disaster. It is far better to set another LAUNCH WINDOW, and wait.

Lawful alignment (gaming): The moral and ethical orientation of CHARACTERS in RPGs that assumes that there is logic and order in the Universe, and that logical beings follow certain rules of life to attain their goals. LAWFUL GOOD CHARACTERS are noble souls, kind and generous, altruistic and gentle, in the words of Chaucer, "a verray parfit, gentil knight." LAWFUL EVIL CHARACTERS are capable of distorting the Law for their own ends, like the Sheriff of Nottingham in the Robin Hood legends. LAWFUL NEUTRAL CHARACTERS tend to sit on the fence, waiting for developments; expediency rules them.

layout (comics): The basic page design for comic strips, done in pencil, also called "roughs." LAYOUTS are finished by the

INKER and the COLORIST; the final product is taken to the editor of the comic for approval and printing.

layout (publishing): The arrangement of the text and illustrations of a book or magazine, whether FAN or PRO. The editor of a FANZINE, and the editors and publishers of PROZINES or books, are responsible for the publication's LAYOUT.

Whether FAN or PRO, the LAYOUT of a magazine should present the work of the writers and artists to the best advantage. Pages should be numbered; art should be placed where it can be most effective in illustrating the story.

A neat LAYOUT can add to the attractiveness and legibility of the 'zine; poor LAYOUT leads to a cluttered or messy-looking item that is hard to read and a disservice to the contributors.

"Lay" story (fan/fanzine): A fan-written story in which the main action involves getting the main character (usually Captain Kirk or Mr. Spock of STAR TREK) into a sexual relationship with a female character (often the author in the persona of MARY SUE). LAY STORIES can be effusively romantic or blatantly pornographic. In most FANZINES, the romance overshadows the porn.

Most of the LAY STORIES of the 1970s were printed in the FANZINES *Grup* or *The Obs'zine*. By current standards, these stories were almost innocent. See also K/S FICTION.

leader (film): Length of blank film or videotape attached to a reel, so that it can be threaded into a projector. Universal LEADER has the name and number of the film or tape printed on it.

Lee, Stan (b. 1922) Comic-book writer; head of Marvel Comics, and the driving force behind the production of SUPERHERO comics. Lee's recent comics are known for high artistic values and story lines in which the SUPERHERO is not as superior as the reader supposed.

Lensman (literary): Series of stories by E. E. "Doc" Smith, beginning with *Galactic Patrol* in 1937. The epitome of SPACE OPERA, the LENSMAN series dealt with space battles against impossibly ferocious BEMS and political intrigue on Earth. They are still very much in print.

lettercol (fan/fanzine): Short for "Letter Column," or "Letters to the Editor"; the central means of communication in a FANZINE, where the readers address the contributors and each other, with the editor as intermediary. Most SF FANZINES are largely devoted to communication between fans, through the LETTERCOL, while MEDIAZINES may devote somewhat less space to letters and more to fiction, poetry, and art.

The LETTERCOL is where readers CRITIQUE the stories and express their opinions on the contents of previous issues of the 'zine. There have been bitter feuds fought out on the pages of a LETTERCOL; literary reputations get shredded or bolstered by the opinions expressed by the LETTERHACKS.

The ultimate LETTERCOL is a LETTERZINE or an APA. See also APA; LETTERZINE.

letterer (comics): The person who adds the word balloons to the final artwork in a comic book, complete with dialog, description, and sound effects. This is not as easy as it appears, since the balloons must be carefully placed, and the dialog must be legible—all this without disturbing the flow of the existing artwork. See also CREATIVE TEAM.

letterhack (fan): A FAN who devotes much time and energy (not to mention postage) to writing letters, both private and public. The private ones go to a network of friends and enemies in FANDOM; the public ones go to various publications, FAN and PRO. Computer NETWORKS and BULLETIN BOARDS are replacing some of the private letters shuttled about by LETTERHACKS, but LETTERCOLS and LETTERZINES are fueled by them.

letterwar (fan): An acrimonious exchange of letters between two or more fans in the pages of a FANZINE, through the LETTERCOL. LETTERWARS have raged over everything from the antics of a particular character in a series of stories to the ethics of reprinting stories taken from FANZINES in mass-media publications. A really hot LETTERWAR may run over several issues of a FANZINE or APA, unless the editor of the 'zine takes a strong stand and instructs the combatants to continue their battle privately.

Occasionally other people are drawn into a LETTERWAR, which may blossom into a full-blown FAN FEUD.

letter-writing campaign (fan): A concentrated effort by a group of fans to urge renewal of a TV SERIES, when said SERIES has announced its cancellation.

The first, and most memorable, campaign was organized by the fans of STAR TREK after its first cancellation was announced in 1967. Led by Bjo Trimble on the West Coast, thousands of letters poured into the NBC offices; the result was mass panic at NBC and a public announcement of STAR TREK's renewal. A recurrence in 1968 led to the third season of STAR TREK, but alas, not even another LETTER-WRITING CAMPAIGN could save the show after that.

Similar campaigns have been organized, with varying results. "Battlestar Galactica" returned, but with a disastrously different format. In 1989, "Beauty and the Beast" was canceled; a LETTER-WRITING CAMPAIGN brought it back, but the SERIES was canceled again after 13 more EPISODES had been filmed.

Producers of TV SERIES are well aware of the power of these campaigns. The office of Steve Cannell has sent out flyers urging that this or that series be saved by a LETTER-WRITING CAMPAIGN. However, most such campaigns are generated by the fans, and are a legitimate expression of preference and concern, and as such, they are taken quite seriously by network bigwigs.

letterzine (fan): An amateur publication devoted to the exchange of opinion through letters on a particular subject. SF

LETTERZINES exist side by side with APAS; the difference is that the APA consists of individual newsletters that may or may not address other members of the APA, while the LETTERZINE is published by an editor who selects the letters, prints them, and is responsible for the distribution of the 'zine.

LETTERZINES tend to be smaller than other MEDIAZINES; some of them may include articles of interest to the readers, or advertisements of FANZINES devoted to the subject of the LETTERZINE in question, or urgent pleas to join a LETTER-WRITING CAMPAIGN.

LETTERZINES print the full name and address of each contributor, for further contact and dialog. They serve as a communications link between FANS who may feel strongly about one particular TV SERIES or film. Currently there are LETTERZINES devoted to STAR TREK, BEAUTY AND THE BEAST, "V," and various other themes and films. They are usually advertised in ADZINES; occasionally they are sold at CONVENTIONS.

level (gaming): Any of several variable factors that affect a CHARACTER'S standing in CLASS or ABILITIES. Class LEVEL #1, for instance, is a beginning adventurer; a CHARACTER who survives many CAMPAIGNS and picks up enough EXPERIENCE POINTS can get up to LEVEL #20 and become a Demi-God!

Spell LEVELS are acquired by magic-users, who can only use those spells for which their LEVEL qualifies them. Again, experience counts, and the DUNGEONMASTER determines the score.

Every skill acquired by a CHARACTER can be enhanced by experience, even as in "real life"; the only ceiling is the CHARACTER'S ABILITIES as determined at the beginning of the game. However, those can also be modified; a CHARACTER with low STRENGTH can build up its muscles through a CAMPAIGN and achieve a higher level than was thought possible.

licensed book (comics): A comic that uses titles, concepts, or characters from another source than the original writer or artist's imagination, usually a film or TV SERIES. LICENSED BOOKS are often ADAPTATIONS of films, taken directly from the SHOOTING SCRIPT. They are the comic book equivalent of a NOVELIZATION, and as such, are officially sanctioned by the production company, unlike the privately printed FANZINES, which are not.

Some LICENSED BOOKS may continue the adventures of the film or TV characters. Currently there are two STAR TREK comic book series, one for the "Classic" characters and one for the "Next Generation." STAR WARS also generated a whole new series of comic book adventures for its characters.

licensing (publishing): The legal use of copyrighted characters by major producers of books, comics, posters, and so on. These extensions of the original product can be extremely lucrative, and the original producers are very much aware of the potential revenue a hit film or TV SERIES can bring in through such oddments as T-shirts, toys, lunch boxes, and computer games. The 1989 *Batman* movie brought with it a scourge of unlicensed dealers in T-shirts and toys, who risked fines and possible jail sentences for the money brought in by BOOTLEG merchandise.

FANZINES fall into a gray area that no one really wants to test in the courts. Most MEDIAZINES include the DISCLAIMER that the publication is not meant to abridge the copyright of the original producers, most of whom permit the publication of such materials under a kind of "gentleman's agreement," knowing that the money generated from FANZINES is minimal compared with that of mass publications, and that to deprive the fans of this creative outlet would be to deprive the producers of the support, both creative and financial, of the fans. See also COPYRIGHT; DISCLAIMER; MEDIAZINE.

liftoff (aerospace): The exact instant at which the rocket leaves the ground. Only a rocket can achieve a LIFTOFF; other craft are launched on the rocket, or are carried by the rocket.

LIFTOFF is probably the most dramatic moment in a space flight. There is an awed hush as the countdown is broadcast; then the roar of ignition, and the clouds of smoke billow from the base of the rocket almost obscuring its flight. A night launch is even more thrilling, with the red flames lighting up the sky for miles.

light speed (astronomy): 186,282.347 miles per second (299,792.458 kilometers per second), as estimated by Ole Roemer in 1676, and established by James Clark Maxwell in

1864. The speed of light is the fastest possible, and until technology manages to break it, we are stuck with it. Of course, SF writers will continue to devise elaborate ways of getting around the difficulty, by imagining FTL DRIVE that utilizes ANTIMATTER or an ION ENGINE, but until technology catches up with imagination, as the button states, "186,282.347 mps: It isn't just a good idea, it's the law." See also IMAGINARY SCIENCE.

light-year (astronomy): The distance light travels in one terrestrial year through a vacuum, the equivalent of 5.8786 trillion miles, or 63,240 ASTRONOMICAL UNITS, or 0.3066 PARSECS. LIGHT-YEARS are used to measure the distance between stars, which is some measure of how very distant they are. Until we can find some way of going faster than LIGHT SPEED, it may be assumed that the only way to reach the stars is in a GENERATION SHIP with or without CRYOGENICS.

limited animation (film): A form of animation in which only a few elements of the drawing are changed in each frame, which may be shot against a static background. The result is that fewer drawings are needed to attain animation, fewer frames are actually shot, and the film is cheaper to make. Much of the animation seen in the SATURDAY MORNING GHETTO is LIMITED ANIMATION.

limited edition (publishing): A PRINT RUN of a book or comic with a set number of copies, often numbered or signed by the author, the artist, or both. LIMITED EDITIONS are often distinguished by a special binding, extra illustrations, or some other expensive feature that will make them collectors' items some day.

limited series (comics): A comic book series with a predetermined number of issues. A miniseries has less than six issues; a maxiseries may have as many as twelve. LIMITED SERIES usually have a particular story to tell, in as many issues as it will take to tell it. The original STAR WARS ADAPTATION, for instance, ran four issues, which was all that was necessary for the story.

limited series (literary): A story told through a number of books with a finite ending. A TRILOGY presumably has a beginning, middle, and end book, in which all the loose ends are tied up. See also OPEN-ENDED SERIES.

lime jello (fan): A catch-phrase that derives from an elaborate practical joke played on an SF writer at a CONVENTION. In an unguarded moment, he revealed that he wanted to bathe in LIME JELLO. A gang of FANS decided to fulfill his desire by filling his hotel-room bathtub with it. The prank has grown to mythic proportions, and even people who were not counted in FANDOM at the time claim to have been part of it. LIME JELLO now has unspeakable connotations, and no one dares to serve it at fannish functions.

line (publishing): A group of books united under the supervision of a particular editor, with a central theme or premise. Often they are distinguished by a unity of design, typeface, or cover art, so that they may be instantly recognized by the readers.

The establishment of a new LINE by a publishing house is announced with fanfares; if the editor is well-known, there is often some kind of official celebration as well. A number of SF writers have become editors of particular LINES.

A SERIES may be part of a specific LINE, but a LINE may also include books that do not necessarily contain interrelated characters or story lines.

lining out (fan): A process of writing a story by reciting it to another person, who will contribute comments, criticism, and may even become a COLLABORATOR. According to the standard texts of writing, this is not supposed to be a good idea. However, it seems to work for SF COLLABORATORS, many of whom do their LINING OUT during the long rides to and from CONVENTIONS. See also COLLABORATION.

"Live long and prosper" (TV): Greeting used on STAR TREK by Vulcans, usually accompanied by a hand gesture with the thumb extended, the index and middle fingers together, and the ring and pinkie together (copied from the ancient Hebrew ritual blessing position that in turn is supposed to imitate the Hebrew letter Shin, which stands for the Name of God). First used by D. C. Fontana in a script for the "Classic" STAR TREK, it is now used as a generalized greeting and farewell between STAR TREK fans.

liveware (computer): A person who works with computers, as opposed to the HARDWARE (the mechanism) or the SOFTWARE (the programming). HACKERS are devoted liveware; a WIZARD is total liveware. See also HACKER; WETWARE.

"living out of the box" (fan/conventions): Using the immediate proceeds of sales to pay for one's CONVENTION expenses. The BOX in this case is the cashbox, into which the DEALER places the day's income.

living world (literary): An entire planet viewed as an organism, a concept that is gaining ground among serious biologists. Such planets as the one depicted in Harry Harrison's *Deathworld* trilogy are psychically attuned, so that every living creature, plant or animal, interacts with every other one. The GAIA THEORY, applied to our own Earth, is similar, although the psychic element may not factor into the idea that all living things on a planet are interrelated, and interference in one area will affect them all. See also GAIA THEORY.

LOC (fan/fanzine): Letter Of Comment; a letter to the Editor, meant for publication in either a FANZINE or a PROZINE, that discusses material in a previous issue in detail, often with a CRITIQUE of stories and artwork. Many FANZINES publish LOCS (pronounced either as letters or as the smoked salmon delicacy), with full addresses for further communication between fans.

LOCS are considered mandatory for recipients of FREEBIES, as a kind of payment in kind. It is through the LOCS that the writers and artists can get feedback from the readers, and thus improve their skills.

Occasionally, a LOC will provoke an answer in the next issue's LETTERCOL that will initiate a LETTERWAR or even a FAN FEUD. All this comes under the heading of communications between FANS, which is what FANZINES are all about.

local group (astronomy): A cluster of twenty known GALAXIES, including our own Milky Way. When the vast distances between them are considered, the term LOCAL is somewhat of a misnomer. There are presumably galaxies even further away than the LOCAL GROUP that can only be seen through radio telescopes, or through the newly established Hubbell Space Telescope. See also GALAXY.

***Locus* magazine** (fan): One of the two major SEMI-PROZINES that provides information about the SF profession. LOCUS was begun as a FANZINE by Charlie and Marsha Brown in 1968; it is now typeset, on slick paper, with paid advertising, and is usually available at SPECIALTY SHOPS and bookstores that cater to SF readers. LOCUS contains book reviews and announcements of forthcoming publications, as well as news articles of interest to SF readers, writers, and publishers. For the address, see Appendix A.

logistics (fan/conventions): The committee of a large CONVENTION that handles things, as opposed to people. LOGISTICS sees to it that film projectors, overhead projectors, slide projectors, screens, and blackboards are in the meeting rooms or auditoriums in time for use by the speakers; they also provide such amenities as pitchers of water and ash trays for panelists. The term was taken from the military, and the requirements for something as large as a WORLD-CON can sometimes rival a military operation.

logo (publishing): The symbol, specific typeface, or decoration that distinguishes a particular brand of merchandise from its competitors. In publishing, this can be the Bantam "Rooster," or the Pocket Books "Gertrude the Kangaroo," or the futuristic typeface used for the STAR TREK film titles, or the *Ghostbusters* Ghost in a circle with a line across its front. LOGOS are counted as trademarks, and are copyrighted; imitation of a LOGO may count as fraud, punishable by fine or imprisonment.

Lost Colony (literary): A Human settlement on a faraway planet whose existence has been forgotten by the very ones who sent them out in the first place! Often the settlers were the victims of a crash, or a navigation error, that sent them off into a hitherto uncharted region of Space. With no way to contact Earth, the settlers are forced to deal with their new home and its biota, often with startling results. When a LOST COLONY is rediscovered by Earthly travelers, a real CULTURE-CLASH may ensue that can run over several stories, and may, in time, produce a full-blown SERIES. See also DARKOVER; PERN; SPACE COLONIES.

Lost World story (literary): A tale of adventure dealing with the discovery of a group of people in a strange place on Earth who have never been contacted by Europeans before. A popular form of early SF in the Victorian era, when the possibility of such a discovery was very real, and occasionally, someone like Hiram Bingham would actually come across a place like Macchu Picchu in Peru. The term was the title of a story by Conan Doyle, first published in 1912, but the genre was around long before that. *Gulliver's Travels*, by Jonathan Swift, for instance, was a satire on such stories, as well as a biting commentary on the politics of 18th-century England. ATLANTIS was postulated as a prime site for LOST WORLD STORIES; others might be found deep in the jungles of South America or high in the Himalayas, as in Hilton's *Lost Horizon*.

Once the Earth was thoroughly explored, the LOST WORLD STORY tended to disappear; the emphasis now is on the strange civilizations that might lie far away from Earth, on some distant planet.

Lovecraft, H. P. (1890–1937): Writer of horror tales. LOVECRAFT's stories often deal with the nightmarish dreams that overwhelm ordinary people. LOVECRAFT began the CTHULHU MYTHOS, which deals with the emergence of ancient forces that once ruled the Earth and now wish to reclaim their heritage.

LOVECRAFT not only created the CTHULHU MYTHOS but he encouraged others to write CTHULHU stories, thus creating the first OPEN UNIVERSE.

Lucas, George (b. 1944): Filmmaker, producer, and director, creator of STAR WARS; collaborator with STEVEN SPIELBERG on the *Indiana Jones* films and JIM HENSON on *Labyrinth* and *The Dark Crystal*. LUCAS revolutionized and revitalized SF film by synthesizing many elements into the STAR WARS Trilogy: the derring-do of the SERIALS of the 1930s, the authenticity of backgrounds of the 1960s, and the mythology of the 1970s. LUCAS has made other films, most notably *American Graffiti*, but the bulk of his influence is felt in the areas of SF film and Special Effects.

Luddite (literary): Someone who is vociferously ANTITECH, ascribing to technology all social evils from poverty to pollution. The term comes from the mobs who tried to stop the Industrial Revolution by wrecking the machinery in the new "manufactories" in the early 1800s. A number of SF novels depict worlds in which technology of any but the simplest kind is highly suspect. See also ANTITECH; HIGH-TECH.

LunaCon (fan/conventions): Vies with PHILCON for the honor of being the largest and most important FAN-CON on the East Coast of the United States. It is run by the Lunarians SF Club every year in March, to coincide with the spring editions of SF books, in the New York City area. LUNACON attracts most of the major editors, writers, and artists in the tristate area of New York, New Jersey, and Connecticut, as well as FANS from all over the country.

lunar base (aerospace): A permanent settlement on the MOON; as yet, still in the planning stages, but supposedly a goal for the U.S. space program in the 1990s.

A LUNAR BASE would involve more than just the buildings. There would have to be provision for atmosphere, food, and living amenities; personnel would include medical, technical, and service staff. A LUNAR BASE might be totally devoted to scientific research, or it might include mining operations.

made-for-TV movie (film): A film whose first showing is on television, instead of in movie theaters. Until the last five years, this was usually a PILOT for a possible TV SERIES, or else what would have been called a B-MOVIE in the 1930s and 1940s. With increased production costs, film producers tend to shy away from a story that doesn't promise immediate dividends; at the same time, CABLE networks are financing entertaining films with bankable (if not major) actors. The result is that many films are now shown on the small screen first.

SF films rarely show up in this form. SFX cost a good deal, and a theatrical showing is necessary to recoup the expense immediately. A few PILOTS for TV SERIES that never quite made it have been shown as MADE-FOR-TV MOVIES; *Something Is Out There* (1988) was a moderately successful PILOT that lasted six EPISODES as a SERIES. A reversal of the trend was the 2-hour PILOT of *Buck Rogers in the 25th Century*, which was shown first in movie theaters and then on television in 1979.

***Mad* magazine:** Leading humor magazine in the United States begun by William Gaines in 1959 as a satire on comic books. Since then MAD has become a purveyor of satire of the American scene for two generations of youngsters. Targets of MAD's "usual gang of idiots" include corruption in government, pollution of the atmosphere, destruction of moral values, and hassles of everyday life; even more telling are parodies of popular TV SERIES and films. A MAD takeoff means that the series or film must be a hit; otherwise, no one would recognize what is being parodied. Copies of MAD with parodies of STAR TREK or STAR WARS are now COLLECTABLES.

Mad Max (film): Character played by Mel Gibson in three films, all directed by George Miller (*Mad Max*, 1979; *Mad Max: The Road Warrior*, 1981; *Mad Max: Beyond Thunderdome*, 1985); he zooms through the POST-HOLOCAUST wastelands of Australia dispensing a kind of Justice and rescuing children from the evils left to them by their parents. The films are violent to the point of parody, using machines as metaphors of our sick society; only the children's colony remains as a last ray of hope in this blighted world. Max himself begins as a policeman trying to maintain order, and becomes the ARCHETYPE of the Knight Errant, who comes along, does his Good Deed for the Day, and leaves on another Quest.

Mad Scientist (literary/film): The STOCK CHARACTER found in comics, films, and early SF, who is not so much psychotic as obsessed. MAD SCIENTISTS in films have tried to reclaim lost loved ones through blood transfusions, or with inoculations of strange hormones that will retain the appearance of youth. Other MAD SCIENTISTS are really inventors, who have come up with DEATH RAYS or similar weapons with which to bludgeon their governments into financing yet more experiments. As played by Boris Karloff or Bela Lugosi or Claude Raines, these characters sent shivers of fear through their audiences.

The archetypal MAD SCIENTIST in literature is Dr. Victor Frankenstein, of Mary Shelley's novel; Wells' Dr. Moreau (*The Island of Dr. Moreau*, 1898) is another. In actual fact, today's scientific researchers are discovering new data about the world that would make most of the MAD SCIENTISTS in film and literature slaver with pleasure, and concepts that at one time were relegated to the pages of PULP FICTION are now part of the daily newspaper.

The MAD SCIENTIST was constantly being warned that "there

are some things that man was not meant to know." This attitude still exists, but better communications and an expanded awareness of humanity and its place in the Cosmos have made the MAD SCIENTIST a figure of parody instead of fear.

magnetic field (physics): Lines of force that surround a planet from north to south, as if the planet was a gigantic magnet. Examination of the planets in our own solar system has shown that all solid bodies have these magnetic properties. The MAGNETIC FIELD leaves traces in the atomic structure of the rocks; with the help of electron microscopes, geologists have been able to plot shifts in Earth's MAGNETIC FIELD over the ages.

magnetic storm (aerospace): A sudden and violent disturbance in a planet's MAGNETIC FIELD, possibly triggered by activity in the sun. A MAGNETIC STORM may appear suddenly, then die down gradually. Unlike an ION STORM, a MAGNETIC STORM is an established phenomenon, observed by astronomers and feared by space travelers as a very real threat. SF writers use MAGNETIC STORMS as a good excuse for space travelers' heroics.

mail auction (fan): A way of SELLING OUT a collection, when the FAN has to weed out items that are no longer wanted or necessary, or when it is time to GAFIATE. A notice is inserted into one or more ADZINES, or a FLYER may be mailed out to people who are known to be collectors, listing the items and their minimum bids. The bidders send back their offers by return mail, and the seller compares prices. This may go on for three rounds, after which each bidder is notified as to what they won, and how much they have to pay for it.

MAIL AUCTIONS are complicated to organize, and the bidders are at the mercy of the POST AWFUL when it comes to delivery of merchandise. A MAIL AUCTION is resorted to only when it is impossible to get to a CONVENTION to sell the collection, or when the collection is so vast as to make it impractical to do so. See also AUCTIONS.

mainframe (computer): The largest kind of computer that controls several other computers, which in turn may control still more computers. The MAINFRAME sits in its own air-conditioned room, attended to like the Queen in a colony of social insects.

SF writers of the 1940s and early 1950s usually had this kind of computer in mind when they wrote tales in which a computer takes over all governmental or business functions and develops a mind of its own.

main-sequence stars (astronomy): Stars whose size, color, and brightness correspond to the diagonal band on the HERTZSPRUNG-RUSSELL DIAGRAM. Most stars fall easily into some area of this diagram, which runs from white giants to RED DWARFS. The stars most likely to have planets capable of supporting life are DWARFS, like our own sun, which are neither too hot nor too cold.

mainstream (publishing): Fiction that does not fall into any particular GENRE, written by someone of literary stature with serious intentions. Popular fiction tends to follow trends and readers tend to enjoy particular types of stories, which are then written for them to read . . . a particularly vicious circle in some cases. Occasionally a MAINSTREAM author decides to break out of the mold and try to set a story in a possible future. John Hersey's *White Lotus* (1965), set in an ALTERNATE UNIVERSE in which China has conquered the United States, is one example. Even more occasionally, a writer known for SF will expand into MAINSTREAM territory, as in the case of Marion Zimmer Bradley's novel of love and death in the circus, *The Catch Trap* (1979).

makeup (costuming): The use of cosmetics, paint, and APPLIANCES to change a person's appearance, to portray a particular character onstage. MAKEUP is part of COSTUMING, and a PRESENTATION COSTUME has to have a suitable MAKEUP to be complete. Theatrical MAKEUP is now sold in most major cities, and there are many books that explain how to use it. A poor MAKEUP can ruin the effect of a costume as much as bad CONSTRUCTION or inept ACCESSORIES.

makeup (printing): The exact way the magazine or book is going to be printed; the full LAYOUT, the typeface, the color of the ink. The printer has to have all this information, whether the material is a 4-page NEWSLETTER or a 500-page HARDCOVER book.

malfunction (aerospace): Sometimes abbreviated to "malf"; anything that goes wrong with a particular mission, from a minor computer GLITCH to a major catastrophe like the *Challenger* explosion. Most MALFUNCTIONS are easily cleared up; some take considerably longer to rectify.

male bonding (biology): The uniting of males into a cooperative force for hunting purposes, disregarding or lowering their natural aggressive tendencies. This phenomenon is seen most clearly in pack animals like wolves who live in packs dominated by one male or female, called the ALPHA-MALE (or ALPHA-FEMALE). The ALPHA-MALE directs the activities of the hunting pack through vocal signals and body language; the lesser males and females will follow the leader.

In human society, MALE BONDING appears to have surfaced early as a mechanism for mutual cooperation in the hunt. Males had to undergo certain mystical rites that literally separated the men from the boys before they were permitted to join in "manly" activities (from which females were excluded). Over the centuries the human male has arranged his society in various ways so as to limit the aggressive tendencies that impede cooperation between males.

MALE BONDING in contemporary American society is best depicted in "Buddy" movies, where two men discover their friendship in spite of their outward differences. The relationship between bonded males is not primarily sexual, although there has been some discussion of a latent homosexual aspect to it. A few females do not understand this; the result is the K/S or SLASH STORY, in which the male-bonded pair do consummate a physical relationship.

MALE BONDING plays an important role in human culture and any story of life in a closed environment usually takes it into account. The Hero of a SPACE OPERA usually has his SIDEKICK; C. L. Moore's Northwest Smith had Yarol the Venusian to rescue him from such creatures as "Shambleau."

The real threat to a male-bonded pair is a woman. Often, the obligatory female turns up, only to leave the two boys to each other's company as she sails off into the sunset (or is conveniently killed by the villain).

Some SF writers have tried to reverse MALE BONDING to apply to women. The result is the WOMAN WARRIOR, whose aggressive posturing seems a little forced.

mando paper (comics): A fine white paper, used in some comics for more expensive editions; because it takes the ink better, the colors look brighter.

manuscript (publishing): The original story, as presented to a PUBLISHER by an author. The MANUSCRIPT should be in the standard FORMAT: typed on one side of white paper, double-spaced, with one-inch margins on all sides of the page. A MANUSCRIPT is the first step in the long process toward eventual publication.

marketing (publishing): The advertising, promotion, and selling of books, comics, films, and so forth, whether SF or anything else. MARKETING includes all means of bringing the item to the attention of the buying public, through advertisements in magazines and newspapers, announcements on TV or radio, or distribution of promotional aids like POSTERS and BUTTONS.

Mars (astronomy): Fourth planet away from the sun in our Solar System; smaller than Earth, and much colder, but seen as the most logical place for life as we know it to develop away from Earth. MARS has been explored by unmanned spacecraft through the Viking landing in 1976, which was hailed as a milestone in space exploration.

In SF, MARS has intrigued writers, either as a launching point for a possible invasion of Earth, as in H. G. Wells' *War of the Worlds* (1898), or as a possible place of origin of strange and wonderful lifeforms, as in Edgar Rice Burroughs' tales of BARSOOM. Ray Bradbury set a series of stories on MARS, collected as *The Martian Chronicles* (1950). MARS has been depicted as a roaring frontier colony, as the seat of GALACTIC EMPIRE, and as a dead or dying world.

In 1990, plans for a manned mission to MARS were announced; whether this will happen in the immediate future is a matter for some debate.

Martians (literary): Hypothetical inhabitants of MARS. So far, despite the best efforts of the CHICKEN SOUP and WOLF TRAP experiments, no evidence exists that there are any. However, there may have been some form of life on MARS in the past; there is certainly evidence of both oxygen and free water, both of which are necessary for life as we know it on Earth to exist.

MARTIANS in literature and on film abound, whether they exist in reality or not. Edgar Rice Burroughs populated MARS (or BARSOOM) with four-armed giants and red reptiles, both extremely intelligent. MARTIANS have been depicted as shriveled and dessicated creatures, and as tall, delicate, beautiful beings of great power. FLASH GORDON found Clay Men in a 1930s SERIAL; the TV series "My Favorite Martian" (1963–1966) starred Ray Walston as a misplaced MARTIAN with several psychic powers.

"Mary Sue" story (fan/fanzine): A story in a FANZINE that deals with the adventures of a perfect heroine, who is obviously the author as she would like to be (almost all such stories are written by women). The term derives from a story submitted to the FANZINE *Menagerie.* The editor, Paula Smith, could not in good conscience print the story, but proceeded to write and print a parody, using the name MARY SUE for the heroine.

MARY SUE is the youngest, smartest, most beautiful ensign on board the USS *Enterprise.* She outwits Klingons, seduces Mr. Spock, reinvents the Warp Drive, ad infinitum, ad nauseum. In short, MARY SUE has become the symbol of the perfect heroine, and when she appears in professional fiction, editors recognize her and insist that she be given a few flaws to make her more human, whether she is or not. (There have been a few Vulcan MARY SUE characters, too.) MARY SUE has a male counterpart, "Marty Su," who is just as obnoxious.

Masquerade (fan/conventions): Also known as a Costume Call; an organized presentation of costumes made and worn by nonprofessional COSTUMERS, for JUDGING by a panel of experts.

The MASQUERADE is a high point of most FAN-CONS and especially the WORLD-CON. It is usually held in the largest room available, on Saturday or Sunday evening (depending on how long the CON is running). Organizing the MASQUERADE involves rehearsing with a tech crew, who may (or may not) have theatrical lights and electrical tape recorders at their disposal; arranging the order of presentations, so that one costume does not negate the impact of another; and providing amenities for the contestants. Photographers must be accommodated as well, since many of the costumers want their creations to be recorded for posterity.

The WORLD-CON MASQUERADE began as a simple parade of people in costume. The competitive element soon entered into the event, with prizes being handed out for "Most Beautiful" or "Most Humorous." By 1969, the musical element had been added, with the introduction of the audio cassette. The costume presentation had become a one-minute minidrama.

The MASQUERADE grew in size and intensity until 1981, when the DIVISION SYSTEM of Peggy Kennedy was adopted; this gave some leeway to the judges, who could form an opinion of a costume based not only on its effectiveness onstage but on the expertise of the maker. In 1983, at the Baltimore WORLD-CON, the MASQUERADE ran nearly four hours, with over 100 entries. Obviously, something had to be done to limit the proliferation of costumes.

In recent years, WORLD-CON MASQUERADES have been more strictly regulated. Costumes must be registered well in advance of the CON, so that there are no last-minute entries that have been thrown together at a moment's notice. There is no use of the microphone by the contestants; all explanatory material must be taped in advance, or read by the emcee. There is usually a technical rehearsal before the actual event, to check light and music cues; this does not always ensure that the production will go smoothly, but at least an attempt has been made.

Local and Regional CONS are not so regimented. Last-minute

entries are the norm, and while the microphone may not be open to the contestants, the audience is much smaller and closer, so that remarks from the stage will be heard, at least in the front rows.

The pressures of mounting a WORLD-CON MASQUERADE are similar to those of a professional producer mounting a one-night benefit. There are even "stars" who will insist on special treatment. A WORLD-CON MASQUERADE shows fandom at its most flamboyantly creative.

mass-market paperback (publishing): A book meant for the widest possible distribution, printed on inexpensive paper, with a paper cover. MASS-MARKET PAPERBACKS are the small-size books that fit into racks so that they can be sold not only in bookstores but on newsstands, in candy stores, in variety stores, in airports, in supermarkets . . . anywhere, in short, where books and magazines are sold.

The history of MASS-MARKET PAPERBACKS is one of the great success stories of the publishing world. Paperback fiction was available by the middle of the 19th century, but most of it was considered trash. In the 1930s, Pocket Books changed that image by introducing well-made inexpensive reprints of successful books, both fiction and nonfiction. During World War II, such books were provided for servicemen overseas, who might not be able to carry larger, HARDCOVER books with them. After the war, paperbacks became even more popular, especially with young readers, who could not afford the HARDCOVER editions.

SF was an especially fertile field for original paperback novels. Ian Ballantine pioneered in publishing SF in original paperback editions; under his leadership, authors like HEINLEIN, ASIMOV, and BRADBURY were able to reach larger audiences than ever before, triggering the demand for their works in the more prestigious HARDCOVER editions. Donald A. Wollheim followed Ballantine into the paperback market. In the wake of their success, other publishers began to issue original SF novels in paperback format, while continuing the tradition of reprinting HARDCOVER editions.

In the 1980s and 1990s, MASS-MARKET PAPERBACK is the major

FORMAT for most SF. There are only a few magazines that publish SF on a regular basis, and some of the major publishing houses are canceling their SF LINES in HARDCOVER entirely, preferring to publish what SF they can in MASS-MARKET or TRADE PAPERBACK format. Occasionally, the novel that originally appeared in paperback will be reprinted in a special hardcover edition by the SCIENCE FICTION BOOK CLUB. The wheel has definitely turned!

master (fan/costuming): The highest level of proficiency in COSTUMING. A MASTER Costumer has won at least three "Firsts" or "Bests" at Regional or WORLD-CON MASQUERADES. Many MASTERS have had experience in theatrical costuming or as professional dressmakers. MASTER costumes tend to be impressive affairs loaded down with sequins, feathers, detailed embroidery, and authentic historical design.

For those costumers who have never quite made it to the WORLD-CON, but whose expertise matches those who have, there is a midway point in Regional costume competition: CRAFTSMAN.

The term comes from the days of the Medieval Guilds, when a MASTER craftsman was an expert at what he was doing, a leader of the Guild, and a person fit to instruct apprentices in the secrets of the craft. For a MASTER costumer, the career apex comes when one is asked to be a JUDGE. See also DIVISION SYSTEM; MASQUERADE.

matte (film): A covering that prevents light from reaching the camera lens. A MATTE may be made of painted glass or mere paper. It may be a traveling MATTE, which seems to move from shot to shot. A good MATTE will blend into the image so completely that its presence will be unnoticed; otherwise, there will be a distinct line where the MATTE and the previous image do not quite join.

matte painting (film): The painted background, often combined with live action, that depicts a vast world in a very small space. If the budget does not permit filming in a desert or a palace or a vast cavern, the MATTE will do the job just as well (or possibly better).

matting (art): Mounting or framing a small piece of artwork in a prepared cardboard frame. Most ART SHOWS specify that each piece must be MATTED or framed before hanging. Art supply stores provide inexpensive standard-sized MATTING, but some artists still prefer to do their own. A well-made MATTE can add to the painting's overall effect, just as the right frame can enhance or detract from it.

"May the Force be with you" (film): Phrase intoned with great meaning in the STAR WARS films of GEORGE LUCAS. In the movie it is used as an all-purpose benediction, often as a heartfelt farewell. "The Force" is the mysterious mystical power that binds the Universe together, at least according to Obi-Wan Kenobi (played with solemnity by Alec Guinness). It is now used as a catchphrase of mock-solemn farewell to someone about to embark on some difficult, dangerous, or downright foolhardy task.

McGuffin (also spelled Maguffin, MacGuffin) (film/literary): The object of the search or the point of the Quest, or whatever it is that sets the PLOT in motion. The term was supposedly invented by master filmmaker Alfred Hitchcock, who used it to describe the Secret Plans, the Mysterious Message, or whatever else everyone in the film was looking for. The MCGUFFIN may be the Ring of Power, or the Holy Grail, or the plans for the Death Star. Whatever it is, everyone in the story wants to get their hands on it, which is the motivating factor of the PLOT. A trivial MCGUFFIN makes the whole effort pointless . . . unless, of course, the point is that there is no point, as in Dashiell Hammett's *The Maltese Falcon.*

media (fan): Refers to anything that originated as film, radio, or TV material, instead of beginning life on the printed page. MEDIA can be a general area of reference or a dirty word, depending on who is using it, and how. See also MEDIA-CON; MEDIA-FAN; MEDIAZINE; MIXED MEDIAZINE.

media-con (fan/convention): A gathering of MEDIA-FANS for the purpose of communication, trading stories, and just plain fun. MEDIA-CONS are broader in scope than FAN-CONS, since they often include elements that are not strictly SF: detectives, spies, Westerns, and general action/adventure film or TV SERIES activities.

MEDIA-CONS began with STAR TREK. The TREKKERS found themselves ostracized from many of the existing CONS, where they were stigmatized as FRINGE FEN. In retaliation, groups of STAR TREK fans organized their own CONS.

By 1980, the MEDIA-CON scene had been complicated by STAR WARS and various other factors. Many of the original actors in the Classic STAR TREK series were now involved in other projects. The scope of MEDIA FANDOM was expanding, and so was the going rate for speakers. The only ones who could afford to pay the hotel and speakers' fees were large organizations who could amortize the cost across several CONS. If one lost money, hopefully the next one would pick up the slack.

In the last ten years, MEDIA-CONS have tried to combine the chummy, friendly atmosphere of a FAN-CON with the glamour of a PRO-CON. Some groups have extended themselves too far financially; others have decided to emphasize FAN-AC and do not depend on a major figure from a TV series or film to attract members.

There are several long-running MEDIA-CONS still going strong. CONS like Shore Leave in Maryland, or KC-Con in Missouri, will attract MEDIA-FANS from all over the country. Probably the largest of the MEDIA-CONS is Media-West Con, held in Michigan and focusing almost entirely on FAN-FIC, FANZINES, and MIXED MEDIA. See Appendix A for addresses.

media fan (fan): One who is more interested in SF as presented in films and TV than in reading SF books. MEDIA FANS were once scorned as illiterates who could not read even if they wanted to; they were treated rudely at SF conventions, and in retaliation, they retreated to their own enclaves, running separate CONS. The situation has changed in the last five years. MEDIA FANS, once considered FRINGE FANS, are now gaining on READERS, and MEDIA SF is acceptable in all but the most rarified SF circles.

MEDIA FANS are the chief perpetrators of MEDIAZINES, and the attendees of MEDIA-CONS.

mediazine (fan/fanzine): A FANZINE that is largely devoted to fiction based on characters developed in TV SERIES and in films. MEDIAZINES started with STAR TREK. The first was *Spockanalia,* edited by Devra Langsam, first published in 1966, and kept continuously in print since then. Other FANZINES shortly followed, all devoted to STAR TREK and its UNIVERSE. When the original series was canceled, fans wrote their own stories, collected them, and sold them to each other, to pay for the cost of printing multiple copies. The MEDIAZINES started to proliferate in the 1970s, when there was no other outlet for STAR TREK fans to exercise their creative talents.

With the emergence of STAR WARS in 1977, a new element entered the MEDIAZINE field. FANS now had a brand-new UNIVERSE to play with. After that, there seemed to be no limit to the extent to which MEDIA-FANS would go. By the end of the 1980s, the field had extended to Westerns (*Ghost Riders*), the military (*Leapin' Jeeps*), and detectives (*Cops and Robbers and Spies, Oh My!*). A recent copy of the ADZINE *Datazine* listed 24 different UNIVERSES represented by MEDIAZINES . . . and that doesn't include the MIXED MEDIA- or GENZINES.

MEDIAZINES differ from the traditional SF FANZINES in several respects. SF FANZINES were used mainly for communication; the publication was given over to the LETTERCOL, to critical reviews of SF books and films, and to discussions of scientific matters of interest to SF readers. Original fiction was rarely featured, on the theory that if a professional publisher didn't want to pay for the piece, it was probably not worth reading anyway. MEDIAZINES may contain reviews or critical commentary, but most of the publications are devoted to FAN-FIC.

Since most of the material used as the basis for fiction in MEDIAZINES is under copyright, it cannot be sold in the mass market, although the quality may be as high as anything in professionally published books. MEDIAZINES are illustrated by talented artists, and printed by the best method the editor can afford. MEDIAZINES tend to be much larger than SF FANZINES;

they therefore cost more to print and the cost is passed on to the buyer.

MEDIAZINES are tolerated by the producers of TV SERIES and films as long as they are kept within certain bounds. They may not compete with the professional product, which means no more than a thousand of any one item may be produced. They may not be sold in bookstores, or in any other mass market, nor may they be advertised nationally. Each copy should contain a DISCLAIMER announcing it is an amateur publication. Aside from that, the content of the MEDIAZINE is up to the taste and discretion of the editor/publisher. A few people new to the world of FANDOM have protested when their characters have been used in MEDIAZINES, but they are quickly told the facts of SF life by more experienced players. A FANZINE means that your SERIES or film has generated enough excitement for fans to use it as a springboard for further creativity. The spate of MEDIAZINES devoted to BEAUTY AND THE BEAST is a tribute to that SERIES' popularity.

The best place to buy MEDIAZINES is at an SF or MEDIA-CON. There are also ADZINES that announce what FANZINES are available for sale, which are about to be printed, and which ones are looking for contributions.

MEDIAZINES have served as the training ground for several SF writers who have since GRADUATED to become major figures in the SF world. Most prominent is Jacqueline Lichtenberg, whose SIME/GEN novels have generated FANZINES of their own.

MEDIAZINES have generated a jargon of their own. See also FAN-FIC; HURT/COMFORT STORY; K/S; MARY SUE STORY; MISSING SCENE STORY.

melee (gaming): A disorganized free-for-all fight in a DUNGEONS AND DRAGONS™ adventure, in which all the CHARACTERS employ direct contact with swords, spears, fists, clubs, or any other weapons permitted by the DUNGEONMASTER. No missiles or spells are allowed, however, and the results of the combat are determined by the DM after a given period of time. There are often ferocious arguments after a MELEE that equal the violence of the imagined combat.

Méliès, Georges (1861–1938): Pronounced MAY-lee-ays; French showman and film pioneer, who created the first SF films in France at the turn of the century. *A Trip to the Moon* (1902) now looks unbelievably quaint, with its cancan girls and bearded professorial astronauts, but Méliès used painted backdrops, speeded-up cameras, split-screen techniques, and stop-action animation to produce SFX that would not be developed in the United States for another 20 years. Méliès spent his money as fast as he earned it and ended his days running a candy stand in the Paris Metro; his influence lasted longer than his affluence.

mercenaries (literary): Soldiers for hire, common through the ages; they are STOCK CHARACTERS in SF and Fantasy stories. MERCENARIES are usually depicted as hard-bitten fighting men (and women) who conceal their true nobility under a veneer of cynicism. Occasionally a MERCENARY becomes too successful, and winds up as a Warlord; then the local peasants hire more MERCENARIES to depose him.

Han Solo is the archetypal SF SPACE OPERA MERCENARY. At the beginning of the STAR WARS saga his aim is to get as much money as he can; by the end of the third film (*Return of the Jedi*) he has become a general in the Rebel Alliance. He eventually marries the Princess and presumably lives Happily Ever After.

MERCENARIES also figure in DUNGEONS AND DRAGONS.™ They can be hired by PLAYER CHARACTERS as Henchmen, to assist in a campaign, at the DUNGEONMASTER's whim.

merchandising (publishing): The selling and promotion of SF books, films, and so forth. See also MARKETING.

Mercury (astronomy): Nearest planet to the sun in our Solar System; as far as we know, it is a blasted rocky body, baked by the sun's radiation to the melting point of lead. Most astronomers and SF writers agree that it is a very unlikely place for life to develop.

Mercury Program (aerospace): The first U.S. manned space effort. Alan Shepherd flew the first manned U.S. mission in May

1961, followed by John Glenn's more spectacular flight a few months later. The MERCURY PROGRAM was a gamble, spurred by the Russian efforts that had launched Sputnik in 1957 and put a man in orbit in 1961. The fierce battles over such matters as whether to put a window into the capsule and the necessity to provide sanitary facilities in space suits have been depicted in the film *The Right Stuff* (1983) and the TV MINISERIES *Space* (1985).

The achievements of the MERCURY PROGRAM were as much psychological as technological. The United States was fighting the Cold War, and the MERCURY PROGRAM was as much a part of it as the Cuban Missile Crisis was.

Once it was shown that people could survive in Space, given the right equipment and the "right stuff," the U.S. space program went on to the GEMINI and APOLLO missions, culminating in the landing on the Moon in 1969.

"mess transit" (fan): A wry comment on Mass Transit, that dying form of transportation used by many fans to get to CONVENTIONS (or anywhere else). Many CONS have been forced into the suburbs, where hotel space is cheaper, but public transportation is minimal. Those who cannot drive, or do not drive, are left to the mercy of whatever bus or train is nearest. A major factor in the location of a CLUB meeting or CONVENTION is the proximity to MESS TRANSIT.

meteor (astronomy): The streak of light produced by a solid particle when it enters Earth's atmosphere. The friction of the molecules in the air produces heat, which in turn produces the light we see in the night sky. The object itself is called a METEOROID or METEORITE.

There are several periods during the solar year when METEORS can be seen in concentrated showers; most easily seen in the Northern Hemisphere are the Perseids, which appear in late July and early August.

meteorite (astronomy): The solid object that we see as a streak of light in the night sky as it falls to Earth. METEORITES have collided with Earth since it first coalesced from whirling gasses some 8 billion years ago; METEORITE craters have been found on other bodies in our Solar System as well. Earth's Moon is scarred with them, so greatly that they can be seen by the unaided eye as the "Man in the Moon."

METEORITES themselves range from tiny pinhead-sized particles to huge boulders that cause vast destruction when they eventually land. It is theorized that one such collision some 63 million years ago may have sent such a shower of dust into the atmosphere as to cause a NUCLEAR WINTER effect that killed off large numbers of animal species including, possibly, the dinosaurs.

Examination of METEORITES has given chemists clues as to the composition of matter outside Earth's atmosphere, and has led to the conclusion that the universe is made up of the same elements as those found on Earth. METEORITES often consist of iron and silicon; it has been surmised that METEORITES were one of the first sources of iron for weapons and tools.

METEORITES are on display in natural history museums and planetariums across the world. One of the largest is a prize exhibit at the American Museum of Natural History's Hayden Planetarium in New York City.

Metropolis (film): Silent film made by Fritz Lang in 1925; one of the first films that tried to depict what a future city would be like. Lang used the Expressionist film techniques of tilted cameras and subdued lighting to tell his story of a future city, run by an aristocratic elite, who suppress the workers, only to find that the workers will eventually revolt against their oppressors. The simplistic but powerful message is played out against the romance between the son of the leader of the elite group and the beautiful leader of the workers.

METROPOLIS has been revived and transferred to videotape with the original score. It is one of the films most often shown at SF CONS. It is the classic and archetypal SF film, using almost all the elements of SF except space travel.

midlist seller (publishing): A book that, when published, was not a runaway best-seller but maintained a respectable and steady rate of sales. Many SF writers and their works fall into this category. While not producing blockbuster status or income, they go on to become staples of a publisher's BACKLIST.

midseason replacement (TV): A SERIES whose first EPISODES are shown after the SEASON has officially begun, usually to take the place of a SERIES that has failed to gain sufficient RATINGS. A few SF SERIES have begun their runs as MIDSEASON REPLACEMENTS. However, it is more likely that the SERIES will be yanked from the schedule in January, and replaced with something else.

mimeozine (fan/fanzine): A FANZINE that is printed on a mimeograph machine. During the 1950s and 1960s, MIMEOZINES were the most common form of FANZINE. The printing process involved typing the text of the 'zine on a wax stencil, then using a printing press to produce copies. The mimeograph process is messy and cumbersome, and in the case of a hand-powered machine, physically exhausting. The paper must be porous to absorb the ink, but this coarse paper tends to become brittle with age. The proliferation of PHOTO-OFFSET franchise stores and the refinements of XEROGRAPHY have led to the abandonment of mimeo as a printing medium for fanzines. Only a very few editors continue to use their old machines.

mind-blind (literary): The sorry state of a nontelepath adrift in a telepathic society. First created as "head-blind" by Marion Zimmer Bradley, and used in her DARKOVER stories as a derogatory description of Terrans by the psychic Darkovans. MIND-BLIND was more euphonic, and has been used by other writers dealing with the same situation.

minder (fan/convention): The person assigned to accompany the GOH around the CONVENTION. The MINDER's main mission is to see that the GOH gets to PANELS, banquets, and so forth on time and in a coherent state. This is not always as easy as it sounds. Many GOH are convivial sorts, who may become engrossed in conversation with FANS or colleagues and lose all track of time. Some MINDERS are so starstruck that they hesitate to tell their charges that people are waiting for them elsewhere, and they have to move! Being a MINDER is a prestigious but delicate chore for a GOFER.

minimum bid (fan/art): The least possible amount that the artist will consider taking for a PIECE in a CONVENTION ART SHOW. Every BID SHEET indicates the MINIMUM BID. Anyone who wants to own the PIECE must write his or her bid on the sheet. Most CONS insist on at least three written bids before the PIECE goes to VOICE AUCTION.

The establishing of a MINIMUM BID is a delicate matter. If the minimum is too low, someone may get a real bargain. If, on the other hand, it is too high, no one may want to bid on it at all. Some artists indicate a QUICK SALE PRICE, which approximates the amount they think the PIECE will sell for at AUCTION. A determined buyer may gain the PIECE by paying this QUICK SALE PRICE, instead of waiting for the AUCTION.

If the buyers do not care to meet the minimum on the BID SHEET, there is still hope for the artist. Some CONS will permit potential buyers to wander about the ART SHOW after the AUCTION, plucking things directly off the wall panels, to be sold at MINIMUM BID.

ART SHOW rules vary from CONVENTION to CONVENTION. Each CON sets everything down clearly in the PROGRAM BOOK and informs the artists of their rules in PROGRESS REPORTS. See also VOICE AUCTION.

miniseries (TV): A dramatic presentation that runs over two or more broadcasting periods. Many MINISERIES are dramatizations of epic novels, or re-creations of major historical events. The form began with *Roots* in 1976, which showed the history of a black family from the 18th century to the Civil War years.

SF has not fared well in this format. The 1980 dramatization of RAY BRADBURY'S *The Martian Chronicles* was considered too cerebral by most American viewers. On the other hand, *V* (1983) and its sequel *V—The Final Battle* (1984) were so popular that the story was expanded into a full-scale SERIES, which fizzled out in 1986 after one season's worth of EPISODES. *Space* (1985), drawn from James Michener's novel, was criticized for its depiction of the astronauts as raunchy fly-boys, and for its emphasis on the emotional life of the characters instead of on the intricacies of the Space Program.

It would seem that the MINISERIES format is both too limited and too large for SF drama on TV. The preference is for either a two-hour MADE-FOR-TV MOVIE, or a full SEASON of one-hour EPISODES, in which characters are allowed to develop and the BASIC PREMISE is fully explored.

Mir (aerospace): From the Russian word for "village"; the Soviet space station currently orbiting the Earth. The MIR station is usually manned by cosmonauts, who are sent up for regular tours of duty on the station. At first it was supposed by U.S. military intelligence to be a spy station; with the relaxation of the Cold War, astronomical data provided by the MIR have been shared with observatories around the world.

A joint U.S.-Soviet SPACE STATION is one option being considered for the future. Until that happens, MIR is the only permanent SPACE STATION in continuous orbit around Earth.

"mirrorshade" SF (literary): Another term for CYBERPUNK. According to popular rumor, the writers of those violent tales all wear mirror-lensed sunglasses, so the rest of the world cannot see their crazed eyes.

missile combat (gaming): A fight during an adventure in which objects are thrown or projected, usually arrows, knives, or spears. All this takes place purely in the minds of the combatants; they describe what they are doing, and what they are throwing, and the DUNGEONMASTER throws the DICE to determine whether they hit anything, and how much damage they did. The resultant scores are added to the EXPERIENCE POINTS of the PLAYERS, calibrated according to each character's ABILITIES. Someone with a high CONSTITUTION rating will be able to endure an injury better than a weaker individual.

DUNGEONS AND DRAGONS™ is played out in a fantasy UNIVERSE in which gunpowder has not been invented (or if it has, it doesn't work). Cannons, rifles, or pistols are not included in the projectiles permitted to characters; however, bows and arrows are allowed, and crossbows can be just as devastating.

MISSILE COMBAT scores are calculated slightly differently than the scores after a MELEE. Neither MISSILE COMBAT nor MELEE allow for any kind of spell-casting, which is another form of combat altogether.

Missing Scene story (fan/fanzine): A story in a FANZINE that tries to explain what occurred between characters in a film or an EPISODE of a TV SERIES, either during a particular scene shown on the screen, or between scenes. Most scripts do not cover every minute of a character's activities; the screenwriter must use a kind of shorthand, and assume the audience will accept the fact that some time has elapsed so that the action can go forward. FANS want to fill in these MISSING SCENES to explain a character's actions, although what the FAN imagines may not be what the actor or original author had in mind.

Occasionally too much EXPOSITION gets cut out of a script; the author of a NOVELIZATION then tries to fill in the MISSING SCENES in the same way. J. M. Dillard does a good deal of this in the NOVELIZATION of the script for *Star Trek: The Final Frontier* (1989).

mixed-mediazine (fan/fanzine): A FANZINE with stories based on a number of different TV SERIES or films, as opposed to a FANZINE that concentrates on one SERIES or film, or on one character, or on the characters played by one actor. MIXED-MEDIAZINES often contain CROSS-UNIVERSE stories, in which the characters from one film or TV SERIES interact with those of another. See also MEDIAZINE.

mock-up (aerospace/film): A full-sized replica of a spacecraft or other object, made of inexpensive materials, for practice purposes. The term was originally used in the theater, and was applied by both film crews and astronauts to the same idea: to practice a technique or procedure on a cheap model until it is ready to be done on the real thing. While a film crew can, and often does, have several tries before the performance is considered perfect, an astronaut may not. The technique must be right the first time; there may not be a second chance.

modem (computer): A device that converts digital data into signals that can be transferred via telephone lines. The term is a contraction of "modulation/demodulation."

MODEM, like fax, is replacing written mail as a form of interpersonal communications. *The Odyssey Files* (1985) is a reprinting of the MODEM communications between A. C. CLARKE and film producer Peter Hyams, regarding the PREPRODUCTION phase of the film *2010*.

module (aerospace): A self-contained unit of a spacecraft or SPACE STATION, to which other units may be attached. The central core of the spacecraft is the COMMAND MODULE, which holds the main instruments for takeoff and landing, the computers, and the crew's quarters. Other MODULES may house supplies or fuel or experiments to be performed during the mission.

module (computer): A set of prepared programs packaged as a unit and often sold commercially. Also known as SOFTWARE.

molinya orbit (aerospace): A global orbit designed so that the communications satellite has maximum time in the North Polar latitudes; named for the Molinya Satellites launched by the Soviet Union in 1965. MOLINYA ORBITS are of the most benefit to the United States and the USSR, whose territories are largely in the Northern Hemisphere.

monitor (computer): The visual display area for a computer system. MONITORS can display their data in monochrome or in color; they can be hooked up in banks, or they can be individual instruments. Most home computers consist of a CPU, a keyboard, a MONITOR, and a printer. Early models used a television set as a MONITOR; the most advanced ones to date can be programmed to organize, rearrange, or revise data.

monster movies (film): Films that depict creatures that are supposed to evoke fear and pity in the audience. In the 1930s, films like *King Kong* (1933) and *Frankenstein* (1931) were able to thrill and frighten audiences with their stories of large and

inexplicable creatures driven mad by the forces around them. After the use of the atomic bomb in 1945, a series of MONSTER MOVIES were made that supposed the radiation from the bomb and the tests that preceeded it had created huge MUTANT ants or bees or whatever else the Special Effects department could come up with. The best of these was *Them!* (1954), which boasted an unusually literate script as well as an excellent cast.

Monsters have had to become more and more horrendous to thrill the modern audience; the ultimate in MONSTER MOVIES are the SLASHER FILMS that show some human being out for revenge for some imaginary or actual misdeeed.

monty hall (gaming): A CAMPAIGN in which large amounts of treasure are given out with little danger to the PLAYER CHARACTERS. This kind of mental combat is just too easy, and the DUNGEONMASTER who devises this kind of game is considered a softy. The term comes from the name of a television game-show host, who gave large prizes to oddly dressed contestants for picking the right box or curtain, or for having some odd item in their possession.

moon (astronomy): A large natural object in orbit around a larger natural object that is not a star; a natural satellite circling a planet. Earth has one large MOON (usually capitalized); for many thousands of years, it was the only one astronomers could see. Not until Galileo discovered the MOONS of JUPITER and SATURN were humans aware that other bodies in our SOLAR SYSTEM had satellites at all.

Earth's MOON is fairly large in proportion to its PRIMARY; it affects our lives in ways that can be immediately seen, such as in its pull on the tides, and in ways that may be more controversial. No one doubts that there are more odd happenings during the times when the most surface of the MOON is visible to us on Earth as a full MOON, but no one is exactly sure why this is so.

The MOON was considered a god in ancient times. Later, the MOON was supposedly the home of any number of living creatures. As late as the 1830s, a New York City newspaper announced that living beings had been found on the MOON.

The landings on the MOON, beginning in 1969 and continuing through 1972, led to enormous advances in technology, as well as adding to our knowledge of the atomic structure of the universe. A LUNAR BASE was supposed to be the next step; however, there has been no manned exploration of the MOON since the last spacecraft left in 1972.

The MOONS of other planets in our solar system have been seen through the photographs sent back by the Voyager PROBE during the GRAND TOUR, 1977–1989. JUPITER and SATURN both have large systems of MOONS, as well as rings of smaller particles. Some of the MOONS of JUPITER may be almost as big as Earth, but they are dwarfed by their enormous PRIMARY. The Voyager showed that distant Neptune also has MOONS, a fact previously unknown.

It is considered highly likely that PLANETS in other systems might have MOONS. Most of the MOONS in our system are lifeless rocks. If life is going to be found on the Earth's MOON, it will probably be in the form of human scientists and technologists at the proposed LUNAR BASE.

Moon (literary): Earth's natural satellite, as the dwelling place of living beings, a theme that has been a part of SF since its earliest beginnings in the myths and legends of the past.

The shadows cast by the mountains and craters on the MOON

can be seen from the Earth, where imagination makes them into the "Man in the Moon." Some of the earliest writings to be called SF were presumptive trips to the MOON, such as the *Somnium* of JOHANNES KEPLER and *The States and Empires of the Moon* of Cyrano de Bergerac. In the 19th century, JULES VERNE and H. G. WELLS each postulated rocket trips to the MOON. VERNE'S spaceship never actually landed, but WELLS wrote of a landing on the MOON, and the discovery of its weird inhabitants.

The idea of a landing on the MOON was a constant theme of SF in the 1920s and 1930s. ROBERT HEINLEIN had a mining colony on the MOON in *The Moon Is a Harsh Mistress* (1967), and had an underground complex on the MOON as the center of a Solar Empire in *Double Star* (1956). Many writers wondered who would be the first humans to step foot on the MOON; none of them predicted that when the event actually occurred, millions would participate in it vicariously through the miracle of TELECOMMUNICATIONS.

Astronomers are now convinced that the MOON is a large and barren chunk of rock endlessly circling our planet. Any living things on it will probably be of Earthly origin. A LUNAR BASE is being discussed, but whether it will be made a reality is yet to be decided.

motif (literary): A constant theme that runs through the work of a particular author, or that recurs in a set of stories by several writers. CYBERPUNK writers often use the decay of modern cities as a MOTIF. Jerry Pournelle has become identified with grim, military tales of warfare in Space, while Piers Anthony often uses the psychology and terminology of game-playing in his stories.

motivation (literary): The underlying rationale for the actions of the CHARACTERS in a story, as shown both by words and by unspoken thoughts. The term is taken from the theater, where the actor must interpret the play to the audience so that the story is believable.

SPACE OPERA and PULP FICTION did not dwell too much on such niceties as MOTIVATION. A HERO was Good, a VILLAIN was Bad, and that was it. Today most CHARACTERS in SF are expected to be

believable, consistent within their own UNIVERSES. A VILLAIN may be exacting revenge for a real or imagined hurt, or a BEM may be a parent protecting its young. The HERO may have a few flaws of character that make him more human, whatever his/her/its species may be. It is important for the writer to let the audience know what makes the CHARACTERS tick, so that they can empathize with them, care about them, and most importantly, want to read to the end of the story to find out what happens to them. See also CHARACTERIZATION.

multiplane (film): Animation technique developed by the Walt Disney studios of *Fantasia* in 1940, in which the camera shoots through several layers of drawings, each set at a slightly different level with a small space between them to give the illusion of depth. The result, when properly done, can be breathtaking, as in the *Nutcracker Suite* sequence of *Fantasia.*

munchies (fan/conventions): Free goodies provided by the CON-COM for members, particularly in the CON SUITE; the term may also be applied to the refreshments at ROOM PARTIES. MUNCHIES can be the standard chips 'n' dips of party fare, or they can be quite hearty, including soups in Crockpots™ or raw vegetables to be dipped in sour cream or melted cheese. Some CON members arrive with minimal cash and GRAZE through the CON, feeding on MUNCHIES for the entire weekend. This is not recommended; a steady diet of MUNCHIES often brings on an attack of the BLORCH.

mundane (fan): Anyone or anything not immediately connected with Science Fiction or FANDOM. The word can be used as either a noun or an adjective. A MUNDANE may be a parent, teacher, employer, or spouse. A MUNDANE job provides the wherewithal for FAN-AC: attending CONS, collecting FANZINES, preparing costumes, and so on.

MUNDANES are regarded with mixed feelings by FANS. On the one hand, there are a lot more of them than there are of FANS; on the other hand, some FANS feel infinitely superior intellectually to most MUNDANES. MUNDANES are not always sympathetic to FANS who show up late for work or school due to extended FAN-AC.

MUNDANES at hotels that have been taken over by CONVENTIONS tend to have mixed feelings about the FANS. Most of them regard FANS with amusement, wondering how sensible adults can go prancing about in HALL COSTUMES, while a few consider the whole SF world a total waste of time.

To be MUNDANE is not fatal, nor is it necessarily permanent. Many FANS were once MUNDANE. A MUNDANE can be converted to FANDOM by a friend or relative. With a little tolerance and good humor on both sides, FANS and MUNDANES can coexist at the same hotel, or even in the same household. See also FREAKING THE MUNDANES.

Murphy's Law (fan): A satiric comment on so-called Laws of Science, to wit, "Whatever can go wrong, will go wrong, and at the worst possible time." There are a number of corollaries and similar formations. A popular BUTTON states "Murphy was an optimist."

mushroom (fan/convention): The person who attends a CON for the sole purpose of watching films or videotapes that would otherwise not be available to him or her. The MUSHROOM spends every hour of the weekend sitting, standing, or even sleeping in the film room, and emerges at the end of three days looking pale and limp around the edges, like a MUSHROOM.

music videos (TV): Short films or videotapes, consisting of a piece of music with accompanying images. MUSIC VIDEOS were meant to sell records when they were first introduced in the late 1970s. They showed performers performing, in a straightforward manner, as if the viewer were sitting at a concert. To attract more attention to the song, surrealistic images were added to the production. MUSIC VIDEOS now use most of the SFX techniques of films, and may include COMPUTER GRAPHICS as well. By the time Michael Jackson recorded *Thriller* and *Captain EO*, the MUSIC VIDEO had become a major vehicle for SF and Fantasy. Many MUSIC VIDEOS may be considered minidramas.

Many CONS sponsor amateur MUSIC VIDEO contests, in which nonprofessional filmmakers combine a piece of music with FILM CLIPS, COMPUTER GRAPHICS, and other imagery to produce a tribute to a favorite SF film or a character in a TV SERIES.

mutants (literary): Major genetic deviations from the human norm. MUTANTS in SF are usually depicted as deformed and pitiable objects, when they aren't superbeings with psychic powers of untold strength, like SLANS. In both cases, the MUTANT is often considered something to be destroyed, on the theory of "Get it before it gets you!"

mutation (biology): The rearrangement of DNA to produce a differentiation in the genetic code of a living being. Natural MUTATIONS occur over a long period of time. Individuals whose MUTATIONS enable them to survive and procreate pass them on to successive generations in the slow process known as evolution.

MUTATIONS often involve energy: heat, chemicals, or radioactivity. It is this latter possibility that intrigued SF writers and filmmakers of the late 1950s and 1960s, who postulated all kinds of horrific beings emerging after atomic explosions or bomb tests. A number of POST-HOLOCAUST stories had hideous MUTANTS emerging after the radioactive dust had cleared. Films like *Them!* were based on the premise that atomic RADIATION would cause an increase in the size of the most harmless of creatures, turning them into horrible monsters.

Humanity has presumably arrived at its present physical state after some millions of years of evolution; in the last eight thousand years or so, culture has taken over the function of physical evolutions, and those MUTATIONS that have actually occurred may be so lethal as to eventually die out entirely with their carriers. See also MUTANTS.

mythology (literary): Stories of gods and other supernatural beings, told by primitive peoples to explain natural phenomena. Most familiar in the Western world are the Classical myths of Ancient Greece and Rome. The names of Greek gods and goddesses, and their Roman counterparts, are part of our heritage. The PLANETS of our SOLAR SYSTEM are named for them, as are many of the star groups we call constellations. MYTHOLOGY explained such phenomena as spiders spinning webs, volcanic eruptions, and the turning of the seasons.

Ancient MYTHOLOGY is often used as the basis of SF or Fantasy. Norse MYTHOLOGY, which is less familiar than Greek or Roman, has also been drawn on. Recent interest in the Far East has led to an increased study of Asian MYTHOLOGY. As more scholars uncover and popularize the MYTHOLOGY of hitherto unknown peoples, SF and Fantasy writers will draw on these tales for inspiration.

SF has been called today's MYTHOLOGY. However, the new stories are often clever retellings and reexaminations of ancient truths that each generation must interpret for themselves.

mythos (literary): The beliefs and legends that comprise a culture's literary heritage, whether written or oral. Much of Western European MYTHOS derives from Classical MYTHOLOGY, as well as the Bible and folklore. SF writers draw on the well of allusion and metaphor for their own purposes. The KING ARTHUR legend, for instance, has been retold as a fantasy by T. H. White, as a historical novel by Rosemary Sutcliffe, and as an epic battle between Paganism and Christianity by Marion Zimmer Bradley.

An important aspect of WORLDBUILDING is the construction of an ALIEN society and its attendant MYTHOS, especially in a Fantasy UNIVERSE, where the PLOT may turn on some arcane point of religion, or on an ancient prophesy.

name tags (fan/convention): Small square or oblong pins, with the wearer's name inscribed on them, ornamented like miniature works of art.

NAME TAGS began as BADGES, issued by CONVENTIONS to identify their members. Artists would embellish their own BADGES by coloring the CON'S LOGO in pencil or crayon, or by adding ornamentation or calligraphy. Individualized NAME TAGS became fashionable for a while; in the mid-1970s they were commonly seen on BNFS, as a sign of prestige.

NAME TAG art is of two kinds: portraiture and generalized. A portrait NAME TAG is often made from an instant photo of the wearer, and some have been used as identification at CONS for the purpose of cashing personal checks, verifying travelers' checks, and so forth. The more generalized NAME TAG illustrations can be almost anything, from a STARSCAPE to a DRAGON (roaring "Service with a Snarl"). Such NAME TAGS are often found in the ART SHOW, as one-of-a-kind miniatures.

NAME TAGS still serve the function of identifying the wearer; they just do it with more panache than a mere CON BADGE.

Narnia (literary): Magical land, created by C. S. Lewis in a SERIES of stories in which Good and Evil fight it out, with Aslan the Lion on the side of Good, and the Witch and her minions on

the other side. NARNIA is reached through a magical wardrobe in *The Lion, the Witch and the Wardrobe* (1950); subsequent books extend and enhance the adventures of the children who penetrate this wonderful realm.

narration (literary): The events of a story and how they are told. NARRATION can be in the third person, as if presented by an omnipotent being, or in the first person, as if one of the participants is relating the story to an audience.

NARRATION provides the glue that holds the story together with descriptive passages, EXPOSITION, and PLOT POINTS. There are a few writers who can tell a story almost entirely in dialogue, but even they need a few words of NARRATION to explain where the CHARACTERS are and what they are doing there.

narrator (literary): The presumed speaker in a story written in the first person; the "I" who is telling the story. Most stories are written in the third person, often from the POINT OF VIEW of an omnipotent being who can see into every CHARACTER's mind, and can inform the reader of what is going on. A NARRATOR may be directly involved with the action, or may be a bystander commenting on it. The first-person NARRATOR has no way of knowing what any other CHARACTER is doing or thinking, other than facial expressions or dialogue. A secondary CHARACTER often acts as the NARRATOR, reporting what was done with an occasional guess as to MOTIVATION. The NARRATOR can sweep the audience into the story, giving a sense of immediacy that third-person NARRATION sometimes lacks.

NASA/National Aeronautic Space Administration (aerospace): The U.S. agency responsible for the U.S. Space Program since 1958. Established by President Dwight D. Eisenhower, NASA (usually pronounced as a word) has had sole control over rocket development and space flight in the United States until very recently, when some privately funded satellites were launched in the late 1980s.

NASFiC (fan/convention): North American Science Fiction Convention, held in the continental United States when the WORLD-CON is held in Europe or Australia. (So far no one in Africa or Asia has tried to host the WORLD-CON.) The NASFIC (pronounced "Nass-fick") entails as much effort as a WORLD-CON, the bidding is often as spirited, and the PROGRAMMING is much the same. If a FAN in the United States cannot afford to travel overseas, the NASFIC is an acceptable alternative.

nebula (astronomy): A region of dust and gas in a GALAXY that appears fuzzy when seen from Earth, hence the name, meaning "cloud" in Latin. NEBULAE may be dark or light, depending on how much light they reflect from nearby stars. They do not generate light themselves, consisting as they do of swirling dust particles. A spacecraft entering such an area would be effectively blacked out from communications with other ships, as in the climactic battle in the film *Star Trek: The Wrath of Khan* (1982).

Nebula Awards (literary): Given by the SCIENCE FICTION WRITERS OF AMERICA (SFWA) to honor excellence in SF writing. The awards are voted on by the membership of SFWA and are presented at an annual banquet. The nominating and voting base for NEBULA AWARDS is smaller than that of the HUGOS, leading some to believe that they are more elitist and/or more prestigious; however, often the same works are nominated for both awards, and may receive both in the final voting.

"neep-neep" (computer): A FAN totally involved with computers to the exclusion of everything else. The term is an echo of the beeping tone used in many computers to alert the user to its functions. See also COMPUTER GEEK; HACKER.

neofan (fan): Often abbreviated to NEO; someone new to SF FANDOM and its subculture. NEOFANS can be seen at CONS with their arms overflowing with FANZINES, trying to catch up on 20 years of FAN-FIC. More often than not, they crowd autograph tables, trying to get the attention of a Big-Name Author. They react riotously when told their favorite TV SERIES is about to be canceled.

NEOFANS are usually taken in hand by more seasoned veterans of FANDOM, and are counseled in the ways they should go. They pick up the vocabulary of SF, and they mend their ways. In time, they too will be BNF, and they can look kindly on the next generation of NEOFANS.

Neo-Pagan Movement (fan): A serious attempt to recover the religious fervor of pre-Christian worship of natural phenomena by re-creating the rituals of Northern Europe and the Middle East. The NEO-PAGAN MOVEMENT gathered momentum in the late 1960s as part of the general uprising of youth against the society of the time that they saw as stultifyingly conformist and out of touch with the natural world. The NEO-PAGANS in Britain have attempted to perform Druidic rites at ancient sites like Stonehenge. In the United States they are regarded as a minor religious sect, whose antics tend more to the farcical than to the maniacal.

Some offshoots of the NEO-PAGANS have been seriously involved in such things as WICCA. NEO-PAGANS strenuously deny any association with Satanism, Black Magic, or any other form of destructive activity. Like many other cults, the NEO-PAGAN MOVEMENT has experienced rifts and heresies, which result in splinter groups.

NEO-PAGANS emerge at WORLD-CONS and may be seen at SCA EVENTS, usually in the robes of some kind of CLERIC. They are largely responsible for THAT REAL OLD-TIME RELIGION, the FILK song of more than 650 verses.

nerd-pack (fan/computer): A plastic pocket protector, full of pens and pencils, worn by people in the COMPUTER field to keep ink or graphite from staining an otherwise pristine plain white shirt. The implication is that only a nerd (a social inept) would wear a white shirt, and only a nerd would care if it got stained with ballpoint pen ink. NERD-PACKS are also worn by a number of perfectly nice MUNDANES who just don't like ink on their shirts.

Net (computer): The central COMPUTER NETWORK that connects business and institutional COMPUTERS to each other, so that someone working in one location can receive information that may be fed into a COMPUTER in another location. The NET is the ultimate interaction of COMPUTERS.

FANS have their own COMPUTER NETS, which have begun to take the place of FANZINES as a means of communication.

network (TV): Large organization that controls many television stations, all of which broadcast the same TV programs at the same time. There are three major NETWORKS in the United States as of this writing: American Broadcasting Company, National Broadcasting Company, and Columbia Broadcasting System. A fourth corporation, Fox, has begun to make inroads into this virtual monopoly of television broadcasting; another alternative is provided by PUBLIC BROADCASTING. There are also several NETWORKS that are only seen on CABLE, such as USA or TNN.

Until the early 1980s, NETWORK television dominated the production of new programs by controlling the funds necessary for such production. A TV SERIES would be developed independently, and presented to the NETWORK by the producers; if it found favor with the NETWORK hierarchy, the SERIES would be given the funds for further production. Should the SERIES dwindle in popularity, the funding would be cut off and the show would be canceled. This happened to STAR TREK, which was saved twice by a LETTER-WRITING CAMPAIGN.

With the emergence of DIRECT SYNDICATION and the development of CABLE NETWORKS, the stranglehold of the broadcast NETWORKS is loosening. However, they still provide the bulk of TV programming in the United States.

networking (computer): The use of computer NETS to exchange information. See also NET.

networking (fan): An extension of the use of NETWORKING in the computer field; the use of social contacts for business purposes. A new word for an old activity; people have been using their social contacts for business since trade began.

Fan NETWORKING can be used as a source of employment opportunities, or as a source of social connections in a strange location. Many FANS try to locate other fans after a move to a new area. FANS tend to congregate in self-protection against the MUNDANES; NETWORKING is another aspect of this kind of activity.

neural networks (computer): A set of HARDWARE that tries to duplicate the physical activities of the human brain, by sending electrical impulses through the system. NEURAL NETWORKS are considered one of the basic necessities in the formation of ARTIFICIAL INTELLIGENCE. So far, the system has not worked, but research is still in its earliest stages.

Neutral alignment (gaming): The ethical and moral orientation in a ROLE-PLAYING GAME that sees all things that exist as part of the entire Cosmos. NEUTRAL CHARACTERS tend to view the Universe as a whole, rather than trying to isolate one set of circumstances over another. A LAWFUL NEUTRAL CHARACTER will uphold order and meaning in the game. CHAOTIC NEUTRAL CHARACTER insists on absolute freedom for each individual. A NEUTRAL EVIL CHARACTER exists for the moment, and uses expediency as an excuse for any action. NEUTRAL GOOD, on the other hand, believes that Law and Order are necessary for the balance of nature. And a NEUTRAL NEUTRAL is the hardest and narrowest character to play, since he believes in total balance of natural and emotional forces.

neutron star (astronomy): A small, dense star, so tightly packed that the protons and electrons in its core have been compressed into neutrons. A NEUTRON STAR may have the mass of our sun, but it will only be a few miles in diameter. It has been theorized that NEUTRON STARS are formed when a SUPERNOVA blows off the outer layers of a star's gasses. In time, the star's gravity will crush even the neutrons and it will continue to shrink until it becomes a BLACK HOLE, from which not even light can escape.

New Age: A set of philosophies and activities dealing with the relationship of an individual to the "inner space," meaning control or self-directed growth of one's emotional, spiritual, and physical being. In their quest for higher consciousness on both the individual and planetary scale, NEW AGE adherents are often involved with meditation and Eastern spiritual teachers, CRYSTALS, CHANNELING, holistic medicine, and bodyworks like yoga and massage. NEW AGE activities may also include examination of various psychic phenomena, age-old mystical religions like Taoism and Shamanism, and environmental issues.

SF has explored such NEW AGE concepts as reincarnation, OUT-OF-BODY EXPERIENCES, ESP abilities, and LIVING WORLDS. It is a moot point as to whether NEW AGE has drawn from SF or SF has expanded NEW AGE.

newsletter (fan/publishing): A small publication, usually no more than eight sides of paper, that contains news items about a particular CLUB, or that announces forthcoming publications of a particular publisher. Most CLUBS distribute a NEWSLETTER to their membership to keep them informed as to the time and place of the next meeting, forthcoming speakers, and other matters of immediate importance. Some NEWSLETTERS also include reviews of current books and films.

Several publishers and bookstore chains also distribute NEWSLETTERS to inform the public about new items, or reissues of old ones. Bantam Books, for instance, includes interviews with currently popular authors in its NEWSLETTER.

NEWSLETTERS may also be called FANZINES, but they are more ephemeral. They are usually limited in distribution to the members of the CLUB, or interest group, and are not generally available for sale outside that group. Occasionally a club may sell off some extra copies of its NEWSLETTERS at a CONVENTION; more often, items of interest to the general population of FANDOM may be extracted from the NEWSLETTERS of a given year, and will be published separately as an Annual.

newsprint (comics): The standard wood-pulp-based paper used by most comics publishers. It's cheap and it takes the ink well, but it turns yellow and brittle with age, and must be protected by a plastic cover against moisture, heat, and cold.

NEWSPRINT was the paper used for the PULP magazines, instead of the more expensive slick paper. A few SF magazines still use NEWSPRINT, although of a slightly finer quality than PULP.

newsprint (printing): Cheap paper made of wood pulp, commonly used for newspapers; PULP magazines are printed on it.

New Wave (literary): SF movement of the late 1960s and early 1970s that emphasized SOFT SCIENCE over HARD SCIENCE, and used writing styles that varied widely from the direct narrative of earlier SF. The term, borrowed from French films of the same era, was first used by Judith Merrill, and applied to mostly British SF stories published around 1964–1965.

Traditionally, SF had concerned itself with problem-solving. HARDWARE STORIES would deal with a dangerous situation on board a starship; SPACE OPERA would depict a heroic battle with ALIEN forces. NEW WAVE writers were more interested in the inner battles than the external ones; their stories would often deal with a psychological conflict that could only be resolved by a total restructuring of Society. There are few certainties in NEW WAVE SF, and ALIENS are regarded in a more reasonable (if not affectionate) light. Battles are not "us against them"; in the spirit of post-Vietnam America, "Us" is as likely to be the Enemy as "Them."

Writers associated with the NEW WAVE were Thomas M. Disch, Philip K. Dick, and Barry Malzberg.

ni var (fan/fanzine): A form of poem, consisting of antiphonal lines or verses, expressing a duality of conceptions, or

the comparison of two otherwise unlike things. The term was invented by Dorothy Jones Heydt, who used it to explain a poem in the fanzine *Spockanalia #1*, printed in 1967. Other people picked up on the term, most notably Claire Gabriel, who used it as the title for a story later printed in the anthology *Star Trek: The New Voyages* (1972).

The form, if not the term, has carried over into the MAINSTREAM; the Newbery Award for 1989 was given to Julian Fleischer for *Joyful Noise: Poems for Two Voices*, which is, in effect, a book of NI VAR poetry.

NI VAR has been extended to apply to any artistic effort that contrasts two aspects of a person or thing.

nonplayer character (gaming): Extra character inserted by the DUNGEONMASTER into an adventure to enliven the proceedings. NONPLAYER characters may include hirelings, henchmen, and followers of the PLAYER CHARACTERS, and various villains, monsters, and even animals. None of these develop or grow into CHARACTERS; they are simply there for the PLAYER CHARACTERS to chop up or lead into battle.

nova (astronomy): A faint star that suddenly flares up into brightness, becoming, in effect a "new" star; one that is seen from Earth where no star had been before. It is surmised that the Star of Bethlehem was such a NOVA. See also SUPERNOVA.

"Nova" (TV series): Science programs broadcast on PUBLIC TELEVISION stations; the series has discussed topics as wide-ranging as the search for Ancient Americans and as particular as the disposal of nuclear waste. Many of the NOVA programs have been put on videotape and are available for viewing through schools and libraries. Some of the most interesting current information on astronomy is disseminated through NOVA.

novelization (publishing): The adaptation of a screenplay to the novel form; the novel is written directly from the shooting script, sometimes by the original writer, but more often by someone who is able to transfer the visual image into the written word.

NOVELIZATIONS usually try to give the reader some of the impact of what was seen on the screen, which is not always easy to do. They may also include material not seen on the screen, but included in the screenwriter's directions to the actors. The NOVELIZATIONS of the STAR WARS scripts included material that GEORGE LUCAS had wanted to put into the films, but could not without destroying the narrative flow and dramatic impact. Scenes in which the young Luke Skywalker talks with his friends about his longings for adventure, for instance, were inserted into the NOVELIZATION. Campbell Black's novelization of *Raiders of the Lost Ark* (1981) includes MISSING SCENES that explain some of the characters' MOTIVATIONS that are murky in the finished film.

Writers of NOVELIZATIONS range from competent HACKS to well-known authors. How much the NOVELIZATION varies from the original script depends on the expertise of the writer. A good NOVELIZATION can often stand on its own, long after the original film has been left on the shelf.

novice (fan/costuming): A Costumer who has never won at a WORLD-CON or someone at a Regional Convention who has never competed at all. There has been a certain difficulty in wording of who, exactly, is or is not a NOVICE. Some costumers compete at the MASTER level at Regional Cons, but have never been to a WORLD-CON. According to the rules, they may compete as NOVICES, but their level of expertise is far above most of the others in their DIVISION.

One win at a Regional or a WORLD-CON moves a NOVICE into the JOURNEYMAN DIVISION.

nuclear bomb (physics): A weapon that depends on atomic fission to detonate an explosion. It has been used twice to date, both times by the United States, in August of 1945; the Japanese cities of Hiroshima and Nagasaki were the targets. In later years, nuclear devices were tested above and below the ground. There was a feeling in the early 1950s that a possible attack by the Soviet Union on the United States was imminent, and bomb shelters were built to shield the population from such an attack. Whether the NUCLEAR BOMB was a deterrent is difficult to say; the threat of such a terrible weapon of destruction has hung over humanity for nearly 50 years, and to date no one has dared to use it again.

nuclear reactor (physics): A device that uses atomic fission as the impetus for the release of energy, either to create electrical power, or to propel a starship through space. NUCLEAR REACTORS on Earth have been the targets of much controversy, especially after accidents at Three Mile Island in the United States and Chernobyl in the Soviet Union created much turmoil and destruction. NUCLEAR REACTORS in space vehicles have been the subject of much speculation, with some writers claiming that they are likely to be the power source for interstellar exploration and others insisting that something less dangerous and more powerful will have to be used to attain FASTER-THAN-LIGHT speeds. Presently, NUCLEAR REACTORS are used in some naval vessels, like the Nautilus submarine.

nuclear winter (biology/astronomy): A condition that may occur after massive nuclear explosions project quantities of debris into Earth's atmosphere. Radiation from the sun would be effectively blocked, causing a general lowering of the temperature of the Earth's climate. Without sunlight, plants would not be able to manufacture chlorophyll, and would die. Without plants, the herbivores would die; without herbivores, predators would die. In time, all life on Earth would be extinguished except for a few simple forms that might survive.

Whether humanity could survive a NUCLEAR WINTER is a point explored by SF writers in various ways. Many presuppose a few small colonies huddled in underground bunkers, or tribal enclaves, cut off from everyone else. POST-HOLOCAUST STORIES often deal with the effects of such a tightly knit society on its young people, who may want to break out of the caves and into the open air (both literally and figuratively).

NUCLEAR WINTER remains a real possibility as long as the threat of nuclear warfare is around. Most scientists agree that no one would survive a nuclear war.

nuke (fan): To destroy something with nuclear weapons. Whether the word passed from SF to the MAINSTREAM or the other way around is moot. There are BUTTONS that proclaim "Nuke the Whales!" or "Nuke the Smurfs!"

The term is also humorously applied to ordinary microwave ovens. A fan may jocularly refer to NUKING dinner, which is being cooked or reheated in the microwave.

null-G (aerospace): Another way of saying ZERO-G; weightlessness, a state of no gravity.

null point (aerospace): A hypothetical point in space where the gravitational pull of one object exactly balances another. Since all bodies in space are constantly in motion, such a point is considered more theoretical than natural.

Nuts 'n' Bolts story (literary): One that deals primarily with technology and problem-solving. Much early SF was written by people who were fascinated with machinery and electronics. These authors fashioned stories around mechanical failures and their repairs, or postulated far-fetched starship engines. CHARACTERIZATION in this kind of SF is overshadowed by the technical details of the situation and its solution. See also HARDWARE STORIES.

obligatory scene (film): A scene that is there because the audience expects it to be there since it is part of the literary convention of the genre. Examples are the one-on-one battle scene in a SPACE OPERA, or the scene in a mystery story in which the detective gathers all the suspects into one room and proceeds to expose the murderer. If a film or novel leaves out these scenes, the audience is vaguely disappointed.

official fan club (fan): One run by the producers of a film or the publishers of a series of novels, to promote their product. LucasFilms runs one such OFFICIAL FAN CLUB to promote its films; Paramount runs another for STAR TREK.

The OFFICIAL FAN CLUB has immediate access to material from the film production office, such as CANDIDS taken during production of an upcoming film, or interviews with directors, writers, and producers. Most OFFICIAL FAN CLUBS provide their members with POSTERS, BUTTONS, and a well-written NEWSLETTER with the latest information on the parent company's newest offerings. Many fan-run CLUBS use this material in their own NEWSLETTERS, which are not necessarily sanctioned by the OFFICIAL FAN CLUB.

An AUTHORIZED FAN CLUB focuses on one particular film or actor, and is run by FANS, with that actor's active consent and participation. The OFFICIAL FAN CLUB is run by the production company itself, using the resources of a major film company's publicity department to produce its publications and memorabilia.

off-world (aerospace): Refers to anything not native to Planet Earth, whether it qualifies as life or not. Moon rocks come from OFF-WORLD; so do METEORITES.

OFF-WORLD is often used by SF writers to refer to anything not native to the particular planet, not necessarily Earth, on which the story is set.

one-shot (fan/fanzine): A FANZINE that is only meant to be for one issue. Many fan-written novels are ONE-SHOTS; so are ANTHOLOGIES that deal with one particular subject, like T'Kuhtian Press's *Dracula*. A few FANZINES are inadvertent ONE-SHOTS that never quite get to their second issue. On the other hand, some ONE-SHOTS prove to be so popular that they become full-blown FANZINES. *Spockanalia*, the first STAR TREK FANZINE, was supposed to be a ONE-SHOT. It ran for five issues, and spawned *Masiform-D*, which is still going strong.

ongoing events (fan/conventions): Activities at a CONVENTION that continue for several hours during the day, so that all members of a CON can attend them. The DEALERS' ROOM, the ART SHOW, and the FILM or VIDEO program are typical ONGOING EVENTS. Their locations and hours are noted in the POCKET PROGRAM.

on-line (computer): A computer database that is instantly accessed by the users. Putting a system ON-LINE can be a tedious process that involves feeding information into the data banks and organizing it so as to be readily available to users.

"Oops" (fan): A humorous pronunciation of UPS, the initials of United Parcel Service, a privately operated rival to the U.S. POST AWFUL, which delivers packages. The pronunciation reflects the attitude of FANS who may not be satisfied with the quality of service provided by this company.

Oort cloud (astronomy): An area just outside the boundaries of the solar system, where comets lurking before their orbits propel them toward the Sun. Named for its discoverer, Jan Hendrik Oort, a Dutch astronomer of the 17th century. The OORT CLOUD is considered a line of demarcation between the Solar System and the rest of the Galaxy.

open-ended series (literary): A SERIES of novels or stories that seems to go on and on as long as people are willing to read them. The characters seem to exist in a timeless place, where they never age and are never changed by experience. The *Conan* novels are of this type; even after the death of Robert Howard, the Barbarian continued to have adventures. On the other hand, E. C. Tubbs' *Dumarest of Earth* series is supposed to come to some kind of conclusion, but the luckless space traveler has never quite found Earth in 35 novels.

SHARED UNIVERSES run the risk of becoming OPEN-ENDED SERIES unless the originators are willing to tie up all the loose ends in one final, climactic volume.

open Universe (literary): A setting or set of characters, created by a particular author, that the originator permits to be used by FANS. Most writers are very careful about this sort of permission. They may extend it to amateur publications, to a point, but will not permit any professional encroachments on their Universe. LOVECRAFT was one of the first to open a Universe in this way, when he allowed August Derleth and others to write about CTHULHU. Later, Marion Zimmer Bradley invited lovers of her DARKOVER stories to "come and play in my garden." She ran a FANZINE of DARKOVER FAN-FIC for several years, and has had the best of the fan-written stories published professionally in several anthologies.

TV and film present different problems, since it is virtually impossible for a television or film producer to impound every FANZINE or prosecute every fan editor who dares to use the characters seen on either the large or small screen. Most film and TV producers tolerate such encroachments, since their appearance means that the fans have taken the film or TV SERIES to their collective bosoms, and will support it vigorously, with LETTER-WRITING CAMPAIGNS and similar encouragement.

All of this applies only to amateur, that is, fan writing. When it comes to professional material, in the mass market, the UNIVERSE is no longer open, and any attempt to re-create it without full legal permission of the originators or their representatives will result in lawsuits. See also CLOSED UNIVERSE; MEDIAZINE.

ops (fan/conventions): Short for "operations center"; the nerve-center of a large FAN-CON, from which the CON-COM directs the multitudinous activities of the CONVENTION. OPS is responsible for people, whereas LOGISTICS takes care of things. It is the OPS center that gives the GOFERS their daily assignments; items for the CONVENTION NEWSLETTER will be handed in there, as will any lost BADGES, lost items, or lost children. A WORLD-CON may split OPS into two subcommittees: Program OPS, which handles changes in scheduling, and Facilities OPS, which takes care of problems with the hotel and/or convention hall. A REGIONAL CON will only have one OPS office to handle all these hassles.

A PRO-CON deals with these matters somewhat differently, since the organization putting on the CON will have its own people who are adept in handling hotel personnel, and the program is not as complex as that of a FAN-CON.

The term OPS is taken from "operations" in the military sense, and the application is quite accurate. A large FAN-CON takes as much organization as a major military campaign. See also LOGISTICS.

opticals (film): Special optical effects in film that use already exposed film to achieve the illusion of endless space, or the feeling of vast expanses of desert or long halls stretching into eternity.

The term OPTICALS may be used for any optical special effects: MATTE or GLASS shots, for instance, or BLUE SCREEN inserts.

orbit (astronomy/aerospace): The path an object takes in space circling another body, held in place by the pull of gravity.

The objects in question may both be natural (Earth and Moon) or one may be natural and one artificial (Earth and MIR Space Station), but their ORBITS will be elliptical, in accordance with KEPLER'S LAWS.

The ORBIT of a spacecraft is carefully calculated. Any deviation might cause ORBIT DECAY, and eventual destruction of the craft.

orbit decay (aerospace): The gradual slowing of a spacecraft in orbit about a planet; the craft may then drop into the atmosphere, where the molecules of gas will cause friction with the craft. Pulled by planetary gravity, the craft will eventually burn up in the atmosphere.

This is apparently what happened to Skylab in 1977; it literally fell to Earth, scattering debris across the planet until it finally came to rest in Australia.

The situation of a spacecraft in ORBIT DECAY is one that many SF writers have exploited for its dramatic tension.

orcs (gaming): Highly unpleasant creatures, deployed by DUNGEONMASTERS as opponents to create difficulties for PLAYER CHARACTERS. Orcs first appeared in TOLKEIN'S *Lord of the Rings*, and have been useful villains ever since. They don't seem to be very smart, but they have a kind of brutish cleverness, and it takes a determined fighter to defeat them.

organ-legging (literary/biology): The repellent crime of removing the organs of still-living patients for use in transplants, without the permission of the donors. The term was invented by SF writer and critic Larry Niven; Alex Panshin called it "thumb-running" in *Starwell.* The practice is graphically illustrated in both the novel and the film *Coma*, in which hospital patients are deliberately kept in comas until their organs are needed for transplants. So far ORGAN-LEGGING remains a literary term.

original art (comics): The actual drawings done by the PENCILLER and the INKER, used to print the comic book. The COLORIST works from the ORIGINAL ART.

ORIGINAL ART may be offered for sale at CONVENTION ART SHOWS, and is highly prized by collectors.

originals (fan/art): The drawings made by the artist, used in illustrating a FANZINE, as opposed to photocopied prints. ORIGINALS must be treated with great care; they should not be folded, spindled, or mutilated in any way, and they should be returned with a free copy of the FANZINE as soon as they have been printed. Many FAN EDITORS will make a photocopy of the ORIGINALS as soon as possible, and return them to the artist, suitably protected. ORIGINALS may be sold at Convention ART SHOWS, where the publication rights may be negotiated.

orphanzines (fan/convention): FANZINES that are not being sold by their own publisher/editors at their own table. They may be said to have no "home." They are often sold by the CONCOM at a Dealers' Table set aside for that purpose; sometimes FANS will carry friends' 'zines to a Convention with their own, and will sell them for a small commission. At least three FANZINE publishers maintain large stocks of ORPHANZINES, becoming major dealers of FANZINES in the process.

ORPHANZINES may be new issues of a FANZINE, or they may be FANZINES that someone is SELLING OUT. In either case, the dealer is responsible not only for selling them but for returning the unsold issues and the profits to the original owner or publisher, less the commission.

Orwell, George, (1903–1950): Pen name of Eric Blair, journalist and political activist, whose two greatest works are the allegory *Animal Farm*, and the grim DYSTOPIA *1984*. ORWELL'S future was one of drab despotism, in which everyone lives under the all-seeing eye of Big Brother. ORWELL has contributed several words and phrases to the English language: "doublethink" and "Big Brother" are now used commonly to mean *twisted thinking* in the first case and *dictator* in the second.

ORWELL'S vision of a war-wracked Britain was dusted off when 1984 actually arrived; even in countries that were ruled by dictators, much of his prediction was far off the mark. This does not negate the force of his vision; it has now become accepted as an ALTERNATE HISTORY.

ose (fan/filking): FILK songs of a long, morbid, miserable content, in imitation of many ballads of the Middle Ages. OSE is an elaborate pun: The joke goes that there is "ose . . . and more-ose (morose)." This was funny in 1981, when it was first used. It is not so funny ten years later, but the term has stuck. OSE songs call for strong voices and stronger stomachs.

outer space (astronomy): Inaccurate and vague term for whatever lies beyond the atmospheric envelope of Earth. Astronomers prefer the terms INTERPLANETARY SPACE (for what lies within the SOLAR SYSTEM) and INTERSTELLAR SPACE (for what lies beyond it).

There is also intergalactic space, which is so far distant as to be virtually unreachable.

outfit (costuming): Any GARB used by the SCA for ordinary dress; an extremely plain HALL COSTUME. Most outfits consist of tunic and trousers for men, long skirt and low-cut peasant-style blouse or bodice for women. Armor may be added by either sex. Weapons used to be obligatory, but recent WEAPONS POLICIES at CONS have limited the knives, swords, clubs, and maces toted about in the name of historical accuracy. See also GARB.

out-of-body experience (parapsychology): The experience of having one's spirit or soul leave one's physical body. The experience has been reported by people who have been declared physically dead after a severe injury or operation, as well as by others who have used meditation or other spiritual techniques to achieve a state of relaxation. OUT-OF-BODY EXPERIENCES have been vouched for by many such people. They are also part of the mechanisms described by SF and Fantasy writers used by ESPERS. Jean Lorrah's *Savage Empire* series describes several such experiences.

out-of-print/OP (publishing): An item that is no longer in production or available for sale by the publisher; pronounced as initials. The term applies to any printed matter, whether a FANZINE or a professionally published book. OP refers only to a particular edition of a book; a paperback reprint of a HARDCOVER book may still be available from another publisher. Many SF books have been reprinted by several publishers in various editions. Many booksellers at CONVENTIONS specialize in selling OP editions of books and magazines, some of which are rare enough to become COLLECTABLES.

out-takes (film/TV): Snippets of film not included in the final product. Some of them may be BLOOPERS, those moments in which actors blow their lines, trip over props, miss cues, and generally act like fools; others may simply be scenes that have had to be cut for reasons of time. Some OUT-TAKES may be restored to the film to produce a "New Edition," as was the case with CLOSE ENCOUNTERS OF THE THIRD KIND. Occasionally a TV showing will also restore the OUT-TAKES to their proper places, as happened to *Star Trek: The Motion Picture* in its TV debut.

Oz (literary): Magical kingdom created by L. Frank Baum, in a series of juvenile novels, starting with *The Wizard of Oz* in 1901. Baum's was a uniquely American sort of fairyland, with a sturdy little heroine in Dorothy Gale who must battle a nasty witch and cope with an incompetent wizard to return her to Kansas.

Baum wrote at least 13 "Oz" novels; at his death, the series was continued for several more by Ruth Plumbly Thompson. The 1939 film *The Wizard of Oz* has crystallized this Universe for the American public.

pad (aerospace): The actual area on which the rocket sits, from which it is launched.

page-turner (publishing): A book that is so exciting the readers will keep turning the pages to find out what happens next. SPACE OPERA is the most prevalent form of an SF PAGE-TURNER, but some CYBERPUNK writing can keep the readers guessing just as well.

panels (art): Sections of pegboard, braced and perforated, for the display of artwork at a CONVENTION. Artists who wish to exhibit at a particular CON may pay a HANGING FEE for a certain amount of PANEL space. Long-running CONS may invest in a permanent set of PANELS, which are stored in the home of one of the CON-COM members between CONS.

panels (fan/conventions): More or less organized discussions scheduled at a CONVENTION, with a group of "experts" who are supposed to expound before an audience on a subject on which they are all familiar. Most PANELS are held in meeting rooms small enough for an interchange of ideas between the panelists and the audience. The panelists may be writers, artists, or editors. They may be experts on rocketry or representatives of the

U.S. or the European space programs. They may even be fans with some experience in FILKING or COSTUMING, who wish to impart the same to NEOFANS. Whoever they are, they are usually announced in advance in the PROGRAM BOOK or POCKET PROGRAM, and they are usually informed by the CON-COM of their participation at least a week in advance of the CON.

Topics for PANELS vary with the emphasis of the CONVENTION. A CON that is heavily oriented toward SF as a literary form will have PANELS on such topics as "How Do I Get Out of This Series?" and WORLDBUILDING. A MEDIA-CON will have PANELS on various SF films or TV series, or discussions of trends in SF on the large or small screen.

In many cases, members of the audience are as knowledgeable on the subject as the panelists, and the so-called PANEL may turn into a wide-ranging discussion that will be carried into the hallways after the time has come to yield the space to the next group.

pantropy (biology): The modification of humans for life on other worlds or in hostile environments here on Earth, through GENETIC ENGINEERING. Since the physical development of homo sapiens appears to have been more or less halted, and the extension of the physical being has been taken over by cultural adaptation (development of tools instead of adaptation of limbs, use of clothing instead of growing hairy pelt), this would have to be done artificially. A few SF writers have played with this idea. James Blish used the term in *The Seedling Stars* (1957). The TV series "The Man from Atlantis" (1977–1978) presented another example of this idea, with Patrick Duffy as a human variant, who evolved underwater.

parallax (astronomy): The change in position of an object when viewed from two different stations. By calculating the difference in the angle of vision, the distance from the object can then be determined, which is how the earliest astronomers were able to calculate the distance between the Earth and its Moon and Sun.

parallel universe (literary): One that may theoretically exist on another ASTRAL PLANE or in the FOURTH DIMENSION. PARALLEL

UNIVERSES, like ALTERNATE UNIVERSES, resemble ours to a certain degree. However, an ALTERNATE UNIVERSE may differ considerably from our own with regard to physical phenomena, whereas in a PARALLEL UNIVERSE the laws of science are as we know them.

There are some writers who postulate that contact can be made between PARALLEL UNIVERSES. Piers Anthony explores this idea in his *Blue Adept* and *Omnivore* series. According to this theory, PARALLEL UNIVERSES may coexist on an infinite number of dimensional levels. Members of the ruling caste of Roger Zelazny's *Amber* series can cross these levels, which they call "Shadows," by psychic transportation.

ALTERNATE UNIVERSES differ from PARALLEL UNIVERSES in that they exist in an entirely different reality. See also ALTERNATE HISTORY.

parking orbit (aerospace): An orbital technique used to increase the accuracy of deep-space probes. The BOOSTER rocket propels the probe to a low orbit. The craft proceeds to a certain point in the orbit, at which time the engines are restarted to establish ESCAPE VELOCITY.

parking orbit (literary): An orbit designated for a particular spacecraft, either chosen by the commander of the craft, or assigned by the planetary authorities. A PARKING ORBIT is much like a berth at a shipyard or a marina, or a slot in a parking lot for a truck. Many writers use the idea of interstellar shipping as the background for tales of ACTION/ADVENTURE on the Space Frontiers, and the spaceships are often left in a PARKING ORBIT while the crew is on the planet below.

parsec (astronomy): A unit of distance, not time; the distance at which the Earth and the Sun would appear to be one second of arc apart. One parsec equals 3.2616 LIGHT-YEARS or 206,265 ASTRONOMICAL UNITS or 19.174 trillion miles or 3.857 trillion kilometers. The fabled boast of Han Solo in STAR WARS that he made the Kessel Run in so many parsecs is a classic SF film boner.

passifan (fan): One who reads SF, or watches SF films, but does nothing further. See FIJAGDH; READER.

patches (fan): Cloth emblems to be sewn or ironed onto a jacket or shirt. They are often produced by OFFICIAL FAN CLUBS for their members, with mottoes like "May the Force Be With You" embroidered on them.

Most highly prized are the emblems made by NASA for each of its space missions; these are sold through authorized agencies, such as the Smithsonian Institution.

PATCHES are among the oddments sold by DEALERS at conventions, along with BUTTONS and BUMPER STICKERS.

payload (aerospace): The working cargo of a space vehicle on a mission, as opposed to the weight of the rocket itself, the fuel, and the combined weight of the crew. The PAYLOAD is carefully calculated for maximum efficiency, so the crew is seriously limited in how much personal gear can be brought aboard. Nevertheless CREWS still manage to smuggle unauthorized personal effects on board.

PBS (Public Broadcasting System) (TV): A loose organization of television stations funded by donations and government grants instead of by advertising. PBS stations do not necessarily follow the same schedule in each area; each station is independent, and may pick from a number of possible SERIES or may choose to present programs of local interest. Viewers in many metropolitan areas may choose from several PBS stations that are available either over the air or on CABLE.

Because they are not bound by a particular schedule, PBS stations often choose to show such British imports as DR. WHO or BLAKE'S SEVEN, which are not available on NETWORK stations. Science programs like NOVA and COSMOS are usually shown only on PBS stations, although they may sometimes be released for viewing on CABLE stations.

Because public broadcasting depends entirely on private donations, corporate grants, and government funds for its operating expenses (rather than selling time to advertisers), many PBS stations organize fund-raising drives several times a year, to generate interest and drum up memberships. PBS stations provide exciting, alternative viewing for SF FANS.

peace-bonding (fan/conventions): The practice of tying down a prop weapon so that it cannot be wielded during a convention. Many fans wander about in HALL COSTUMES, using swords, knives, ZAP-GUNS, and so forth as accessories. In the past, the wearers of these accoutrements insisted on flourishing them or displaying them, causing grave risk to the life and limbs of anyone within reach. After a few serious incidents, one CONCOM after another reluctantly agreed that weapons had no place in a peaceful society, and that if the costume looked bare without them, they had to be lashed down so that they could not be used for anything but display.

There was a certain unhappiness about this decision. A few disgruntled swordsmen tried to organize a "Weapons-Con," at which everyone was supposed to be armed! However, most fans agree that in today's climate of social unrest, with so many working weapons about, PEACE-BONDING is necessary. See also WEAPONS POLICY.

peanut butter (fan/costuming): A catch-phrase for any unpleasant, dangerous, or disgusting material used for costume purposes. PEANUT BUTTER was actually used by an entrant in a WORLD-CON MASQUERADE; the costume was supposed to represent a COMMIX character called "The Turd," and it was just as revolting as it sounds. By the time the costume was ready to be presented, it had disintegrated to the point where the wearer left his mark on the carpets, the chairs, and anyone who got near him. There is now a rule in all MASQUERADES: NO PEANUT BUTTER.

penciller (comics): The person who does the pencilled illustrations, based on the artist's conceptions, which the INKER then fills in. Some PENCILLERS do their own inking, but the two techniques are somewhat different, and many CREATIVE TEAMS split the two chores.

Pennsic Wars (fan/SCA): A week-long encampment of the SOCIETY FOR CREATIVE ANACHRONISM, during which mock battles are fought, feasts are given, and the members try to re-create the atmosphere of a medieval tourney. Since this event usually takes place in August on a campsite near Pittsburgh, Pennsylvania, when the weather tends to be damp and cold at night, the participants may long for such modern amenities as indoor plumbing and antibiotics. For an idea of the goings-on, and a tongue-in-cheek description of the participants, read *Murder at the Wars*, by Monica Pulver (1986).

penny-dreadfuls (publishing): Cheap novels, written by HACKS, turned out in bulk during the late 1890s and early 1900s. They actually sold for a penny or two, and the literary merit was about the same. Early SF and HORROR stories began as this sort of fiction. See also PULP FICTION.

people-movers (fan/convention): The committee members or division in charge of distributing gofers throughout a WORLD-CON. The term was first used during the Boston World-Con, NorEasCon II, in 1980. The PEOPLE-MOVERS have lists of areas where GOFERS will be wanted; it is their duty to see that GOFERS are assigned to those locations. Some chores are more attractive than others. GOFERS are usually more willing to work as MINDERS than they are to guard doors or help LOGISTICS move heavy equipment.

perfect-binding (printing): Also called self-binding; the method of putting a FANZINE together that comes closest to professional bookbinding. The pages are attached to a WRAP-AROUND COVER by squirting hot glue into the space between the cover and the tightly packed pages. The result is a neatly cut, squared-off book or magazine.

PERFECT-BINDING is used most often for large-scale MEDIAZINES that may run well over 200 pages. It is much more expensive than side-stapling, but it makes the FANZINE look better and makes it more salable.

peripherals (computer): Equipment linked to a CPU to allow for input and output of data. Printers, terminals, and MODEMS are PERIPHERALS.

Pern (literary): Planet created by Anne McCaffrey as the setting for a series of novels, beginning with *Dragonflight* in 1968. The first inklings of PERN were seen in several short stories printed in various magazines in the early 1960s; they were later incorporated into the PERN novels. Several of the PERN novels may be found in the CHILDREN'S ROOM GHETTO, since they deal with young people and their problems in growing up in a semifeudal society.

PERN was settled by Earth people, but their origin was soon forgotten, as they tried to cope with their new environment. One feature of the local scene was Thread, a deadly spore that dropped from space every 200 years or so. The only way to fight it was with the Firelizards, or Dragons, who could burn the fatal spores with their breath. Dragons could bond mentally with selected people, who became their riders; they could move through space and time by going into a cold area called "Between," which may be a form of HYPERSPACE. The PERN novels emphasize this psychic bond between the dragons and their riders, and the society that has been built up around the isolated Weyrs, or settlements.

PERN has been the subject of many costumes, artistic efforts, and even a FANZINE or two. McCaffrey permits fans to use PERN as a setting for FAN-FIC, but will not allow them to continue the adventures of characters she herself has created. The SERIES is still being expanded; the most recent addition is *Renegades of Pern*, printed in 1989.

persona (fan/costuming/gaming): The character someone is portraying during a CONVENTION, which may be taken from a story or TV series or film, may be a CHARACTER developed in a ROLE-PLAYING GAME, or may simply be a character developed by the fan for CONVENTIONS. The term was first used in the Ancient Greek theater, and meant the mask used by the actor. Like the ancient mask, the PERSONA is an ALTER EGO for the FAN. In effect, the FAN becomes the CHARACTER he or she is RUNNING, and behaves accordingly.

The SCA takes this a step further. Many members create a PERSONA based on historically accurate data; the members then dress and behave as this person (or PERSONA) would. See also HALL COSTUME.

personal computer: The product of the revolution of the 1970s and 1980s made possible by the invention of the microchip, and the ensuing reduction in the cost of equipment. Thanks to the PERSONAL COMPUTER, we can play games, organize our banking, and even shop, all without leaving our homes. Among all their predictions, SF writers seem to have missed this one.

personalzine (fan): A FANZINE devoted to the thoughts, writings, and activities of the editor. PERSONALZINES are a way of communicating with one's friends without necessarily writing a letter to each one. PERSONALZINES rarely run more than 4 to 8 pages, and are usually sent out free to a selected group of friends of the editor. In return, the recipient is supposed to send back comments, which may or may not be printed in the next issue. Arthur Hlavaty has been sending out his PERSONALZINE for nearly 20 years, for which he is perpetually nominated for a HUGO AWARD as Best Fan Editor.

perturbation (aerospace): A disturbance in the regular orbit of a body in space, due to any one of a number of factors. The irregular shape of a planet's MOON can cause natural PERTURBATION, while a GLITCH in its programming can cause a satellite to veer off-course.

Pete Seeger's Antidote: See FRANK HAYS DISEASE.

PhilCon (fan): The annual convention run by the Philadelphia Science Fiction Society; it vies with LUNACON for the title of longest-running East Coast SF CONVENTION. PHILCON is usually held in the late fall, to coincide with the winter releases from SF publishers. The GOH is usually a writer or artist of wide reputation. Like LUNACON, PHILCON draws its membership from across the country, but especially from the New York and Baltimore areas.

photon (physics): A quantum of radiant energy, with no mass. PHOTONS are theoretically capable of being used to power a spacecraft, assuming there is some way to control them.

"Photon torpedoes," the weapons mentioned in the STAR TREK TV series, films, and novels, are encapsulated PHOTONS that expand with great force when they encounter anything solid, for instance, another starship. Physicists doubt whether such a use for PHOTONS will ever be a reality, but so far it makes for spectacular Special Effects.

photo-offset (printing): A printing process that involves photographing the material to be printed and then reproducing the negative. It's the most popular method of printing FANZINES today, since the copies are indistinguishable from the ORIGINALS, and the proliferation of franchised printing shops makes it easy and relatively inexpensive. PHOTO-OFFSET printing is more expensive than mimeographing, but less expensive than photocopying.

photo-ref (fan): Photographs of actors in films or TV series, to be used as reference material for artists who illustrate the stories in MEDIAZINES. Certain publicity photos are endlessly reproduced by artists, who simply reinterpret the same pose. Some artists need scenes from episodes of the series to use as models for ILLOS. Artists may request PHOTO-REFS if they are not familiar with the characters in a particular TV series, or the minor characters in a particular episode (on which the story may be based). Some writers like to "cast" their characters, mentally giving them the faces of certain actors or actresses; these, too, may demand PHOTO-REFS.

PHOTO-REFS are not necessarily returned. Most artists who work in FANZINES maintain a file of them, taken from magazines, STILLS, and bubble-gum cards.

picaresque novel (literary): A story that follows the adventures of a rogue (*picaro* in Spanish, where the form arose). SF is a fertile field for them; many SPACE OPERAS are simply the escapades of a semi-outlaw. The *Domenic Flandry* novels of Poul Anderson are typical of the form.

The picaro is usually shown as being clever, rather than brilliant; he is outside the law, but not vicious, and, like Robin Hood, he has a kind heart and prefers to plunder the rich to give to the poor (himself). Occasionally the picaro comes to a sad end, but more usually he escapes the clutches of the Law and there's a HERE WE GO AGAIN! ENDING to give promise of more adventures to come.

pick, pass, or play (fan/filking): A procedure used in organizing a FILK-SING, so that each person in the room gets a turn to PICK a song for someone else to sing, PASS and not take a turn at all, or PLAY a song of his or her own choosing. It usually works out well. However, a crowded room may mean that a player might have to wait an hour to play something, although anyone can join in on a picked song, or someone may PICK a song for one of the guitarists to sing. See also BARDIC CIRCLE.

piece (fan/art): Any item in a CONVENTION ART SHOW. A PIECE may be as small as a miniature sculpture or as large as a full-sized carved desk or chair. It may be a framed oil painting, a matted watercolor, or even an unframed print. It may be a quilt, a crocheted sweater, or a full suit of armor. Whatever it is, it must be documented before it is entered in a CONVENTION ART SHOW. It will need a CONTROL SHEET and a BID SHEET, a MINIMUM BID, and a QUICK SALE PRICE.

pilot (TV): The opening episode of a proposed TV series that must explain the BASIC PREMISE and introduce the characters to the prospective audience. Until quite recently, independent film producers would finance PILOTS and exhibit them to the network executives, hoping to sell the idea and get the funding necessary to produce more EPISODES. Recent developments have changed this procedure. Many TV SERIES are not developed for NETWORKS, but are sold to CABLE or local stations through DIRECT SYNDICATION. One hour may not be enough to establish the characters and their setting, particularly if the PILOT is supposed to take place on another planet or in the far future. In this case, the PILOT may be funded as a MADE-FOR-TV MOVIE. If it proves to be popular, more episodes will be made. *V* began as a MINI-SERIES, which was then developed into a short-lived TV SERIES. *Buck Rogers in the 25th Century* was shown in theaters, and then became a SERIES.

Occasionally the PILOT may sell the PREMISE of the SERIES, but there may be cast changes due to the schedules of the people involved. There may even be changes in the basic PREMISE! The PILOT for STAR TREK underwent several changes before the SERIES achieved its final format; however, the film of the EPISODE itself was saved, and was later shown as the EPISODE titled "The Cage," now considered one of the best in the SERIES.

PILOTS that do not make the grade are often aired during the summer months as a kind of "Showcase." Occasionally, one of these becomes a surprise hit, and may become a REPLACEMENT series if one of the scheduled SERIES does not get the RATINGS desired by the NETWORK executives.

pixillation (film): An ANIMATION technique that uses STOP-ACTION photography to achieve a jerky motion, usually for humorous effect. Mike Jittlow's *Wizard of Space and Time* is a film that uses PIXILLATION. The term is a short form of "titillated pixy," which is what people filmed in this fashion look like.

plane of the ecliptic (astronomy): The plane in our SOLAR SYSTEM in which all planets except Pluto have their orbits. The plane extends outside the SOLAR SYSTEM, dividing the GALAXY into an arbitrary "horizon." Stars may be located "above" or "below" this imaginary line.

planet (astronomy): A nonluminous body circling a star, possibly with smaller bodies circling it. PLANETS may be TERRESTRIAL, like Earth, consisting of solid rock, or they may be GAS GIANTS, like Jupiter, made up of banks of frozen or liquid gas swirling around a dense core. Our SOLAR SYSTEM is made up of nine PLANETS and their attendant MOONS. There may be other PLANETARY SYSTEMS circling other stars in the Galaxy, and there may be sentient life-forms on one of them; certainly this is the premise of countless SPACE OPERAS and tales of GALACTIC EMPIRES.

planetary probe (aerospace): An unmanned spacecraft sent from Earth to examine a planet on a FLYBY. There have been several such probes sent through our system; the Soviet probe Venera landed on Venus and lasted about two hours before it melted. The Voyager probes made the GRAND TOUR, sending back invaluable information about Jupiter, Saturn, Uranus, and Neptune before sailing through the OORT CLOUD into INTERSTELLAR SPACE.

There are many people who feel that PLANETARY PROBES should be the extent of our exploration of the SOLAR SYSTEM and beyond, since probes do not need air, food, or medical attention. Others feel that PLANETARY PROBES cannot do the work of human hands and eyes and brains. Debate still rages. Meanwhile, SF writers prefer to deal with humans rather than mechanical PROBES.

planetary system (astronomy): The preferred term for a star and its attendant PLANETS. Our own Sun and its planets form the SOLAR SYSTEM, named for our sun, Sol.

planetoid (astronomy): A nonluminous body circling a star that is larger than an ASTEROID and smaller than a PLANET. PLANETOIDS are about the size of MARS or MERCURY. In SF stories, they may hold an atmosphere, regardless of whether or not they physically should, and they may be populated by whatever settlers the writer chooses to put there. PLANETOIDS are often spots where space travelers are marooned, or SPACE COLONIES may be established on them, or they may be the far outposts of GALACTIC EMPIRES.

planetology (astronomy): The study of planets, as astronomical bodies: what makes them, how they function, and whether there are any other planetary systems in this GALAXY.

planetscape (art): A painting of a landscape on some faraway PLANET, depicted with as much realistic detail as the artist can squeeze into the scene. PLANETSCAPES of MARS and VENUS have been derived from information received from the Voyager and Venera PROBES. Other PLANETSCAPES are derived from scenes depicted in SF novels or films, or may come directly from the artist's fertile imagination. PLANETSCAPES are classed with ASTRONOMICALS in CONVENTION ART SHOWS.

player character (gaming): A CHARACTER created by a player in a game of DUNGEONS AND DRAGONS.™ Before a game can start, each player must create the CHARACTER he or she is going to RUN, using the DICE to determine the character's ABILITIES, selecting the character's RACE and CLASS and ALIGNMENT, and finally, picking a name for the CHARACTER. These PLAYER CHARACTERS will proceed to interact with each other under the direction of the DUNGEONMASTER.

The DUNGEONMASTER may introduce NONPLAYER CHARACTERS, such as monsters or villains or even henchmen, for the PLAYER CHARACTERS; these, however, are not developed in the course of the game, but merely exist as figures for the PLAYER CHARACTERS to defeat or lead, as the case may be.

play-testing (gaming): Trying a new game out on a selected group of players before launching it on the open market. New games may be PLAY-TESTED at CONVENTIONS, where a number of expert players will be readily available. If these experts cannot manage to figure out the game, it goes back to the drawing-board for reworking.

plot (literary): The events in a story, whether on the page or on the screen, that should lead to the climax. There are many kinds of PLOT, some of which have become so standardized as to be typified in this book.

The PLOT usually involves CHARACTERS, who interact with each other. The events of the PLOT may be carried forward through NARRATION, dialog, or description. The PLOT should be able to involve the audience in the characters' lives, so as to provide an escape and a catharsis, and possibly, an insight into current problems and events.

SF PLOTS often hang on one of several threads. There are HARDWARE stories that deal with a technological problem and its solution. FIRST CONTACT stories are based on the problems of communication with a new and unusual life-form. In CULTURE-CLASH stories, the PLOT may involve characters of two different and conflicting societies, each of whom is right according to the customs of his or her own people. SPACE OPERA often has a simplistic PLOT, in which there is a danger to one of the main characters, and the others have to rescue him (or more usually, her).

Some SF stories have vast, sprawling PLOTS that seem to take forever (or at least 500 pages) to organize. Others are so diffuse that it takes three novels to reach a satisfactory conclusion, which explains the prevalence of TRILOGIES in SF, and even more particularly, in Fantasy. See also ADAM AND EVE STORY; LAST MAN ON EARTH STORY; MARY SUE STORY; TOMATO SURPRISE ENDING.

plot hole (literary): An error or omission in the events of the PLOT that causes the reader to lose SUSPENSION OF DISBELIEF. Often the PLOT HOLE is some minor discrepancy in CHARACTERIZATION or a flaw in the scientific background of the story that makes the rest of the story unbelievable. When the otherwise all-knowing Wizard does not notice the Hero creeping up on him, that's a PLOT HOLE. If it's bad enough, it might even be called a Great Gaping PLOT HOLE.

plot point (literary): An element in a story that carries the PLOT one step further. It may be a line of dialog, or an action performed by one of the CHARACTERS, or a piece of information given by the author in a descriptive passage. Whatever it is, it enables the reader to proceed with a deeper understanding of the CHARACTERS and their actions.

PLOT POINTS in films are underscored by the camera, which may emphasize one particular element in the picture. In a novel or story, the writer must make sure the information is delivered to the reader. If these connecting links are not forthcoming, the story becomes obscure. A missing PLOT POINT can result in a PLOT HOLE.

plotter (comics): The person who originates the plot line for the comic. This may not necessarily be the same person who writes the dialog, who will follow the outline given by the PLOTTER. See also CREATIVE TEAM.

plotter (computer): A device that draws lines, shapes, and so forth under computer control for GRAPHICS. PLOTTERS may be among the PERIPHERALS that come with a particular computer.

pocket program (fan/convention): The daily listing of events at a CONVENTION, designating where each event is being held, at what time, and with whom. A CONVENTION may have several ONGOING EVENTS, like the ART SHOW and DEALERS' ROOM, plus special events like a MASQUERADE, plus daily PANELS, in several TRACKS. All of these will be listed in the POCKET PROGRAM, together with any special rules pertaining to the CON (WEAPONS POLICY, for instance).

The POCKET PROGRAM is usually printed just before the CON, so that it is as accurate as possible. However, even the most tightly organized CONVENTION will have a few program changes. The day's revisions will be posted near REGISTRATION where everyone can see them.

pocket Universe (gaming): A limited set of events, characters, and so on that pertain only to one particular game. DUNGEONS AND DRAGONS™ is a generalized Universe; a lesser-known, or derived game will be a POCKET UNIVERSE.

Poe, Edgar Allan (1809–1849): American poet and short story writer, best known for HORROR STORIES, but also an early developer of SF and detective stories. With E. T. A. Hoffmann, POE is considered the originator and master of the GENRE. POE is known primarily for such chillers as "The Telltale Heart" and "The Fall of the House of Usher," but he also wrote several stories of the LOST WORLD variety, such as "The Narrative of A. Gordon Pym," and is credited with inventing the modern detective story as well. H. P. LOVECRAFT's eerie tales are very much in the POE tradition.

Many of POE's stories have been translated into films. ROGER CORMAN's "The Masque of the Red Death" combined several POE tales.

portfolio (fan/fanzine): A section of artwork within a FANZINE, either illustrations on a theme by several artists, or a selection of works by one artist on several themes. PORTFOLIOS are meant to be a showcase of ILLOS, to the glory of fan artists. Often prints of the PORTFOLIO ILLOS may be sold by the editor of the FANZINE. See also FILLOS.

portfolio (publishing): A collection of several high-quality art PRINTS, either by several artists on a theme, or by one artist as a showcase of his or her talents. PORTFOLIO PRINTS are often signed and numbered to increase their value; they are packaged carefully, so as not to damage them, and are usually advertised as "suitable for framing." If a FAN cannot afford an ORIGINAL, a

PORTFOLIO is the next best way to obtain a selection of an artist's work.

possession (parapsychology): The replacement of a person's spirit or soul by that of someone or something else; the taking over of an individual's physical body by another being. This theme recurs in horror fiction as well as in Fantasy and SF.

Primitive peoples had a dread of losing control over their own souls, and those whose speech or actions were unlike the rest of their society were deemed mad and were considered posessed by evil spirits.

The theme of POSSESSION is still able to thrill us. The Jewish legend of the "dybbuk" who takes over the body of a living person is only one of many variations on this theme. There are endless novels about children being posessed by the spirits of uneasy ghosts. *Players at the Game of People* (1980) by John Brunner presupposes a group of ALIENS, who take posession of the bodies of selected humans for a short time, rewarding their hosts with various perks such as money and long lives.

Post Awful (fan): Also called "Pest Awful" and (when it has been unusually remiss) "Post Offal." The Postal Service, which sometimes seems to be entered into a conspiracy against FANDOM. FANS depend on the postal service for communications. PROS must send their manuscripts and artwork to editors somehow. Postal rates go up and up, and service in many localities has been cut. It's no wonder SF people have coined this nickname. See also OOPS.

poster (publishing): A large reproduction of a drawing, advertisement, or other piece of graphic art. POSTERS may be used to publicize a film or TV series; they may be a way to promote a particular actor or actress.

Advertising POSTERS have been around since the mid-1800s, when cheap lithography became available. POSTERS were made into a legitimate art form by painters like Toulouse-Lautrec and Mucha. They have been used for propaganda purposes by both sides in both world wars. During the 1960s, POSTERS became a part of youthful decor, as a sign of protest against high-priced art. Now, those same inexpensive POSTERS are considered rare and beautiful artifacts, and sell for several times their original price.

POSTERS of characters from films and TV series are offered for sale at CONVENTIONS, as well as through bookstores and variety stores across the country. POSTERS advertising films are COLLECTABLES, particularly those from the 1930s and 1940s, which were often thrown away after they were used in movie theaters.

POSTERS are among the FREEBIES handed out at CONS. They are avidly grabbed up by DEALERS, who will hang onto them to see if the film they advertise will be the next STAR WARS. Even if the film turns out to be a dud, the POSTER may be attractive enough to remain on some FAN's wall.

Post-Holocaust Story (literary): A film or novel set in a hypothetical future when Earth has been through some kind of cataclysmic destruction, and only a remnant of Humanity remains. The Holocaust in question was a nuclear war in stories of the 1960s and 1970s; in the 1980s, the destruction was often caused by pollution or a natural disaster like a massive chain of earthquakes or volcanic explosions. In either case, the result is the same: a general breakdown of all forms of social order, with a tightly knit group surviving by grimly hanging onto whatever supplies they have, and repelling anyone who tries to take them away. The "Mad Max" films are set in such a POST-HOLOCAUST world; so is SURVIVALIST FICTION. POST-HOLOCAUST STORIES tend to be thoroughly depressing, with only one or two characters who survive to the end of the story, usually by being more unpleasant than anyone else.

postproduction (film): The work that goes into a film after the actual photography has been completed. It involves putting all the little bits and pieces together, adding the special effects and the sound, coordinating all of this with the SCORE, and generally making sense out of what might be several million feet of exposed film. See also PREPRODUCTION.

potboiler (literary): A story or film made solely to make money (to keep the creator's pot boiling). Much PULP FICTION was written for this very purpose; that it later turned out to have literary merit was often as much a surprise to the writer as it was to the critics who once scorned it.

There are plenty of POTBOILERS around in MASS MARKET PAPERBACK; they are matched on the screen by B-MOVIES or MADE-FOR-TV-MOVIES. See also FORMULA FICTION; HACK.

POV (Point of View) (literary): Pronounced either as initials or as a word: "pohv." The way the actions of a story are perceived by both the audience and the characters. A story may be seen through the eyes of one of the characters, who then serves as NARRATOR, or it may be told to the audience from the POV of an omniscient, godlike being, who sees and knows everything. A midway point may be the "over-the shoulder" POV, which tells the story as it affects only one CHARACTER.

Some stories cannot be told one way or the other; the author may combine two POV, alternating chapters in which one part of the story is told in the first person by a NARRATOR, with chapters that relate events that the NARRATOR would have no way of knowing. Whatever the POV, it should be consistent within a unit of the story. If a NARRATOR is speaking, that person cannot know what is going on inside someone else's head (unless, of course, the NARRATOR is a telepath . . .).

In some stories, a change in POV is indicated by a row of asterisks, which replace the film technique of cross-cutting from one scene to another.

precognition (parapsychology): The ability to know of events before they occur; also called "prescience." Many so-called psychics insist that they have this ability. The tabloid press often prints long lists of these predictions. A hard look at them after the event shows that very few of these predictions ever come to pass.

PRECOGNITION is found in some SF stories; more often, it appears in FANTASY as a PLOT POINT, in which the character in question either is given a prophetic text or has a dream that presages some key event in the story.

True PRECOGNITION is often brought on by a stressful situation, and is regarded by parapsychologists as a possible warning of danger to a loved one.

premise (literary): Also known as the BASIC PREMISE; the "what if . . ." that underlies the rationale of a story. A typical PREMISE is "what if we could meet beings from another world . . ."; what follows may be a FIRST CONTACT STORY. Often one PREMISE builds on another, until a BACK-STORY is made up. Put together a complex BACK-STORY, and you'll have to write a PREQUEL.

preproduction (film): The work that goes into setting up a film, before the cameras start to roll. To begin with, the SCRIPT must be written. Once that is done (sometimes even before that is done), the financial backing must be secure. Casting the parts, organizing the technical aspects of the film, and selecting sites for location shooting (if any) must be done well in advance.

The PREPRODUCTION phase of film may take months or even years before a single frame of film is shot. The first STAR TREK film was framed as a film, a MADE-FOR-TV MOVIE, and a PILOT before it finally reached the screen.

The dialog via MODEM of ARTHUR C. CLARKE and Peter Hyams during the PREPRODUCTION phase of *2010* is related in *The Odyssey Files* (1985).

prequel (publishing): A story or film that deals with events that presumably occurred before the beginning of an already existing work. The writer may have so much BACK-STORY that another book or film must pick up the pieces so that we know how we got to the starting point of the first work.

There are a number of SERIES written in this way. If the series gets too complicated, the writer will have to include a TIME-LINE with each book, so that readers will know just where they are in the history of the place.

prescience: See PRECOGNITION.

presentation costume (fan/costuming): An elaborate costume meant to be formally entered in a MASQUERADE competition. PRESENTATION COSTUMES tend to be gaudy affairs, dripping with sequins, feathers, jewels, and embroidery. The entrant has 60 seconds to impress the JUDGES with the artistry or humor of the costume, and will use music, lighting effects, and a cast of thousands to do it.

PRESENTATION COSTUMES are an offshoot of the early costume calls. At CONVENTIONS of the 1950s and 1960s, attendees in costume just paraded across the stage. Music was first used by Karen and Astrid Anderson at a WesterCon in 1969; after that, the presentations became so elaborate that a time limit had to be set and the open microphone became a thing of the past.

Most PRESENTATION COSTUMES are so elaborate that they are downright uncomfortable to wear. The MASQUERADE contestants are usually assigned a dressing room where they can shed some of the heavier parts of their accoutrements, but even so, once the competition is over, most of the Masqueraders head for the elevators, so that they can get back into T-SHIRTS and jeans.

press kit (film): A packet of publicity material distributed by the producer of a film or TV series to advertise it well in advance of its opening date. PRESS KITS usually contain STILL photos, information about the cast, a brief synopsis of the story, a press release, and anything else that will make people want to see this particular film. PRESS KITS may be sent to critics on newspapers and magazines, so editors of FANZINES may find themselves on the list to receive them.

Once the film has been shown, the PRESS KITS become COLLECTABLES, particularly if the film (or TV series) is a hit. The original PRESS KITS for STAR WARS may be sold for as much as $50 each if they are complete and in good condition.

press-type (printing): Letters with adhesive backing, mounted on waxed paper, used by people who do not have the advantage of having an artist to letter their FLYERS or FANZINE covers. PRESS-TYPE is available at most business stationery stores, in a variety of typefaces and sizes. It is used extensively by FANZINE editors for title pages to add variety to the LAYOUT.

primary (astronomy): A large body in space, around which a smaller body orbits. Earth is the PRIMARY body of the Moon; the Sun is the primary body of the Earth.

print (fan/art): A reproduction of a work of art, on high-quality paper, sold either individually or as a set, often numbered and signed. Many artists reproduce their own COVER ART and sell the PRINTS at CONVENTIONS. Such multiple copies cannot be displayed in the ART SHOW, but they are often sold in a Print Shop, run by the Art Committee. If you can't get an ORIGINAL, a good PRINT is the next-best thing.

printout (computer): The actual words, diagrams, and so forth imprinted on paper that were first entered onto a disk or diskette; also known as HARD COPY. Until there is a PRINTOUT, the data remain locked into the electronic memory of the computer.

print run (publishing): The number of copies of a publication (books, magazines, or FANZINES) printed at one time. The term holds for both professional and amateur publishers; both of them speak of a PRINT RUN of a certain number of copies. The difference is the size of the PRINT RUN. FANZINES rarely run more than 500 copies at a time, whereas PROZINES run thousands of copies. Books can have PRINT RUNS ranging from a few hundred copies to a million, depending on the popularity of the author.

"Prisoner, The" (TV): Surrealistic TV series created by Patrick McGoohan, first seen in the United States in 1967, and revived on PBS stations from time to time. The Prisoner is being held in The Village, a combination resort and prison, where he is constantly questioned to find out what he knows. Presumably the Prisoner was involved in highly secret and suspicious government activities; part of the appeal of the series is its ambiguity. The series did not do well in its first showings, but the post-Watergate paranoia of the 1970s led to its reputation as a cult TV series. There are "Prisoner" fan clubs and FANZINES.

pro (fan): Professional, that is, someone who receives money for what they do. PRO can also be used as a prefix; a PRO-NOVEL is one that has been published by a professional publisher, and a PROZINE is distributed on newsstands and takes paid advertising.

PROS in SF often rise from the ranks of FANS. They consider themselves lucky to be able to earn a living doing something they really enjoy. Occasionally a PRO comes into SF without having any experience in FANDOM; the shock of exposure to so many admiring readers has led to stories told at the DEAD DOG PARTY.

Most fans aspire to become PROS. Although a few of them can become nuisances, badgering PROS to read manuscripts, or asking them for the name of a good AGENT, kindly PROS are tolerant; after all, it might not have been so long ago that they were in the same boat.

The line between FAN and PRO is very thin in SF, more so than in any other writing genre. The interaction between FAN and PRO is best seen at a FAN-CON, where the give and take is kept on a friendly and helpful level.

probe (aerospace): Also called a PLANETARY PROBE. A mechanical device designed to enter a planet's atmosphere and relay information back to Earth about conditions therein. Much of what we know about the surface of VENUS and MARS comes from the probes Venera and Viking. A PROBE like the Voyager may not actually enter the atmosphere, but may instead FLYBY.

There is considerable controversy about the direction in which the U.S. space program should concentrate its efforts in the 1990s. Many people feel that unmanned probes are just as effective in relaying information, and are considerably cheaper to build and maintain than rockets and SPACE STATIONS. Others believe that humanity has a place among the stars, and while PROBES are useful, they are, after all, only tools. Only time will settle this particular debate.

pro-Con (fan/conventions): A gathering of FANS run by a professional entrepreneur for the purpose of promoting SF films, TV series, and comics. PRO-CONS are usually held in centralized locations in various cities, where they can attract attention from the local news media. The GOH is usually the star of a popular TV SERIES or a featured player in a popular SF film, who can answer questions from the audience and sign autographs. There will be a well-stocked DEALERS' ROOM, and possibly a film room as well.

PRO-CONS are often lavish with their FREEBIES, distributing promotional BUTTONS and POSTERS to advertise the latest films, books, and TV SERIES. Although some PRO-CONS only distribute a single sheet of PROGRAM information, some of the larger organizations like the Creation Cons will have a PROGRAM BOOK with interviews, CANDID photos, and information about upcoming CONS. Attendees may get HAND STAMPS instead of BADGES. There will usually be one or, at the most, two TRACKS of PROGRAMMING. The PROGRAM will tend to emphasize MEDIA, although a writer may be included in the weekend's schedule.

PRO-CONS tend to attract a broad range of people, from the sincere SF fans to those who just want to pick up an autograph and have a few minutes to talk to the Star. They provide a means of publicizing upcoming events, informing as well as entertaining the audience. Often, there may be several PRO-CONS a year in a large city, such as New York or Los Angeles.

There are several organizations that run PRO-CONS. Creation Conventions is the largest, running CONS across the United States and around the world, but there are others, like Bulldog and Dreamwerks, that run PRO-CONS in more localized areas.

PRO-CONS began in the mid-1970s as an outgrowth of the well-publicized STAR TREK CONVENTIONS. The earliest was probably the StarTrektacular organized by Lisa Boynton in Chicago in 1975. The same promoter tried the same stunt in New York City the following year, with staggering results. Over 30,000 people tried to get into an auditorium that could only hold 5,000 bodies. The resulting bedlam is still being discussed 15 years later.

There has been a rivalry between the FAN-CONS and the PRO-CONS as to which is more truly representative of SF at large. The fan-run CONVENTIONS tend to become sniffy about the lack of literacy on the part of the attendees of PRO-CONS, while the organizers of PRO-CONS tend to resent the snobbery of the fan CON-COMS.

However, in many locations, the PRO-CONS are the only game in town for SF FANS of whatever stripe, and they do bring fans together, which is the basic purpose of all SF CONS, whether FAN or PRO. For more information on CONVENTIONS, see Appendix A.

pro-ed (fan): A professional EDITOR, presumably one who works for a major SF publication or a publishing house. PRO-EDS often begin as FANS, who use their experience with FANZINES in their professional life. Many SF PRO-EDS are also SF writers. Frederik Pohl has edited *Galaxy* magazine and *If* magazine, in addition to writing a vast body of influential SF novels and short stories.

PRO-EDS are very important in the SF milieu. They are the ones who spot new talent, nurture it, and develop the next generation of SF writers.

proficiency (gaming): A CHARACTER'S learned skills, not necessarily defined by CLASS or RACE, which enable it to rise to various LEVELS as it participates in more adventures. A CHARACTER can overcome handicaps by accumulating EXPERIENCE

POINTS, and gaining skills that negate the low scores of the DUNGEONMASTER's dice.

program book (fan/conventions): The souvenir booklet handed out at a FAN-CON. It is often a thing of beauty, illustrated by the Artist GOH, with laudatory remarks about the other GOH from their friends. A really good PROGRAM BOOK might even include a short piece of SF written by the GOH.

PROGRAM BOOKS vary in size and quality, from a simple four-page folder to the elaborate volume handed out by the WORLD-CON. They usually contain such vital information as the names of the GOH and their accomplishments, the rules of the CONVENTION, the location of local eateries, and whatever other information the CON-COM remembers to put into them. They do not contain the details of the PROGRAM; that is often a last-minute decision, and is found in the POCKET PROGRAM.

programming (computer): The feeding of information and/or instructions into a COMPUTER. PROGRAMMING is a skilled operation, and experts who work at it are known as HACKERS or WIZARDS. Most day-to-day computer users rely on prepackaged PROGRAMS, which are now proliferating so it is possible to buy a computer program that will do almost anything. See also SOFTWARE.

programming (fan/convention): The organized events at a convention, as listed in the POCKET PROGRAM. There may be several TRACKS of PROGRAMMING: ongoing events, PANELS, and films.

ONGOING EVENTS run more or less continuously during the CON, like the ART SHOW, DEALERS' ROOM, and VIDEO ROOM. PANELS may be scheduled in blocks, or simply according to who is available when. Autographing sessions are a major part of the PROGRAMMING of both FAN-CONS and PRO-CONS. Special events like the GOH speech and the MASQUERADE may be scheduled for the evening hours; there may also be a late-night showing of a CULT FILM.

PROGRAMMING for a weekend CON usually begins on Friday

evening with some kind of social event (a "Meet the Pros" party, for instance). PANEL discussions and WORKSHOPS may take up most of Saturday, with the MASQUERADE as the high point of the CON. Things tend to taper off on Sunday, with the Art AUCTION on Sunday afternoon, after which the fans go home, mentally stimulated, if physically exhausted.

PROGRAMMING at a PRO-CON will run slightly differently. Events usually begin at 10:30 or 11 A.M. on a Saturday, and continue until 7 P.M., at which time the CON is effectively closed. Most PRO-CONS do not schedule events in the evening, unless the GOH has decided to initiate some particular performance. The GOH will speak and sign autographs (or not, as the case may be), and most FANS will leave once that is done.

PROGRAMMING is what a CON is supposedly about. A few CONS try to do without it altogether, and call themselves RELAX-A-CONS. Some CONS go to the other extreme, and forget to schedule time to eat and sleep. And a WORLD-CON has something to do at every hour for five whole days. Now that's PROGRAMMING!

progress report (fan/convention): A newsletter sent out at regular intervals before a CONVENTION to give the membership such vital information as the location of the CONVENTION hotel, the registration procedure for the MASQUERADE or ART SHOW, and the names of people seeking roommates. PROGRESS REPORTS vary from a two-sided FLYER to the elaborately illustrated WORLD-CON PROGRESS REPORTS, which become COLLECTABLES in their own right.

Most FAN-CONS try to get PROGRESS REPORTS out to the membership at least a month in advance of the CON, especially if there is some event that needs preregistration, like a banquet or WORKSHOP.

Project Blue Book (aerospace): The official dossier on UFO, maintained by the U.S. Air Force. PROJECT BLUE BOOK lists all UFO sightings and reports on the ensuing investigations. In almost all the cases, the investigation leads to the conclusion that the sighting was a mistake, a fraud, or just an error in judgment. However, there are a few sightings that are still question marks in the BLUE BOOK.

promos (film): Short for "promotional films"; those short excerpts from upcoming films, shown at CONVENTIONS or movie theaters to advertise the films and whet audience interest in them. Some PROMOS may include OUT-TAKES or candid shots of the actors and director; some may merely be one key scene in the film. They are used extensively at PRO-CONS, and are eagerly awaited at MEDIA-CONS. See also TRAILER.

proofreader (publishing): The person who goes over the pages before the book goes to press, correcting the TYPOS. FAN editors have to do their own proofreading, which is not always accurate, because the editor may have been the one who typed the manuscript in the first place. It is always a good idea to have someone PROOFREAD the copy before it goes to press.

props (fan/costuming): Immobile stage bits and pieces that can make up a complete PRESENTATION COSTUME onstage. Most costumers prefer not to use them; they tend to be bulky, and often are too large for the space allotted to them. Nevertheless, the temptation to use a full-sized T.A.R.D.I.S. or a working spaceship may be too much. Then the problem is to get the thing on and off the stage in time for the next person's presentation.

The term comes from the theater, where props is short for "properties." What the costumer carries onstage is an ACCESSORY; if it just sits there, it's a PROP.

protostar (astronomy): A mass of gas, in the process of coalescing into a star. As the gas contracts, the molecules that form it begin to agitate, generating heat. Eventually, they achieve enough density to begin to radiate energy, and after millions of years, a new star emerges into the GALAXY.

prozine (fan): A professional magazine, that is, one that is readily available through newsstands or bookstores and accepts paid advertising. The GOLDEN AGE OF SF (1938–1946) saw the rise and fall of many PULP magazines. The current financial scene has limited the professional SF magazine market to three or four major publications, among them ISAAC ASIMOV'S *SF*

Magazine, The Magazine of Fantasy and Science Fiction, and *Analog*. Since a large proportion of the available space in PROZINES must go to already-established writers, it is becoming harder and harder for a beginner to break into the SF field by contributing to a PROZINE. However, the SMALL PRESS remains the training ground for beginning SF writers. See also SEMI-PROZINE.

pseudoscience: A system of belief based on fallacious premises, no matter how reasonable they sound. Because of this, PSEUDOSCIENCE, unlike IMAGINARY SCIENCE, is regarded by the SF world as unproven at best, and downright stupid at worst. See also ASTROLOGY.

psionics (parapsychology): The practical application of mental powers beyond the five senses. Most commonly studied is mental TELEPATHY, the direct transfer of information from one person to another without the use of verbalization. PRECOGNITION, the knowledge of events before they occur, and CLAIRVOYANCE, the knowledge of events as they occur, are also being studied. The most useful of all the psychic talents is TELEKINESIS, the ability to move physical objects without touching them.

Several SF and Fantasy writers have used the idea of a caste or specialized group of people with such powers as the basis for a whole series of stories. The DERYNI of Katherine Kurtz are such a group; so are the ruling class of Marion Zimmer Bradley's DARKOVER. The Exotics of Gordon Dickson's *Childe Cycle* novels possess PSIONIC powers, much to the dismay of their enemies on other planets.

The term was first used by John W. Campbell in the sense of "something special that the mind can do, involving unknown mental powers, which can be focused as reliably as radio." Scientific investigation of PSIONIC powers has barely started. While some people deride PSIONICS as PSEUDOSCIENCE, there is considerable evidence that some people may have such abilities.

psychic healing (parapsychology): The ability to correct malfunctions in the human body by means not directly connected with physical phenomena. There is considerable controversy generated over PSYCHIC HEALING in current medical practice, with one group of practitioners labeling it PSEUDOSCIENCE and another group insisting that it often works where more orthodox medicine fails.

PSYCHIC HEALING is often included as one of the PSIONIC talents used by TELEPATHS in SF stories. The Adepts of Jean Lorrah's *Savage Universe* novels are able to manipulate the tissue of the human body, as well as other physical matter, and one of the key scenes in the series is the excision of a tumor from the brain of one of the main characters.

psychobabble (parapsychology): High-sounding gobbledygook of a weighty nature, dealing with matters of the mind. Adherents of NEW AGE philosophies tend to employ it to overwhelm opponents.

Public Broadcasting: See PBS.

pulp fiction (literary): ACTION/ADVENTURE stories, often featuring dauntless heroes battling unspeakable villains, of the sort written for PULPS in the late 19th and early 20th centuries. PULP FICTION is not necessarily bad writing. Often the stories have a broad dramatic sweep that carries away any deficiencies in CHARACTERIZATION or MOTIVATION. SPACE OPERA is the epitome of SF PULP FICTION.

pulps (publishing): Professional magazines printed on cheap paper, made from coarse wood pulp, which has a grainy finish that yellows quickly and disintegrates easily. PULPS were the most common form of mass-market fiction in the late 19th and early 20th centuries; they were written mostly by HACK writers, who wanted to appeal to the lowest common denominator of reader. The result was a proliferation of detective stories and SPACE OPERA SF.

These early SF magazines are now COLLECTABLES; their value is far in excess of the dime or quarter they cost when they were new.

pulsar (astronomy): A radio source that emits short pulses of radiation at regular intervals, presumably from a NEUTRON STAR.

Over 100 PULSARS have been discovered by astronomers using advanced radiotelescopes.

PULSAR emissions are as regular as clocks, but after a mere 10 million years of activity their emissions fade out.

punker (literary): A fan of CYBERPUNK, who tends to dress and behave like his literary counterparts. SF FANS are willing to accept almost anything at a CON; the PUNKER is considered to be the 23rd-century equivalent of CONAN THE BARBARIAN, and is treated accordingly.

puppet animation (film): Animation of three-dimensional models and puppets, using stop-action photography. PUPPET ANIMATION is largely used for short films for children, although some SF TV SERIES, like "Thunderbirds," have used this technique.

JIM HENSON has extended the use of puppets far beyond the simple stop-action animation. His work in *The Dark Crystal* (1982) and *Labyrinth* (1986) combines electronics, costuming, and puppetry so well that the SUSPENSION OF DISBELIEF is complete, and the audience can enter into the imaginary world of the film totally.

puppetry (film): See Puppet Animation.

quantum theory (physics): Theory used in 20th-century physics to describe atomic particle behavior. First stated by Max Planck in 1900, the theory holds that all electromagnetic radiation is emitted and absorbed in units called quanta that are made up of PHOTONS. The activities of these quanta produce the effects that we call light and heat.

quark (physics): A subatomic particle, even smaller than an electron. The term was coined by physicist Murray Gell-Mann in 1961, from a passage in James Joyce's *Finnegan's Wake.* QUARKS can be up, down, or strange; charm, beauty, or truth. Each QUARK has its own "flavor."

No one has actually seen a QUARK, but its presence has been surmised from the behavior of electrons. So far no one has ventured to guess at anything that might be smaller than a QUARK.

quasar (astronomy): An object that appears to be a starlike point of light, but emits more energy than an entire GALAXY. The name is a contraction of Quasi-Stellar Object.

QUASARS were first recognized in 1963. Since then, over 200 of them have been located. It is probable that a QUASAR is the central region of a GALAXY too far away to be seen, even with the most powerful telescope.

Quest story (literary): A tale in which a group of CHARACTERS gathers and goes in search of some valuable object; in the course of the search, each CHARACTER meets with challenges and overcomes them with the help of his companions. The QUEST has become an ARCHETYPE, and a staple form of FANTASY, from the legends of Jason and the Golden Fleece to *Lord of the Rings* by TOLKEIN.

quick-sale price (fan/art): A price set by the artist at which a PIECE may be sold immediately, without going through the BIDDING or AUCTION process. Most artists prefer to have their work go to AUCTION, but some buyers will snap up a favorite PIECE at the QUICK-SALE PRICE rather than risk getting outbid. The QUICK-SALE PRICE will be higher than the MINIMUM BID, but it may be lower than the eventual VOICE AUCTION price. It's up to the artist to decide whether to set a QUICK-SALE PRICE or not.

race (gaming): A CHARACTER's species: human, elf, dwarf, gnome, or halfling. The character's RACE is determined by the PLAYER with the assistance of the DUNGEONMASTER. RACE is a factor in determining the character's CLASS and ABILITIES; some professions are only open to human characters, while others seem to be more universal. A Paladin must be human, while a Rogue can be almost anything.

radar (physics): High-frequency radio waves used to detect the existence of objects at a distance. RADAR was first developed in the early 1940s; since then it has become a vital part of the aerospace industry.

radiation (physics): The emission of nuclei of certain particles from minerals or gasses, at a fixed rate. RADIATION was detected in the late 1800s by physicists Bequerrel and Curie, among others, and further studies led to the discovery of radium, and, eventually, to the harnessing of atomic power.

radiation belt (astronomy): See VAN ALLEN RADIATION BELT.

radiation sickness (biology): An adverse reaction of human tissue to bombardment by subatomic particles. The symptoms may include sores that do not heal, burns on exposed areas, and, in the long run, destruction of the immune system. RADIATION SICKNESS is a definite possibility in Space, where unknown types of radioactive minerals may be encountered. Most space vehicles are shielded against the more standard types of RADIOACTIVITY, but one of the points against manned exploration of the solar system is the risk to human life involved.

radiation storm (astronomy): A wave of electrified particles, hurled out of a star during a solar flare. Any space traveller caught in one would run the danger of RADIATION SICKNESS, unless the ship were properly shielded.

These storms may be the origin of the ION STORM, used in SF stories to disable spacecraft and set up dangerous situations for space travellers to overcome.

radioactive decay (physics): The gradual loss of atomic particles over a period of time by a particular mineral. Since each mineral has its own rate of decay, the age of a particular item can be determined by measuring the decay of the minerals in it. The isotope Carbon-14 is found in all organic matter; once its rate of decay was determined, it was possible to date organic remains found by archeologists, who otherwise would have had to make an educated guess, based on the local legends and geology.

radioactivity (physics): The emission of highly charged particles from certain minerals, like radium and uranium, measurable by tools like the Geiger counter. An otherwise inert mineral may be rendered radioactive by exposure to the RADIOACTIVITY of an atomic blast. Areas used for nuclear testing have been rendered uninhabitable for years.

One of the POST-HOLOCAUST scenarios is the world rendered totally sterile by a NUCLEAR WAR; only a tiny remnant of humanity survives, usually by burying itself deep in some kind of underground bunker.

ramjet (aerospace): A means of propelling a spaceship through vacuum by means of a jet-propulsion engine fueled by atomic waste. The idea was first explored by R. W. Bussard in 1960, and was later used by SF writers as one possibility for FTL DRIVE.

ramscoop (aerospace): A form of starship propulsion, using hydrogen atoms collected from space itself, to fuel a fusion drive. The "scoop" would collect the atoms, using a kind of magnetic "net." The idea was first presented by Robert Bussard in 1960. Of all the schemes for FTL DRIVE, this is the most likely to be attempted by researchers.

ratings (film): A guide to the suitability of a film for a particular audience. A "G"-rated film is for "General Audience," meaning that there is nothing in it to frighten or upset a very small child. "PG" means "General, with Parental Guidance"; this sort of film may have bad language, a certain amount of violence, and possibly some risque situations that might baffle a 10-year-old. "PG-13" is a film that may contain gory scenes and strong language, and can be seen by anyone over the age of 13. An "R" rating indicates a film is "Restricted"; viewers must be over age 18, because there may be profanity, partial nudity, and gore. An "X" rating indicates something totally unacceptable, usually pornography. A recent court ruling has led to the "A-17" rating, designating a film that would otherwise be rated "X," but that its makers feel is of artistic and social worth.

The present movie RATINGS system grew out of several attempts to censor the contents of films over the years. The tight restrictions of the old Movie Code of the 1930s and 1940s were loosened in the more permissive 1960s to the point where some people were offended by nearly everything on the screen. Parents were especially upset when a film that had been recommended for children turned out to have foul language or too much violence. The current system is not perfect, but it seems to work. Most parents can take small children to "G" films without risking nightmares, while adults can enjoy more sophisticated "R"-rated fare.

Outside the United States, other countries also use some kind of RATINGS system. Interesting variations indicate different cultural biases. STAR WARS, which was "PG" in the United States, has been rated as Adult fare in some Scandinavian countries because of excessive violence.

ratings (TV): The number of people assumed to be watching a particular TV program at a given time, determined by the Nielsen Rating Service. The actual sampling is done by a cross-section of the population, who have a small device attached to their TV set that records what programs are being watched, although it does not say who is doing the watching.

The RATINGS determine the broadness of the audience for a particular program, which, in turn, determines how much the NETWORK can charge its advertisers for the opportunity to sell their products to those TV watchers. A highly rated series will be able to charge more. If the RATINGS are low, the SERIES will be canceled and replaced with something that will, presumably, attract more people to watch and generate more advertising revenue.

This sort of thinking annoys a number of SF FANS as well as producers and writers. GENE RODDENBERRY has been extremely vocal about his problems with network executives and their obsession with RATINGS. When he decided to produce "Star Trek: The Next Generation," he bypassed the NETWORKS altogether, and sold the programs directly to local stations through DIRECT SYNDICATION, which has its own RATINGS system. Occasionally, a network executive will have faith that a TV SERIES will find an audience, and will ignore the RATINGS.

Most SF SERIES are, by their very nature, limited in appeal. Even STAR TREK was not considered a hit SERIES in its first run. It is only after 20 years of RERUNS that the SERIES has attained near-legendary status.

reader (fan): A person who insists he is not a FAN; he "only reads the stuff." READERS haunt bookstores, looking for obscure early works of their favorite authors. They subscribe to PROZINES, and occasionally even to SMALL PRESS. However, they scorn anything FANNISH, as being "amateur," and not worthy of their attention. See also PASSIFANS.

reader (publishing): Term for person who scans the SLUSH PILE for publishable material for a PROZINE. In book publishing, this job belongs to an editorial assistant. Such a person wades through vast piles of dross looking for the nugget of gold that indicates a major writing talent about to be discovered.

Although it is a mostly thankless task, every so often a future best-seller is found that makes the job worthwhile.

re-creation costume (fan/costuming): A costume that attempts to reproduce an already existing costume from a film, TV series, or play, or one that attempts to reproduce a costume seen in a comic or on a book cover. RE-CREATION is a specialized art, and as such, it is judged by different standards than other costumes.

A RE-CREATION costumer is limited in materials, whereas the original creator of the costume may have had access to a material made expressly for that film, play, or TV series. In the case of re-creating a comics character, the costumer has to insert a physical body into something that may have existed only as a drawing; the attempts to reproduce SUPERHEROES in leotards and tights are sometimes rendered ineffectual by the body beneath the outfit.

Some judges insist that the contestant provide them with a picture of the original costume, so that they can decide if the RE-CREATION faithfully copies it, or if it falls short of total imitation.

red dwarf (astronomy): A star with a low surface temperature, and a diameter about half that of our sun. RED DWARFS are long-lived as stars go, because of their low energy output. However, any planets circling them will not be warmed as well as those of yellow or white stars.

red giant (astronomy): A star with a low surface temperature, and a diameter between ten and one hundred times that of our sun. RED GIANTS are considered fairly young as stars go; they are brighter than our sun, and their planets may be just forming. As the star's gasses burn off and its core begins to solidify, it gradually turns yellow and then white. Further stellar burning reverses the coloration, until the star has become a RED DWARF.

red shift (physics): The amount by which wavelengths of light and other forms of electromagnetic radiation are increased, because of the expansion of the universe. RED SHIFT is one example of the Doppler effect, caused by the motion of a light source along the line of sight.

Regency Ball (fan/convention): A popular event at some CONVENTIONS that attempts to duplicate the atmosphere of the English Regency (1795–1815). Why such an event should be part of an SF CONVENTION is one of the great mysteries of FANDOM. Possibly the artificiality of the milieu attracts the same people who read Fantasy stories. For whatever reason, the REGENCY BALL has become a feature of FAN-CONS like Boskone.

Recorded music is usually provided by the Dancing master, who instructs the attendees in the intricacies of contradances (something like square dancing) and reels (Virginia Reel being the most popular). Attendees are expected to wear an approximation of Regency dress: a high-waisted, long-skirted, short-sleeved gown for the ladies, and either knee-britches or formal dress for the gentlemen. (Everyone at a Regency Ball is supposed to be of the Gentry at the very least.)

The REGENCY BALL may be scheduled in the middle of the afternoon, around tea-time; in that case, a light collation will also be provided. REGENCY BALLS may charge each attendee a small fee. In this, they are quite within the scope of the period; the Assemblies that they are trying to imitate were often supported by subscriptions.

regional con (fan/convention): A FAN-CON that draws its attendance from a particular region, as opposed to the WORLDCON, which is presumably attended by anyone who can possibly get to it. Most FAN-CONS qualify as REGIONAL CONS, also known as regionals. They are often run by an SF club or group based near the location of the CON, and they tend to request SF writers living in the vicinity to sit on PANELS, along with the GOH.

REGIONAL CONS like LUNACON in the New York area or Windycon in Chicago have a wider pool of panelists to draw on; some REGIONAL CONS have attracted members from across the country.

registration (fan/convention): The process of actually checking CONVENTION members into the CON; also, the people who do it, and the area in which it is done. Each member usually receives a PROGRAM BOOK and/or a POCKET PROGRAM and a BADGE, with whatever notation is deemed necessary. DAY-TRIPPERS may get a BADGE with a particular mark on it, or one of a different color than the full members. DEALERS, Guests, and CON-COM may get badges with ribbons attached, proclaiming their status.

REGISTRATION is usually the first CON function set up, since nothing can happen until the people are there. REGISTRATION procedures can be as simple as having each member sign a computer-generated checklist, or they can involve entering the member's name and address into a computer, for later communications. A sure sign of CON-COM organization is how well they handle REGISTRATION.

The REGISTRATION desk is also the place where general communications are placed. Any PROGRAM changes will be noted on a bulletin board near REGISTRATION, and any lost or found items may be turned in there.

regular (astronomy): Said of a natural satellite that maintains a nearly perfect circular orbit around a planet. An irregular satellite will have an orbit that verges on the eccentric.

rejection slip (publishing): The way an EDITOR informs a prospective contributor that a manuscript is not acceptable for publication. REJECTION SLIPS may consist of anything from a brief note to a long letter stating exactly why the material is being turned down.

No one is immune to REJECTION SLIPS; even ISAAC ASIMOV has received them. The only recourse is to take a good look at the story and rewrite it, then submit it elsewhere, and hope that the next EDITOR will accept it.

Relationship story (fan/fanzine): A story that deals with interpersonal relationships, rather than problem-solving or ACTION/ADVENTURE; many of these stories assume the reader already is familiar with the characters through exposure to them in a TV series or films. They are primarily found in MEDIAZINES, rather than in SF-oriented FANZINES. They have also penetrated into the world of PROZINES, through SOFT SF.

Many of the stories in MEDIAZINES are RELATIONSHIP STORIES. They explore the interaction of the CHARACTERS in an already existing situation, instead of setting up the situation and inserting the CHARACTERS into it. The RELATIONSHIP is often a deepening friendship between two antagonistic men, which may develop further into a MALE-BONDING situation, or, if it is extended far enough, into a SLASH situation.

HURT/COMFORT stories began as a combination of RELATIONSHIP and ACTION/ADVENTURE. The two main characters would be in a life-threatening situation; one would be hurt, while the other would have to give comfort, and the relationship would determine the outcome.

RELATIONSHIP STORIES may not necessarily be SF; however, the proliferation of the SOFT SCIENCES into SF has increased the number of SF stories that include RELATIONSHIP interactions.

relax-a-con (fan/conventions): A small local or regional convention, with a limited program; an extended party for less than five hundred members. RELAX-A-CONS are deliberately low-key, with one GOH (or perhaps none at all), and one TRACK of PROGRAMMING. The emphasis is on fun, rather than on either SF as literature, or SF as entertainment.

A CONVENTION may be deliberately advertised as a RELAX-A-CON, but may develop into something larger than the CON-COM intended. On the other hand, a CONVENTION that was supposed to have attracted a much larger audience may dwindle into a RELAX-A-CON, much to the dismay of the committee.

remainders (publishing): Books sold by the publisher to dealers at a fraction of their retail cost. REMAINDERS are surplus HARDCOVERS that no one wants to buy at full price after the same book has come out in a cheaper PAPERBACK edition. REMAINDERING means that the book is still popular enough for people to buy at a price still higher than a PAPERBACK. The alternative to REMAINDERING is pulping (when surplus books are destroyed).

Just because a book is REMAINDERED doesn't necessarily mean it was a flop; sometimes, it is quite the contrary. There are bound to be surplus books of a HARDCOVER best-seller that sold 500,000 copies if the publisher printed 501,000. Buying these books is an inexpensive way to build up a good SF HARDCOVER collection. Many public libraries also buy REMAINDERS of elaborate art and science books.

Ren-Faire (fan/convention): Short for "Renaissance Fair"; a gathering of craftspeople, actors, and musicians who attempt to reproduce the atmosphere of a medieval fair for a paying audience. REN-FAIRES have been organized by various groups, for various reasons. Occasionally local or regional artistic or theatrical organizations decide to mount a REN-FAIRE to generate income for the group. More frequently, they are financed by entrepreneurs, who take over a park for several weekends, charge a sizable admission fee, and hope it doesn't rain.

REN-FAIRES are colorful events, with gaily colored tents set up for the various craftspeople and vendors and costumed SCA members strolling about, lending color and verisimilitude to the scene. The time period that is being re-created is roughly 1450–1550. In Italy, this was considered the Renaissance, while in northern Europe, the period has been called the High Gothic. No one really cares about historical accuracy, though; the emphasis is on pageantry, not pedantry.

REN-FAIRES may be found across the United States during the summer months. One of the largest and best-known is held at Sterling Forest Gardens, in New York State.

repro (fan/fanzine): Short for reproduction method. Early REPRO was by hectograph or mimeo; the results were blurry, with practically unreadable type and foggy-looking illustrations. Currently, most FANZINES use PHOTO-OFFSET for REPRO, with results that are more attractive to prospective readers. A few FANZINES are laser-printed; these almost look like professionally typeset publications.

rerun (TV): The popular term for what is more accurately known as SYNDICATION, the showing of TV programs after their initial broadcast. When this is done during the SEASON, the show is labeled a repeat EPISODE. The practice of repeating the EPISODES has become so common that many SERIES have to announce that a particular EPISODE is "all-new."

Retief (literary): The leading character in a series of stories by Keith Laumer, based on his experiences in the U.S. Armed Forces, and as a professional diplomat. First seen in *Envoy to New Worlds* in 1963, Retief is a clever and resourceful career diplomat, who gets shuttled off to different worlds, where he usually pulls off some diplomatic coup against the vile Groacii. His incompetent superiors inevitably take the credit for Retief's accomplishments, leaving Retief to pick up and take off for the next planet. The Retief stories reflect the "Ugly American" attitude of the late 1960s.

rimworld (astronomy/literary): A planet circling a star on the extreme edge of our GALAXY, where star systems are few and far between, and any contact with more centralized systems is problematical at best. SF writers usually describe such planets as frontier settlements, analagous to the American West or the far-flung outposts of the British Empire at its height.

ring binding (printing): Also known as comb binding; plastic strips, inserted into perforations in the pages of a book or FANZINE by a machine and pressed into place with a heating machine. RING BINDING looks very professional; it allows the pages to lie flat, which is useful if the FANZINE runs to more than 200 pages. However, RING BINDINGS take up more room than either side stapling or SADDLE STITCHING and the plastic tends to unwind, leaving the pages loose. For some editors, however, the professional look of RING BINDING is worth the added expense.

Ringworld (literary): Planet created by Larry Niven for a series of novels, beginning with *Ringworld* in 1968. The RINGWORLD is an artificially constructed environment, completely encircling the equator of its star, something like a limited DYSON SPHERE. In this extended SPACE STATION, representatives of three different species encounter adventures in various environments.

robinsonade (literary): A story in which a stranded traveller must fend for himself in a hostile environment; the term comes from Daniel Defoe's *Robinson Crusoe*, which was widely imitated in the early 1800s. The theme has continued to fascinate writers, although the literary term has fallen into disuse. Many of the early SF stories depicted survival on a strange planet on which the hero would triumph through superior strength and wit.

robot (literary): A mechanical device, meant to do work usually done by humans. The term was first used by playwright Karel Capek, in *R.U.R.* (first produced in 1921); he took it from the Czech word for "laborer." In his play, the mechanical men revolt against their masters, and take over the factory that made them.

ROBOTS became a staple theme in SF. They were often seen as tools of a ruthless dictator, who used them as soldiers who could not be wounded. Occasionally, a ROBOT appeared as a

SIDEKICK of the hero of a SPACE OPERA, but most of the early views of mechanical men were unfavorable. The point was endlessly made that mechanical men were, after all, mechanisms, and they lacked the intuitive senses of humanity. In Robert Sheckley's story *Watchbird*, for instance, a device that was supposed to prevent one human from harming another cannot distinguish between murder and cutting the power to an electrical appliance . . . or between a mugger stabbing his victim and a doctor using a scalpel on a patient.

Much of the change in attitude is due to the stories of ISAAC ASIMOV, who is best known for his ROBOT stories, beginning with "Robbie" in 1940.

Famous film ROBOTS have varied from the purely mechanical Robbie of *Forbidden Planet* (1956) to the almost-human C3PO of STAR WARS (1977). This snippy, if not downright snotty, ROBOT has become a STOCK CHARACTER of SF, both written and filmed.

ROBOTS have moved out of SF and into Reality. Many factories use ROBOTS to do chores that were once performed by humans on assembly lines. A ROBOT need not necessarily look like a human if all that is needed to do the job is a pair of arms.

The science of using ROBOTS is called Robotics, a term invented by ISAAC ASIMOV, who postulated the Three Laws of Robotics: (1) A ROBOT may not injure a human being, or, through inaction, cause a human to come to harm. (2) A ROBOT must obey the orders given to it by humans, except where those orders conflict with the First Law. (3) A ROBOT must protect its own existence, as long as this does not conflict with the First or Second Laws.

The technology of Robotics is barely getting started. ROBOTS are already performing many of the standard tasks in industry. They have been sent out as PLANETARY PROBES to explore the SOLAR SYSTEM. Eventually, the dream of a household ROBOT may become a reality. See also ANDROID; ARTIFICIAL INTELLIGENCE; CYBORG.

rocket (aerospace): An engine used to propel a vehicle into space, outside the pull of the Earth's gravity and beyond the Earth's atmosphere. ROCKETS work on the reaction principle: Forward propulsion is achieved by reaction to a jet of gasses, forced through a nozzle at tremendous pressure. ROCKETS are meant to work in atmosphere; any ROCKET that is fired in space must carry liquid oxygen to allow the fuel to burn.

The earliest forms of ROCKETS were those developed by the Chinese, used primarily in fireworks displays. Later experiments produced unreliable but spectacular weapons, used during the Napoleonic Wars. Theorist KONSTANTIN TSIOLKOVSKY and practical experimenter ROBERT GODDARD paved the way for today's gigantic Saturn ROCKETS, which launch SPACE SHUTTLES and SPACE STATIONS into orbit.

ROCKETS became the primary vehicle for literary space travel early in the history of SF. H. G. Wells and Jules Verne both described the primitive ROCKETS used by their imaginary explorers to get to the Moon. The tapered shape of the ROCKET was meant to thrust easily through the atmosphere; once in the vacuum of space, a ROCKET ship could have any shape an artist cared to draw . . . and many of them were extremely odd indeed!

Over the years, various means of attaining FTL DRIVE have been described by SF writers: HYPERSPACE, SOLAR SAILS, RAMJETS, and RAMSCOOPS. Nevertheless, the ROCKET ship has become the very symbol of SF; the much-valued HUGO AWARD is a statuette in the shape of a ROCKET.

rocketry (aerospace): The science and technology of building ROCKETS. Model ROCKETRY is a hobby for millions of enthusiasts, who arrange launches in open spaces, and try to perfect their tiny craft to extend their range.

Rocky Horror Picture Show (film): 1975 film starring Tim Curry, Barry Bostwick, and Susan Sarandon that is a parody of horror movies, SF movies, musicals, and pornography; it has become the #1 CULT FILM of all time. Showings take place in theaters across the United States, usually at midnight, with the audience dressing up like the characters, reciting the dialog, throwing things at the screen, and generally participating in the action.

Roddenberry, Gene (b. 1921): TV and film producer and writer; creator of STAR TREK. RODDENBERRY's original idea was to present contemporary ideas in the guise of futuristic drama. He fought successfully for concepts that later became standard procedure in SF drama on TV: a multiracial, multiethnic crew; women in positions of authority; literate scripts based on valid personal and scientific concepts. When the SERIES was canceled after three seasons, RODDENBERRY tried several other concepts, but none of them seemed to click. In 1979 STAR TREK moved to the Big Screen, and then back to television as a "Next Generation" in 1987.

RODDENBERRY set most of the precedents for cooperation with FANS as well. He permitted his characters to be used for FAN-FIC, and understood the need to nurture fannish enthusiasm for a TV SERIES. He has maintained connections with fans through OFFICIAL FAN CLUBS, and through various NEWSLETTERS. RODDENBERRY's hand is felt on almost anything professionally produced with the STAR TREK name on it.

role-playing games (also called RPG): Games in which players assume roles, as if they were characters in a story that is being created as they play. The players are given a situation, which is often a QUEST for a particular object, or a rescue attempt, set in a specific UNIVERSE. They announce their actions, whereupon the referee, that is, the DUNGEONMASTER, tells them what the results of those actions are. Most ROLE-PLAYING GAMES resemble the original, DUNGEONS AND DRAGONS,™ and follow the same sort of procedures.

There are some groups that continue their game over months and even over years. There are also limited ROLE-PLAYING GAMES that are run during a CONVENTION weekend. Some players like to use props, models, and so forth to keep their characters clear in their minds, while other games insist on being purely cerebral. There are even ROLE-PLAYING GAMES that are conducted through the mail.

By far the most popular role-playing game seems to be D&D.™ All you need for the game are a Player's Guide, three or four friends, and a lively imagination.

One offshoot of ROLE-PLAYING GAMES is the proliferation of Fantasy novels that read as if some player had simply written out his or her last CAMPAIGN.

role reversal (literary): The assumption of one GENDER ROLE by another. The most commonly used idea is that of women assuming the dominant role that Western culture has attributed to men. This assumption of the male-dominant role underlies much of the early Greek myths of the Amazons, who may very well have been matriarchal societies who rebelled against being enslaved by male-dominated war-parties.

The idea of the "masculine" woman and the "effeminate" man may be taken to extremes, for comic effect. On the other hand, many FEMINIST SF writers went to extremes in depicting women as fighters, to the point that the WOMAN WARRIOR has become almost as much a cliche as her swaggering male counterpart.

A good example of ROLE REVERSAL is in the *Chanur* novels of C. J. Cherryh, which depict a species somewhat resembling lions on Earth. Like lions, the females are the hunters; the males are considered too emotionally unstable for anything but providing home life for the young.

ROM (computer): Read-Only Memory; the permanent store of information that tells the computer what to do. Most computers must have this ROM inserted on a hard disk before they can be operated. Others may need SOFTWARE to provide the DATABASE for operation.

roman cycle (literary): A series of novels with interrelated characters, each of which can be read as an entity of its own. The novels need not be written in sequence; a writer may begin the SAGA with the culmination of a situation, then go back and describe what led up to it in a number of PREQUELS. The term comes from the French word for novel, *roman*, pronounced with the accent on the second syllable.

room party (fan/conventions): A gathering of fans at a CONVENTION, held in one of the private rooms being used by the membership. ROOM PARTIES are announced by FLYERS spread throughout the hotel, often to the annoyance of the hotel management, who remove them from walls and elevators as fast as they are put up.

ROOM PARTIES may be held by a group of FANS interested in some particular TV SERIES or some aspect of SF or of FANDOM. They may be held to promote a WORLD-CON BID. They may even be held to celebrate some personal event with one's FANNISH friends. They are usually open to anyone with a CON BADGE. Entertainment at ROOM PARTIES ranges from chips 'n' dips and conversation to the showing of videotapes of old TV SERIES. At one time FILKING was a feature of ROOM PARTIES; complaints from other inhabitants of the hotels led to the removal of the FILKERS to the main program area of the CONVENTION.

For many fans, the whole purpose of going to a CONVENTION is not to attend the PANELS but to attend the ROOM PARTIES.

roomstuffing (fan/conventions): The practice of allowing several people to stay in a hotel room that has only been registered to one person. The extra people may be accommodated in sleeping bags on the floor, or on mattresses torn from the beds, or even in the bathtub. The idea is to share the cheaper cost of a single room among as many people as possible. While ROOMSTUFFING is not strictly legal, some hotels do turn a blind eye to it, on the theory that the SF CONVENTION is a yearly event, held at the same place, and a good working relationship is hard to find.

ROOMSTUFFING is for the young; as a fan grows older, privacy assumes more importance, and the advantages of a mattress overweigh the disadvantage of paying the full cost of the room.

Rotsler's Rules of Costuming (fan/costuming): Informal guide for would-be costume contestants at FAN-CONS, drawn up by William Rotsler, SF writer and fan. Most of ROTSLER'S RULES are plain common sense. ROTSLER'S RULES are usually included with preregistration papers for WORLD-CON MASQUERADES. For the full text, see Appendix C.

round robin (fan): A story created by several contributors, each of whom writes a section and passes it on to the next writer. The result is sometimes funny, sometimes spotty, like a Victorian parlor game. Occasionally, a ROUND ROBIN is started at a CON, where each member gets a chance to add another bit to the story. The final result is read out at the DEAD DOG PARTY.

RSN (fan): "Real Soon Now," or whenever the EDITOR/CON CHAIR can find the time. It's a common excuse when contributors want to know when their story will see print.

runner (fan/convention): The GOFER who displays the PIECE being bid on at the VOICE AUCTION, who literally runs up and down the aisle to wave the item tantalizingly before the prospective buyer. The PIECES are usually lined up before the VOICE AUCTION, and each RUNNER gets a PIECE in rotation. RUNNERS must be extremely careful with the more delicate PIECES of sculpture or craftwork. If they break a PIECE, it's theirs, and at the QUICK-SALE PRICE, too. Being a RUNNER takes strong legs and a steady hand.

running a character (gaming/literary): Creating and playing a CHARACTER in a ROLE-PLAYING GAME. Since so much time and effort goes into creating the CHARACTER, a player will continue to run the character through several adventures, presumably picking up EXPERIENCE POINTS as the CHARACTER goes from escapade to escapade, until the CHARACTER reaches a point of no return, being either killed or deified.

The term has carried over into the literary field; the writers of a SHARED UNIVERSE are said to RUN THE CHARACTERS they themselves have created. Anyone who wants to use those CHARACTERS in another part of the story must consult with the originator.

running gag (film): A recurrent comic situation, joke, or action in a story or film; the term comes from burlesque, where the same joke might be told throughout the show, with different reactions each time. A typical RUNNING GAG might involve a particular action, which is funny twice, only to produce groans the third time it is repeated.

rushes (film): One day's shooting, reviewed by the director and producer before editing. Each scene may have been shot several times, and it is by viewing the RUSHES that the director must make the choice of which one to use in the finished film.

S

saddle stitching (printing): Binding a FANZINE or any other publication so that the staples are in the center of the sheet of paper that is then folded over to form a readable book. FANZINES are often collated by hand and stapled by the editor/pulisher, and SADDLE STITCHING is one of the preferred means of putting them together. The alternatives to SADDLE STITCHING are SIDE-STAPLING, RING BINDING, or PERFECT-BINDING. Most PROZINES are either SADDLE STITCHED or PERFECT-BOUND.

saga (literary): Originally, SAGA referred only to the epic poems of the deeds of Norse heroes, dating back to the oral tradition of the Scandinavian peoples before the incursions made by Christian missionaries in the 11th and 12th centuries AD. The term has been extended to include any series of adventure stories, particularly those set in a mythic past or feudal future.

SAGA has become an overworked term. Almost any set of stories with interrelated characters can be called a SAGA. George Lucas' STAR WARS films have been termed the STAR WARS SAGA. CONAN THE BARBARIAN is certainly the hero of a SAGA, but it is difficult to see ISAAC ASIMOV'S soft-spoken ANDROID detective, R. Daneel Olivaw, in such a position. Nevertheless, ASIMOV'S novels in which this character appears are occasionally marketed as *The Robot Saga*.

Sagan, Carl (b. 1934): American astronomer and biologist, whose television series COSMOS helped popularize scientific concepts such as the GREENHOUSE EFFECT and NUCLEAR WINTER. SAGAN has written Science Fiction as well as Science Fact, and often acts as a spokesperson for the scientific community when one is called for, during transmission of new data from Space after the VOYAGER PROBE transmissions, for instance. SAGAN is an enthusiastic proponent of scientific research into matters such as ARTIFICIAL INTELLIGENCE and the possibilities of life on other planets elsewhere in the GALAXY.

Salyut (aerospace): Soviet SPACE STATION in use from 1971 to 1982; it was augmented by the MIR SPACE STATION in 1986. SALYUT 7 is still in orbit as of 1990. Soviet crews have been ferried back and forth to the SALYUT by SOYUZ shuttlecraft over the last 20 years; some crews remained in space for nearly a year, with no major physical harm. See also SPACE STATION.

same-sex relationship stories (literary): An extremely roundabout euphemism for homosexual. No one wants to step on anyone's toes, and this way, no one's feelings are hurt. Most SAME-SEX RELATIONSHIP STORIES in FANZINES come under the heading of SLASH FICTION. See also K/S FICTION.

samizdat (literary/publishing): From the Russian: the Soviet press that until recently had to operate under secretive conditions to disseminate Western literature. Under the present regime, the SAMIZDAT press has emerged from hiding, ready to fulfill its task of criticizing the government, satirizing the bureaucracy, and helping the populace to improve itself.

By extension, in the United States, SAMIZDAT has come to mean any politically oriented nonprofessional publication, often with a radical left-wing orientation. Very few FANZINES qualify as SAMIZDAT, although the PERSONALZINES and individual APAS may very well propound such philosophy as their writers wish to share with their readers.

SASE (fan): Self-Addressed Stamped Envelope; can be pronounced as initials or as "Say-See." An absolutely necessary

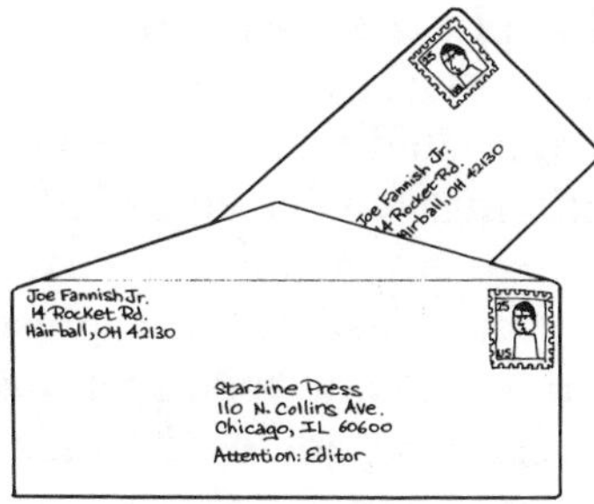

enclosure with any request, inquiry, manuscript, or anything else sent to an editor or publisher, whether FAN or PRO. Between the exigencies of time and money, both FAN and PRO are appreciative of the person who includes the SASE. It means the recipient of the request does not have to decipher someone's handwriting, find an envelope, and find a stamp before answering the request. When it comes to MANUSCRIPTS, a SASE is even more important, since the cost of mailing back the MANUSCRIPT may come to several dollars. Many editors simply do not answer any query that does not include a SASE.

Some writers include a SASP (Self-Addressed Stamped Postcard) with their MANUSCRIPT, so that the editor can reply on that and the MANUSCRIPT need not be returned. That's all right, too.

satellite (astronomy/aerospace): Any nonluminous object in orbit around another, larger, nonluminous object in Space. Most SATELLITES in our SOLAR SYSTEM are natural ones, termed MOONS. In 1957, the Soviet Union launched the first artificial SATELLITE, SPUTNIK, and ushered in the Space Age. The United States did not put a SATELLITE in orbit until 1958, when Explorer was successfully launched.

In the past 30 years, SATELLITES have become an integral part of Earth's technology. In the 1990s, SATELLITES provide information on everything from the pollution of the oceans to the deployment of missiles. They facilitate communications between nations, closing the gap between peoples. The successful emplacement of the Hubbell Space Telescope will enable astronomers to learn even more about the Universe beyond our GALAXY. The ultimate SATELLITE may well be a SPACE STATION.

Saturday morning ghetto (TV): The morning hours of Saturdays in the United States that are given over to the most mindlessly violent animated cartoons seen on broadcast television. Most of the offerings have been criticized for such flaws as simplistic plot lines, stereotyped characters, and overemphasis on material goods; even worse, the unsophisticated audience is ripe for exploitation by toy and food manufacturers, who submit the young viewers to an endless barrage of advertisements for expensive toys and sugary breakfast foods.

Occasionally, the SATURDAY MORNING GHETTO comes up with a gem. Much JAPANIMATION was originally broadcast in the United States during this time period. The "Star Trek Animated" episodes were also shown during the morning hours of Saturday during the 1973–1974 season. Occasionally a live-action series will be shown, usually depicting a young hero or heroine overcoming adversity or working with clever, cuddly friends to thwart a story-book style witch or evil wizard.

Since most adults are either sleeping or doing chores during this time period, and the hungy maw of the advertisers must be filled, it is unlikely that the situation will change. As long as there are cartoons available, the SATURDAY MORNING GHETTO will provide this sort of mindless entertainment to children, who will undoubtedly be delighted by it. See also CHILDREN'S ROOM GHETTO.

Saturn (astronomy): Sixth planet from the sun in our Solar System; second largest after JUPITER, and the last of the planets visible without a telescope. SATURN is best known for its spectacular system of rings, which extend from the planet's equator and into space for 170,000 miles (275,000 km). Between the rings (which appear to be made up of asteroids, moonlets, and rocky space debris) and the full-sized MOONS (10 large ones and at least 12 smaller ones), SATURN forms a minisystem all its own.

Alas, SATURN is too far from the Sun to have enough heat to generate life as we know it. However, the MOONS, rings, and other bits and pieces make excellent sites for space pirates to lurk. Alan Nourse's *Raiders from the Rings* (1962) presupposes such a den of iniquity. Other writers have used SATURN's moons as the site of mining colonies as well as political refugee camps.

SATURN was one of the planets examined by the Voyager PROBE in its GRAND TOUR.

Saturn (rocket): U.S. space launchers, developed by the team led by Wernher Von Braun after 1958. SATURN rockets were used to launch the APOLLO missions; they now launch SPACE SHUTTLES.

SCA (Society for Creative Anachronism): Pronounced either as initials or as "skah." A group founded in 1966 by several SF and Fantasy writers and their friends in Berkeley, California, to re-create the Middle Ages as they would have liked to have lived them. Among the founders of the SCA were Diana Paxton, Fred Hollander, and Poul Anderson. The SCA has been incorporated as a nonprofit educational organization, whose membership now includes well-known writers, artists, historians, and ordinary folk who enjoy dressing up and living in a fantasy world for a few hours a week. The current membership is greater than 10,000 worldwide, and the SCA boasts "Kingdoms" in Germany and Denmark. There is even an active group aboard an aircraft carrier.

The SCA has a Board of Directors who take care of such MUNDANE matters as taxes and the internal administrative affairs of the organization. There are 13 Kingdoms divided by major geographic areas; within each Kingdom, there may be Principalities, Baronies, Shires, or Cantons, depending on the body count. The local groups are run by a King, who wins the title by Force of Arms, in a more or less bloodless tourney, and by various appointed functionaries, who deal with such problems as arranging for meeting space, speakers, and finances.

Each subgroup, whether Principality or Shire, encourages its members to create their PERSONAS, based on historical research. Many groups require their members to attend meetings in GARB, which must be as authentic as possible. A number of SCA members have become adept at such medieval skills as handweaving, brewing, and manuscript illumination, and offer their products for sale to finance their group's activities.

SCA members have become especially prominent in the summer REN-FAIRES that have begun to spring up all over the United

States. They add color to the proceedings, and are often used by the promoters of the event as performers.

SCA members also pop up in costume at SF CONVENTIONS, where they draw particular attention if they are in either full armor (male) or full feather (either sex, if Tudor). SCA costumes are meant to be authentic; in addition, many of the more luxurious ones are truly spectacular, using beads, embroidery, and exquisite fabric to great effect. A few MASQUERADES have had to rule that SCA garb may not be entered into the competition.

There has been some criticism of the SCA. Detractors point out that the members tend to ignore some of the less pleasant aspects of the period 450–1650 AD. No one really wants to recreate the sanitary or medical practices of the time, nor can the standard middle-class 20th-century American understand a mindset that automatically assumes that anyone not exactly like oneself in all ways must be inferior and possibly not even quite human.

However, the SCA members assert that all their activities are done for fun, and their pageantry does add a good deal of color to SF CONVENTIONS.

The SCA has evolved its own jargon, which is noted in this Dictionary. See also EVENT; FEAST-GEAR; PENNSIC WARS.

Science: The systematic exploration of natural phenomena, through observation and experimentation. SCIENCE provides the theoretical knowledge that is then put to practical use through technology.

SCIENCE attempts to explain the workings of the Universe. New evidence is being brought to light daily that contradicts what is already known; when that happens, perceptions must change to accept the new information. This is not always easy, and there is a distrust of scientific endeavors that comes out in MONSTER MOVIES and HORROR STORIES, in which some experiment goes terribly wrong and death and destruction threaten to engulf humanity.

When scientific research breaks previously held ideas, and disturbs the status quo, an innovative thinker like Galileo might be forced to recant "heresies," just as the theories of natural selection expounded by Charles Darwin were mocked and misinterpreted in a later era, and the theories of physics proposed by Albert Einstein were deemed too esoteric for the average person to understand.

The STOCK CHARACTER of the MAD SCIENTIST was part of SF from its very inception. The antiscientific strain in FANTASY and HORROR fiction is one that has its counterpoint in the enthusiastic espousal of technology by early SF writers. Both attitudes are found in SCIENCE FICTION, and both have their current adherents.

Science Fantasy (literary): A story that combines the technological background of SF with the brooding atmosphere of FANTASY. SCIENCE FANTASY is especially effective on film, where the atmosphere can be evoked by music and costumes. JIM HENSON's delightful film *The Dark Crystal* (1982) can be viewed as a SCIENCE FANTASY, combining the technology of another world with fantastic characters. C. L. Moore's story, "Shambleau," is a much darker SCIENCE FANTASY, evoking the myth of Medusa in the setting of a frontier settlement on Mars.

Science Fiction: A type of Fantasy based on scientific credibility, often dealing with possible future developments on this planet or on other worlds. (In this book Science Fiction is abbreviated SF.)

The term was first used by Hugo Gernsback in 1929, to describe the type of stories he printed in *Amazing Science Fiction* magazine, but the ideas and conventions used in SF had been established long before. Jules Verne had been writing technology-based adventure stories since the 1860s; H. G. Wells had produced stories that postulated future developments in society beginning in the 1890s. Even earlier, Mary Shelley's FRANKENSTEIN (1818) explored the possibilities of scientific research and its horrendous aftermath.

Today, SF encompasses a wide range of topics and writing styles. It is more than a literary GENRE; SF is a way of life.

Science Fiction Book Club: A division of Doubleday Publications that provides SF books through the mail, often in special editions or omnibus volumes that are unavailable elsewhere. Begun in 1953 in both Britain and the United States, the

SF BOOK CLUB has become a powerful distribution factor in the SF world. A sale to the SF BOOK CLUB automatically guarantees an author a wide audience, many of whom never get near a bookstore or a CONVENTION.

Selection of items for the SF BOOK CLUB is a delicate matter, balancing popularity of the author with the salability of the book and the possibility of a newcomer reaching superstar status. The SF BOOK CLUB maintains a large BACKLIST as well, so that members can order materials they may have missed earlier.

The SF BOOK CLUB offers at least four new items every month. Members must buy at least six items a year to maintain their good standing. Bargains are offered at various times, and there are often special editions of older books or omnibus editions of SERIES books that can be bought only through the SF BOOK CLUB.

While the SF BOOK CLUB has been criticized for sticking too close to the middle of the artistic road, and pandering to popular taste in its selections, the general SF reading public appreciates the opportunity to acquire these items through the mail, at reasonable prices, and in well-bound, well-printed editions.

Science Romance (literary): A story that deals largely with the betterment of society through technology, as depicted in the works of Jules Verne and his followers: *20,000 Leagues Under the Sea* (1870) is the most typical of Verne's SCIENCE ROMANCES. While the adventures of Professor Arronax, Ned Land, and the mysterious Captain Nemo are the basis of the PLOT, the real fun of the story lies in the detail with which the workings of the "submarine boat" are described, and the specifics of life underwater.

scientifiction (literary): An early form of SF, as written and fostered by HUGO GERNSBACK, who defined it as "a charming romance intermingled with scientific fact and prophet's wisdom." SCIENTIFICTION was supposed to be a tool for teaching SCIENCE as well as for promoting a vision of the future that would encompass a benign technology and an optimistic outlook on life. Few of these stories have stood the test of time; the sourer DYSTOPIAS seem to have had better luck in sustaining reader popularity.

Sci-Fi (literary): Abbreviation for Science Fiction first used by FORREST ACKERMAN in the 1930s. Most MUNDANES (including many book and film critics, alas) persist in using it. TRUFEN prefer SF (which is the form used in this book).

score (film/TV): The music that accompanies the action in a film or TV program. It can be written specifically for the film, as JOHN WILLIAMS' well-known themes for STAR WARS (1977) and *E.T.* (1982), or it can consist of previously written and performed selections interposed on the action, such as *Also Spracht Zarathustra*, the tone-poem by Richard Strauss that sets the scene for *2001: Space Odyssey* (1968).

The SCORE can set the mood for the entire film, evoking feelings of awe and grandeur, as in James Horner's *Star Trek: The Motion Picture* (1979). Occasionally, the SCORE takes on a life of its own, and the music becomes totally identified with the film or TV program. Such has become the case with the theme by Alexander Courage used for the original STAR TREK episodes, the John Williams' themes used in the STAR WARS trilogy, and the eerie ping-pong notes that introduced the EPISODES of THE TWILIGHT ZONE (1959–1964).

Scott, Ridley: British filmmaker, who has imprinted his dark vision of the future on several SF films, most notably *Blade Runner* (1982). SCOTT's hallmarks are his attention to detail and his unified approach to the film. In *Blade Runner*, for instance, the magazines on a newsstand had to be exactly as he envisioned the current products would be 50 years from now, even though the viewing public might not even notice them.

scratchpad (computer): Small, fast, reusable memory that acts like the paper on which the user can scribble ideas, which may later be expanded on, or erased.

screening (film): A free showing of a soon-to-be-released film to a limited or preselected audience, often for critical analysis prior to its general distribution. Attendance at private SCREENINGS is usually by invitation, given to members of the press for reviewing the film. These private showings are usually held in small SCREENING rooms, rather than in theaters.

There are also open SCREENINGS of CULT FILMS at theaters across the country. THE ROCKY HORROR PICTURE SHOW is often shown as a Midnight Screening, complete with its enthusiastic audience participation.

Occasionally, there will be a SCREENING of a film or series of films at an SF CONVENTION. One of the features of the WORLD-CON in recent years has been the SCREENING of all the films nominated for the HUGO AWARD in the category of "Best Dramatic Presentation."

screening (printing): A process whereby ink is applied to paper or another medium through a mesh or screen. The result is a very fine stippling, and a delicate gradation of color. SCREENING is often used for individual works of art; however, it is not a preferred technique for FANZINE illustration, because it is not always easy to reproduce the delicate stippling.

screenplay (film): The dialog written for a film, without any technical or stage directions. The SCREENPLAY is not exactly the same as the SCRIPT, since it contains the words but not necessarily the actions that go with them. Actors receive the SCREENPLAY; directors work from the SCRIPT.

script (film/TV/literary): The full text of any dramatic presentation, whether for the stage or on film, with all technical and stage directions.

The SCRIPT of a film may begin as the work of one person, but the finished product is likely to be a team effort, with a certain amount of dialog sometimes being "ad lib" during the filming. Certain talented producers or directors write their own SCRIPTS. George Lucas wrote the first STAR WARS SCRIPT, although he funneled his ideas through other writers for *The Empire Strikes Back* and *The Return of the Jedi*. Television scripts are even more likely to be team efforts, particularly in this era of arcs and multiple-plot story lines in television SERIES.

Some dealers manage to get copies of the SCRIPTS of popular films or of EPISODES of well-known TV series, which they sell at

MEDIA-CONS. A real find is an "original" script; one that has the actor's hand-written notes may be sold as a COLLECTABLE.

The term SCRIPT may also be used to describe the MANUSCRIPT an author delivers to a publisher that will eventually become a book.

scripter (comics): The person who writes the final story and dialog for the comic; this may or may not be the same person who invented the PLOT. The scripter and the PLOTTER are responsible for the story line that the various artists will depict graphically. See also CREATIVE TEAM.

scrod (fan): Miscellaneous oddments, presented for sale at a CONVENTION DEALERS' ROOM. The term arose during a dinner at the WORLD-CON in Boston in 1980, when some FANS were dining at a seafood restaurant and came across the item on the menu, where it means immature codfish. The diners had trouble eating the fish, and tried to imagine the creature from which it was taken. Eventually they decided it must have been that one-eyed monster that inhabits the garbage dump in the first STAR WARS film (all that is seen of it is one tentacle and an eyeball). A spate of SCROD jokes followed. By the time the joke had run its course, the term had passed from the monster to its habitat. The name SCROD has managed to become synonymous with the FANNISH equivalent of flea-market items.

season (TV/publishing): The period of time during which new releases will be presented to the public, whether they are previously unaired EPISODES of a TV SERIES, or new publications.

The concept of beginning a theatrical SEASON in the fall dates back to the pre-air-conditioned era. In those days, all theaters closed down operations during the summer months, when the heat made any kind of theatrical production impossible. Television production took many of its conventions from the theater, and new television SERIES were supposed to be presented somewhere between the first week in September and the last week in October.

This has changed considerably in recent years. What with writers' strikes, MINISERIES, and the current practice of yanking a

SERIES off the air if it does not produce instant RATINGS, new SERIES may be offered at any time, and RERUNS may be common as early as November.

Book publishing SEASONS vary from two to four a year. Fall is traditionally the most important SEASON due to the arrival of December holiday gift-giving sales. The publishing year begins in September. Publishers who work with two SEASONS publish from September to February (Fall/Winter) and have another SEASON that begins in March and runs through August (Spring/Summer). Those with three or more lists per year divide up the months accordingly. However they are divided, the publishing SEASONS always begin in September. As for MASS-MARKET PAPERBACKS, they are issued month after month, all year long.

second-generation fan (fan): The child of someone who is active in SF FANDOM. Until the 1980s, youngsters were rarely seen at CONS. However, as FANS grow older, the SECOND GENERATION is produced, and makes its appearance at a startlingly young age.

SECOND-GENERATION FANS are often encouraged to read and write as soon as possible. Any sign of artistic or scientific talent is fostered by their eager parents. FANDOM is like their extended family.

Of course, rebellion is part of the growing process. A few SECOND-GENERATION FANS retaliate against their weird parents by becoming aggressively MUNDANE and refusing to have anything to do with FANZINES, CONVENTIONS, COSTUMING, or any of the other activities their parents indulge in. As I heard one child moan, "Mother, when are you going to grow up!"

second-generation tape (film/TV): A videotape reproduced from an existing tape; often, a copy of a copy. By the time the electronic impulses have been through five or six machines, the image they project is less than clear, and the sound is worse. The SECOND-GENERATION TAPES are reasonably good; it's the fourth, fifth, and sixth generation that can be totally distorted. However, for many fans, SECOND-GENERATION TAPES are the only chance they will get to see such gems as *"Sapphire and Steel"*

(1979–1982), *"The Professionals"* (1978–1983), and other British SERIES rarely shown in the United States. See also BOOTLEG TAPES.

Security (fan/conventions): The people responsible for the protection of persons and property from theft and physical damage at CONVENTIONS. It is unfortunate that they should be needed at all, but there are always people who will become obstreperous or unpleasant, and there is the risk of some light-fingered individual removing small objects from the DEALERS' ROOM.

There were several paramilitary groups that provided SECURITY for conventions during the 1970s, among them, the Klingon Diplomatic Corps, the Dorsai Irregulars, and the VSR. They were gaudily costumed and often carried side-arms that looked extremely convincing. Most CONVENTIONS now prefer to have less conspicuous SECURITY people around, who may only wear an extra ribbon on their BADGE to distinguish them from the rest of the crowd. Their duty is to see that no one at the CONVENTION is hurt or robbed, and most of the time they succeed admirably.

self-binding (printing): See PERFECT-BINDING.

self-publishing: See VANITY PRESS.

selling out (fan): Getting rid of a large collection of FANZINES, memorabilia, or whatever, either because the seller has lost interest or because there is simply no more room in the house or apartment, and something has got to go!

SELLING OUT is often a painful process. A fan may have been collecting items for some twenty years, and parting with them may be like parting with a piece of one's soul. However, if it must be done, there are several ways to go about it.

Some fans advertise in one of the ADZINES. Some prefer to send out FLYERS. Others simply tote their SCROD to a CONVENTION and leave it with whoever is running the ORPHANZINE table.

Some NEOFANS haunt MEDIA-CONS to find out who is SELLING OUT; for many of them, it may be the only chance to acquire some of the FANZINES of the 1970s.

selling out of the room (fan/convention): The practice of turning one's hotel room into a salesroom at a CONVENTION, instead of buying a table in the DEALERS' ROOM. Most DEALERS would prefer to be in the DEALERS' ROOM, but there are some CONVENTIONS where table space is next to impossible to get, since the same people attend year after year, and they often buy tables for the following year on the last day of the CON.

At these CONVENTIONS, the CON-COM may set up a "Dealers' Row," with the help of the hotel management, which will assign rooms on a particular floor to those requesting such space. The people using the rooms for sales may keep whatever hours they choose, and are not bound by the hours set by the CONVENTION. However, SELLING OUT OF THE ROOM involves a certain amount of risk. There is no ready-made clientele eagerly picking over the stock. Signs must be posted, directing prospective customers to the merchandise, which can run afoul of hotel policy regarding taping signs to walls. Someone must be in the room during selling hours. And, of course, the room must be kept neat.

Given the choice, most DEALERS definitely prefer buying a table in the DEALERS' ROOM.

semi-prozine (fan): A publication that has a circulation of about 5,000 or more, or that accepts paid advertising, or that pays its contributors, or that decides to call itself a SEMI-PROZINE. The category was inserted into the World Science Fiction Society by-laws in 1985 in the section regarding nominations for the HUGO AWARDS, because several publications had been nominated for years on end as FANZINES, even though their circulation and format were no longer in the FANZINE category. LOCUS and SCIENCE FICTION CHRONICLE are two SEMI-PROZINES that specialize in news and reviews of the SF world; *Pandora* and *Aboriginal SF* are the two leading SEMI-PROZINES that publish fiction as well as articles and reviews.

sensawunda (literary): A deliberate slurring of "sense of wonder"; the feeling of breathless awe that SF writers try to convey as they describe the wonders of the universe, majestic scenery on faraway planets, or cities built by humans in a distant future. Much early SF was full of this atmosphere, but nowadays, the term has taken on an ironic overtone. Space exploration has stripped away much of the mystery from the SOLAR SYSTEM, but there are other stars and other systems with unimaginable scenes yet to excite our SENSAWUNDA. Film manages to do a better job of SENSAWUNDA.

sensor (aerospace): Any device that will approximate one of the human senses in Space; anything that will inform the crew of a starship or the monitors on Earth of what is beyond the skin of the craft. Telescopes, sound receivers, even devices to collect and identify the particles that produce aromas, all may be called SENSORS, since they "sense" information and deliver it to the "brain," that is, the central monitoring computer system, for analysis. SENSOR is a nice, general term that covers all kinds of electronic gizmos; its first popular use was on the TV series STAR TREK in 1966, and it has become a standard aerospace term.

sentience (psychology): Self-awareness; a being's sense of its own identity and place in the universal scheme of things. This is now considered the touchstone of humanity, the dividing line between "them" and "us" in the natural world. INTELLIGENCE, which was once considered the realm of humans, has been found in apes and dolphins. Many animals, previously considered too simple to solve complex problems, have managed to do so (among them, octopi). Some apes have even been taught to communicate through sign language, and monkeys have been observed teaching particular behaviors to their young.

However, so far, no wild animal has given evidence of SENTIENCE, and when we meet another species capable of communication with us, SENTIENCE will have to be the standard against which it will be judged.

sequel (literary): A continuation of a previously written or filmed work. SEQUELS are tricky things to handle. The first book or film may be a wild success, leading the writer and publisher (or the director and his producer) to hope that lightning will strike twice in the same place. The result may or may not be as good as the original, particularly if the original had been meant to be taken as a whole work in the first place. Very occasionally, the SEQUEL may outstrip the first film; ALIEN (1979) was a very good, very violent film; ALIENS (1986) was considered by critics to be a better film with a slightly different approach to the same material.

A SEQUEL may actually be the second part of a TRILOGY. The problem there is that the middle section often cannot come to a complete resolution, since there is one more part of the story left to be told. The audience must wait for the third part of the story to tie up all the loose ends.

A SEQUEL that recounts the events that led up to the first story is called a PREQUEL; get enough of them, and you've got a SERIES.

sercon (fan): A combination of "serious" and "constructive"; a FAN who is trying to use SF to improve the world, perhaps a little too hard. One of the first FAN FEUDS was in the late 1930s, between a group of SERCON FANS who felt that SF readers were honor bound to use their political clout (such as it was) to work for better living conditions for the poor, improvements in labor relations, and so on, and another group who felt that SF was for fun, and political activity was best left to the politicians. World War II answered that question for those particular FANS, but the point has been raised from time to time, and many SF fans have been both serious and constructive about taking action to improve their environment and encourage social action. SF FANS spearheaded efforts to popularize the space programs of the 1960s and 1970s. Many are now active in environmental protection.

Many SF writers have used their books to propound their particular political agendas, beginning with H. G. Wells and continuing through the works of Robert Heinlein, Jerry Pournelle, and even some of the recent CYBERPUNK writers. SERCON fans try to carry through some of these visions, to make a better world.

series (literary): A number of interrelated stories or novels, usually by one author (or collaborative pair), tracing the adventures of a person or set of persons in a particular setting, or tracing the history of a particular place. SERIES are sometimes planned, but often, like Topsy, just grow. Marion Zimmer Bradley tells how her DARKOVER series evolved to the point where she had to rewrite the novel that started it in the first place. Anne McCaffrey has only just published the story of the settling of her planet, PERN, after tracing its history through some dozen or more novels and stories.

Occasionally a SERIES will be continued long after the death of its original creator. Robert Howard died in 1930, but the adventures of CONAN THE BARBARIAN are still being written.

The publication of SF books as SERIES is not a new phenomenon; PULP FICTION throve on juvenile SERIES like *Tom Swift*. One of the first serious adult SERIES was ISAAC ASIMOV'S FOUNDATION, which presented the readers with several long stories set in a particular UNIVERSE, with CHARACTERS who might reappear at several points in their lives, and a story line that encompassed many generations.

Many readers enjoy SERIES books for their familiarity; one feels one knows the characters and their world as well as one's own. In fact, many readers attempt to re-create that world, sometimes to the chagrin of the original author. If the creator is Marion Zimmer Bradley, the would-be imitator may be invited to "come and play in my garden." If it is someone else, the imitator may perhaps do well to keep the new material to himself or herself.

The books in a SERIES form the basis of a UNIVERSE, which may be CLOSED or OPEN, depending on whether the original writer or writers will permit others to use the characters and locale that they have created. Occasionally, the originators of an OPEN UNIVERSE will collect the stories of these imitators into an ANTHOLOGY that will be published for the Mass Market, as Andre Norton has done with WITCHWORLD, and as Marion Zimmer Bradley has done with DARKOVER. More often, an author will permit limited use of the characters in FANZINES, which "don't count" as far as COPYRIGHT is concerned. And some authors will react to any incursion into their domains with instant lawsuits. See also UNIVERSE.

service module (aerospace): The section of a spacecraft that contains the engines for maneuvering in space, the electrical systems, and the air and water supplies; in short, the nonliving section of a spacecraft. The COMMAND MODULE contains living quarters for the crew.

set (film/TV): The stage on which a drama is performed for filming. A motion picture may have several SETS, all elaborately decorated and "dressed," that may be torn down to make room for others. A TV SERIES will use several SETS that remain "standing" until the SERIES ends. The standing SETS may be redressed for different scenes, so as to get extra use out of them. The control room of the USS *Enterprise*, whether in 1966 or 1990, is a "standing set" for STAR TREK.

setting (literary): The time and locale of the action of a particular story. An SF story may take place almost anywhere, at any time. The SETTING may be on any PLANET, or on a spacecraft plying between the PLANETS. It may take place in the distant past or the far future or even the DAY AFTER TOMORROW. Whatever the time or place, it is the task of the writer to inform the readers of when and where the action is taking place, and to make them feel a part of it.

SF (fan): The preferred abbreviation for Science Fiction (and the one used in this book). Many critics use Sci-Fi, and FANS wish they would not.

SFWA (Science Fiction Writers of America): Often pronounced as a word, SIFF-wah. The major organization for professional writers and editors of Science Fiction in the United States, formed in 1965 under the leadership of SF writers Damon Knight and Lloyd Biggle, to inform SF writers of matters of professional interest, and to help them deal with contracts, agents, and other legal hassles. SFWA is only open to those who have sold at least three short stories or one novel to major publishers, which effectively shuts out those who have only been published in SMALL PRESS or FANZINES.

SFWA provides its members with a number of publications that further communication between writers and the publishing establishment. New members receive a handbook that contains samples of typical contractual agreements, and articles by long-established SF writers on various aspects of the writer's business. SFWA also publishes a monthly bulletin, with more information for new (and established) writers.

Among SFWA's most important contributions to SF is the establishment of the NEBULA AWARDS, given annually for excellence in SF. The awards are voted on by the membership of the organization, so that they represent the opinion of the PROS, unlike the HUGO AWARDS, which include nonprofessionals among the voting population.

Membership in SFWA represents a major step in a writer's career. After attaining full membership, a writer can call himself or herself a PRO.

SFX (film): Pronounced as initials, which is shorthand for "Special Effects" ("eff-ecks"). Any camera magic that makes for strange things seen on the screen: people that move in and out of walls, bright lights and outlines, things going faster or slower than usual. Some SFX are barely noticeable: inserting a landscape into an otherwise blank wall, for instance, or making a castle hall out of a short corridor. There are several techniques used in SFX, such as MATTE or BLUE SCREEN, that extend the limitations of a flat wall in this manner.

More dramatic SFX may involve large objects crashing into even larger ones, with satisfying explosions, bright flames, and thunderous booms and crackles throughout the theater. STUNTS may also be used to enhance the SFX.

An SF film is often judged on the brilliance (or lack of it) of the SFX.

Sharecropper Universe (literary): A SERIES of stories with a pre-determined setting and characters, written by several authors, who forego the usual royalties and accept the assignment as WORK FOR HIRE. The novels are usually published under a general title, as MASS MARKET PAPERBACKS.

The idea of using several authors to produce novels under one pseudonym has been around since literacy became general in the mid-19th century. No less a personage than Alexandre Dumas was accused of harboring a writing-factory on his country estate. The TOM SWIFT novels were produced by the Stratemeyer Syndicate, which was also responsible for the popular "Nancy Drew" mysteries.

SHARECROPPING has been decried by some SF writers as encouraging young writers to imitate other peoples' ideas instead of formulating their own UNIVERSES. On the other hand, several people who have accepted SHARECROPPER contracts point out that there is considerable latitude within the GUIDELINES set down by the originators of the various UNIVERSES, and the writers have plenty of room to develop their own characters and situations. The popularity of such SERIES as *Star Trek* and *DragonLance* has given many rising writers an opportunity to attract an audience that they might otherwise not get. See also SHARED UNIVERSE.

Shared Universe (literary): A SERIES of stories written by a number of different authors, all set in a particular time or place devised by one of the editors or writers. Each writer in the UNIVERSE receives a set of guidelines that give the physical peculiarities of the place, and explain the "rules" by which its people exist. Each of the writers in that UNIVERSE must work within those guidelines, using only the established milieu and its characteristics.

The first professionally published SHARED UNIVERSE was "THIEVES' WORLD," which appeared in 1979, with Robert Asprin as Editor, although the MEDIAZINES may be said to have originated the concept, as various writers created different adventures for the STAR TREK characters. Since then, there have been several other SHARED UNIVERSES, among them, "Hell," "The Fleet," and "Merovingen Nights."

A SHARED UNIVERSE offers writers an opportunity to work with each other in a cooperative way; it might be called the ultimate in COLLABORATION. Each writer RUNS a particular CHARACTER or set of characters, and any other writer in the group must check with the first writer before using them. Killing off someone else's CHARACTER is considered very bad form; it leads to all sorts of complications later on.

The real creative burden falls on the one who has to bring all these stories together and make them a unified whole. When it works, the result has been called "a novel written by a committee."

shirt-sleeve environment (aerospace): A comfortable place fit for humans to inhabit in Space, without special protective equipment. The people inside a SPACE SHUTTLE work in overalls and shirts, instead of in bulky G-SUITS.

The SHIRT-SLEEVE ENVIRONMENT is one of the "givens" of most SF stories set on spaceships.

Shrink-Pak Law (computers): The notice of COPYRIGHT on a commercially prepared package of SOFTWARE, stating that if the seal on the package is broken, the buyer accepts the terms of COPYRIGHT. The SOFTWARE within may not be copied for resale to a third party, under pain of legal penalties. See also SOFTWARE PIRACY.

shuttlecraft (literary): A small spacecraft, used for short-range space travel. SHUTTLECRAFT are often referred to when a story calls for several large spacecraft to exchange personnel. SHUTTLECRAFT are also depicted as a kind of space-going taxi service that provides transportation between a planet and a SPACE STATION.

sidekick (film/literary): The loyal companion of the HERO, who acts as a backup in case of danger, or as a second-in-command, or as a servant, depending on the circumstances. The sidekick is often depicted as a comic foil to the steadfast HERO, who is deadly serious. A SIDEKICK in SF may be nonhuman (Chewbacca the Wookiee in the STAR WARS saga is typical) or even nonbiological. He or she is there to support the HERO or heroine.

The term comes from the thieves' slang of the late 18th century. Pickpockets had an elaborate language to describe their craft. A trousers pocket was a "kick"; a SIDEKICK was often squeezed shut by the pressure of the body within. A person who clung tightly to another was dubbed a SIDEKICK.

side-stapling (printing): Binding a book or FANZINE by staples, rivets or brass fasteners along the left-hand side of the page. SIDE-STAPLING is cheap and easy, requiring no more equipment than a mechanical stapler that can be bought in almost any stationery store, and a strong arm to wield it. It is the most common method of FANZINE binding, but it has certain disadvantages. There is a limit as to how many pages can be stapled together without losing legibility. Staples have a way of working loose and stabbing the fingers of anyone handling the item. And metal staples can rust and discolor the paper around them.

A few FANZINE publishers use RING-BINDING or PERFECT-BINDING. However, most FANZINES are SIDE-STAPLED.

"Sime/Gen" Universe (literary): SERIES of stories and novels, initially created by Jacqueline Lichtenberg and continued by Jeah Lorrah and others. The stories take place in a future when humanity has mutated into two separate species: the Gens, who create life-energy, and the Simes, who take it from them, often destroying the Gen in the process. The novels cover several hundred years of human history, during which the Simes and Gens find a way to live together cooperatively. The SERIES has spawned at least two FANZINES, many FILK songs, and COSTUMES.

Skylab (aerospace): The first U.S. Space Station, placed in orbit in 1973. It circled the Earth until its orbit decayed in 1979, when it fell spectacularly to Earth, showering debris across Australia.

Slans (literary): Superhuman successors to homo sapiens in a SERIES of stories by A. E. Van Vogt, beginning in 1925 with *Galactic Lensman.* Early SF FANS wore BUTTONS that announced "Fans Are Slans!"

slan-shack (fan): A semicommunal living arrangement of young SF FANS, who share the rent on an apartment or house, usually while they are unmarried and unattached. SLAN-SHACKS have appeared at various times and in various locales; there was a very popular one during the 1970s near the University of Maryland at Silver Spring, inhabited by a group of young people who have since become well-known in FANDOM as WRITERS, EDITORS, and FILKERS.

SLAN-SHACKS are, by their very nature, temporary arrangements, but they work well enough while they last.

slasher movies (film): Films that depict with gruesome accuracy the misdeeds of a deranged person, usually out for revenge, who commits heinous murders in bizarre ways until someone realizes what is going on, stops the murders, and presumably destroys the murderer . . . until the next film. SLASHER MOVIES are an outgrowth of the MONSTER MOVIES of the 1930s. However, in these films, the monster is quite human (or was human; a few of these killers seem to have as many lives as the original FRANKENSTEIN).

SLASHER MOVIES are marginally SF. Occasionally the killer is regenerated through some weird sort of genetic or radioactive accident that sets off yet another wave of gore. See also GRAND GUIGNOL; SLICE 'N' DICE.

slash fiction (fan): Not to be confused with SLASHER MOVIES. When the slash is placed between the names of a well-known MALE-BONDED pair, it indicates a degree of intimacy not usually fostered by most such buddies. SLASH FICTION is written mostly by women, to the intense disgust of many straight men and to the amusement of the gay community.

The first objects of this peculiar form of literary affection were STAR TREK'S James T. Kirk and his loyal First Officer, Mr. Spock.

Later pairs included Starsky/Hutch and even Napoleon Solo/ Ilya Kuryakin, of "The Man from U.N.C.L.E."

There is very little anyone can do to stop this sort of writing, short of confiscating every FANZINE in which it is printed. Gene Roddenberry tried to stem the tide with a footnote in his NOVELIZATION of *Star Trek: The Motion Picture* (1980). George Lucas vented his irritation through his OFFICIAL FAN CLUB. Other actors, writers, and producers tend to shrug and laugh, realizing that the writers of this kind of fiction are a very small minority as compared with the great number of writers who concentrate on other areas of MEDIA FANDOM. See also K/S FICTION.

sleeper (film): A movie that attains hit status through sheer excellence. Many of today's CULT MOVIES began as SLEEPERS. TV SERIES can also start out as SLEEPERS. "Alien Nation" was a surprise critical SF hit of the 1989–1990 season, despite its lowly position on the RATINGS totem pole.

sleeper ship (aerospace/literary): A space vehicle that carries a contingent of settlers for a far-off star system in CRYOGENIC containers until they reach their destination. SLEEPER SHIPS travel at LIGHT SPEED or close to it; the settlers realize that wherever they land, they will never see Earth again.

SLEEPER SHIPS are another way around the unpalatable fact that no group of colonists traveling at the speed of light can expect to reach its destination in less than four Earth years, and it will probably take a good deal more than that. Unlike a GENERATION SHIP, a SLEEPER SHIP can be maintained by a small crew, who can take turns in the CRYOGENIC freezer, or even by ROBOTS, programmed to wake the sleepers when the ship arrives at its preordained destination.

slice 'n' dice (film): A grimly humorous description of SLASHER MOVIES, taken from the name of a popular household appliance that shreds vegetables or meat.

slicks (publishing): Magazine publications that use expensive glossy paper instead of cheap, coarse paper made of wood pulp. SF has traditionally been part of the PULP magazine tradition;

even now, most of the professional SF magazines are printed on pulp paper (albeit, a better quality than NEWSPRINT). SLICK paper takes color ink better, so that the magazine can print illustrations (and advertisements) in full color, instead of sticking to black and white.

As of 1990, the most prominent SF magazine printed as a SLICK is *Omni.* Several popular scientific publications that provide the basic material from which SF writers concoct their stories also can be called SLICKS.

A few SF writers have appeared in generalized SLICKS. Some of Robert Sheckley's stories first appeared in *Playboy.*

slipcase (publishing): A cardboard protector for a high-quality HARDCOVER book, often decorated with a sample of the illustrations within. Special editions of classic SF novels or PORTFOLIOS of SF PRINTS may be protected in this way. The SLIPCASE adds to the cost of the book, but if the binding is so unique, the book may warrant the added protection.

slush pile (publishing): Unsolicited MANUSCRIPTS sent to a publisher directly instead of through an agent. Many book publishers will not accept SLUSH. They insist on dealing through a recognized AGENT or packager. Magazine EDITORS are more forbearing; they will hire a READER to wade through the SLUSH PILE, winnowing out the dross and searching for that nugget that will presage the next HEINLEIN or ASIMOV or ELLISON. Of all the possible markets for unsolicited MANUSCRIPTS, the SMALL PRESS is probably the most accessible, but it is also the one that pays the least.

The term dates back to the days of sailing ships, when the grease used in cooking was poured into a barrel, to be rendered down. The resulting fat was then sold for the benefit of the crew. The term SLUSH became associated with refuse and the gains accrued from it; hence the political SLUSH fund that is at the disposal of the candidate and his assistants.

Literary SLUSH is sometimes referred to as coming in "over the transom." This term dates back to the days when air conditioning was only a dream in an SF story. To aid in air circulation, the publisher's office door was furnished with a movable glass panel, called a transom. The image is that of MANUSCRIPTS stealthily being chucked through this window over the door by would-be writers.

SLUSH PILES tend to grow to horrendous heights unless they are read regularly. FAN EDITORS and SMALL PRESS editors do this themselves. Readers for PROZINES get to do this all the time. Editorial assistants have this job at major publishers.

Small Press (publishing): Also called "Alternative" or "Limited Interest" Press; those publishers of books and magazines who are not involved with major distribution of a wide variety of materials, but are more interested in publishing materials that may be limited in range, and are more intensely involved in their subject matter. SMALL PRESS encompasses a wide variety of publications: books and magazines, art prints, comics, and even audio and video tapes. The SMALL PRESS periodicals are occasionally called "Little" magazines; this may refer to their circulation, but not to their size, or their impact.

Science Fiction has several varieties or subgenres of SMALL PRESS endeavors within its ranks. There are publishers of books of critical analysis who specialize in SF. There are many SMALL PRESS magazines that print fiction as well as reviews, articles, and general news of the genre. There are publishers of books that rescue obscure works that would otherwise be forgotten from the cellars and attics of collectors. There is the vast amount of amateur publication: FANZINES, APAS, and NEWSLETTERS. There are even publishers who specialize in reprinting SF illustrations, selling them as PORTFOLIOS or as individual copies. All of these exist, and all of them are represented at SF CONVENTIONS.

The professional SF market is limited by economics. Publishers must produce material that will sell in order to continue to publish at all. SMALL PRESS publications may not necessarily provide the sole livelihood of their producers, who may have other, MUNDANE jobs to keep body and soul together. Therefore, SMALL PRESS publications can take artistic chances that the more prestigious and larger distributors cannot. Many new writers get their start in SMALL PRESS, and many established writers may offer something to a SMALL PRESS that is too specialized for a larger organization.

Between them, the FANS and the SMALL PRESS account for a sizable portion of the SF being written and published today. See also FANZINE; SEMI-PROZINE.

Small Press Writers and Artists Organization (SPWAO): An association of SMALL PRESS writers, artists, and editors, founded in 1977. The group concentrates on SF in SMALL PRESS, and tries to differentiate SMALL PRESS from FANZINES in terms of professional quality of product by promoting high standards in art and writing. SPWAO produces an annual collection of SF by its members, as well as a bimonthly newsletter that explores various matters of interest to SF writers and artists. For the address of this organization, see Appendix A.

SMOF (fan): Pronounced as a word, Smoff; "Secret Master Of Fandom," one of those who know Who's Who and What's What in SF FANDOM and its internal workings.

When FANDOM was smaller, there might have actually been such people. By 1990, the SF world has expanded to include a number of groups who would have been consigned to the Siberia of FRINGE FANDOM 20 years before. The term SMOF has begun to lose whatever luster it ever had; it is now used somewhat derisively, to imply that the person referred to is not as knowledgeable as he or she thinks.

There is a core group of people who have run CONVENTIONS for a number of years, who may find themselves suddenly recruited by a distraught CON-COM to get out of a tight situation. If any one group deserves the name SMOF, they do.

The word can also be used as a verb. SMOFFING is behaving like a SMOF: exchanging FANNISH gossip, giving the impression that one knows what is going on behind the scenes in FANDOM, in SF publishing, or anywhere else. There are sometimes signs in the CON SUITE that read "No Smoffing!" See also BNF.

SMOG (fan): Pronounced like the atmospheric condition; "Secret Master of Gaming." A SMOG is like a SMOF, only worse. The SMOG is sure he or she knows every rule of every game ever invented, and can tell who is inventing new ones. The SMOG can tell you what new games are being marketed, and by whom. The

SMOG can even impart the "real" story behind each and every game. Most real GAMERS are in the GAME ROOM by this time.

Smurfs (comics): Cuddly blue-skinned humanoids who have become the epitome of saccharine cuteness within SF FANDOM. They began as "Schtrumphs" in a comic strip in the Netherlands, and were translated into English in the 1970s. By 1980 the SMURFS had invaded the United States, where they proliferated into stuffed toys, T-SHIRTS, lunch boxes, and anything else that could hold their images.

To SF the SMURFS were so sweet as to be sickening. Costumes like "Smurf-hunter" (carrying stuffed dolls and a club) or "Super-Smurf" (in a cape and tights) were seen at MASQUERADES. A FILK song called "Nuke the Smurfs!" was written. Cartoons appeared in FANZINES showing SMURFS as everything from Captain Kirk to Darth Vader. SMURFS are beginning to become more cliche than cute.

soft sciences: Sciences dealing with human relationships, as opposed to those dealing with the manipulation of matter. Psychology, sociology, anthropology, and archeology seem to be the major areas indicated by the term. Biology seems to fall somewhere in between.

Early SF largely ignored the psychological aspects of storytelling, focusing instead on either technology or adventure. Under the editorship of Herbert Gold, *Galaxy* magazine initiated the extension of SF into stories with a deeper emphasis on interpersonal relationships within an SF context. The NEW WAVE writers often concentrated on the personalities of their characters as they worked their way out of their various dilemmas. FEMINIST SF deals largely with the motivations of people in the context of their surroundings.

The current SF picture leans toward the inclusion of psychological and sociological material in the story. Some writers will interweave historical figures into their stories. HARD-SCIENCE advocates like Hal Clement will try to describe the psychology of their creations as well as their physiology.

It is generally accepted in current SF that the SOFT SCIENCES are as valid as the HARD ones, and a good story about beings (human, alien, or mechanical) and their activities is readable in any GENRE.

soft sculpture (art): The use of fabric as a medium for artistic three-dimensional expression. A SOFT SCULPTURE is not a doll or a stuffed toy, although it may depict a person or imaginary beast. SOFT SCULPTURES often use fabrics like satin, brocade, or embroidered linen for their effects. They have no armature or inner stiffening, but are stuffed with foam rubber, cotton batting, or even horse hair.

There has been considerable controversy regarding SOFT SCULPTURES and other so-called crafts and their inclusion in SF ART SHOWS. Most artists agree that these items are one-of-a-kind decorative art, and should be considered as seriously as any other piece of sculpture, whether in metal, stone, wood, or clay. However, the question of "is it art or is it craft" may depend on the artist's intent, and how many of an item the artist has made. Some SOFT SCULPTURE has been banished to the DEALERS' ROOM.

soft SF (literary): Stories that deal with the human or humane problems of interactions between individuals, whether of Earthly origin or any other. The term came into use during the 1970s to distinguish the spate of NEW WAVE stories from the traditional HARDWARE STORIES that dealt with technology and problem-solving.

SOFT SF need not necessarily be soft-hearted. Barry Longyear's *Enemy Mine* deals with two stranded warriors of different species, who learn to trust each other in the face of a mutual enemy. Ursula LeGuin's *Left Hand of Darkness* (1969) explores the society in which sexuality is ambiguous.

SOFT SF coexists with HARD-CORE SF, often blended into the same story. There will always be room for both kinds of story in the SF publishing scene. See also SOFT SCIENCES.

software (computer): The instructions that guide the computer and tell it exactly what to do. There is now a wide variety of mass-produced SOFTWARE for almost any model of home computer, which can be bought through computer outlet stores, electronics stores, or even bookstores and variety stores.

SOFTWARE packages are copyrighted under the SHRINK-PAK LAW, and may not be copied for resale.

The computer itself is just a box. It takes the SOFTWARE to make the computer "go." See also HARDWARE; PROGRAMMING.

software piracy (computer): The copying for resale of prepackaged computer programs, that is, SOFTWARE. This was a knotty point for several years until the Law caught up with Technology. It has now been established that the rights to a computer program belong to the manufacturer, and that no one may copy said program for resale without the permission of said manufacturer. This is especially important when it comes to video games, which form a large part of the prepackaged SOFTWARE market. Buyers of SOFTWARE are informed that under the SHRINK-PAK LAW they may not copy the contents of their package for resale. (Of course, this does not apply to home use of the program.) See also COPYRIGHT.

software rot (computer): A decay in the efficiency of prepackaged computer programs. The diskettes or disks tend to disintegrate over a period of time if they are not used or stored properly.

solar sails (aerospace): A large lightweight surface designed to receive thrust from solar radiation pressures, to be used as the propellant force of a spacecraft once ESCAPE VELOCITY has been attained, in much the same way that a sailing vessel on Earth catches the prevailing breeze. Several designers have proposed this method as a means of saving fuel during interplanetary flights.

Solar System (astronomy): The star we call Sol, or the Sun, and its attendant planets, one of which is Earth. By extension, any star and its attendant PLANETS, their MOONS, and all the assorted rocks and bits of space debris within the star's gravitational field may also be termed a SOLAR SYSTEM. However, technically, the term should only be used to refer to the one that includes Earth. All others are PLANETARY SYSTEMS.

solar wind (astronomy): The continuous stream of protons and electrons constantly emitted by a star, and most particularly, our Sun, extending in all directions. The SOLAR WIND may be affected by such variations in the sun's temperature as are caused by sunspots, and may, in turn, affect the Earth in ways that are only now being understood. Presumably, other stars will emit similar radiation, with differing effects on possible life on PLANETS that may be circling them.

Soyuz (aerospace): Soviet manned spacecraft used for long-duration flights since 1967. The SOYUZ is the mainstay of the Soviet space effort; it was a SOYUZ craft that linked up with one of the Apollo craft in the U.S.-Soviet linkup in 1975.

space colony (literary): A human settlement on another world, presumably at some time in the future. The colonization of areas of Earth by groups of people who have left their homes for reasons of war, famine, or social reform has left us a number of possible parallels such settlements might take.

In many stories, the settlement of humans on otherwise barren PLANETS is seen as a natural extension of human history. The PLANET in question may be adapted to human existence through TERRAFORMING, or the settlers may find themselves adapting to their new environment physically as well as culturally. Some writers have envisioned native species of other PLANETS as being dangerous enemies who must be exterminated before humans can remain there. Others have suggested that native species may be adapted to human needs, or possibly even combined with Terran genetic material to produce hybrids beneficial to both worlds.

Heightened sensitivity to minorities in our own world has been mirrored by writers who use SF to echo the concerns of modern life. A number of writers pit the local sentients against the invaders from Earth. Many FIRST CONTACT stories deal with attempts by colonists to coexist with the beings already in possession of the place. C. J. Cherryh's *Downbelow Station* (1981) depicts a group of nonhumans caught up in a human war zone; the "Downers" try to understand the odd creatures that have taken over their world, while the humans continue their battles over and around them. On the other hand, in *40,000 in Gehenna* (1983), by the same author, the planetary environment re-shapes the colonists, almost against their will.

Several writers have based their ideas of colonization on the early history of the United States, presupposing small groups who try to find self-contained settlements in which they can live by their own particular customs or laws. Gordon Dickson's *Childe Cycle* novels use this PREMISE; each settlement has chosen to base its culture on one or two principles of human society. Many writers extend their ideas into a description of a "perfect society," a UTOPIA. When another human society meets with the isolated one, the result is often a CULTURE CLASH.

SPACE COLONIES may be viewed as isolated fragments of humanity, unable to reach their home base on Earth. They may be LOST COLONIES whose existence has been forgotten. They may be connected into a GALACTIC EMPIRE, on the march in a campaign of conquest and expansion. They may even be the decaying and decadent remains of what was once a great civilization, but is now overextended and dying. However they are depicted, SPACE COLONIES are an integral part of what readers expect of SF.

space marines (literary): Armed forces that will presumably fight the battles of the future. They may be armed with ray guns, LASERS, or other far-fetched devices. They may be fighting at the orders of a respected and revered leader, or they may be mere MERCENARIES fighting for pay, loot, or adventure. Whatever they are, they are usually male (although the WOMAN WARRIOR has become as much a macho cliche as her male counterpart in current SF), and they are especially prevalent in SPACE OPERA.

Space Opera (literary): An ACTION/ADVENTURE story in a futuristic setting, with a hard-jawed muscular HERO, a dastardly VILLAIN, a loyal SIDEKICK, and occasionally, a sweet heroine to be rescued from direst peril. In other words, a typical Western melodrama with ray guns instead of six-shooters.

The term derives from "horse opera," a Western melodrama, which in turn derives from "soap opera," a dramatic radio or television presentation that presents a continuing tale of domestic upheaval for entertainment. The "opera" came from the highly emotional nature of the plots; the "soap" referred to the sponsors of the dramas as presented first on radio and later on television.

SPACE OPERA has a long tradition of adventure story-telling behind it, going back to the first recounters of myth and legend around campfires in the earliest of human settlements. People have always been enthralled by the adventures of some larger-than-life character who undergoes great trials of strength and character before winning the battle and, in addition, the fair maiden. SF changed the locale of the story, but not its ingredients or its basic character types.

SPACE OPERA has sometimes been derided as mere entertainment. *Entertainment,* yes; *mere,* no. It takes as much expertise to create a successful adventure hero as it does to concoct a tale of technological marvels, and the SPACE OPERA series like E. E. "Doc" Smith's *Lensman* stories are kept in print, and still give enjoyment to their readers. GEORGE LUCAS' STAR WARS films are SPACE OPERA at its best. See also BAT DURSTON STORY.

spaceships (aerospace): Any form of spacecraft, but particularly those that can traverse the vast areas between the stars. SPACESHIPS have been the mainstay of SF since Jules Verne's *The Trip to the Moon,* written in 1869.

SPACESHIPS have been given many forms and many means of propulsion. Early experiments by ROBERT GODDARD led to the idea that a SPACESHIP should be needle-shaped, so that it might best cleave through the Earth's atmosphere. The ROCKET has been the symbol of SF since the 1920s. However, once the ship is loose in the weightlessness of Space, it may take any configuration that seems logical. SPACESHIPS have been depicted in films as disc-shaped, as in *Forbidden Planet* (1956), or shaped like a 20th-century battleship in dry-dock, as in the STAR WARS films. The most famous spaceship in television history, the Starship Enterprise of STAR TREK, is shown as having a saucer-shaped main hull and two cylindrical extrusions that presumably keep the engines away from the crew.

SPACESHIPS are used symbolically in SF as examples of Earth's domination over lesser technologies, or as the instruments of a superior culture over us. They may be run by computers, ANDROIDS, or maybe just one scruffy pilot and his faithful semihuman friend.

SPACESHIPS now being designed are still close to the original needle-shaped idea of GODDARD. They still have to escape Earth's atmospheric envelope. However, the future is still before us, and no one will know what a working SPACESHIP will look like until we build one.

space shuttle (aerospace): The reusable spacecraft currently being used by the United States to deploy SATELLITES, perform research, and generally explore the universe outside Earth's atmosphere. The prototype was named *Enterprise* after the famous starship on STAR TREK. Later shuttles were named *Discovery, Atlantis, Columbia,* and *Challenger.* The future of the U.S. space program is geared to the SPACE SHUTTLE, which will ferry materials and personnel into space to construct a permanent SPACE STATION, presumably by the year 2000. See also SHUTTLECRAFT.

space station (aerospace): A large orbiting spacecraft meant for long-term human habitation. Currently, the only such spacecraft is the MIR, being maintained by the USSR. Plans are being made for a joint U.S.-Soviet station orbiting Earth that will enable astronomers to make accurate observations about the universe outside of the distortions of Earth's atmosphere. SPACE STATIONS have also been heralded as the first step toward the colonization of the Moon and Mars.

SPACE STATIONS are likely settings for SF novels. One plan calls for each station to develop its own culture, much as the 13 Colonies did when separated by the Atlantic Ocean from the Mother Country. Other stories depict SPACE STATIONS as being run by oligarchies, interested only in perpetuating their own profits. SPACE STATIONS may be established around other PLANETS, particularly if the PLANET surface is not hospitable to human life.

The first U.S. space station, SKYLAB, fell to Earth in 1976, after it was abandoned. However, if the current plans are followed through, there is every likelihood of a SPACE STATION becoming a permanent fixture around Earth by the 21st century. See also LAGRANGE POINTS.

space suit (aerospace): Fully enclosed protective gear for space exploration; a garment that can provide life-support for a human being in a vacuum. Early SPACE SUITS were based on G-SUITS designed for underwater exploration. They were bulky and made no provision for basic human necessities other than breathing and warmth. Today SPACE SUITS have been refined to the point where their wearers are able to exist in them for extended lengths of time.

space warfare (aerospace): Aggressive or defensive acts conducted either in space or from space to the Earth. SPACE WARFARE has been a staple ingredient of SPACE OPERA from the earliest days of PULP FICTION. Earth has been a target for invasion, beginning with H. G. Wells' *War of the Worlds*, published in 1898. In retaliation, perhaps, there have been endless tales in which some force from Earth goes out to do battle with some nasty invader from Planet X. Other plots involve battles between the central powers on Earth and a rebellious gang of outlaws on one of the outer PLANETS, or even in a SPACE COLONY. A reversal of this plot is the one where the government of Earth has become a repressive dictatorship, and the colonists see themselves as the Americans did in 1776: fighting for their freedom.

Whether as self-defense, aggressive conquest, or civil war, most experts believe that SPACE WARFARE works better on the page than in a vacuum. Most SF people, writers and FANS, are working to make a world where SPACE WARFARE will not be necessary.

space warp (literary): A concept that, like HYPERSPACE, postulates that space is not continuous, but contains bends and folds. Presumably, if a means could be found to cut across these warps, a SPACESHIP could surpass the speed of light, cutting hundreds of LIGHT-YEARS off a voyage. Astronomers are dubious about the existence of SPACE WARPS, but SF writers continue to use them. Probably the best explanation of SPACE WARP is given in Madeleine L'Engle's novel for young people, *A Wrinkle in Time* (1962).

specialty shop (bookselling): A bookstore that concentrates on selling COMICS, SCIENCE FICTION, and FANTASY books, together with the associated oddments that go with them: buttons, posters, prints, and so on. Most major metropolitan areas have at least one such store. Some are located in shopping malls, and some are situated in small towns. The owners of SPECIALTY SHOPS are often FANS themselves who attend SF CONS as DEALERS. Such stores often act as a magnet for SF FANS, where the owners provide a bulletin board for local club announcements, distribute NEWSLETTERS, and generally serve the FANNISH community.

Spielberg, Steven (b. 1946): American filmmaker, especially known for films that place ordinary people in extraordinary situations. *E.T.* (1983) tells of a small boy's relationship with a visitor from another planet; *Close Encounters of the Third Kind* (1977) deals with a blue-collar worker who becomes involved with the FIRST CONTACT of a non-Earth species to our planet.

SPIELBERG teamed up with his friend GEORGE LUCAS to produce the *Indiana Jones* trilogy, probably the most popular adventure films of the last 20 years. SPIELBERG has made films outside the SF and ACTION/ADVENTURE genre, most notably *The Color Purple* (1985) and *The Empire of the Sun* (1987). However, his greatest successes to date have been in the SF genre.

spine (printing/publishing): The edge of the book along which the pages are joined. A book will have the title, author, and publisher imprinted on its SPINE; a FANZINE may or may not have this information, depending on the style of binding or the thickness of the magazine (also called its bulk).

spiral binding: A way of joining pages together with a single wire or plastic coil, which is wound through the pages by a machine. SPIRAL BINDING is often used for books that are meant to be held open, such as cookbooks or books of instructions. FANZINES rarely use SPIRAL BINDING; staples, RING-BINDING, or PERFECT-BINDING are more practical.

splatter movies (film): Also called SLASHER MOVIES or SLICE 'N' DICE. The modern answer to GRAND GUIGNOL; films in which some person (male or female) wreaks bloody revenge upon selected individuals until stopped by someone who destroys the killer . . . until the next film in the series. The term was coined by director George Romero.

Spock Enslaved (fan): Novel by D. T. Steiner, first published in 1972. One of the earliest and most notorious of the fan-written STAR TREK stories, in which Mr. Spock is captured and humiliated by a society of women. It became the focus of attention when it was analyzed in depth by Jacqueline Lichtenberg in *Star Trek Lives!* (1972). See also GET 'EM STORY.

spot illos (fan): Small illustrations used purely for decoration in a FANZINE. SPOT ILLOS are found in other publications, where they are sometimes called "casuals," "fillers," or "toons." SPOT ILLOS do not depict events in any particular story or poem; they are simply there to decorate the page and fill up otherwise blank space. COVER ART may be the ultimate in SPOT ILLOS. CREEPY-CRAWLIES are SPOT ILLOS with horror content. See also FILLOS.

Sputnik (aerospace): The first artificial satellite launched by the Soviet Union in 1957, thus initiating the Space Age. The launching of SPUTNIK sent the U.S. military establishment into a collective tizzy, and spurred the funding of the U.S. space effort.

stage ninja (fan/convention): A GOFER who assists at a MASQUERADE, dressed in black shirt and pants, so as to be inconspicuous as he or she helps contestants on or off the stage, picks up PROPS that may have been discarded, and generally keeps the MASQUERADE running smoothly. STAGE NINJAS are named for the legendary Japanese assassins who also wore black and could infiltrate any stronghold without being seen.

Starlog: Most prominent professionally produced magazine that deals with SF films and television in a serious manner. STARLOG began its publishing history in 1976 with a heavy emphasis on STAR TREK. Under the editorship of Dave McDonald,

STARLOG has become the leading media-oriented PROZINE. Recently, the magazine has expanded its scope by printing extended interviews with leading SF writers and artists.

starscape (art): A painting that depicts a group of stars, as seen in INTERSTELLAR SPACE. The stars may form a known constellation, or may be superimposed on another image, such as an animal or person. STARSCAPES are often technically quite exact, based on astronomical observations and photographs taken by PROBES. Like PLANETSCAPES, STARSCAPES are classed as ASTRONOMICALS in ART SHOWS.

starship: See SPACESHIPS.

"Star Trek" (TV): American TV series, first aired 1966–1969, and kept alive in SYNDICATION and video cassettes ever since. Probably the most important SF event of the 1960s, overshadowing such landmark films as *2001: Space Odyssey* in its influence over the media and SF FANDOM.

STAR TREK depicted the adventures of a multiracial, multinational spaceship crew, led by staunch Captain James T. Kirk, abetted by his loyal First Officer Mr. Spock. The series, conceived, produced, and written by GENE RODDENBERRY, was the first adult continuing drama that used an SF background to present literate stories by good writers that dealt with the issues of the day. If the message got heavy-handed at times, that was the spirit of the times. There were stories about racial discrimination, pollution, and the senselessness of war; there were also stories that pitted the crew of the Starship against beings with superior powers or against their own psyches.

STAR TREK was supposed to have been canceled after its first season, but the fans launched the first LETTER-WRITING CAMPAIGN that sent thousands of letters to the NBC offices, and kept the show on the air for another 50 episodes. Not even the efforts of the fans could keep the series in production after that . . . but the story was only beginning.

The enthusiasm of the STAR TREK FANS evinced itself in creative efforts; if they could not get new episodes on the air, they'd write them themselves! FANS organized special CONVENTIONS, modeled after the SF CONS they had already attended, which soon developed into MEDIA-CONS, later taken over by professional producers as PRO-CONS. STAR TREK books were published in both MASS-MARKET PAPERBACK and HARDCOVER formats: first collections of short stories, written by James Blish and based on the original episode scripts, then original full-length novels by various professional writers. Nonfiction appeared as well: technical manuals, a concordance that listed every person, place, or thing in all the original EPISODES, even diagrams of the USS *Enterprise.* A series of animated EPISODES was filmed in 1973, and run during the SATURDAY MORNING GHETTO.

Meanwhile, the actors had to scramble to find work. GENE RODDENBERRY had made several other films for television; the actors and writers had found other projects. Nevertheless, all throughout the 1970s, all of the people concerned with the show came back to STAR TREK.

The enthusiastic response to GEORGE LUCAS' STAR WARS made the executives at Paramount think again about RODDENBERRY'S plans for a STAR TREK motion picture. Through a complex series of takeovers, Gulf-Western now owned the Paramount studios, which had taken over DesiLu, the original producer of the show. The result was not as satisfactory as either the FANS or RODDENBERRY wished, but in 1979 *Star Trek: The Motion Picture* was first shown. It reunited the original cast; it used spectacular SFX; it revamped one of RODDENBERRY's pet ideas, the battle between pure logic and human emotion; and it was a financial success.

The rest, as they say, is history. There have been five STAR TREK films. There is now a second STAR TREK on television, with a "Next Generation" cast and a slightly different outlook, but with the same dedication to quality scripts and the same optimism that made the "Classic" what it was.

STAR TREK changed the way people regarded SF, not only on television but in FANDOM. For one thing, it made SF more accessible; one did not have to be an intellectual giant to understand what was going on. Women were given more prominence in STAR TREK, not just as set decorations but as part of the crew, and a vital part at that. Minority actors were seen in key roles, not as "Black" or "Oriental" but as "the Admiral" or "the Scientist" or even "the Security guard."

STAR TREK FANDOM fostered writing talent especially among women. Two of the women writers to come out of the FANZINES are Jacqueline Lichtenberg and Jean Lorrah, both of whom have written SF tales well outside the scope of STAR TREK.

STAR TREK has inspired young people for two generations, and it looks as if it will continue to do so for another generation to come. As they say . . . "Star Trek Lives!"

Star Wars (film): Omnibus term that includes three films produced by GEORGE LUCAS: *Star Wars* (1977), *The Empire Strikes Back* (1980), and *The Return of the Jedi* (1983), which are supposedly the central trilogy in a grand series of nine possible films, all set "Long ago, in a Galaxy far far away," in which a doughty band of rebels fights against the tyranny of the greatest of GALACTIC EMPIRES.

GEORGE LUCAS amalgamated the derring-do of 1930s' serials with the mysticism of the 1960s in the trilogy. His hero, Luke Skywalker, learns of "The Force," that mysterious bond that unites all things in the universe. The Jedi Knights could learn to control their psychic talents and use that knowledge to fight for Good against Evil . . . or so goes the philosophy of Obi-Wan Kenobi (played by Sir Alec Guiness) and the 900-year-old Jedi Master, Yoda (designed and played by Frank Oz, of Muppet fame). The three films show the maturing of young Luke, his fight with the epitome of Evil, Darth Vader, and his eventual realization that the true evil lies within oneself, and the battle against it is never over.

STAR WARS came along just as the fans of STAR TREK were beginning to wonder if there would ever be another source of inspiration like it. When it hit, it hit like a bomb. Almost before the film was in the theaters, stories began to emerge in MEDIAZINES. The fans of STAR WARS battled the fans of STAR TREK in the pages of LETTERZINES and through the PANELS of MEDIA-CONS. At one point, every mention of one or the other would bring out vociferous arguments, no matter which side was present.

At first the higher-ups at 20th Century Fox, the production company of STAR WARS, didn't know what to make of all this unauthorized use of the characters they had so carefully tried to market via posters, comic books, buttons, and so forth. There were rumors (possibly true) of government agents snooping through the merchandise for sale at PRO-CONS, trying to ferret out the bootleg books. However, the "Official Star Wars Fan Club" was quickly formed, and the FANZINES were tacitly permitted to continue to publish (although LUCAS suggested that he would like a copy of each issue).

A story, possibly apocryphal, has circulated, to the effect that when the FANZINES began printing STAR WARS stories GEORGE LUCAS went to GENE RODDENBERRY (who had, after all, been through it before) and asked what to do about it. Said RODDENBERRY, "Do nothing . . . and they will make you a millionaire."

Whether or not this story is true, STAR WARS FANDOM has extended itself widely, so that the characters of the films have become as famous as those of its predecessor, STAR TREK. A political cartoon shows the caped and helmeted figure of Darth Vader boarding one of the SPACE SHUTTLES, while a mechanic sighs, "That's what you get for letting the military into the Space Program." Mel Brooks has used the STAR WARS films as the basis for his uproarious film parody, *Spaceballs*. There have been professionally published novels based on the Han Solo and Lando Calrissian characters, as well as novelizations of the three films. Like STAR TREK, STAR WARS has spawned nonfiction as well as fiction, with many volumes of detailed drawings, maps, and diagrams of the people, places, and things shown in the three films.

There are rumors that GEORGE LUCAS is preparing to make the PREQUELS to his original TRILOGY. If this proves true, we may expect a whole new influx of fannish creativity.

Star Wars (military): Also known as Strategic Defense Initiative. A use of the title of the film that infuriated GEORGE LUCAS, who went so far as to try to take legal steps to prevent its use in the public media.

The basic idea behind the Strategic Defense Initiative was to prevent Soviet missiles from approaching the United States by stopping them in midair through a series of satellites that would project an energy shield that would deflect the oncoming warheads back into Space. It was a pet project of President Ronald Reagan, who tried vehemently to get funding for it, and pressed for research into its possible production. However, as of 1990, the technology behind the scheme has been revealed to be unworkable, and the political climate has changed so drastically that its use may not really be necessary.

While the Strategic Defense Initiative was still being researched, SF writers were often divided on its possible use. As of now, the question has been shelved.

stationary orbit (aerospace): A circular orbit around the equatorial plane of a planet, with a rotational period equal to that of the planet, so that an object holding such an orbit appears to be fixed in place from the point of view of someone on the ground. Most SATELLITES are placed in STATIONARY ORBITS, so that they may receive radio or television signals and relay them to particular receivers on the ground.

stereotype (literary): A hackneyed character, usually with ethnic or class characteristics, used in a story as a STOCK CHARACTER. The term comes from a technique for reproducing etchings on NEWSPRINT. The CHARACTERS are simply interchangeable duplications of one another. See also STOCK CHARACTER.

stills (film): Posed photographs of scenes from a particular film or TV SERIES, as opposed to CANDIDS, which present the actors and other people connected with the film or series just being themselves, out of character, and away from the SET. STILLS are a primary source of PHOTO-REFS for fan artists. There are usually several dealers in STILLS at any MEDIA-CON or PRO-CON; they are less likely to be found at a fan-run SF CONVENTION, where the emphasis is on books rather than MEDIA. These STILLS make up an integral part of a PRESS KIT.

stock character (literary): A standard type (if not a STEREOTYPE) found in a particular GENRE; the term comes from the theater, where the same types of characters would be played by actors who were known for taking those particular parts, as if they were part of a merchant's stock-in-trade. STOCK CHARACTERS in SF may include the naive youngster who joins the Space Force/Academy/Marines and survives brutal reality to become the Hero; the laconic Space Marine/Mercenary/Warrior; the MAD SCIENTIST (even if he's only mildly obsessed) and his idiotic assistant; the loyal SIDEKICK of the hero; and the Damsel in Distress. Any or all of these may appear in current SF, but they are usually depicted with some variation on the standard formula, to take the story out of the realm of SPACE OPERA and move it closer to true literary entertainment.

A common twist is to substitute a Heroine for a Hero, who must prove herself in various ways against terrible odds to attain her true destiny. Robin McKinley's Newbery Award-winning *The Blue Sword* (1985) uses this variation on the formula, with stunning effect. Barbara Hambley's *Ladies of Madrigyn* prove to be considerably more able to rescue their husbands than the men thought.

STOCK CHARACTERS populate most PULP FICTION, whether it be on the page or on film. However, good writing can enliven the most banal of these CHARACTERS, and breathe life into an otherwise standard plot. Most readers of today's SF demand no less.

stock footage (film): Scenes of places, actions, and objects stored in a film library that may be inserted instead of being photographed specifically for that film. For instance, a filmmaker may use a stock scene of a desert to set the stage for a planet with very little water. The films of the Voyager spacecraft have been used to prepare the audience for a story of adventure in INTERSTELLAR SPACE. Occasionally, the STOCK FOOTAGE may include historical material; the TV MINISERIES *Space*, based on James Michener's novel, used newsreel footage of bombing raids and early experiments by the U.S. rocket experts to add verisimilitude to the production.

Most SF films are so original that they use very little STOCK FOOTAGE. However, a really cheap filmmaker may try to cut corners by inserting OUT-TAKES or background shots of one film into another. Many knowledgeable FANS watch out for this kind of thing.

Stop-Action/Stop-Motion Photography (film): An animation technique that requires the starting and stopping of the camera during shooting to produce a desired effect. Most often, the camera is stopped and an alteration is made in a model, which is then shot, and the camera stopped again, until the model appears to be moving onscreen. The models must be moved precisely and carefully, otherwise the movement will seem jerky and artificial.

story conference (literary): A meeting between a writer and an EDITOR or COLLABORATOR to discuss a particular piece of fiction. The term comes from the world of film, where SCRIPTS are often written by a team.

STORY CONFERENCES can take place at any time, in any place where SF writers (PRO or FAN) can get together: at SF CONS, en route to a CON in a plane, train, or automobile, in bars or restaurants, or even cross-country via telephone, fax, or MODEM.

strength (gaming): The ABILITY of a CHARACTER to carry a physical load, determined by the DUNGEONMASTER's dice at the beginning of the game. A useful trait, especially when hauling off treasure, although not absolutely necessary for a ROGUE or a WIZARD.

stunts (film): Dangerous activities performed by a trained athlete and acrobat, who takes the place of the actor who is assumed to be fighting, falling, or whatever else the SCRIPT calls for. Some actors insist on doing their own STUNTS. STUNTS may be quite simple, like a choreographed fight scene, or very elaborate, involving explosions, large moving objects, and/or animals. The STUNTS in the *Indiana Jones* films are spectacular, in every sense of the word.

Sturgeon, Theodore (1918–1987): Writer of romantic SF and Fantasy, whose influence is especially felt in SOFT SF. His masterpiece is *More Than Human* (1952), which explores the possibility of an advanced form of humanity, made up of individuals with extraordinary psychic powers who combine their talents. STURGEON's stories often verge on ALLEGORY.

Sturgeon's Law: As formulated by THEODORE STURGEON, "90% of everything is garbage." (The last word is a euphemism;

substitute your own obscenity.) A truism that is often uttered philosophically by READERS wading through a SLUSH PILE.

style sheet (publishing): A list made by the COPY EDITOR of words and style rules pertaining to a particular manuscript. The list ensures that consistency for these items will be maintained throughout the manuscript. For example, BACK-STORY is capitalized and hyphenated in this Dictionary. The COPY EDITOR listed this word on the STYLE SHEET so that it would always appear this way.

subracial memories (psychology): Theory, expounded by psychologist Karl Jung, that deep within the subconscious mind each human being harbors the total memory of the species. This is supposed to account for the almost universal human dread and fascination with snakes, for instance, since most primate species are preyed on by snakes. The prevalence of DRAGONS in folklore is laid down to SUBRACIAL MEMORIES of dinosaurs. The existence of such memories is controversial, and writers are still debating the theory.

subs (fan): Short for subscriptions; advance sales of a FANZINE prior to its actual publication. Very few FANZINES are produced on anything like a regular schedule; usually CLUBZINES and NEWSLETTERS are the only FANZINES that accept SUBS. However, there are some FAN-EDS who feel they can only afford to print their 'zine if they have a guarantee of selling enough of them to cover the initial investment. They will announce the publication date and wait for SUBS to come in. If they don't arrive, the FANZINE is scrapped, and the money collected for it must be returned.

subspace (literary): Another variation on the HYPERSPACE theory, similar to SPACE WARP. This theory holds that Space is not infinite and amorphous, but is shaped into folds and warps. If a means could be found to chart those folds and warps, a space-going vessel could cut across the LIGHT-YEARS, and emerge at a given point in less time than would be possible traveling at LIGHT

SPEED. The vessel would drop into an area known as WARP, HYPERSPACE, or SUBSPACE.

Scientists are dubious about the existence of SUBSPACE. This does not prevent SF writers from using it in their stories.

subtext (literary): The meaning behind the author's words; what the writer was really trying to say, especially in an ALLEGORY. GEORGE ORWELL's *Animal Farm* (1945) is ostensibly about some barnyard creatures who attempt to set up a perfect society. The SUBTEXT, on the other hand, deals with the Communist Party of the Soviet Union, its squabbles and probable ending. Occasionally FANS read more into the SUBTEXT than the creators intended; this is one explanation given for K/S or SLASH FICTION.

supergiant (astronomy): A very large star, usually blue-white in color, at the extreme upper end of the H-R DIAGRAM. SUPERGIANTS are often the product of a NOVA or SUPERNOVA, and may boil off and collapse into a BLACK HOLE in a short space of time (astronomically speaking). They are unlikely to attract planets.

superhero (comics): A CHARACTER with extraordinary powers, usually dressed in a tight-fitting costume that displays musculature to perfection. SUPERMAN was the prototype for SUPERHEROES that followed. SUPERHEROES are sometimes explained as the products of GENETIC ENGINEERING, although they are more often described as the last escapees from a dying world, or ordinary folks who have come into possession of a magic device that grants them super strength, hearing, or flying ability. Often the SUPERHERO hides behind a secret identity, to emerge in moments of need to save the world from SUPERVILLAINS.

SUPERHEROES are the staple fare of comic books. They have joined forces to form Leagues or Gangs or Bands. They usually use their powers to fight the Powers of Evil, be they Nazis, Commies, or MAD SCIENTISTS out to take over the world.

Of late, SUPERHEROES have been used to warn their readers of the dangers of drug abuse and the virtues of literacy.

Superman (comics/film/TV): Comic book character who has become the prototype for all subsequent SUPERHEROES. SUPER-

MAN first appeared in *Action* Comics in 1938; he has been updated and redrawn several times since. On television he was played by Steve Reeves; Christopher Reeve played him in three films between 1980 and 1986.

SUPERMAN is really the son of Jor-El and his wife Lara, of the faraway planet Krypton. He was launched into space by his parents as his PLANET destructed when he was just an infant, and landed on Earth in the Midwest. He was found by the Kents of Smallville, USA (his exploits are chronicled in *Superboy* comics). As he grew older, he became a reporter for the *Daily Planet* in Metropolis. As Clark Kent, SUPERMAN must hide his muscles under a sloppy suit and his X-ray vision behind thick glasses. However, when danger threatens, Kent ducks into any handy hiding place (often a telephone booth) and emerges triumphant dressed in SUPERMAN's trademark leotard and tights, ready to save the day.

SUPERMAN's foes have included kingpins of crime and dastardly MAD SCIENTISTS. Occasionally, nasty remnants of his planet's violent past make their way to Earth, where SUPERMAN must battle them to the death. SUPERMAN sometimes comes to the rescue of ordinary people, especially Lois Lane, his colleague at the *Daily Planet.*

SUPERMAN's powers are . . . well, superior. He has X-ray vision, which can see through anything except lead. He is stronger than most humans. He is "able to leap tall buildings at a single bound!" He is indestructible to anything except kryptonite, the metal native to his home planet. Best of all, he can fly! SUPERMAN is the totality of every dream any youngster ever had.

Once the SUPERMAN character was introduced into comic books, he became a smash success, and inspired endless imitators. His deeds were the stuff of legend, and indeed, there have been not only television and radio programs but even a Broadway musical comedy based on the character. As played by Steve Reeves on television, SUPERMAN was noble to the point of boredom. Christopher Reeve (no relation) brought a touch of goofy naivete to the part. His SUPERMAN was willing to give up all his powers to be an ordinary husband to fellow reporter Lois Lane. (Of course, he got them back again, when the time came to use them to battle for Truth, Justice, and the American Way!)

SUPERMAN has been called everything, from the ideal of American Youth to a dangerous fascist threat. Nothing seems to alter the basic fact that SUPERMAN represents comic book story-telling at its most definitive, and the character's popularity hasn't diminished in over 50 years. See also SUPERHERO; SUPERVILLAIN.

supernova (astronomy): A star that explodes, ejecting its mass at high velocity; the energy thus released is at least a million more times that of a mere NOVA. A SUPERNOVA may be visible from Earth as a sudden bright spot in the sky. It is surmised that the fabled Star of Bethlehem might have been such an explosion.

After the SUPERNOVA dies down, its mass may boil away completely, or the star's central core may collapse into a NEUTRON STAR. The particles that make up the core may collapse further, forming a BLACK HOLE, from which not even light can escape.

supervillain (comics): The Bad Guy against whom the SUPERHERO must pit his extraordinary powers. SUPERVILLAINS tend to have odd names and odder looks. BATMAN in particular finds himself fighting strange people with schemes to take over the United States (or the whole world). The Joker, for instance, is a criminal who devises practical jokes with very nasty climaxes: an electric buzzer that electrocutes its victims, or a disappearing ink that doesn't disappear, but spreads itself over priceless works of art.

It is the job of the SUPERVILLAIN to devise some plan to disarm the SUPERHERO, using the one item that will harm him. Of course, the SUPERHERO then manages to get out of the trap and destroy the SUPERVILLAIN . . . until the next time. Comic book SCRIPTERS are kept busy thinking up ever more devilish schemes for SUPERVILLAINS to perpetrate on humanity.

survivalist fiction (literary): Grim stories, set in a POST-HOLOCAUST future, in which all semblance of law and order has broken down, and a tiny band of humans must fend off anyone and anything that will deprive them of food and water. Most of these works are the products of HACK writers.

SURVIVALIST FICTION usually focuses on one male protagonist, who must fight off threats to his community both from without and within. The women are usually depicted as being either subservient to the men, or so tough that they must be destroyed. The landscape is threatening, the politics are those of the Far Right, and the plots are so hackneyed as to be interchangeable. Nevertheless, there is a steady market for this sort of FORMULA FICTION; there are several SERIES in print, and the demand hasn't stopped.

suspension of disbelief (literary): Occasionally amended to "willing suspension of disbelief"; the critical item in the enjoyment of SF. The reader must willingly admit that some parts of what is being read cannot take place, but will accept them as part of the story anyway. SUSPENSION OF DISBELIEF is what makes such literary conventions as FTL DRIVE or HYPERSPACE or ALIENS possible. The reader does not argue with the writer, but uses a kind of DOUBLETHINK that accepts the writer's viewpoint for the duration of the story.

There are many ways that a writer can bolster the realism of a story, so that the reader may suspend disbelief. Details of life on board a starship or on another PLANET may be piled high, so that the reader understands where the CHARACTERS are and what they are doing. The CHARACTERIZATION and the MOTIVATION of the characters may draw the reader into their world. All of this makes demands on the writer as well as the reader. It's not enough to set the story on Space Colony X anymore; readers want to be able to feel that they know all about Space Colony X and its people, so that they can suspend disbelief and enter into the life and reality of its people.

The reverse is also true. SF writers must be careful not to throw in too many mistakes in the "science," or their "fiction" will be revealed, and the reader will not be able to suspend disbelief, and will turn to something else.

sword and sorcery (literary): Another term for HEROIC FANTASY; those stories set in mythical kingdoms where magic works and gunpowder hasn't been invented yet. The term was coined by Fritz Lieber in 1960, who used it to deride the whole pseudomagical genre in which he himself participated. However, the genre goes back much farther than that. CONAN THE BARBARIAN is a typical SWORD AND SORCERY hero.

synchronous orbit (aerospace): An orbit in which a satellite or other small body (either natural or artificial) moves around a planet at the same rate as the object moves on its own axis. The result is that only one side of the object is visible from the planet at any given time. Our MOON circles the Earth in a SYNCHRONOUS ORBIT.

syndication (TV): Selling the EPISODES of a TV SERIES to be replayed after the NETWORK has released them. Many classic SF SERIES have been rebroadcast for years, thanks to SYNDICATION, enabling FANS to enjoy THE TWILIGHT ZONE or STAR TREK on local stations or CABLE. Some long-running TV SERIES may sell their early EPISODES to SYNDICATION, even while the show is still producing new EPISODES for the NETWORKS.

SYNDICATION has allowed some SERIES to develop new FANS long after the original EPISODES were first broadcast. Some independent producers prefer to bypass the NETWORKS altogether, and go into DIRECT SYNDICATION.

syzygy (astronomy): An arrangement of the planets whereby they are all lined up along the same radius and along the same orbital plane extending from the sun. This does not happen very often in a PLANETARY SYSTEM. When it does, astronomers want to take advantage of it, as did NASA when it sent the Voyager spacecraft on its GRAND TOUR. See also ALIGNMENT (ASTRONOMY).

T

tachyons (physics): Hypothetical faster-than-light particles, invented by physicists who saw no reason why they should not exist, even though there is no evidence that they do. TACHYONS have been evoked by SF writers who want to use them in such matters as communications or transportation at FTL speeds.

TAFF (Trans-Atlantic Fan Fund) (fan): A fund begun in Britain in 1953 and financed through AUCTIONS, sales, and donations, whose purpose is to send a deserving fan across the Atlantic, usually from Britain to attend the WORLD-CON in the United States. The earliest recipient of the award was Irish FAN Walt Willis. Other TAFF beneficiaries have been Bob Shaw and Wilson Tucker, both of whom went on to become well-known writers. See also DUFF.

talking heads (fan): Portrait illustrations in FANZINES, used to depict standard characters from popular TV SERIES or films; most often, the characters of STAR TREK or STAR WARS. Many STILLS are endlessly reproduced by fan artists, to be used by the editors of MEDIAZINES. The artists protest that they must work from photographs, and the posed pictures are the only ones available to them; the editors of the FANZINES insist that while the portraits are very well done, what is really needed is an illustration that relates to the action of the story. Readers are caught in the middle of all this.

The term comes from television, where TALKING HEADS is used derisively for any program that consists of several people in a discussion. The matter may be engrossing, but the visual impact is nil.

TANJ (literary): "There Ain't No Justice!" An acronym invented by Larry Niven and used extensively in his *Ringworld* novels as an all-purpose expletive. It sounds explosive and has no connection to natural functions, either eliminative or procreative, which makes it an expletive that does not have to be deleted.

TANSTAAFL (fan): A fannish dictum: "There Ain't No Such Thing As A Free Lunch." Or, in short, "You get what you pay for." First credited to ROBERT HEINLEIN. It has been adopted by the general public, to the extent that a member of the Senate Finance Committee, when questioned by the Press about funding for future space efforts, said, "There ain't no such thing as a free launch."

tapes (audio/fan): Usually in the form of cassettes, easily portable and used to record the pearls of wisdom that drop from the lips of the experts of PANELS at CONVENTIONS, or the musical doings at FILK-SINGS. There are also semiprofessional TAPES of FILK songs offered for sale at CONS or through the mail. See also FILK-TAPES.

tapes (video): See BOOTLEG TAPES; CLONING PARTIES.

techie (fan): A FAN who is enthralled with technology, especially when it is used in his or her own daily life. TECHIES are often COMPUTER GEEKS who enjoy playing with the COMPUTERS and other gadgets more than they enjoy interacting with other people. TECHIES tend to read HARDWARE STORIES rather than Fantasy or SOFT SF.

techno-thriller (literary): A suspense story set in the immediate future that features technology and its ramifications in its central plot often dealing with international espionage and Cold War strategems. Most TECHNO-THRILLERS may be called DAY AFTER TOMORROW STORIES; *The Hunt for Red October* by Tom Clancy is typical.

Recent developments in international politics may have made the TECHNO-THRILLER obsolete; however, some of them can be read on their own merits, as top-notch ACTION/ ADVENTURE tales.

tectonics (geology): Also called plate TECTONICS. The study of the movement of continental masses of a planet. Until the last 10 years, the whole theory of plate TECTONICS was considered totally far-fetched, the dream of one Alfred Wengener, a German geologist who realized that the outlines of the continents seemed to fit into each other like a jigsaw puzzle.

The theory of plate TECTONICS has been proven by underwater explorations that have revealed deep-sea fissures through which the internal molten rock that makes up the core of the Earth wells up. TECTONICS may be incorporated into the geology of a faraway planet and used in WORLDBUILDING.

telecommunications (electronics): The ability to communicate over vast distances by means of electronic devices, SATELLITES, and so on. One of the dreams of early SF that has come to pass through the technology of COMPUTERS and microchips. Thanks to TELECOMMUNICATIONS the entire world was able to share in the Apollo Moon Landings in 1969, in the Viking Mars Landing in 1977, and in the *Challenger* Disaster in 1986.

telekinesis (parapsychology): The ability to move objects without touching them physically, presumably with mental power. The most disputable of mental powers, because it is the most easily tested and the least likely to be falsified, TELEKINESIS is also the one most misinterpreted in SF films and stories.

Practitioners of TELEKINESIS are supposedly able to start fires (as in Stephen King's *Firestarter*, 1980); they can remove tumors from brains (as in Jean Lorrah's *Savage Empire* series); they can even move themselves from place to place.

Whether TELEKINESIS works is a moot point. It is one of the powers most commonly claimed for ESPERS in SF.

telepath (parapsychology): One who uses mental powers to communicate or to receive communications from others. The idea of a society of TELEPATHS is one explored frequently by SF writers. Those unfortunate persons who find themselves caught in such a society may be called MIND-BLIND by those who can communicate directly without such clumsy intermediaries as words. See also EMPATH.

telepathy (parapsychology): The ability to communicate with other beings without the use of vocalizations, signals, or any other devices; in other words, thoughts are projected directly from one brain to another. There have been many instances reported of such communications, but it is difficult to verify them.

TELEPATHY is one of the most common mental powers claimed by SF writers for their superior species. Mere mortals have to flounder about, trying to put their thoughts into speech; SLANS, for instance, can simply project their thoughts into the minds of others.

There are variations on the theme of TELEPATHY. STAR TREK'S Vulcans, for instance, are TOUCH TELEPATHS; they must be in physical contact with the person with whom they are trying to communicate. Other means of TELEPATHY might employ an object on which to focus one's thoughts, such as the "starstones" used by the TELEPATHS in Marion Zimmer Bradley's DARKOVER.

terminal (computer): The complete computer setup, whether in a private home or a business situation. A TERMINAL usually consists of a keyboard, a MONITOR, and a printer. How elaborate this arrangement is depends on how much information the computer is expected to store and process, and how much money the owner is willing to spend to achieve the expected results.

Terra (astronomy): The name given to Earth in various SF novels. TERRA means "earth" in Latin, and is the most logical way to refer to the planet on which life has evolved in the SOLAR SYSTEM. As a result, the inhabitants of Earth are often referred to as TERRANS or some variation of the word.

terraforming (biology): The alteration of a planet's natural ecology to suit the needs of humans. The term was first used by Jack Williamson in 1942, although the concept had been around since the 1920s.

TERRAFORMING has been considered as an alternative to the use of protective gear in the settlement of other planets in our SOLAR SYSTEM, particularly MARS. While such a project might take years, if not centuries, the result would be a place in which humans could exist without SPACE SUITS, domes, or other special equipment. On the other hand, there are many people who feel that whatever has evolved on another PLANET belongs there, and humans are interlopers who should adapt themselves to the environment instead of the other way around.

"That REAL Old-Time Religion" (fan/filk): A FILK-SONG with over 650 verses, sung to the familiar camp-meeting tune, that chronicles the doings of the gods and goddesses of MYTHOLOGY with wild and woolly puns. "Master Class Old-Time Religion" is a game played at FILK-SINGS; the object is for each person in the group to sing a different verse from memory, without missing a beat. The song's fame has spread beyond FANDOM; Joseph Campbell quoted a verse of it in one of his "Conversations with Bill Moyers," broadcast on PBS. For a few of the more popular verses, see Appendix B.

Thieves' World (literary): A SERIES of novels and ANTHOLOGIES edited by Robert Asprin, beginning with the first THIEVES' WORLD ANTHOLOGY in 1979. THIEVES' WORLD was the first SHARED UNIVERSE, a collaboration of several writers who use the same SETTING for interrelated stories.

The THIEVES' WORLD saga has a complex story line that incorporates Byzantine Imperial politics, invasions of strange peoples from over the seas, and interference by Gods in the affairs of Men. The 12th volume of short stories was published in 1989; there are also several full-length novels, three GRAPHIC NOVELS and a ROLE-PLAYING GAME.

three-sheet (publishing): The largest size of POSTER for advertising books and films, taken from the world of the theater. See also TWO-SHEETS.

throw-away dialog (literary/film): Bits of information conveyed by dialog to the reading or viewing audience. THROW-AWAY DIALOG lets the audience know where the action is taking place, the names of various characters, their relationships to each other, and their places in the PLOT. PLOT POINTS can be made in THROW-AWAY DIALOG; it takes a careful reader to pick up on them.

The term comes from the theater, where such information was given in tones that implied that it was not particularly important. The information was literally "thrown away," and it was up to the audience to catch it.

tie-ins (comics/literary): COMIC BOOKS that contain stories relating to other stories in other COMIC BOOKS; a CROSS-UNIVERSE concept used in comics, often with the direct assistance of the CREATIVE TEAMS of both story lines. A new CHARACTER or set of characters may be introduced in a TIE-IN, to go on to more adventures on their own.

The term may also refer to NOVELIZATIONS that are published to coincide with the release date of a film or TV program.

time-line (literary): A table provided by the author listing the stories in a SERIES in chronological order that may not necessarily be the order in which they were published. A SERIES like the SIME/GEN stories that ranges over several centuries of human history demands a TIME-LINE to keep all the SEQUELS and PREQUELS straight. A very complex SERIES may also need a list of CHARACTERS as well as a TIME-LINE.

time machine (literary): A device for traveling backward or forward in time. The term was the title of a novel by H. G. WELLS, first published in 1895. WELLS did not specify how the machine worked; later writers have attempted to explain their devices in terms of advanced physics. See also TIME TRAVEL.

time travel (literary): The moving of a being or its mentality to a period either before or after the presumptive date of the original action of the story. The idea of traveling into the past or future has been a theme used in SF since H. G. WELLS' novel *The Time Machine.*

One example of TIME TRAVEL is Poul Anderson's *Time Patrol* SERIES, in which a group of humans is trained to "correct" errors that might lead to an ALTERNATE HISTORY. Another possibility is explored in the TV SERIES "Quantum Leap," based on the idea that an experimenter's mentality is being lodged in the bodies of various people in the experimenter's past.

TIME TRAVEL is one of those literary CONVENTIONS that HARD SCIENCE claims cannot possibly be done. Writers still like to use TIME TRAVEL to make philosophic points, or just to have fun with history.

Tolkien, J. R. R. (1898–1973): Fantasy author, folklorist, and historian, best known for his *Lord of the Rings* TRILOGY. TOLKIEN invented a UNIVERSE, chronicled its peoples, organized its language, and described its geography. In *The Hobbit* and *The Lord of the Rings* TOLKIEN described the two QUESTS that located and destroyed the Ring of Power.

TOLKIEN'S UNIVERSE is probably the most completely documented Fantasy universe in literature, spawning costumes, artwork, poetry, and music. Donald Swann, best known for his collaboration with Michael Flanders, has set some of TOLKIEN'S poems to music. Many FILK-SONGS extol the events in TOLKIEN'S tale. There is an active TOLKIEN Society, as well as other groups that meet regularly to discuss the works of the Master.

Tomato Surprise ending (literary): A so-called "surprise ending" that comes as no surprise to anyone, except perhaps the author, who thought it had never been done before. Typical TOMATO SURPRISE ENDINGS are the ADAM AND EVE STORY, the one in which the horrible monsters are only three inches tall, or the one in which the whole PLOT turns out to be a dream.

Many TOMATO SURPRISE ENDINGS turn up in the SLUSH PILE. It is up to the READER or EDITOR to point out to the writer that this idea was new and astonishing when it was first conceived (possibly in 1925), but by now the surprise has long gone and the story is a cliche.

The term was first used by George Scithers in the REJECTION SLIP he sent out when he was editing *Isaac Asimov's SF Magazine.*

Tom Swift (literary): Leading character in a series of juvenile novels, beginning with *Tom Swift and his Airship* in 1910, published under the name of Victor Appleton (possibly the pseudonym of H. R. Garis). TOM SWIFT was a "boy inventor," who came up with ingenious devices in his basement workshop, such as ROCKETS and communications devices. The SERIES has remained popular, although the devices have been updated to include SATELLITES and other marvels of technology. TOM SWIFT has become the epitome of the HARDWARE STORY for young people.

'toon (film): Cartoon, either in animation or art. 'TOONS are used as FILLOS in FANZINES and are seen in movie theaters before the feature presentation. The Golden Age of the 'TOON was 1940–1960, honored in the 1989 film, *Who Framed Roger Rabbit?*

touch-plates (computer): The electronic pads on COMPUTERS that have largely replaced buttons. Buttons have many parts that can break or wear out; TOUCH-PLATES are activated by the pressure of a finger on the circuitry.

touch telepath (parapsychology): A being that communicates its thoughts by placing them directly in the mind of another being through physical contact. Without the contact, the TOUCH TELEPATH must resort to verbal communication like the rest of us. STAR TREK's Mr. Spock and his fellow-Vulcans are TOUCH TELEPATHS. See also TELEPATHY.

tracking (fan/conventions): The centering of a series of PANELS or WORKSHOPS around a particular theme at a CONVENTION. FAN-CONS may run several tracks of PROGRAMMING. One may deal with the practical aspects of SF writing, while another will be aimed at a critical analysis of the works of the GOH, and a third may focus on FAN-AC. There may be separate TRACKS for film/video or art. A WORLD-CON may have as many as five TRACKS, including the film program and the Special Events.

The term has been adopted from the education system (in which many FANS find employment), where it is used to mean the practice of directing children into classes and activities suitable for their intellectual abilities.

trade paperback (publishing): A compromise between the cheaply produced MASS-MARKET PAPERBACK and the HARDCOVER; a book printed on paper of the same quality as a HARDCOVER but with a perfect-bound paper cover instead of the more durable cloth-covered cardboard used in HARDCOVER bookbinding. A TRADE PAPERBACK sells for less than the HARDCOVER edition, but costs more than the smaller MASS-MARKET PAPERBACK. Many TRADE PAPERBACKS are sturdy books that will stand a good deal of wear. There are no hard-and-fast rules as to which FORMAT works better with any one book. The publisher has to decide which is most suitable for the subject area and audience of the book.

trailer (film): A short piece of film with scenes from a forthcoming production, taken to CONVENTIONS by a promoter to generate interest in the film. TRAILERS are shown in theaters and on television as "coming attractions," with the same idea in mind. They are sold by dealers at CONVENTIONS. Occasionally a commercially prepared videotape will include TRAILERS of upcoming films from the same company.

transit (astronomy): The passage of a smaller body, such as a planet or an artificial SATELLITE, in front of a larger one, such as a star, so that the smaller body appears to cross the face of the larger one. If the smaller body is positioned close enough to the Earth to block out light from the larger one, the phenomenon may be called an ECLIPSE. The TRANSITS most likely to be seen from the Earth are those of MERCURY and VENUS against the Sun. A viewer on MARS might be able to witness the TRANSIT of EARTH against the Sun.

transponder (electronics): A device that receives a signal and automatically sends a response; quite useful as a tracking device, which is how it is used today. The idea was used in SF long before it became a gadget used by modern police and espionage agents.

transporter (aerospace): A hypothetical device that will break an object into its component atoms and reassemble it in a given spot. The idea of transporting matter (organic or not) has been thrashed around in SF since the 1920s. So far no one has been able to make a device that will reassemble the object once it has been demolished. However, the TRANSPORTER or something like it has been a staple device used in SF films, TV SERIES, and books since it made its appearance in the first STAR TREK episodes in the 1960s, if for no other reason than because it gets the CHARACTERS from one place to another in very little time, permitting them to get on with the play.

transwarp (literary): Another variation on HYPERSPACE.

Trekker (fan): A serious FAN of STAR TREK, who participates in FANNISH activities such as writing FAN-LIT, buying FANZINES, devising costumes, attending MEDIA-CONS, and generally using STAR TREK as a springboard for various creative and purposeful activity. The term was coined by Joan Winston, a TV producer and writer, in response to the use of the word TREKKIE by the press.

Many of the people working on the current "Star Trek: The Next Generation" series began their artistic careers as TREKKERS. TREKKERS have adapted computer programs first written as STAR TREK games for use by the disabled. They have become artists and writers, computer specialists and research scientists, or perhaps just happy human beings, through their interaction with each other through STAR TREK FANDOM.

TREKKERS take their STAR TREK seriously, which makes them a target for satire. Even William Shatner, the erstwhile Captain Kirk, was able to scream "Get a life!" at a supposed gang of them in a comedy skit on "Saturday Night Live."

Do not call TREKKERS "TREKKIES."

Trekkie (fan): A very young and enthusiastic FAN of STAR TREK. First used by critics in the 1960s, derived from "teeny-bopper," a young and enthusiastic lover of popular music. The "Trekkie-bopper" was soon reduced to a TREKKIE, and a stereotype: a breathless, overweight young woman with a mad passion for Mr. Spock and very little literary discrimination. This STEREOTYPE and the name for it became distasteful to FANS of STAR TREK, who were offended by its implications. The preferred term is TREKKER.

trilogy (literary/publishing): Three interrelated novels or films that tell one coherent story. Many very long and complicated tales can only be done in this manner, especially Fantasy stories set in a mystical and magical land that requires much BACK-STORY to be explained before the PLOT can get underway.

TRILOGIES were the norm in the Victorian era, when novels were read aloud around the parlor table. Many of the great works of the 19th century were deliberately written in this format. The real Age of the TRILOGY in SF may be said to begin with TOLKEIN's *Lord of the Rings*.

TRILOGIES present certain structural difficulties for the writer. The first book must present the BASIC PREMISE and introduce the main CHARACTERS. The last book must tie up the loose ends and bring the PLOT to a satisfactory conclusion. The book in the middle is the real problem, since it does not have a real beginning (which was done in the first book), and it cannot come to a real conclusion (which is going to be done in the next book). In films this is even more devastating; one of the weaknesses of *Star Wars: The Empire Strikes Back* is that there is no definite conclusion. GEORGE LUCAS hung up millions of his fans for three years until he finished the TRILOGY with *The Return of the Jedi.*

If a TRILOGY receives a good response, the publisher may request more of the same from the writer, who then finds he or she has a SERIES on his hands.

trucking shot (film): A scene photographed by a moving camera. The result is a feeling of movement in what would otherwise be a static confrontation scene. Directors may use a TRUCKING SHOT to show reactions of a number of people to some event or statement; they may also use TRUCKING SHOTS to generate action where none really exists.

trufan (fan): Plural, trufen; one who is seriously and completely immersed in the SF subculture. A total and committed FAN who reads and often writes SF, who may be involved in various forms of FAN-AC, who attends SF CONS, and who generally fits his or her life around SF instead of the other way around. See also FANDOM; FIAWOL.

T-shirts (fan/merchandise): Pullover short-sleeved cotton shirts, first used as undergarments, now used as a form of portable advertising for almost everything: films, CONVENTIONS, particular brands of food and drink, even philosophy. Many of the slogans found on BUTTONS may be imprinted on T-SHIRTS.

T-SHIRTS (also spelled tee-shirts) became part of the standard dress of American youth in the 1960s, when wearing cheap undergarments as outer wear was considered a political statement against the materialistic culture that valued objects because of their high price.

Many FAN-CONS produce a distinctive T-SHIRT that will be sold at the CON to produce extra operating revenue. The shirt will be distributed to the CON-COM, and will often be kept as a souvenir by those who have attended the CON.

The latest wrinkle in the T-SHIRT is the hand-painted one-of-a-kind item that may be entered into the ART SHOW as a legitimate piece of textile art.

Tsiolkovsky, Konstantin (1859–1914): Russian chemist and founder of Soviet rocketry, who designed a rocket in 1903 that would have been powered by heated gasses produced by mixing liquid oxygen and liquid hydrogen. TSIOLKOVSKY was a theorist, not an experimenter; he did not live long enough to see the Soviet space program take shape after World War II. ROBERT GODDARD's experimental work in the United States in the 1920s may have been based in part on TSIOLKOVSKY's theories, but GODDARD concentrated on the practical aspects of space flight.

Tullamore Dew (fan): A brand of Irish whiskey, supposedly far more potent than any other. Whether this is true or not is beyond this writer's ability to tell; however, TULLAMORE DEW or "Tully" is now a FANNISH icon by which all other liquor is judged.

Twilight Zone, The (TV): U.S. TV ANTHOLOGY SERIES, written and hosted by ROD SERLING, featuring stories of SF, Fantasy, and the supernatural. The series ran from 1959 to 1965 in several formats. At first, each episode ran 30 minutes, shot in black and white. Later, the episodes were expanded to a full hour, and finally, the series was shot in color.

Most of the stories dealt with ordinary people being sucked into some strangeness that changed their lives forever. A pool hustler plays with the Devil for his soul; a derelict steals a pair of shoes from a dead man that turn his body into a vehicle for the deceased; a seemingly benign visit from Aliens has shocking implications. The original episodes often featured actors who were to go on to leading roles in films and television series; William Shatner (later seen as Captain Kirk on STAR TREK) played a man who thinks he sees something (or someone) strange on the wing of an airplane.

The eerie nature of the stories was enhanced by the ping-pong musical theme, which has become an aural cliche in popular culture for any kind of weird or unusual behavior. Each episode was introduced by ROD SERLING himself, whose emphatic delivery provided fuel for comic impersonators for years.

The term TWILIGHT ZONE has moved into the general language, meaning any strange occurrence or sequence of events, or any unusual behavior on the part of a friend, relative, or enemy. Someone acting oddly is said to have gone into THE TWILIGHT ZONE.

two-sheets (publishing): Mid-sized advertising POSTERS, not as large as THREE-SHEETS, but large enough to exploit whatever the publisher or filmmaker wants to sell.

typos (printing): Short for "typographical errors," mistakes in the printing due to misplaced or transposed letters, or misspelled words. Some of these have become classics, and some are inadvertently humorous; a few may be almost Freudian slips. This writer once wrote "contentious objectors" instead of "conscientious objectors" when discussing the political implications of the Vietnam War.

Most editors, whether FAN or PRO, pick carefully through the manuscripts to eliminate typos; their presence indicates sloppy proofreading.

UFO (aerospace): Unidentified Flying Objects, reported regularly by people who range from amateur astronomers to bona fide mental cases. Each sighting has been followed up and noted in PROJECT BLUE BOOK by the U.S. Air Force. Most of them have proved to be balloons, birds, or atmospheric disturbances, easily laughed off by hard-headed observers. There have been a couple of exceptions that might possibly have been objects from other worlds; those exceptions are still under investigation.

The possibility of a visit from another species, whether benign or aggressive, is a staple ingredient of SF; bringing the fictional into the realm of fact is another matter entirely. See also ALIENS; FIRST CONTACT STORY.

umbilical (aerospace): A length of tubing that attaches a space-traveller to his or her craft during EVA, in the same way that the umbilical cord connects the growing infant to its mother's body.

undergrounds (comics): Comic books published by a SMALL PRESS in the 1960s as part of the counterculture of the decade. Most of them were meant to be shocking, advocating the use of marijuana or other stimulants, and expounding on the joys of sex. Today some of these attitudes seem quaint, while others are downright dangerous.

The UNDERGROUNDS were the training ground for some of the comic artists who emerged in the 1970s, particularly Robert Crumb and RALPH BAKSHI.

unicorns (mythology): Graceful beasts in the shape of a horse with one horn projecting from their forehead. UNICORNS have been described in myth and legend dating back to Greek and Roman days.

There has been much speculation as to how the myth began. One answer may lie in a rare and beautiful antelope of the Arabian Peninsula, the oryx, that bears two (not one) spiral-striated horns. From a distance, and from the side, the animal could appear to have a single horn. The twisted tusk of the narwhal, a small whale with a single tooth emerging from its upper lip, may have been sold as a "unicorn's horn" by Norse traders.

UNICORNS were said to have magical powers. Only a virgin could catch one; it would lay its head in her lap, and be powerless to resist its captors. This legend was depicted in medieval tapestries and illuminated bestiaries.

SF artists are particularly enthralled with UNICORNS, to the point where SF writers are beginning a kind of backlash. The magnificent animal with its single horn has been depicted in so many dreamy landscapes that writers like Piers Anthony and Jack Chalker have rebelled and inserted carnivorous or savage UNICORNS into their fantasy Universes. The classic FANTASY story about UNICORNS is *The Last Unicorn*, by Peter Beagle, published in 1972.

UNICORNS are among the standard subjects found in ART SHOWS at CONVENTIONS.

UNIVAC (computer): Universal Analog Computer: the first commercially available stored-program electronic digital device in the United States, beginning in 1951 and superceded by more efficient computers in 1958. It filled an entire room and was waited on by devoted slaves. No wonder SF writers regarded it and its subsequent adaptations with awe, fear, and loathing!

UNIVAC has been relegated to a museum piece; the current version of a MAINFRAME does ten times the work in half the space.

Universe (astronomy): Everything that exists, anywhere and at any time: stars, PLANETS, or space debris; organic, inorganic, or in between; sentient or nonsentient. The UNIVERSE as we know it has no beginning and no end. It simply is, and it is the business of humanity to find out all we can about it, through observation, experimentation, and deduction.

Universe (literary): The aggregate of people, places, and things pertinent to the works of a particular author, or to a particular film or set of films, or to a TV SERIES. A UNIVERSE may encompass the CHARACTERS who are directly involved in the action, as well as the ones who are peripheral to it, and may even come to include mythological or historical beings who may be described by the CHARACTERS. A UNIVERSE will take place in a particular milieu that may or may not exist on Earth at this time (or any other). The objects handled by the CHARACTERS in that milieu as described by the creator or creators of the UNIVERSE are also part of that UNIVERSE.

The development of a particular UNIVERSE over a SERIES of novels and/or films is a characteristic of SF writers, who build their societies and worlds carefully over a period of time, so that their readers feel that this place could actually exist somewhere, somehow.

A UNIVERSE can be OPEN to other writers; more often, it is CLOSED, since the creator has a particular vision of FUTURE HISTORY, and knows exactly where he or she wants the UNIVERSE to go. It can be a SHARED UNIVERSE, in which many writers use the same PLANET or starship as the background for their stories, and a central EDITOR makes sure that everyone's details match. When a CHARACTER from one UNIVERSE meets someone from another UNIVERSE, the result is a CROSS-UNIVERSE story.

MEDIAZINES often indicate in which UNIVERSE their stories take place, so that readers may be able to pick the ones in which they have the most interest. ADZINES indicate the UNIVERSE (or UNIVERSES) most pertinent to the 'ZINES they are advertising by coded references. A recent copy of one ADZINE listed some 25 separate UNIVERSES.

Unix (computer): The most commonly used computer operating system, developed and marketed by IBM.

Urban High Fantasy (literary): The latest twist in an old metaphor, with the City acting as the Forest Primeval in SF or Fantasy tales of battle, murder, and sudden death. The 1989 *Batman* film is the best example of URBAN HIGH FANTASY. An SF version is Ridley Scott's film *Blade Runner* (1982). See also FILM NOIR.

user-friendly (computer): A COMPUTER that is easily operated and understood, even by MUNDANES. Most people prefer a home COMPUTER that answers this description.

user-hostile (computer): A COMPUTER that is difficult, if not obstreperous, toward its operator. USER-HOSTILE COMPUTERS have been designed by COMPUTER GEEKS to do strange and wonderful things that no ordinary person would expect them to do. They also come with instructions in Japanese.

Utopia (literary): A perfect society, as devised by the writer. The term was first used as the title for a work by Sir Thomas More in 1516, in which he described the ideal society as he saw it. There is some debate as to exactly what More meant by the title, which is from the Greek. If he meant "U-Topia," he was talking about "Another Place"; if, as might be inferred from the text, he meant "Eu-Topia," he was talking about a "Better

Place," in which case the antithesis would be a DYSTOPIA, or a "Worse Place."

Many writers have tried to formulate the perfect society, both before and after More. Most of them describe a place in which every person may have peace and tranquillity; at what cost to the individual depends on the writer's philosophy. SF writers like H. G. WELLS have tried to postulate what a future society might be; most of them fall far wide of the mark, since technological or sociological factors of which they could have no foreknowledge may intervene in the best-laid scheme of things.

The main problem with a UTOPIA is that it is often so peaceful as to be totally boring.

vacuum (aerospace): A state of total absence of atmosphere, as in INTERSTELLAR SPACE. There is no friction in a VACUUM, so that a spacecraft does not need to be shielded against it; on the other hand, there is no atmosphere in space, hence no resistance, so there is no necessity for streamlining a vessel.

The very existence of a VACUUM was difficult to understand until the beginning of the 19th century, when scientists began to experiment with the properties of air and its absence.

Vallejo, Boris (b. 1940): Peruvian-born American SF artist, known for Fantasy portraits in the tradition of FRANK FRAZETTA. VALLEJO's muscular males and well-developed females have adorned everything from book covers to POSTERS and calendars.

vampires (mythology): Evil beings who exist by sucking blood from living men and women. Legends of VAMPIRES have been traced through the Balkans, into Slavic mythology. There is some evidence that the characteristics of VAMPIRES (hatred of daylight, elongated incisor teeth, need to ingest blood for nutrition) may be the symptoms of a rare blood disease brought on by a nutritional deficiency. There are historical incidents of people who believed that drinking the blood of young women would make them young and beautiful. The nobleman known

as Vlad Tepes DRACULA was considered violent and bloodthirsty, even for his times, but it was not until Bram Stoker put all the legends together into a brew of adventure, horror, and slightly disguised sex called *Dracula* that the character of the VAMPIRE entered SF and Fantasy literature as a STOCK CHARACTER.

Several writers have used VAMPIRES as the central characters in their stories. Fred Saberhagen managed to mix DRACULA and Sherlock Holmes in one CROSS-UNIVERSE story (*The Holmes-Dracula File,* 1978), and extended the range of the venerable VAMPIRE in *An Old Friend of the Family* (1988). Chelsea Quinn Yarbro writes of Radozy Saint-Germain (who may be based on a historical figure) in his march through human history. The VAMPIRES of George R. R. Martin's *Fevre Dream* (1982) are not so genteel. Anne Rice's *Vampire Lestat* becomes a rock star, while his lover, *The Queen of the Damned,* uses her powers to gain and lose fortunes.

VAMPIRES may be depicted as evil beings who destroy human lives and souls for their pleasure, or they may be described as misguided creatures who must kill to exist. In either case, the public's fascination with them has not abated.

Van Allen Radiation Belt (astronomy): Two zones of high-energy charged particles trapped in the Earth's magnetic field.

Until the Apollo Moon Landings in the late 1960s and early 1970s, no one knew whether they represented a barrier to further human exploration of the SOLAR SYSTEM or not. So far, there have been no adverse effects observed in those who have passed through the VAN ALLEN BELTS.

vanity press (publishing): Producers of HARDCOVER books who publish the works of hitherto unknown writers for a fee. The writer must bear the cost of printing and publicizing the book, which presumably feeds the writer's ego. This is not quite the same as self-publishing, since the writer expects the publisher to do the physical labor of producing the book.

FAN publishing is self-publishing, but not necessarily VANITY publishing, since the FAN expects to MARKET the product.

vaporware (computer): A product that has been promised but is not yet delivered. It may not even be in existence. It is, so to speak, made of vapor! The term is derived from HARDWARE and SOFTWARE.

VCR (electronics): Video-Cassette Recorder, a device that has changed SF MEDIA FANDOM. When connected to a television receiver, the VCR can record a TV transmission, store it on magnetic tape, and retain it for later retrieval. Films may be recorded and stored similarly, which means that the average FAN can build up a personal library of SF films and favorite EPISODES of TV SERIES. FANS can share their stores of EPISODES through CLONING PARTIES. Unfortunately, some people abuse the possibilities of the VCR by trying to make illegal copies of films that are protected by COPYRIGHT. See also BOOTLEG TAPES.

Venus (astronomy): The planet second closest to the Sun, about the same size as Earth, but much, much hotter. It is now known to be a hellishly poisonous planet, possibly the victim of a runaway GREENHOUSE EFFECT that trapped the planet under a blanket of carbon dioxide, keeping the surface so hot that there was no possibility for water to collect in a liquid form.

Until the Soviet PLANETARY PROBE Venera landed, VENUS was still considered a possible site for life to develop, albeit in a different form than it did on Earth. ROBERT HEINLEIN imagined vast, intelligent beings wallowing in primeval swamps. C. L. Moore's VENUS is the home of ancient and evil civilizations. C. S. Lewis called VENUS "Perelandra," and set his Utopian fantasies there.

Given what we now know of VENUS, it is highly unlikely that there will be a manned SPACE COLONY there.

Verne, Jules (1828–1905): French writer of adventure stories, generally considered one of the two founders of modern SF (the other is H. G. WELLS). VERNE was an unsuccessful writer of stories toiling in an office job when he was asked to write a tale about a balloon expedition. The result, *Five Weeks in a Balloon* (1863), combined the latest technology with a roaring adventure, and was an instant hit. It was followed by such classic tales as *20,000 Leagues Under the Sea* (1870) and *Around the World in 80 Days* (1873). VERNE's stories used as much technical material as he could find, to add to the SUSPENSION OF DISBELIEF. A few of VERNE's gadgets became realities, particularly the "submarine boat" described so lovingly in *20,000 Leagues Under the Sea*, and the rocket of *From the Earth to the Moon*.

VERNE lived long enough to see some of his predictions become reality . . . and was not at all surprised that they did.

video room (fan/convention): A room at an SF CONVENTION designated for nonstop showings of SF films or selected EPISODES of TV series that may not be available locally. Many British SF SERIES received their first showings in VIDEO ROOMS. The VIDEO ROOM is usually set up with multiple VCRS and television sets. The tapes may be donated by the CON-COM or may be brought to the CON by the members.

The person who sits in the VIDEO ROOM throughout the CON, emerging only for meals and natural functions, is called a MUSHROOM.

vignette (literary): A short piece of prose that illuminates a single moment in the life of a character, either fictional or not. From the French; the literal meaning was "a little vine," a drawing of which might be used to fill in blank space on a page.

FANZINES specialize in this sort of piece; many of them are MISSING SCENES that fill in the blank spaces left by the scriptwriter or director of a film or TV EPISODE.

Viking (aerospace): PLANETARY PROBE that landed on Mars in 1976, providing the population of Earth with the first view of the surface of a planet other than our own. The landscape was a shock for those who had imagined great cities or canals on Mars. For endless miles all that could be seen around the landed craft were rocks and sand. The VIKING PROBE carried several experiments that were supposed to answer the question, "Is there life on Mars?" As far as the CHICKEN SOUP and WOLF TRAP tests were concerned, there wasn't.

The VIKING PROBE sent pictures back to Earth that are still being studied. If there is going to be a colony on another planet in our SOLAR SYSTEM, MARS is the most likely place.

villain (literary): The "bad guy" against whom the HERO must pit his strength, cunning, and ineffable hopes. VILLAINS abound in SF, as they do in life. Over the years, their nature has changed, as readers' expectations and society's mores have changed.

SPACE OPERA was full of nasty VILLAINS: brutal pirates, greedy officials, and especially BEMS. There are still plenty of them around, usually in comic books.

Readers of SF novels these days demand more of their writers. It is not enough to announce that Governor Xargk is evil; it must be shown how evil Xargk is . . . and why! Even VILLAINS need MOTIVATION. Evil for evil's sake rarely works, even in the "Hell" UNIVERSE run by Chris and Jan Morris.

The word VILLAIN originally meant no more than "the one who lives near the villa," the fortified country house of an official of Ancient Rome. After the Empire fell, the "villa" became a "village" and the people who lived near it were "villeins." A VILLAIN was usually an unlettered sort, who might be coarse and crude in his manners, unlike the polished city dweller. By Shakespeare's time, the VILLAIN was not merely a clod; he (or she) was just plain bad.

Shakespeare could get away with having Richard of Gloucester announce "I am determined to prove a VILLAIN." SF readers want more, and SF writers usually accommodate them by creating really dandy "baddies." Most of the villainy tends to stem from pride or greed; occasionally there is a justification of the evil, on the grounds of revenge for past crimes committed by the family of the HERO.

Whatever the reason, most readers want the VILLAIN to pay for the evil that has been done. More often than not, the VILLAIN is far more interesting than the hero.

virus (computer): An intentional MALFUNCTION of a COMPUTER PROGRAM, which can mean anything from malicious mischief to vicious sabotage. VIRUSES are the bane of all computer programmers.

voice auction (fan/conventions): The open sale of artwork or other items by means of oral competitive bidding. The VOICE AUCTION is one of the high points of an SF CON, scheduled late in the weekend so that most of the attendees can view the artwork and place their written bids on the BID SHEETS.

The VOICE AUCTION provides entertainment even if one is not actively bidding on something. There is always the possibility of a BIDDING WAR, with two people raising the price on a PIECE while the artist holds his or her breath until someone gives up.

The auctioneers at the VOICE AUCTION are responsible for keeping things moving. Usually they will begin the classic "Going once . . . going twice . . ." after three bids are called, unless the sparring is particularly lively. See also ART SHOW.

voiceover (film/TV): Narration by an unseen person, while images are seen by the viewer. VOICEOVERS are used to great effect in films like *Blade Runner* (1982), which imitate the tone of the FILM NOIR of the late 1940s. Often a film may include a VOICEOVER introduction to set the scene, or a final epilog that explains what happened to all these interesting people. The most mundane example of the VOICEOVER is the ubiquitous commercial advertisement.

Von Braun, Werner (b. 1912): German-born engineer and rocket specialist, who developed the U.S. Space Program in the late 1950s. VON BRAUN and his team were criticized for having begun their careers by working on the German weapons that devastated Britain at the end of World War II, but their later efforts led directly to the success of the U.S. efforts in reaching the Moon. VON BRAUN, thinly disguised, is one of the characters in James Michener's epic novel, *Space,* and is a less admirable figure in Thomas Wolfe's *The Right Stuff.* He was also the target of a satiric song by Tom Lehrer.

WAHF (fan): "We Also Heard From . . . ," pronounced as initials or as "waff." Used in FANZINES, LETTERZINES, and APAS to indicate that the people in question sent brief letters that aren't worth reprinting, or sent letters that are so long that there isn't time to reprint them all.

waldoes (aerospace): Mechanical arms with pincers on the end that extend into radioactive chambers to handle dangerous materials. The name was taken directly from a novel by ROBERT HEINLEIN.

War of the Worlds, The (literary/radio/film/TV): Initially, *The War of the Worlds* (1898) was a short novel by H. G. WELLS that described an attack on Earth by indescribably horrible beings from MARS. The book was turned into a radio play by the young Orson Welles and turned loose on an unsuspecting public on October 31, 1939, when it became famous as the "Night That Panicked America." By using the radio news format to introduce the drama, Welles gave millions of people the impression that other-worldly forces actually had landed in Grover's Mill, New Jersey.

There have been at least two more attempts at dramatizing *The War of the Worlds.* One was a film, first shown in 1953,

starring Gene Barry; the other is a TV series, in DIRECT SYNDICATION, which is still in production as of 1990. Neither of them has had the impact of the Welles broadcast.

warlock: See WITCH.

waterhole (aerospace): The range of the electromagnetic spectrum most likely to pick up signs of extraterrestrial life. Various groups are monitoring the WATERHOLE with electron telescopes and radio antennas, but so far there has been no answer to the signals.

weapons policy (fan/conventions): A written statement in a CONVENTION PROGRESS REPORT or PROGRAM BOOK describing what may or may not be worn or carried during an SF CON, either as an ACCESSORY to a costume or as a working part of SCA GARB. Most SF CONS have decided on a simple WEAPONS POLICY: If it looks like a weapon, it is a weapon, and it is not to be carried at all. Occasionally an exception will be made for a sword or mock-up pistol that can be PEACE-BONDED. Too many people were waving sharp-edged objects without proper training in their use, and innocent bystanders were getting in the way. Most CON-COMS have decided that the best way to keep the CONVENTION safe is to eliminate the opportunity for accidents by eliminating the weapons entirely.

Wells, H. G. (1866–1946): British writer and philosopher, who, with JULES VERNE, is said to be one of the founders of modern SF. Wells tapped into several veins of material that have become standard ploys in SF. *The Time Machine* (1895) explores time travel. *The War of the Worlds* (1898) describes the invasion of the Earth by beings from another planet. *The Island of Dr. Moreau* (1896) is an early discussion of mutation and genetic engineering.

In his later life, WELLS became involved in political philosophy, some of which is expounded in his SCREENPLAY for the 1936 film, *Things to Come*. He lived to see some of his early ideas taken over and explored by others. It is said that he refused to watch the bombing of London in 1941, since it did not in the least resemble his vision in the film.

werewolves (mythology): Either a man who becomes a wolf, or a wolf who becomes a man, depending on which version you believe. The myth of the being that can change shape at will appears throughout human literature, in all societies. Ancient Greek gods took the form of animals, plants, or even mere mortals. Other cultures might revere animals who could appear in human form. The wolf was especially feared, since it seemed to imitate human social behavior by running in a pack and obeying a leader.

The stories of VAMPIRES were linked to those of WEREWOLVES (also called lycanthropes, or loups-garous) in the HORROR MOVIES of the 1930s, to produce the popular idea of the WEREWOLF. Presumably, the WEREWOLF is a human who has run afoul of some WITCH or WIZARD, and has been punished for his presumption by being forced to take on the shape of a wolf and go rampaging about the countryside whenever the moon is full.

Lon Chaney, Jr. played *The Wolfman* in the first film in 1932. *Curse of the Werewolf* (1962) had Oliver Reed as a Spanish WEREWOLF, and Rutger Hauer was a noble knight who became a wolf when the sun went down in *Ladyhawke* (1985). WEREWOLVES in novels are less prominent, although Daniel Manus Pinkwater has little Larry Talbot tell his woes in *I Was a Second-Grade Werewolf* (no one believes him) and Peter David has written of a wolf who becomes a man in *Howling Mad* (1988).

WesterCon (fan/conventions): The oldest and largest of the West Coast SF CONVENTIONS, especially patronized by FANS involved in MEDIA.

wet-ware (computer): Mental programming, that is, the human brain. A back-creation, from SOFTWARE and HARDWARE. While many COMPUTER GEEKS deplore the need for WETWARE, most of the rest of humanity prefers the human brain to the electronic one.

"Whips and Chains" story (literary): Fiction with a decidedly sadomasochistic bent, often found in FANZINES. WHIPS AND CHAINS STORIES in professional publications soon become targets of satire, until, like John Norman's GOR novels, they are treated as a joke. FANZINE WHIPS AND CHAINS STORIES are often far nastier than the ones found in PROZINES, since the only rein on the writer's imagination is the taste and discretion of the editor. See also HURT-COMFORT STORY.

white dwarf (astronomy): A star whose diameter is only one percent that of our Sun, but whose luminosity is 10,000 times less. WHITE DWARFS represent the final stage in stellar evolution; they are old and cold, and so are any planets they may have accumulated in their billions of years of existence.

white hole (astronomy): A star whose core has collapsed, like that of a NEUTRON STAR, so that no light can escape. A WHITE HOLE may be connected with a BLACK HOLE, but no one has gotten close enough to one to find out.

white-out (printing): Generic name for the white correction fluid that effectively blanks out typing errors, permitting corrections; a necessity for FANZINE editors bent on eliminating TYPOS. Now that PHOTO-OFFSET has replaced mimeo as the primary printing medium for FANZINES, WHITE-OUT has taken over the position once held by COR-FLU.

Wicca (mythology): Also called "the Old Religion"; the worship of fertility deities and the powers of nature, carried on at the present time. To the Christians of the 15th, 16th, and 17th centuries, the practitioners of WICCA were witches, and were treated accordingly. Most of them are now aligned with the NEO-PAGAN Movement, and are treated as practitioners of a slightly odd religious sect. They are adamant on one point: They are not involved with Satanism or any similar ritual of destruction. See also WITCHCRAFT; WITCHES.

Williams, John (b. 1930): American conductor and composer of some of the best-known SF film SCORES on the current SF scene. WILLIAMS actually incorporated music into the script of *Close Encounters of the Third Kind* (1977), where contact with the Aliens is made through a glorified electronic organ. His grandiose music for STAR WARS has almost become a musical cliche. Williams combines his film chores with an active career as the conductor of the Boston Pops Orchestra, in which position he often plays orchestral suites from his own film music.

wisdom (gaming): A character's ability to exercise intuitive judgment, common sense, and willpower, as determined by the DUNGEONMASTER'S dice. WISDOM is a prerequisite for a CLERIC or a PRIEST; a WARRIOR can get away with being less than brilliant if he has enough STRENGTH.

Wish-Fulfillment story (literary): One in which the characters achieve their goals without any special effort, through magical means, and without particularly deserving their good fortune. WISH-FULFILLMENT STORIES are mostly written by beginners, and serve more to satisfy their writers than their readers, who demand more of the characters than just good luck. Even in FAIRY TALES, the hero or heroine usually performs some good deed before being granted their wishes.

witchcraft (parapsychology): The use of unknown, possibly arcane or psychic forces, to attain physical ends. WITCHCRAFT can be taught; more often, the point is made that WITCHCRAFT depends in part on the natural abilities of the WITCH. One is reminded of CLARKE'S LAW: "Any technology sufficiently advanced is indistinguishable from magic."

A division is made between WITCHCRAFT meant to harm and WITCHCRAFT aimed at benign purposes. Most modern practitioners make a point of emphasizing that their actions are meant to cure illness or heal a rift between people, not to harm or destroy, and certainly not to call down evil powers on any person or persons.

There is a tendency to lump all occult studies under the heading of WITCHCRAFT. Practitioners and researchers make a clear definition between WITCHCRAFT and Satanism. See also WICCA.

witches (parapsychology): Those who use arcane means to achieve physical ends; often, the name is given to those who observe the rituals of WICCA, the fertility religion that prevailed in Europe before Christianity.

People have claimed to use supernatural powers since the beginning of recorded history, and probably before that. Those who could control natural forces were regarded with superstitious awe, and some of them undoubtedly used that awe to further their own success by whatever means they could. In the years after the Roman Empire was destroyed, the Christian missionaries characterized the followers of the Old Religion of nature worship as WITCHES. They were accused of all sorts of heinous acts, some of which may have been ancient rituals meant to increase the fertility of the fields or produce animals for hunting. By the middle of the 15th century, a determined effort was made to eliminate the so-called WITCHES, many of whom were wealthy women with no strong male ties.

The WITCH in folklore is often such a woman. She is shown as being elderly. She has great power, often through objects or animals. She literally eats small children, as in *Hansel and Gretel*, collected by the Grimm brothers, or in the Slavic *Baba Yaga* tales. She can be defeated by an innocent child, who uses cleverness to turn the WITCH's minions against her. Several psychological studies of fairy tales have concluded that these stories are meant to frighten and correct unruly children, who are then reassured that they can defeat the wicked WITCH (i.e., the powerful grown-ups in their lives).

WITCHES crop up in modern FAIRY TALES too. Frank Baum's

Land of Oz is ruled by both good and bad WITCHES, who focus their powers through objects like Dorothy Gale's Ruby Slippers. WITCHES in Fantasy stories often use sex to get their way; an ARCHETYPE is the woman who seduces, then abandons the hero.

The point is often made that a WITCH is born, not made. One must have the talent before one can use the tools. Modern WITCHES insist that what they are doing is simply exercising talents they already possess; they are not performing miracles or worshipping the Devil. WITCHES and WITCHCRAFT still play an important role in many Third World societies to this day. WITCHES are usually depicted as female. The male equivalent is called a WARLOCK.

Witchworld (literary): A series of novels and short-story ANTHOLOGIES created originally by Andre Norton and extended by others into a limited SHARED UNIVERSE. *Witchworld* (1963) deals with an ALTERNATE UNIVERSE in which 16th-century WITCHCRAFT really works, and is still practiced.

wizard (computer): An extremely proficient COMPUTER PROGRAMMER, who can correct a faulty system after one brief look at the COMPUTER. By extension, the most proficient person in a given company is designated the WIZARD, and is given sole responsibility for the COMPUTER and all its workings.

Many WIZARDS begin as mere HACKERS; they achieve WIZARD status by hard work, diligent study, and a talent for talking to COMPUTERS.

wizards (literary): Students of magic, who can control outside forces by means unknown to the greater part of society. In the past, those who studied natural phenomena might gain the reputation of being WIZARDS; today's equivalent is the research scientist.

WIZARDS in fiction often tend to be irascible, tetchy, professorial types. TOLKEIN's Gandalf, from *Lord of the Rings*, is typical. So is Merlin, in any or all of the versions of the KING ARTHUR legend. The WIZARD in Jack Chalker's "... Dancing Gods" novels is a jolly sort, given to practical jokes, who thinks nothing of hauling a couple of unwitting humans off to a PARALLEL UNIVERSE to help him get revenge on a fellow WIZARD.

WIZARDS are scholars. They have mastered their craft after much training. Unlike WITCHES, they may or may not have innate gifts; most of their power comes from knowing how to use magical talismans, spells, and the like. One must be born a WITCH or a WARLOCK, but one can learn to be a WIZARD.

Wolf trap (aerospace): One of the experiments sent on the VIKING Mars Mission in 1976, devised by Dr. Wolf Vishniak to see if there is life as we know it on Mars. The WOLF TRAP takes soil and atmosphere samples, seals them into a receptacle, and introduces them into a chemical solution. It is hoped that any possible organism will ingest the nutrients in the solution, thus displaying evidence (if somewhat negative) of its existence. The WOLF TRAP works in the snows of Antarctica, proving the existence of bacterial life-forms even in that inhospitable wasteland. It did not work on Mars, which would tend to indicate that there was nothing there to ingest the nutrients . . . unless the Martian bacteria simply didn't like Earthly chemicals. See also CHICKEN SOUP.

woman warrior (literary): The female equivalent of a literary BARBARIAN; a muscular, aggressive, trained fighter, who can take on all comers, of any size, shape, or sex. The WOMAN WARRIOR was seen in the Greek legends of the Amazons, and there have been many women who assumed men's clothing in times of war and went off to fight under assumed names. Anne Bonney and Mary Read were women who became pirates and fought alongside the likes of Calico Jack Rackham in the early 1700s. The WOMAN WARRIORS of SF, however, are not trying to pose as men. They are rambunctiously female, part of the movement in FEMINIST SF toward total equality of the sexes and evenness of GENDER ROLES.

It is refreshing at times to see women being depicted as actively participating in fight scenes, rather than being crowded off into a corner (where they might conveniently drop a large

vase onto the villain's head), but it is also nice to see a woman (or a man) who can get what she (he) wants without resorting to violence. See also GENDER ROLES; ROLE REVERSAL.

work for hire (publishing): The commissioning of a piece of writing or artwork that is done specifically for a particular publisher; the work is paid for outright, and the COPYRIGHT then belongs to the publisher. Many JUVIE SERIES books are WORK FOR HIRE. WORK FOR HIRE is not necessarily done by HACKS, nor is it always FORMULA FICTION. Several well-known SF writers and artists have taken on WORK FOR HIRE at some stage in their careers. See also SHARECROPPER UNIVERSE.

workmanship (fan/costuming): The effort involved in constructing and decorating a costume, whether a PRESENTATION or HALL COSTUME. WORKMANSHIP counts for a good deal in JUDGING of costumes. Details of tailoring, embroidery, and trimming add to the effectiveness of a costume, as do the decorative arts and crafts such as leatherwork, beading, and metalwork. The overall effect can make or break a costume. Shoddy WORKMANSHIP may be glossed over in a PRESENTATION COSTUME, but any costume that falls apart or molts feathers and sequins as it goes by is going to leave the wrong impression on those who see it. CRAFTSMANSHIP AWARDS given at MASQUERADES are the reward for superior WORKMANSHIP.

workshops (fan/conventions): Classes in writing, editing, or art, held during an SF CONVENTION for the instruction of would-be writers, editors, and artists. WORKSHOPS are often taught by well-known practitioners of writing, editing, or arts and crafts; they may require a fee, in addition to CON membership, and usually require preregistration, with submissions of sample work as well. WORKSHOPS are often of the HANDS-ON variety.

Writing WORKSHOPS may be offered as concentrated classes in writing during the summer. The most famous of them is the CLARION WORKSHOP, which offers six weeks of instruction in all aspects of SF writing.

worldbuilding (literary): The creation of alien biospheres by SF writers, in such a way that the reader can enjoy both SUSPENSION OF DISBELIEF and SENSAWUNDA.

WORLDBUILDING requires a good background in the geology and ecology of Earth, with careful attention to such matters as chemistry and physics. The inhabitants of an imaginary planet must be made to fit their environments, and they should be able to fill their proper ecological niches.

World-Con (fan/conventions): The World Science Fiction Convention, held each year in a different location and attended by all the SF people who can possibly get there.

The WORLD-CON began in 1939, just before World War II, as a gathering of young men who were interested in SF. The War interrupted the progress of the WORLD-CON; most histories of SF FANDOM count WORLD-CONS from 1946.

In the years since the early WORLD-CONS, FANDOM has grown considerably. WORLD-CONS were once attended by less than a thousand people; the 1989 WORLD-CON in Boston attracted over 8,000 members, including guests and DAY-TRIPPERS. As a result, the WORLD-CON represents a major attraction for a host city, and since the venue changes each year, the bidding for the WORLD-

CON can be furious. The sponsoring organization, the World Science Fiction Society, has divided the world into various sectors, of which three are in the United States, where most of the SF FANS tend to reside.

Because the WORLD-CON attracts so many people in so many areas of SF, the PROGRAMMING can get complicated. There may be as many as five different TRACKS, aimed at various segments of the SF population. One TRACK may cover the business of writing fiction (SF or any other) for sale; another may focus on literary criticism; a third may deal with scientific background for SF; and a fourth TRACK may cover the history of SF FANDOM itself. There will be SCREENINGS of films, including those nominated for HUGO AWARDS, which are determined by the votes of all members of the WORLD-CON. Evening PROGRAMMING may include FILKING, a REGENCY BALL, the MASQUERADE, and the HUGO AWARD presentations. The ART SHOW will attract professional artists who want to display their latest work and aspiring amateurs who want to attract notice. The DEALERS' ROOM will have every sort of merchandise, from FANZINES to rare EDITIONS of OUT-OF-PRINT books. There may be special areas for GAMERS and COMPUTER WIZARDS. There may even be provision made for SECOND-GENERATION FANS, with on-site baby-sitting and special PROGRAMMING for children. Most of all, the WORLD-CON is a place where FANS can meet PROS on terms of equality. The line between amateur and professional is crossed frequently at the WORLD-CON.

The WORLD-CON is advertised extensively for at least a year in advance in most of the major SF PROZINES. Day visits are possible, even if a full five-day stay is not. Anyone interested in SF should try to attend at least one WORLD-CON.

WORLD-CONS have developed their own jargon. See also LOGISTICS; OPS; PEOPLE-MOVERS; SECURITY.

world-wrecking (literary): The capacity of an author for destroying a planet, either through natural disasters or by warfare. The planet most often destroyed is our own Earth, but the technique works elsewhere, too. Having built up the imaginary planet, the writer then gleefully starts to take it to pieces; the story that results may be grim, but it will be interesting. See also DOOMSDAY STORY.

worm hole (astronomy): The hypothetical passageway between a BLACK HOLE and a WHITE HOLE; a means of circumventing space totally. Since no one has gotten near enough to either a BLACK HOLE or a WHITE HOLE to find out if WORM HOLES exist, their presence must continue to be theoretical.

wraparound cover (printing): An illustration on the cover of a FANZINE or book that goes across both the front and the back of the publication.

writer (comics): The person who concocts the plot and the dialog of a comic book. The two functions are often split between the PLOTTER and the SCRIPTER, while the art chores are taken over by the ARTIST, the INKER, the COLORIST, and the LETTERER. The group as a whole is the CREATIVE TEAM.

Writer's Digest: A monthly publication aimed at the person who wants to write professionally. Articles and regular columns give instruction in all forms and formats of writing: fiction, nonfiction, poetry, screenwriting, even the technique of inventing clever captions for cartoons and sentimental verse for greeting cards. The magazine also provides information on current markets for all kinds of writing, both fiction and nonfiction, and sponsors various contests in all areas of writing. WRITER'S DIGEST produces books on all aspects of the writing profession, containing hard, practical advice on how to construct a good story in any of a number of genres, including SCIENCE FICTION.

WRITER'S DIGEST is governed by an Editorial Board that includes several major SF writers and editors. It is a necessary addition to the library of anyone interested in writing as a profession.

Writer's Market: An annual listing of publications looking for contributors, publishers looking for manuscripts, and agents looking for clients, used extensively by writers looking for markets. The volume solicits information from as many publishers and publications as it can find, and lists the information according to type of publication.

Writers and would-be writers may find copies of *Writer's Market* at their local public library.

Xanth (literary): Setting for a series of novels by Piers Anthony; an imaginary land with the outline of the state of Florida, where trolls, ogres, fairies, and similar beings go on QUESTS, discover magic rings, and generally go through their paces. The XANTH novels are full of puns and other verbal high jinks; the plots are mostly nonsense, but they have a large following. Piers Anthony gives full rein to his gamesmanship tendencies in the XANTH stories.

xenobiology: Sometimes called EXOBIOLOGY. The study of life-forms existing somewhere besides Earth. So far, in spite of all efforts, no such life-forms have been found, but scientists are still looking for them. See also CHICKEN SOUP; WOLF TRAP.

xenophobia (psychology): The fear of the unknown, especially unknown beings with untold mental and physical powers. XENOPHOBIA was a powerful motivation behind much of the SF produced during the 1950s; the themes of invasion by overwhelming beings and destruction of the Earth by nuclear warfare run throughout the written and filmed stories of that era. XENOPHOBIA has been tempered in the last 10 years, but it still tends to creep up on us.

xerography (printing): A process whereby an image is impressed on paper with a dry ink and sealed by heat. The Xerox Corporation was the first to patent the process. In fact, the process itself began to be called "Xerox" by the public at large, much to the dismay of the Xerox Corporation, which mounted a campaign to remind consumers that the word "Xerox" was neither a common noun nor a verb. Nevertheless, most people still say "Xerox" when they mean "photocopy." Thanks to XEROGRAPHY, printing has become quick and cheap.

X-Men (comics): A group of SUPERHEROES, supposedly MUTANTS, who combine their powers to fight Evil SUPERVILLAINS. The individuals may vary, but the group persists as one of the better-known gangs in the comics field.

X-rays (physics): Light rays that extend into the long end of the spectrum; one of the first forms of radiation discovered by researchers in the 1880s. X-RAYS are able to penetrate flesh and leave the shadows of bones on prepared plates, giving rise to one of the most useful of modern medical tools. The so-called "Roentgen" machine was being demonstrated in 1901 when President William McKinley was shot; had it been used, it might have been possible to locate the bullet and save the man by removing it. The process was considered too radical to permit its use on the body of the stricken statesman, who died after five days of agony; Theodore Roosevelt, the then vice-president, ascended to the presidency, and into the history books. Of such small details is history made.

yarn (literary): A long, rambling story that winds its way through detail after detail until it reaches some kind of end without reaching any kind of a point. Many YARNS are written as if being told in a bar; Spider Robinson's *Callahan's Crosstime Saloon* (1977) is an example of a collection of YARNS.

Z

zap-gun (fan/convention): A small toy pistol modified so that it shoots a ray of light instead of a pellet, used in LASER WARS. ZAP-GUNS have been largely abandoned, along with LASER WARS; the few that remain are usually PEACE-BONDED.

"Zap" stories (fan/fanzine): British term for what American fans call GET 'EM STORIES.

zero-gee (aerospace): A state of no gravity; total weightlessness. Also called NULL-G.

zip-a-tone (printing): Sometimes modified to "zippy-tone." Gummed paper, stippled and striped in various patterns, to be used as background in ILLOS when the artist does not feel like filling in all those little dots and dashes. ZIP-A-TONE comes in many brands and sizes, and can be found at stationery stores.

Zodiac (astronomy): A set of patterns in the night sky of the Northern Hemisphere that rise and set along the PLANE OF THE ECLIPTIC at specific times of the year. Each so-called sign is supposed to affect the people born when that pattern was prominent in the sky; this is the basis of the PSEUDOSCIENCE of ASTROLOGY.

zombies (parapsychology): Artificially revived corpses, as described in the folklore of Haiti. ZOMBIES are supposed to be servants of their master, who controls them through magical powers. The idea of a living corpse sends a thrill of horror down the spine of most people, who prefer that the dead remain dead. Of course, with advances in CRYOGENICS, ZOMBIES may yet become reality.

APPENDIX A

Useful Addresses

Publications

There are many Science Fiction periodicals, newsletters, fanzines, and Small Press magazines. A full list would fill another book the size of *FutureSpeak*. However, below is a partial list of some of the more outstanding SF publications. Several are available on newsstands and in bookstores. Others may be distributed at Conventions.

Aboriginal Science Fiction (prozine)
P.O. Box 2449
Woburn, MA 01888-0849

Analog Science Fiction/Science Fact (prozine)
Davis Publications
380 Lexington Ave.
New York, NY 10017

The APA Master File (listings for amateur press associations)
c/o Tim Gatewood
P.O. Box 12921
Memphis, TN 38182–0921

Con News (newsletter for conventions, distributed free at Cons)
Privateer Publishing
7735 Osceola St.
Westminster, CO 80030

Datazine (adzine, lists current media fanzines)
P.O. Box 24590
Denver, CO 80224

Dragon (semi-prozine for role-playing games)
P.O. Box 110
Lake Geneva, WI 53147

Factsheet Five (adzine, lists fanzines, alternate press, and small press publications)
c/o Mike Gunderloy
6 Arizona Ave.
Rensselaer, NY 12144–4502

Fandom Directory (mailing lists; fan publication addresses)
FanData Publications
7761 Asterella Court ASF
Springfield, VA 22152–3133

Isaac Asimov's Science Fiction Magazine (prozine)
Davis Publications
380 Lexington Ave.
New York, NY 10017

Locus (semi-prozine, with news of the SF world)
Box 13305
Oakland, CA 94661

Magazine of Fantasy and Science Fiction (prozine)
Box 56
Cornwall, CT 06753

Pandora (semi-prozine)
2844 Grayson
Ferndale, MI 48220

Scavenger's Newsletter (market information and reviews of small press publications)
c/o Janet Fox
519 Ellinwood
Osage City, KS 66523–1329

Science Fiction Book Club
Subscription Office
6550 E. 30th St.
P.O. Box 6367
Indianapolis, IN 46206–6367

Science Fiction Chronicle (semi-prozine, with news, reviews, and other information of the SF world)
P.O. Box 2730
Brooklyn, NY 11202–0056

Starlog (prozine, specializing in SF media news, interviews, etc.)
475 Park Ave. South
New York, NY 10016

Writer's Digest
F&W Publications
1507 Dana Ave.
Cincinnati, OH 45207

Organizations

There are many local SF clubs that usually advertise themselves through flyers at conventions, or through local specialty shops. These listings are for national organizations, which may have smaller local divisions.

First Fandom
c/o Ray E Beam
2209 S. Webster St.
Kokomo, IN 46901

Lucasfilm Official Fan Club
P.O. Box 111000
Aurora, CO 80011

National Association of Fan Clubs
2730 Baltimore Ave.
Pueblo, CO 81003

National Fantasy Fan Federation
c/o Lola Ann Center
1920 Division St.
Murphysboro, IL 62966

Science Fiction Writers of America (SFWA)
P.O.Box 4236
West Columbia, SC 29169

Small Press Writers and Artists Organization (SPWAO)
c/o Audrey Parente
328 Timberline Trail
Ormond Beach, FL 32174

Society for Creative Anachronism (SCA)
P.O. Box 260743
Milpitas, CA 95035–0743

Star Trek Official Fan Club
P.O. Box 111000
Aurora, CO 80011

Star Trek Welcommittee
Box 12
Saranac, MI 48881

Star Trek Welcommittee Directory (lists fan clubs, fanzines, etc.)
P.O. Box 75
Cooper Station
New York, NY 10276

Conventions

Convention Listings can be found in many SF publications. *Starlog* lists Pro-Cons and Media Cons; *Isaac Asimov's SF Magazine* and *Analog* list Fan-Cons; *Locus* and *Science Fiction Chronicle* list a year's worth of conventions, plus the World-Con. For those who need more information, these are some of the long-established conventions:

BaltiCon (Fan-Con)
Box 686
Baltimore, MD 21203

Creation Cons (Pro-Con)
145 Jericho Tpke.
Mineola, NY 11501

Dreamwerks (Pro-Con)
Box N
Crugers, NY 10521

LunaCon (Fan-Con)
P.O. Box 338
New York, NY 10150-0338

MarCon (Fan-Con)
Box 1101
Columbus, OH 43221

PhilCon (Fan-Con)
P.O. Box 8303
Philadelphia, PA 19101

SF Convention Register
c/o Erwin S. Strauss
Box 3343V
Fairfax, VA 22038

Shore Leave (Media-Con)
P.O. Box 8808
Towson, MD 21385

WesterCon (Fan-Con)
Box 5794
Portland, OR 97228

Costuming

International Costumers' Guild
P.O. Box 683
Columbia, MD 21045

APPENDIX B

Filk Distributors

Filk-tapes and Filk-books are found at many conventions. However, the following distributors handle Filk:

The Filk Federation
c/o Margaret Middleton
P.O. Box 45122
Little Rock, AR 72214

Firebird Arts & Music
P.O. Box 14785
Portland, OR 97214

Thor Records (Filk-tapes)
P.O. Box 403121
Downey, CA 92039-1312

Wail Songs (distributes Filk-tapes, Filk-Books)
P.O. Box 29888
Oakland, CA 94604

SUGGESTED BILL OF RIGHTS AND RESPONSIBILITIES FOR FILKERS (Revised Version 1.1)

I. AS A HOST (at a housefilk):

A. The right to edit the guest list or to have an open filk and the responsibility to do the dirty work.

B. The right to ask someone to leave and to ban a person from the household.

C. The responsibility to post household rules, if any, in a conspicuous place, i.e., the fridge or front door.

D. The responsibility to provide advance notice on invitations or flyers to filkers for items E through O below.

E. The responsibility to alert guests to potential hazards, i.e., fuzzies, rug rats, whatever.

F. The right to specify "NO SMOKING--PERIOD!".

G. The right to declare any space "OFF LIMITS", i.e., spare rooms, fridge, etc.

H. The right to declare an "Adults Only" filk.

I. The right to specify starting and ending times as desired--you're not locked into "4:00 PM to ?????".

J. The right NOT to provide a feast or crash space.

K. The responsibility to provide the maximum seating space available, i.e., large living room or family room, plus (if available) alternate space for those who wish to converse.

L. The responsibility to provide a serving area for food/drink/munchies.

M. The responsibility to provide paper/plastic eating/serving supplies.

N. The right to pass the kitty, if you wish, to help defray food costs (local customs may differ).

O. The right/responsibility to set the filksing style (i.e., bardic circle, Midwest, host's rules, etc.) and to clearly define/announce the filk rules, especially for the neos (let's avoid interrupting the filk for rule explanations).

P. The right/responsibility to run the filk and/or appoint demighod(s).

Q. The responsibility for ensuring that guests who are not crashing overnight depart for home before they become incapacitated by fatigue (or alcohol if there is drinking).

II. AS A GUEST (at a housefilk):

A. The responsibility to respect and honor the host's declared and posted houserules.

B. The responsibility to contribute to the evening's munchies or the kitty in accordance with local customs.

C. The responsibility to help clean up the filksite both before and after the filk.

D. The responsibility to get host's OK in advance to bring smalls/minors/pets.

E. The right to arrive and/or depart at any point during the announced hours.

F. The responsibility to honor the host's chosen style of filksing and demighod.

G. The responsibility to depart for home if not crashing overnight before becoming incapacitated by fatigue (or alcohol if there is drinking).

III. AS A PERFORMER (anywhere):

A. While performing, the right to the undivided attention of filkers present.

B. The responsibility to be ready with a song when it's your turn--don't keep the rest of us waiting, please.

C. The right to entertains the rest of us with your musical talents. If you have something to sing/perform, take your turn.

D. The responsibility NOT to be a filkhog. Let others have a chance to perform too.

E. The right to pass or decline a request WITHOUT HARASSMENT.

F. The right to choose your form of torture, be it filk, folk, synthesized, accompanied, a capella, instrumental, OSE, bawdy, whatever.

G. The responsibility to announce any caveats to your performance. Some people are offended/upset by some types of filk, such as OSE, bawdy, etc. This is neither their fault nor yours. Don't let it stop you from performing, but allow them to leave gracefully (see Listener C).

H. The responsibility to keep your introduction short and to the point. Your song should stand on its own merits without apologies or long explanations (see Listener G).

I. The right/responsibility to define/request your desired accompaniment, i.e., vocals/no vocals (it's a solo, general sing-along, chorus only, etc.) and instruments/no instruments (solo, harmonizing, all together now, etc.). If nothing is said, anything is fair game!

J. The responsibility not to cut-off or talk over someone else's song or intro.

IV. AS A LISTENER (anywhere):

A. The responsibility to give the performer your undivided attention and to respect her/her choice of music (i.e., NO chitchat in the filkroom during the music!).

B. The responsibility NOT to hog any down time (time between performers), i.e., don't rush in to fill the void with conversation.

C. The right/responsibility to leave the filkroom if you don't like the song/performer/whatever (see Performer G above).

D. The responsibility to leave the filkroom quietly so as not to disturb the rest of us who are enjoying the performance. (Hint: If you leave frequently, sit near the exit.)

E. The responsibility to respect the performer's choice of accompaniment and NOT to join in without invite/consent. (If not immediately clear, ASK FIRST before joining in.)

F. The responsibility to move to an alternate room/space if you want to converse.

G. The right as an audience (en masse) to short circuit an unpleasantly long intro (see Performer H above).

Printed courtesy of *The Filking Times*, Deborah Leonard and Rick Weiss, editors, 13261 Donegal Drive, Garden Grove, CA 92644-2304. Your comments and suggestions are welcome.

Filk-Songs

"That REAL Old-Time Religion"

(These are only a sampling of this song's 659 verses.)

Chorus: Give me that Old Time Religion,
Give me that Real Old Time Religion,
Give me that Real Old Time Religion,
It's good enough for me.

We will worship Aphrodite
Though she's rather young and flighty,
And she doesn't wear a nightie,
But she's good enough for me.

We will run the Lupercalia
In our leathern paraphernalia
Substitute for genitalia,
And NOT good enough for me!

We will burn our joss to Buddha,
Of all gods there is none cuter,
Comes in silver, brass, and pewter,
And he's good enough for me!

We will now go pray to Loki,
He's the old Norse God of Chaos
Which is why this verse doesn't rhyme or scan,

But it's good enough for me.
We will all bow down to Allah,
When we do he will not holler,
'Cause he's got the Petro-dollar,
And he's good enough for me.

We will never worship Ares
Though his chest a mat of hair is,
He hates Pinkos, Wogs, and Fairies,
And they're good enough for me!

We will worship with the Druids,
Drinking strange fermented fluids,
Running naked through the woo-ids
Which is good enough for me!

For a full text of all 600+ verses, write to John Boardman, 234 E. 19th St., Brooklyn, NY 11226.

Banned from Argo

Words and music: Leslie Fish

G C G
When we pulled in - to Ar - go port in need of R. and R., The
C G D7
crew set out in - ves - ti - ga - ting ev - ery joint and bar. We
G C G
had high ex - pec - ta - tions of their hos - pi - tal - i - ty, But
C G D7 G
found too late it was - n't geared for spa - cers such as we. And we're
C G C
banned from Ar - go ev - ery one. Banned from Ar - go just for
G 3 D7 G D
hav - ing a lit - tle fun. We spent a jol - ly shore leave there for
C G D7 G
just three days or four, But Ar - go does-n't want us an - y more.

When we pulled into Argo Port in need of R. and R.,
The crew set out investigating every joint and bar.
We had high expectations of their hospitality,
But found too late it wasn't geared for spacers such as we.

CHORUS: And we're banned from Argo, every one.
Banned from Argo, just for having a little fun.
We spent a jolly shore leave there, for just three days or four,
But Argo doesn't want us any more.

The Captain's tastes were simple, but his methods were complex.
We found him with five partners, each of a different world and sex.
The Shore Police were on the way—we had no second chance.
We beamed him up in the nick of time—and the remnants of his pants.

CHORUS

Our Engineer would yield to none at putting down the brew.
He outdrank seven space marines and a demolition crew.
The Navigator didn't win, but he outdrank almost all,
And now they've got a shuttlecraft on the roof of City Hall.

CHORUS

Our proper, cool First Officer was drugged with something green,
And hauled into an alley, where he suffered things obscene.
He sobered up in Sickbay and he's none the worse for wear,
Except he's somehow taught the bridge computer how to swear.

CHORUS

The Head Nurse disappeared awhile in the major Dope Bazaar,
Buying an odd green potion "guaranteed to cause Pon-Farr".
She came home with no uniform and an oddly cheerful heart,
And a painful way of walking—with her feet a yard apart.

CHORUS

Our lady of Communications won a ship-wide bet
By getting into the planet's main communication net.
Now every time someone calls up on an Argo telescreen,
The flesh is there, but the clothes they wear are nowhere to be
seen.

CHORUS

Our Doctor loves Humanity; his private life is quiet.
The Shore Police arrested him for inciting whores to riot.
We found him in the city jail, locked on and beamed him free—
Intact except for hickeys and six kinds of V.D.

CHORUS

Our Helmsman loves exotic plants; the plants all love him too.
He took some down on leave with him, and we wondered what
they'd do.
'Til the planetary governor called and swore upon his life
That a gang of plants entwined his house and then seduced his
wife!

CHORUS

A gang of pirates landed, and nobody seemed to care.
They stamped into the nearest bar to announce that they were
there.
Half our crew was busy there, and invited them to play,
But the pirates only looked at us, and turned and ran away.

CHORUS

Our crew is Starfleet's finest, and our record is our pride.
And when we play we tend to leave a trail a mile wide.
We're sorry about the wreckage and the riots and the fuss;
At least we're sure that planet won't be quick forgetting us!

The Westerfilk Collection, Off—Centaur Pub. 1981.
Used by permission

Hope Eyrie

Words and Music: Leslie Fish

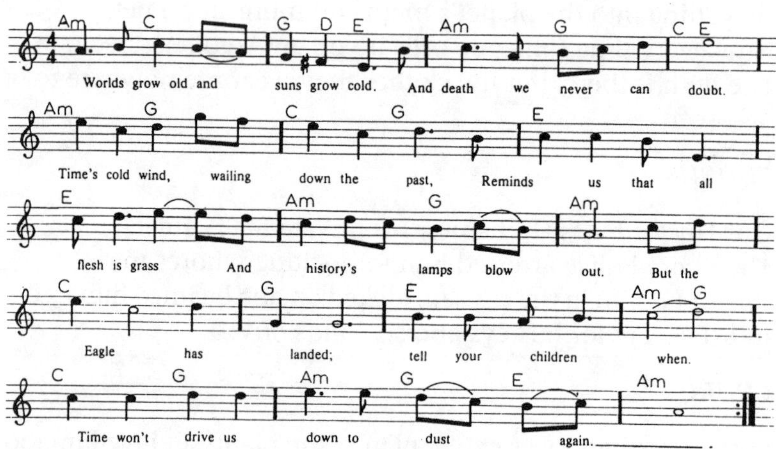

Worlds grow old and suns grow cold
And death we never can doubt.
Time's cold wind, wailing down the past,
Reminds us that all flesh is grass
And history's lamps blow out.
    But the Eagle has landed; tell your children when.
    Time won't drive us down to dust again.

Cycles turn while the far stars burn,
And people and planets age.
Life's crown passes to younger lands,
Time brushes dust of hope from his hands
And turns another page.
    But the Eagle has landed; tell your children when.
    Time won't drive us down to dust again.

But we who feel the weight of the wheel
When winter falls over our world
Can hope for tomorrow and raise our eyes
To a silver moon in the opened skies
And a single flag unfurled.
    But the Eagle has landed; tell your children when.
    Time won't drive us down to dust again.

We know well what Life can tell:
If you would not perish, then grow.
And today our fragile flesh and steel
Have laid their hands on a vaster wheel
With all of the stars to know
    That the Eagle has landed; tell your children when.
    Time won't drive us down to dust again.

From all who tried out of history's tide,
Salute for the team that won.
And the old Earth smiles at her children's reach,
The wave that carried us up the beach
To reach for the shining sun.
    For the Eagle has landed; tell your children when.
    Time won't drive us down to dust again.

Minus Ten and Counting, Off—Centaur Publications, 1985
Used by permission.

APPENDIX C

ROTSLER'S RULES FOR MASQUERADES

1: There should be a weight limit for the purchase of leotards.
2: Every contestant should first see himself/herself from the rear.
3: Learn to manage your props, accessories and music.
4: Select costumes and characters suited to your personality and/or body type.
5: No name tags on costumes.
6: Thy shoes shall match thy costume.
7: Parts of your costume should not be edible or smell. Parts of your costume should not fall off accidently, brush off against other contestants, or be left lying around on the stage.
    Kathleen Sky's Corollary: Multiple any discomfort you have wearing the costume by the number of hours you are going to be in it.
8: Consider carefully before going nude or semi-nude. What looks good in the bedroom or bath may not be spectacular on stage.
9: Numbers alone do not make a coherant group.
    Bjo Trimble's Corollary: A group is only as good as its weakest costume.
10: No fire, explosives, loud noises or dangerous weapons without full and proper clearance from the masquerade committee.
    Marjii Ellers' Corollary: Effect is everything.
11: Carry a repair kit with appropriate tools and materials.
12: Whether prince or pauper act like it. Stay in character.
13: Speak distinctly, but not at length...or at all. Learn to use the microphone--or don't.
14: Do not lecture your audience. This is show biz. You are not there to make long statements about your particular passions, but to entertain yourself and others, to show off, to exhibit a character and/or a costume, not to convert, harangue, or bore.
15: When in doubt, keep your mouth shut.
16: Remember, some people can grow a beard and some cannot.
17: Hand in a legible entry card, even to the point of writing out phonetically any difficult or unusual words. Do not assume either the narrator, the judges or the audience know all these words.
18: If you have the slightest doubt that your costume--based on a cover, a story description or media origin--might be unfamiliar to the judges, do not hesitate to supply them with visual materials or a copy of the passage in the text.
19: Give the judges sufficient time to examine your costume from all angles, giving special time to any particularly interesting aspect or design or construction.
20: If you have something for the narrator to read, keep it brief, eliminate as much as possible all unpronouncible, incomprehensible made-up names and terms. Do not duplicate on microphone what the narrator has already said.
21: If you are thinking of doing something you intend to be amusing, try it out on honest friends.
    Craig Miller's Corollary: Short is better than long; funny is better than non-funny; short and funny is best.
22: If you are going to try a costume cliché, you must either do it better than ever before, or have a good variation, preferably comic.
23: Presentation can make a mediocre costume and break a good one.
24: Keep all presentations short. Action is better than words.
25: Do not commit the one unforgivable sin: *Do Not Be Boring.*
26: Rehearse! *REHEARSE!* REHEARSE!
    Len Wein's Law: Those who think these rules do not apply to them are wrong.

I encourage the distribution and reproduction of these "rules," not out of ego, but because it is my belief—and the belief of many others—that if they are followed we will *all* have better masquerades to enjoy. These "rules" should be published *prior* to any convention, masquerade or fashion show—in the Progress Report, for example—so as not to reflect on the contestants in that costume event.

NEBULA AWARD RULES AS OF JANUARY 1989

Please keep this copy of the current Nebula Rules on file and refer to it first when you have a question.

1. The Nebula Award year shall run concurrent with the calendar year, January 1 to December 31.

2. Awards will be made in the following categories:
   a. **Short Story**: less than 7,500 words
   b. **Novelette**: at least 7,500 words but less than 17,500 words
   c. **Novella**: at least 17,500 words but less than 40,000 words
   d. **Novel**: 40,000 words or more

3. Works in categories (a) through (d) are eligible if they were published for the first time in the United States of America in a periodical dated in the award year or in a volume published in the award year. Serialized works are eligible if the last installment meets the foregoing requirements.

4. Works are eligible whether or not their authors are members of the Science Fiction Writers of America. Previous publication in another country or in a foreign language does not make a work ineligible.

5. The author of any eligible work may withdraw it from consideration in a given year and request that a later edition be considered for the Nebula, but no work may be eligible in more than one year. A written withdrawal must be received by the Nebula Award Report editor within a month of publication for a work to be considered withdrawn.

6. All active members of SFWA in good standing are entitled to make recommendations and may vote on award ballots.

7. Works may not be recommended by their writers, editors, or publishers.

8. The SFWA President shall appoint a Nebula Awards Report editor to compile, publish and distribute to members a list of recommendations of works to be considered for the awards at intervals during the award year.

9. A Nomination or Preliminary Ballot, being a list of all works receiving five (5) or more recommendations during the award year, shall be published and distributed to active members by 10 January of the year following the award year.

10. Members shall nominate no more than five works in each category on the Preliminary Ballot. These ballots shall be returned to the Nebula Award Report editor or independent accountant before the Preliminary Ballot closing date, which shall be not less than 28 days and not more than 30 days after the date of distribution of the Preliminary Ballot. The five works in each category receiving the most nominations shall be placed on a Final Ballot.

11. A Nebula Award Jury may by a majority vote add one candidate to any of the categories on the Final Ballot. The jury shall be selected by an affirmative vote of at least five of the following: the current officers and two past presidents. It shall consist of not less than five (5) nor more than seven (7) persons chosen for their interest in and knowledge of the field of science fiction. The jury may not add to the ballot a work written by a member of the jury.

12. The Final Ballot shall be published and distributed by the Nebula Award Report editor to all active members within 10 days after the Preliminary Ballot closing date.

13. Members cast numerically ranked votes for works on the Final Ballot, writing 1 for the first choice in each category, 2 for the second, and so on; or, instead of ranked votes for nominated works, members may vote for "No Award." If any ranked vote is cast in a category, a vote for "No Award" in the same category will be disregarded. Members may leave any category completely unmarked; their ballots will only be counted in categories in which they have cast ranked votes or votes for "No Award."

14. Votes for "No Award" are counted before ranked votes are counted. If forty percent or more of the ballots received are marked only for "No Award" in a particular category, then no Nebula Award will be given in that category, in which case no count of votes for works in that category will be performed.

15. Ranked votes for nominated works are counted by the "Australian ballot" method defined in this paragraph. On the first count of ranked votes for nominated works in a category, only first-ranked choices are counted. If any work is the first choice of a majority of the ballots cast for works in that category, it is declared the winner of the Nebula Award for that category. If no work has received a majority of first-ranked votes on the first count, additional counts will be made, as follows: The work which received the lowest number of best-ranked votes on the latest previous count is removed from further contention. Each ballot cast for the removed work is now counted for the work, still in contention, which received the next-best-ranked vote on that ballot. If no work that is still in contention has been marked with a ranked vote, that ballot is not counted again for that category. Additional counts will be made, removing the last-place work from contention each time, and adding next-best-ranked votes from its ballots to the totals for the works still in contention, until one work receives a majority of the votes cast in the latest count in that category, in which case that work is declared the winner of the Nebula Award for that category; or until only two works remain with exactly the same number of ballots counted in their favor, in which case the work, of those two, which received the greater number of first-ranked votes on the first count is declared the winner of the Nebula Award. If both works also had the same number of first-ranked votes on the first count, the voting is declared a tie, and both works receive the Nebula Award.

16. The Final Ballot will be tabulated by an independent agency. To be counted, properly prepared Final Ballots will be received by the Final Ballot closing date, which shall be not less than 28 days and not more than 30 days after the date of distribution of the Final Ballot.

17. A Grand Master Award may be presented to an individual for his/her work within the field of science fiction. The President shall nominate a person for this award, and it shall be given upon approval of a majority vote of the SFWA officers. No more than six (6) such awards may be given during a ten (10) year period.

18. The officers of SFWA, at their discretion, may propose additional awards in special categories to be voted on by the active members. These additional awards will not be a Nebula Award, but consist of a plaque.

19. The President shall appoint a three (3) person committee to rule on questions pertaining to the Nebula Award Rules. The Nebula Award Report editor will serve as a secretary to this committee, but shall not be a voting member. Decisions of the committee may be appealed to the SFWA officers, whose decision shall be made by a majority vote.

20. The Nebula Award Rules may be amended by a majority of the active membership or a majority of the officers.

APPENDIX D

Award Rules

Science Fiction Achievement Awards (the Hugo Awards)

Section 1: Selection of the Science Fiction Achievement Awards, known as the Hugo Awards, shall be made as follows in the subsequent Sections of this Article.

Section 2: *Best Novel:* A science fiction or fantasy story of forty thousand (40,000) words or more appearing for the first time during the previous calendar year. A work originally appearing in a language other than English shall also be eligible in the year in which it is first issued in English translation. A story, once it has appeared in English, may thus be eligible only once. Publication date, or cover date in the case of a dated periodical, takes precedence over copyright date. A serial takes its appearance to be the date of the last installment. Individual stories appearing as a series are eligible only as individual stories and are not eligible taken together under the title of the series. An author may withdraw a version of a work from consideration if the author feels that the version is not representative of what said author wrote. The Worldcon Committee may relocate a story into a more appropriate category if it feels that it is necessary, provided that the story is within five thousand (5,000) words of the new category limits.

Section 3: *Best Novella:* The rules shall be the same as those for Best Novel, with length between seventeen thousand five hundred (17,500) and forty thousand (40,000) words.

Section 4: *Best Novelette:* The rules shall be the same as those for Best Novel, with length between seven thousand five hundred (7,500) and seventeen thousand five hundred (17,500) words.

Section 5: *Best Short Story:* The rules shall be the same as those for Best Novel, with length less than seven thousand five hundred (7,500) words.

Section 6: *Best Non-Fiction Book:* Any non-fictional work whose subject is the field of science fiction or fantasy or fandom appearing for the first time in book form during the previous calendar year.

Section 7: *Best Dramatic Presentation:* Any production in any medium of dramatized science fiction or fantasy which has been publicly presented for the first time in its present dramatic form during the previous calendar year. In the case of individual programs presented as a series, each program is individually eligible, but the series as a whole is not eligible; however, a sequence of installments constituting a single dramatic unit may be considered as a single program (eligible in the year of the final installment).

Section 8: *Best Professional Editor:* The editor of any professional publication devoted primarily to science fiction or fantasy during the previous calendar year. A professional publication is one which had an average press run of at least ten thousand (10,000) copies per issue.

Section 9: *Best Professional Artist:* An illustrator whose work has appeared in a professional publication in the field of science fiction or fantasy during the previous calendar year.

Section 10: *Best Semiprozine:* Any generally available non-professional publication devoted to science fiction or fantasy which has published four (4) or more issues, at least one (1) of which appeared in the previous calendar year, and which in the previous calendar year met at least two (2) of the following criteria: (1) had an average press run of at least one thousand (1000) copies per issue, (2) paid its contributors and/or staff in other than copies of the publication, (3) provided at least half the income of any one person, (4) had at least fifteen percent (15%) of its total space occupied by advertising, or (5) announced itself to be a semiprozine.

Section 11: *Best Fanzine:* Any generally available non-professional publication devoted to science fiction, fantasy, or related subjects which has published four (4) or more issues, at least one (1) of which appeared in the previous calendar year, and which does not qualify as a semiprozine.

Section 12: *Best Fan Writer:* Any person whose writing has appeared in semiprozines or fanzines.

Section 13: *Best Fan Artist:* An artist or cartoonist whose work has appeared through publication in semiprozines or fanzines or through other public display during the previous calendar year. Any person whose name appears on the final Hugo Awards ballot for a given year under the Professional Artist category shall not be eligible in the Fan Artist category for that year.

Section 14: *Extended Eligibility:* In the event that a potential Hugo Award nominee receives extremely limited distribution in the year of its first publication or presentation, its eligibility may be extended for an additional year by a three-fourths (3/4) vote of the intervening Business Meeting of WSFS.

Section 15: *Additional Category:* Not more than one special category may be created by the current Worldcon Committee with nomination and voting to be the same as for the permanent categories. The Worldcon Committee is not required to create any such category; such action by a Worldcon Committee should be under exceptional circumstances only; and the special category created by one Worldcon Committee shall not be binding on following Committees. Awards created under this Section shall be considered to be Science Fiction Achievement Awards, or Hugo Awards.

Section 16: *Name and Design:* The Hugo Award shall continue to be standardized on the rocket ship design of Jack McKnight and Ben Jason. Each Worldcon Committee may select its own choice of base design. The name (Hugo Award) and the design shall not be extended to any other award.

Section 17: *No Award:* At the discretion of an individual Worldcon Committee, if the lack of nominations or final votes in a specific category shows a marked lack of interest in that category on the part of the voters, the Award in that category shall be cancelled for that year. In addition, the entry "No Award" shall be mandatory in each category of Hugo Award on the final ballot. In any event, No Award shall be given whenever the total number of valid ballots cast for a specific category is less than twenty-five percent (25%) of the total number of final Award ballots (excluding those cast for No Award) received.

Section 18: *Nominations:* Selection of nominees for the final Award voting shall be done by a poll conducted by the Worldcon Committee, in which each member of either the administering or the immediately preceding Worldon as of January 31st of the current calendar year shall be allowed to make five (5) equally weighted nominations in every category. Nominations shall be solicited for, and the final

Award ballot shall list, only the Hugo Awards and the John W. Campbell Memorial Award for Best New Writer. Assignment to the proper category of nominees nominated in more than one category, and eligibility of nominees, shall be determined by the Worldcon Committee. No nominee shall appear on the final Award ballot if it received fewer nominations than the lesser of either: five percent (5%) of the number of nomination ballots cast in that category, or the number of nominations received by the third-place nominee in that category.

Section 19: *Notification and Acceptance:* Worldcon Committees shall use reasonable efforts to notify the nominees, or in the case of deceased or incapacitated persons, their heirs, assigns, or legal guardians, in each category prior to the release of such information. Each nominee shall be asked at that time to either accept or decline the nomination.

Section 20: *Voting:* Final Award voting shall be by mail, with ballots sent only to WSFS members. Final Award ballots shall include name, signature, address, and membership-number spaces to be filled in by the voter. Final Award ballots shall standardize nominees given in each category to not more than five (5) (six (6) in the case of tie votes) plus "No Award." The Committee shall, on or with the final ballot, designate, for each nominee in the printed fiction categories, one or more books, anthologies, or magazines in which the nominee appeared (including the book publisher or magazine issue date(s)). Voters shall indicate the order of their preference for the nominees in each category.

Section 21: *Tallying:* Counting of all votes shall be the responsibility of the Worldcon Committee, which is responsible for all matters concerning the Awards. In each category, votes shall first be tallied by the voter's first choices. If no majority is then obtained, the nominee who places last in the initial tallying shall be eliminated and the ballots listing it as first choice shall be redistributed on the basis of those ballots' second choices. This process shall be repeated until a majority-vote winner is obtained. The complete numerical vote totals, including all preliminary tallies for first, second, ... places, shall be made public by the Worldcon Committee within ninety (90) days after the Worldcon.

Section 22: *Exclusions:* No member of the current Worldcon Committee nor any publications closely connected with a member of the Committee shall be eligible for an Award. However, should the Committee delegate all authority under this Article to a Subcommittee whose decisions are irrevocable by the Worldcon Committee, then this exclusion shall apply to members of the Subcommittee only.

Bibliography

Books

Advanced Dungeon Master's Guide, G. Gygax, ed. (TSR, 1979) Lake Geneva, WI.

Advanced Dungeons and Dragons Player's Handbook, 2nd edition, D. Z. Cook, ed. (TSR, 1989) Lake Geneva, WI.

Complete Film Dictionary, I Konigsberg, ed. (NAL, 1987) New York, NY.

Critical Terms for Science Fiction and Fantasy; A Glossary and Guide to Scholarship, Gary K. Wolfe (Greenwood, 1986) Westport, CT.

Dictionary of Popular Slang, Anita Pearl (Jonathan David, 1990) Middle Village, NY.

Dictionary of Literary Terms, J. Cudden, ed. (Doubleday, 1977) Garden City, NY.

Glossary of Literary Terms, M. H. Abrams, ed. (Holt, Rinehart and Winston, 1961) New York, NY.

Harry and Wally's Favorite TV Shows, H. Castleman and W. Podrazik (Prentice Hall Press, 1989) New York, NY.

Illustrated Encyclopedia of Astronomy and Space, I. Ridpath, ed. (Crowell, 1976) New York, NY.

The Joys of Jargon, Tom Fahey (Barron's, 1990).

The Language of Space, P. Turnill, ed. (John Day, 1971).

Loose Cannons and Red Herrings, R. Claiborne, ed. (Ballantine, 1988) New York, NY.

Man in Space Dictionary, M. Caidin, ed. (Dutton, 1963) New York, NY.

Movies on TV and Videocassette, S. Scheuer, ed. (Bantam, 1990) New York, NY.

New Encyclopedia of Science Fiction, J. Gunn, ed. (Viking, 1989) New York, NY.

Newspeak: A Dictionary of Jargon, J. Green, ed. (Routledge and Kegan Paul, 1984) New York, NY.

The Science Fiction Book, F. Rottensteiner, ed. (Seabury, 1975) New York, NY.

The Science Fiction Encyclopedia, P. Nichols, ed. (Doubleday, 1979) New York, NY.

The Science in Science Fiction, P. Nichols, ed. (Knopf, 1983) New York, NY.

Slang! The Topic-by-topic Dictionary of Contemporary American Lingoes, P. Dickson (Pocket Books, 1990) New York, NY.

The Visual Encyclopedia of Science Fiction, B. Ash, ed. (Harmony, 1977) New York, NY.

Word Origins: The Romance of Language, C. Hunt (Citadel, 1962) Secaucus, NJ.

The World of Science Fiction: The History of a Subculture, L. Del Rey (Ballantine, 1979) New York, NY.

Writing and Selling Science Fiction, SFWA, ed. (Writers' Digest, 1976) Cincinnati, OH.

Fanzines and Newsletters (Privately Printed)

Comic Shop News, Collectors' Guide, 1989.

Domino Theory, Newsletter of NolaCon (World Science Fiction Convention), 1988.

The Fantastically Fundamentally Functional Guide to Fandom, by Susan Garrett, 1989.

The Neofan's Guide to Fandom, by Joan Verba.

The Neofan's Guide to Science Fiction Fandom, by LASFS, 3rd, 5th, and 6th editions.

SFWA Membership Guide.

STREKfan's Glossary of Abbreviations and Slanguage, by M. J. Fisher, 1979.

About the Author

Roberta Rogow began her love affair with Science Fiction at the age of ten and became the quintessential SF fan some two decades later when, in 1973, she attended one of the first Star Trek conventions in New York City. There she discovered fan-written and fan-published "fanzines."

Eventually Rogow rose from fan obscurity to fan celebrity status as the compiler of six volumes of Trexindex (an index of Star Trek fan stories) and as the editor or coeditor of three long-running fanzines. She is also the author of over one hundred fanzine stories and the singer, performer, producer, and/or publisher of hundreds of "filk-songs." In addition, Ms. Rogow has modeled her award-winning costumes and "hawked" her own printed and recorded creations as well as fanzines from fellow publishers all over the country at conventions.

Roberta Rogow crossed the barrier from amateur to professional writing when four of her stories were published in the C.J. Cherryh anthologies of "Merovingen Nights."

When she is not writing stories or filk-songs, creating and sewing new costumes, publishing fanzines, performing and recording new audio cassettes, or attending conventions, Rogow is a full-time municipal librarian in Union, New Jersey, where she uses her singing and storytelling talents in the children's department. She lives in Fair Lawn, New Jersey, with her husband of nearly three decades, Murray, a freelance promotion consultant. Roberta and Murray are the parents of Miriam, a travel agent, and Louise, a computer wizard, both of whom have been active in fandom since childhood.